MUSIC AND WESTERN MAN

MUSIC
AND WESTERN MAN

Edited by Peter Garvie

*The Canadian Broadcasting
Corporation Series*

DENT

LONDON · TORONTO · VANCOUVER

PREFACE

USIC is both something heard and something lived, and the two cannot be dissociated. Hearing a piece of music may seem a simple experience; the sounds are received by the ear and made meaningful by the mind. Certainly the immediacy, the excitement, the sense of a direct communication between composer and listener are valuable, and without them music would probably cease to be an experience —something that we live—and become only a subject for study. But when we say we are listening to Beethoven we are only expressing a part of the truth. We are using a metaphor that simplifies a complex experience. For the variables of the musical experience are infinite; the more we know of them, the better we know the masterpiece itself, and the more it will mean to us.

There is, theoretically at least, an ideal relationship between the listener and the music, almost an identification. Yet to attain this a listener would have to know everything there is to know, first, about the work itself, and then about the work in relation to the composer who wrote it, the society of which he was a part, and the whole history of music of which the work is a part. And that is only one side of the equation. There is also the listener's background; in time and place, the kind of person he is and the beliefs he holds, his general attitude to music, and all the occasions on which he has heard this particular work before.

Nevertheless, we do not despair of music or of ourselves. Perhaps we conceive the truth of a particular work (the truth or reality of it for each listener) as at the centre of a maze, and we know we will never reach the centre; yet we still go on. It is one way in which we distinguish a masterpiece from a commonplace; a masterpiece is inexhaustible and continues to reveal aspects of itself, however familiar it is to us; a commonplace work of art has no reserves of meaning, and we know all about it all too quickly. We look into great works and always see something new; we look at ordinary works and see through them.

Most of our exploration of a great work is by listening to it,

but a valuable part, the part that gives the work its context, is
founded upon commentary. The less familiar the work the less
we are likely to know of its context. If we know how and why and
for whom a work was composed we can at least approach it from
the right direction. We turn for counsel to those who have
special knowledge or special gifts of understanding, and the ability
to communicate their understanding to us; and we apply all that
we can learn from them to illuminate the music and enrich our
experience of it. Expert commentary can re-create the context
for us, though it should never be regarded as in any sense replacing
the music. The purpose of commentary is to enable the music
to speak for itself to a mind that is prepared to receive it.

This defines too the purpose of *Music and Western Man*—the
book and the series of broadcasts from which it is drawn. A
chief responsibility of a national radio system like the Canadian
Broadcasting Corporation is to attend to the needs of music lovers,
and they are a surprisingly high percentage of the total radio
audience. This responsibility cannot be discharged simply by
offering the standard concert and recital repertoire; that is, the
more familiar part of a mere two centuries' music. We have
more than twenty centuries of western music as our legacy, and in
a country like Canada, with its small centres of population in a
great area, the organization that can best reveal this legacy is the
national radio system. Isolated performances of earlier music
can do little but indicate that these works exist. Commentary
is needed at the initial stage, for the works must be given a context.
Accordingly, in 1955 the Canadian Broadcasting Corporation
organized a series of fifty one-hour programmes to be broadcast
weekly. Each programme would consist of commentary and
recorded musical illustrations, and each programme would be
repeated the following day. Later in the week music of the
period under discussion would be broadcast as a supplement to
the lectures.

A committee of four drew up the outline for the series. This
outline went through many drafts, and while it is by no means the
only way in which such a series could be organized, it seemed to
my colleagues and myself the best way. The contributors were
then chosen, and in each case an expert knowledge of the subject
was the first requirement. A glance at the list of contributors
will show their quality. As a rule each contributor recorded his

talk wherever he was and sent it to Vancouver, and he also chose his music examples. For this book some abridgment of the scripts has been necessary, but any changes have been approved by the contributors. The music examples have been retained in the text so that the references to records are adjacent to the discussion of that particular piece of music. So the record collector can, as it were, *play* through the book as well as read it. At the end of the book a short list of books for further reading and a list of other relevant records has been added.

It was decided to give the broadcasts permanent form for a number of reasons. A great many listeners tuned in to the repeat of each broadcast and wrote to ask for copies of the scripts and for information about records heard. A number of universities, too, expressed great interest in the series. The tributes of listeners were reinforced by the judges at the Institute for Education by Radio-Television at Ohio University, who conferred a first award upon the series. Most important, *Music and Western Man* seems to have fulfilled a need; a need for a history of music that would be scholarly and not academic, lucid in style, and accessible to every inquisitive listener without condescension towards him.

When we first study the role of music in earlier societies we may be startled, for we tend to regard our contemporary musical life as the norm. We discover, for instance, that western man lived for centuries without finding contemporary music a 'problem'; indeed, contemporary music until recently meant more to him than the music of the past. We discover that concerts and concert audiences, as we know them, are rather late developments, and it is only recently that passive listeners have so outnumbered performers. The decline of the amateur and his influence and the growth of other media for the dissemination of music—notably broadcasting and records—have radically altered, or soon will alter, music's part in our lives, both for good and for ill. The constant and indiscriminate availability of music of all sorts may have an effect upon our ears like that of billboards upon our eyes, and the passivity of our experience of music may make our relations with it much less direct—to the detriment of music and ourselves. On the other hand, twentieth-century scholarship and the mass media have provided every interested person with a long view of music that was not to be had before. We may hope that exploration within that perspective, and the fact that the works of music themselves do not change as do our circumstances, but offer the same challenge and promise the same reward, will maintain a resilience of mind in our society to ensure the continuing significance of music and the arts in general. If we ignore the legacy and decline the effort of exploration, music may become just a soothing routine, like hot baths. We perhaps lack the talent and training to participate in music directly as composers or performers, but we can at least apply ourselves as *active* listeners to the study of the unfamiliar and the not easily apprehended; a study that will reveal to us as much about the familiar as about the new.

Each of us brings his special knowledge and interests to such a study, and it is perhaps surprising to find how relevant and useful they can be. The historian will discover how peoples expressed themselves in music at different periods, and the influence of the structure of society upon music, and vice versa. Not the least fascinating aspect is the coincidence of historical events and the appearance of works of art, literature, and music. So we find that Machaut composed his great *Mass of Notre Dame* in Chaucer's lifetime, and that both lived through the Black Death: that Leonardo da Vinci was almost the exact contemporary of Josquin des Prés, and that their lifetimes took in the discovery of America, the end of the Wars of the Roses, Sir Thomas More's *Utopia*, and the first days of the German Reformation; that the first operas were contemporary with the later plays of Shakespeare; that Hogarth and Pope were contemporaries of Bach and Handel; and that Wordsworth and Beethoven were born in the same year.

If we have not been aware of such coincidences in time, it is doubtless because the history of man and the history of the various arts are quite separate in our minds, and because the close of one period and the transition to a new one in political history does not often correspond exactly to a similar stage in the evolution of music. Indeed, the more one studies the history of music, the less one relies upon specific dates to mark the beginning or end of a style or period. Tangible things can be ascribed to a particular year— a work is composed or published, a decree is issued by prince or prelate that affects music—but the main current flows over our marked segments of time and only gradually discloses its direction. There are so many factors in any change, and they are complicated by national distinctions and the presence of both conservatives and adventurers in any generation of composers. For example, scholars detect the beginnings of the baroque style in the music of Giovanni Gabrieli at Venice, and Gabrieli, who lived in the latter part of the sixteenth century and early part of the seventeenth, is accounted a Renaissance composer. He died in 1613, and yet sixty years later in the early music of Purcell we see the survival of the string style of Renaissance England.

The student of architecture, like the historian, will find many points at which his interests are involved in this account of music; the influence of acoustics upon the single line of Gregorian Chant or upon the splendid music of Gabrieli and other composers associated with St Mark's in Venice. The student of literature may trace the relations of music and poetry from the troubadours to the present time; the student of theatre may be absorbed by the growth and development of opera. Those whose interests are theological may find a new illumination of their subject in the many different approaches to liturgical texts by composers at different periods. Those interested in painting and sculpture can trace parallels of style between what was drawn, painted, and carved and what was sung or played at various moments of history.

Less important than special interests, however, is the interest that all readers will presumably share in music and in western man. This book aims to provide a history of music in western civilization and to explore western civilization through one of its aspects, music. It is always as well, when we speak of western civilization, to know its constituents; our values derive from individual masterpieces, not from abstract categories. So perhaps the most valuable part of this account is that it directs our attention to certain works of music and illuminates them so that we may experience them directly for ourselves. The tradition will cease to be a succession of trends and periods and names and will become instead a range of masterpieces and near-masterpieces which we have heard and come to know and understand. It will become a living reality, and thus the more valuable, because it will have a variety of individual meanings and emphasis for each of us. The tradition lives in individual experience: the music must matter enough in our own lives. This book is offered as a means to that end.

PETER GARVIE.

Vancouver, October 1955.

*

THE CONTRIBUTORS

Wilfrid Mellers

English musicologist and composer. Staff tutor in music to the extra-mural department of Birmingham University. His compositions include three operas: *The Tragicall History of Christopher Marlowe*, *The Trial of the Jewelled Peacock*, and *The Shepherd's Daughter*. He has written many articles for periodicals, and his books include *François Couperin and the French Classical Tradition*, *Music and Society*, and *Studies in Contemporary Music*.

Egon Wellesz

Austrian composer and musicologist. He studied with Schönberg and lectured on music history in Vienna before the First World War. As a musicologist he has specialized in baroque opera and Byzantine music. He settled in Oxford in 1939 and is now University Reader in Byzantine Music. His long list of compositions includes six operas, two symphonies, seven string quartets, choral works, and ballets. His books include studies of Byzantine music and a collection of essays on opera.

Alec Robertson

English scholar and critic. He has made a special study of plain-song and published a standard book on the subject. He is music editor of the *Gramophone*, has contributed to a number of journals and to *Grove's Dictionary*, and is well known in Great Britain as a lecturer and broadcaster. In 1945 he was elected a Fellow of the Royal Academy of Music.

Denis Stevens

English scholar and critic. Studied music and musicology at Oxford University. Later joined the B.B.C. Music Division, where he produced many hundreds of pre-classical music programmes and talks. His lecture tours have taken him through Europe and America, and in 1955–6 he was Visiting Professor of Music at Cornell University and Columbia University. His publications include *The Mulliner Book*, *Thomas Tallis: Complete Keyboard Works*, *Altenglische Orgelmusik*, *Tudor Church Music*, and *Thomas Tomkins*.

Willi Apel

German-born musicologist, now resident in the United States.
Studied mathematics and the piano and gave recitals in Germany.
Taught at various American colleges and is now Professor of Musicology
at Indiana University. His publications include *The Notation of
Polyphonic Music, 900–1600*.

Paul Henry Lang

American musicologist, born in Hungary. He was educated in Buda-
pest, Paris, and at Cornell. Since 1933 Professor of Musicology at
Columbia University. President of the International Musicological
Society. Editor of the *Musical Quarterly*. Music critic of the *New
York Herald Tribune*. His publications include the monumental
Music in Western Civilization.

Gustave Reese

American musicologist. Professor in the Graduate School of Arts
and Science at New York University. Director of Concert and Opera
Publications of Carl Fischer Inc. He was one of the founders and is a
past president of the American Musicological Society, and is a member
of the Committee on Musicology of the American Council of Learned
Societies. His publications include the comprehensive *Music in the
Middle Ages* and *Music in the Renaissance*.

J. A. Westrup

English musicologist. He was editor of the *Monthly Musical Record*
and has been a music critic. Later Professor of Music at Birmingham
University and currently Professor of Music at Oxford. He has been
active in the production of unfamiliar operas there. General editor
of the *New Oxford History of Music*. His publications include books
on Purcell and Handel.

A. K. Holland

Music critic of the *Liverpool Daily Post*. He has lectured widely,
chiefly on English music. Author of books on Purcell and the songs
of Delius.

H. Wiley Hitchcock

American scholar. Studied in France with Nadia Boulanger and
recently spent a year in Italy for studies in the history of the oratorio.
His particular field of interest is French and Italian baroque music.
He is Professor of Music at the University of Michigan.

Arthur Hutchings

English scholar. Professor of Music at Durham University. His books include studies of Schubert, Delius, and the piano concertos of Mozart.

Anthony Lewis

English musicologist and conductor. Studied with Nadia Boulanger and later served on the music staff of the B.B.C. He is general editor of *Musica Britannica* and has edited and conducted much early music. Barber and Peyton Professor of Music in the University of Birmingham.

Lionel Salter

English pianist, harpsichordist, conductor, and critic. Music critic of the *Gramophone*. Well known as a radio speaker and has often conducted for the B.B.C. and abroad. Now Director of Music Productions for the B.B.C.'s Television Service.

Karl Geiringer

Austrian musicologist. He studied in Vienna and Berlin. Now Professor of History and Theory of Music at Boston University. His publications include books on the Bach family, Haydn, Brahms, and musical instruments.

Alfred Frankenstein

American music critic. Studied at University of Chicago and at Yale. Instructor in music, University of Chicago. Music and art critic, *San Francisco Chronicle*, since 1934. Has lectured on American music and art at a number of universities. Guggenheim Fellow, 1947–8. His publications include *After the Hunt*, a monograph on William Harnett and other American still-life painters.

William Mann

English music critic. Studied at Cambridge and with Matyas Seiber and Ilona Kabos. Assistant music critic of *The Times* since 1948. He is associate editor of *Opera* and has contributed to a variety of books. He is currently engaged on a study of Richard Strauss.

Andrew Porter

English music critic. Organ scholar at University College, Oxford. Music critic of the *Financial Times* and associate editor of *Opera*. Contributes to the *Gramophone* and other periodicals and broadcasts for the B.B.C.

Aaron Copland

American composer. Studied with Nadia Boulanger. His compositions have included scores for films and ballets and a wide variety of other works. He is himself an accomplished pianist. He has written articles on aspects of contemporary music and his books include *Our New Music* and *Music and Imagination*.

Peter Garvie

Born in London and educated at Repton and Clare College, Cambridge. Now makes his home in Vancouver, B.C., where he is a producer with the Canadian Broadcasting Corporation. He has produced concerts, recitals, dramas, and talks programmes and inaugurated the C.B.C.'s weekly programme of commentary on music, *Music Diary*, which has now been on the air almost four years. He was in charge of planning and producing the series, *Music and Western Man*, which in 1956 received a first award from the Institute for Education by Radio-Television at Ohio State University.

In addition, the C.B.C. has included a selection of his poems and a short story on its programme of new writing and has produced his two radio plays, *The Flight of Janus* and *The Summer School*. He has also contributed articles to the *Canadian Music Journal*.

A NOTE ON BOOKS AND RECORDS

FOUR recorded anthologies were used in the broadcasts:

(i) THE HISTORY OF MUSIC IN SOUND.
RCA VICTOR (10 LP records) or HMV (78 r.p.m.).

(ii) MASTERPIECES OF MUSIC BEFORE 1750.
HAYDN SOCIETY (3 LP records)
These are recordings of the fifty musical illustrations in the book of the same title.

(iii) ARCHIVE SERIES.
DEUTSCHE GRAMMOPHON GESELLSCHAFT: released by DECCA in North America. (Still in progress.)

(iv) ANTHOLOGIE SONORE.
Many of the records have been transferred to LP in North America.

The recorded musical illustrations used in each broadcast are identified in the body of each chapter. The appendices contain a list of recommended books and additional records for study in connection with each chapter; these lists have been prepared by the editor in consultation with the contributors. They are not meant to be exhaustive, but simply to be suggestive. Those who wish to explore further can best do so through the comprehensive bibliographies in some of the books cited and through the current record catalogues.

The records listed are there because of the music they contain. No attempt has been made to evaluate each record on the basis of performance and quality of recording. But it should be remembered that each record used as an example in the broadcasts was chosen by the contributor, and where alternative records are listed the one mentioned first is the contributor's choice.

Not all the records used in the broadcasts were easy to obtain, but they have all been listed since they illustrate points made by the contributor. In order to extend the range of usefulness of both the records used as illustrations in the broadcasts and of those given in the appendices, an effort has been made to quote both the

North American and the English catalogue numbers. Where there is no equivalent on the English market of a record from an American source, an alternative has been suggested where available. In the texts of the broadcasts the references are usually to the American numbers, and where the same record is also available in England, its English number is quoted in brackets.

Where a record is not available to the English public an alternative recorded version of the music in question is, where possible, quoted. In such cases the alternative is clearly marked as such. It has not been found possible always to find an equivalent or an alternative; but even here the reader need not despair, because American and continental records can often be found in the stocks of specialist British dealers, or in the private advertisement columns of such magazines as the *Gramophone*.

In the case of the appendices, much the same system has been adopted. Unless otherwise stated, the first listing is by the American number, and its English equivalent, if there is one, follows in brackets. Where no English equivalent is available a particular effort has been made to list an alternative; but in this case it is not necessarily indicated as such. It is thus safe to say that all numbers quoted in brackets refer throughout to the English numbers; and in the case of labels like DECCA and COLUMBIA, which have different meanings in North America and Great Britain, the difference is always marked, when the number is not enclosed in brackets, by the prefix ENGLISH. In some cases the North American and English numbers are identical: VOX is a case in point. Where this is so availability on the English market is indicated by (E) following the number. In the case of OISEAU-LYRE the numbers are also identical; but here availability on one continent implies a similar availability on the other, so no distinction is required. In a few cases also, records available in England have been marked for deletion. These are always quoted when they are equivalents of the American first choice, and even if an alternative is included; but where possible they have been marked with an asterisk. Naturally, the task of finding a suitable alternative is more difficult in the case of the older, and much less extensively recorded, music. But the progressive growth of the DGG Archive Series has been most helpful here, and where possible the latest additions have been incorporated.

There is really no satisfactory way to indicate degrees of

accessibility to the record buyer.   It is broadly true that 78 r.p.m. disks are becoming progressively harder to obtain, and much material on them has not yet been transferred to LP.   Accordingly, the appendices are restricted (with only a few exceptions) to LP records that are obtainable in North America and/or Great Britain. In spite of the gaps in the repertoire (to which attention is drawn) the reader should have no difficulty in collecting his own recorded anthology.

In addition to the books dealing with specific subjects, periods, or composers indicated in the appendices, the following general works are to be recommended:

WILFRID MELLERS: *Music and Society.*

PAUL HENRY LANG: *Music in Western Civilization.*

CARL PARRISH AND JOHN F. OHL: *Masterpieces of Music before 1750.*

SIR DONALD TOVEY: *Musical Articles* (from the *Encyclopaedia Britannica*).

DAVISON AND APEL: *Historical Anthology of Music* (Harvard).

Grove's Dictionary of Music and Musicians, 5th Edition, ED.

SHAWE-TAYLOR AND SACKVILLE WEST: *The Record Guide and Supplement.*

ACKNOWLEDGMENTS

MY first thanks must go to the contributors whose enthusiasm, helpfulness, and courtesy have made my work so agreeable. They have had to contend with the special demands of broadcasting and the editing of their broadcast scripts for publication—not to speak of the complications arising from the thousands of miles between them and Vancouver.

I also owe a special debt to Mr Leonard Wilson and Mr Lawrence Cluderay, who not only served on the planning committee, but have throughout a period of two years given generously of their time and trouble. They have been available to comment and advise at all times during the broadcasting of the series and during the preparation of the manuscript.

My thanks must also go to Mr Robert Harlow, Director of Radio for the Canadian Broadcasting Corporation in British Columbia, who encouraged the project from first to last; and to Dr Robert Turner, also of the C.B.C., for his help on the planning committee.

Miss Maxine de Felice and Miss Margaret Fielder of the C.B.C.'s London and New York offices respectively did the work of recording the contributions. Miss Wendy Livett of the C.B.C. in Vancouver typed the manuscript and in addition attended to all the correspondence. They, and many other members of the C.B.C. staff, have done a great deal to make this book possible.

For permission to include copyright material acknowledgments and thanks are made to the following:

The Clarendon Press, Oxford, for an extract from *The Legacy of the Middle Ages*; the Columbia University Press for an extract from *A Short History of Opera* by Donald Grout; J. M. Dent & Sons Ltd for an extract from *Mozart* by Eric Blom; the Oxford University Press Inc. for an extract from *Mozart* by Alfred Einstein; Routledge & Kegan Paul Ltd for an extract from *Some Musicians of Former Days* by Romain Rolland; Simon & Schuster Inc. for an extract from *Chronicle of My Life* by Igor Stravinsky.

It would be impossible to thank everyone by name for their help in a great variety of ways, but they will probably recognize their contributions in the text; certainly the editor has been constantly reminded of their part as he has prepared this book. Finally, acknowledgment must be made of the many letters from radio listeners to the broadcast series; their comments encouraged us all.

CONTENTS

I

Wilfrid Mellers

MUSIC AND SOCIETY

WHEN I first started to write music I composed because, as they say, I had to. I wanted to create something, and the medium in which I happened to be able to create most effectively proved to be sound. I found —and I gather that my experience is not unique—that it is only after one has grown into a better or at least a more efficient composer that one begins to face up to the central problem. As one begins to discover what one wants to say and how to say it in sound—the two discoveries being at bottom identical—one comes to see that in the process of composition something other is involved than one's own personality. A language implies someone willing to understand it, someone at the other end of the telegraphic system. Music is willy-nilly a social and perhaps a religious act; and this remains true even though the telegraphic system may, in our day, have got a bit tangled. And so at the beginning of this large-scale survey of the growth of Europe's music, I want to discuss the relationship between a musical idiom and the human experience which it embodies. We are concerned not only with what music is, but with what it is for.

However different the musical techniques of different ages may be, they will have in common certain features which derive from the physical nature of sound. Music exists in time, not space; and it involves the alternation of varying degrees of tension between aural vibrations. (High degrees of tension we call dissonances, relatively low degrees of tension we call consonances.) One might perhaps say that the forms of music are the means whereby men have organized in terms of time the aural relations between tension and relaxation. It is, however, obvious that the ways in which composers have used these basic resources of sound have varied greatly from generation to generation: and that they have varied according to men's preconceptions about music's significance and purpose. Let us consider, from this point of view, a few pieces of music chosen from widely separated periods of European history.

First, a typical example of medieval music, a plain-song melody.

Gregorian Chant. (See Chapter 3 for a selection of recorded examples).

The first thing we shall notice about this chant—bearing in mind that music is an alternation of tension and relaxation moving in time—is that it is written in a single unaccompanied line. There is thus no harmony to provide any conflict between tones sounded simultaneously. But more than that, the melody itself avoids any intervals which could *imply* harmonic stress; it moves mainly by step, or by very smooth intervals which involve the minimum of tension. Its modality is derived from the phrases the human voice naturally sings. Then again, the rhythm is free, non-metrical, and the cadential phrases usually fall by a whole tone, never rise by a semitone, which would give an impression of finality. All this means that the music conveys almost no sense of time, or of conflict and drama. This is just what the composers were after, for they were trying to create not a music that expressed their own passions, but rather a music that helped one to lose the self in the contemplation of God. Even when a thirteenth-century composer such as Pérotin put several lines together in an organum or motet he regarded the additional parts as extensions and embellishments of the original melody. The melody remained fluid and the harmony avoided any acute tensions. The music still suggests a dissolution of the self into eternity. Order was imposed on the concourse of parts by almost mathematically conceived rhythmic patterns which embodied in sound what seemed to be the immutable laws of the cosmos.

Pérotin: *Organum triplum.* ANTHOLOGIE SONORE AS 1 (AS 65, 78 r.p.m.).

Now let us jump more than two hundred years to the *Agnus Dei* of Byrd's five-part Mass.

Byrd: *Mass for five voices.* LONDON LL 888 (DECCA LXT 2919).

In this music each vocal part preserves its independence, and the 'form' of the piece appears to be the growth of melody, fugally imitated in all the parts. If you examine each of the vocal lines separately, it seems to be similar to the unterrestrial serenity of plain-song. The intervals are smooth and vocal, the rhythm non-metrical, the movement unaggressive. Yet not only are the lines modified by a desire for sensuous richness of harmony; but the traditional partiality for independent part-writing is now itself a means of creating some of the most remarkable harmonic effects. Thus, while the music preserves the old-style liturgical polyphony, it uses the technique in a new way. The composer has to think simultaneously of the purely melodic beauty of his lines: and of the emotional possibilities of tension and relaxation between the chords that these lines create. The music is at once liturgical and an expression of the humanist spirit. It acquires a much more 'personal' quality than the Pérotin example—what one might almost call a Shakespearian tragic pathos.

Plain-song and Pérotin's polyphony are 'monistic' acts of praise to God. In Byrd's polyphony each individual part has, while preserving its melodic freedom, to think of the harmonic rights of the others: polyphony has become, as it were, a communal act. We can see this in the changing conception of rhythm. Each part, individually considered, remains freely vocal in rhythm; but the behaviour of the parts when they are sung together depends on the implicit existence of a 'strong' and a 'weak' beat on which the dissonances are prepared and resolved. Dance metre has come to complement vocal rhythm as a basic principle of construction.

When we move on more than another hundred years to our next example we find that dance metre now reigns supreme. In the aria *He shall feed His flock* from Handel's *Messiah* the tonality is unambiguously our modern major and minor, and the clauses are grouped in symmetrical periods dominated by *siciliano* dance rhythm, rounded off by clearly defined cadences.

Handel: *Messiah: He shall feed His flock.*

Here, instead of the continuously evolving texture of polyphony, we have a structure which depends on the architectural grouping of phrases, involving simple changes of key. The balanced repetition of the clauses resembles the symmetrical, terrace-like structure of eighteenth-century gardens and buildings. The lucid system of tonality and the imposition of dance patterns canalizes harmonic passion: just as classical civilization wishes to impose a rigid, state-dominated order on the perversities of individual beings.

Handel's conception of order is harmonic rather than melodic, but it is still based on creative unity; his movements have usually only one theme and a consistent figuration. When we turn to the sonata epoch, and especially to Beethoven, we find a radically different principle of construction. Consider the last movement of Beethoven's Seventh Symphony. Here there is no unified song-melody. There are striking thematic motives in dynamically obsessive rhythms; and the structure of the music is a dramatic conflict between heterogeneous motives and contradictory keys, on which Beethoven imposes order by the sheer force of his will.

Beethoven: *Symphony No. 7 in A* (Finale).

We have heard this music so often, perhaps, that we can no longer fully experience these savagely abrupt modulations, these sudden pauses and silences, the sheer physical impact of the orchestration, with its fanatically barking horns. Yet if we can listen afresh we shall find this one of the most terrifying pieces of music ever written, far more scarifying, after a hundred and forty years, than Stravinsky's *Rite of Spring* after forty. If it is 'joyful,' it can only be the blood-curdling joy of battle: for it is a revolutionary piece which hammers out a new world. Its order is dualistic, whereas that of Handel—or Byrd or plain-song—is monistic.

For our last example let us take the Prelude to Act I of Wagner's *Tristan und Isolde*.

Wagner: *Tristan und Isolde* (Prelude).

We shall immediately notice that the explosive metres of Beethoven have disappeared; instead, we have a continuous surge of sound. Moreover, whereas the orchestration of the classical age had aimed at the clearest definition of the main melody, in Wagner's orchestration melodic definition is intentionally submerged in the rich flood of harmony. Soon we shall notice a further point: this continuous surge of sound negates the structural principle—the exposition, development, and recapitulation—which had characterized the classical sonata up to Beethoven's last works, and negates also the key-system on which that form depended. Expressive thematic fragments take the place of developed melodies, and the logic of the music tends to become equated with the succession of harmonic tensions, corresponding to different degrees of nervous sensation.

The music's overwhelming intensity derives from the fact that Wagner concentrates on the dissonant harmony at the expense of its resolution; note how it is always the dissonant chord that falls on the strong beat. Moreover, the effect of the passage as a whole depends on the way in which the brief yearning phrase, underlined by its dissonance, is repeated at progressively rising intervals. This building up of tension, followed by only a partial resolution, is used repeatedly by Wagner, and just such a combination of passionate yearning with frustration is the essential theme of his adaptation of the Tristan story, between which and his own life there is a more than usually direct connection. In effect Wagner is saying 'My feelings *are* life; there is nothing except them and death.' This is the triumph of subjectivity; Wagner has created a myth and a world out of his own passion. Music and the opera are now not so much an expression of the values and beliefs of a civilization as a projection of the individual's ego. The deification of the ego could hardly go further than the Wagner cult at Bayreuth, where a temple is built in which to perform the master's creations—instead of the music being composed to serve the needs of the temple, as was Byrd's to serve God or Handel's to serve the State. Wagner thus effects a curious inversion of the religious attitude to music.

I have tried to show, however elliptically, that basic changes in musical technique are not fortuitous. In plain-chant we have a purely melodic, almost conflictless unity whereby the composer strives not to express himself, but to become unified with God. In Byrd's polyphony we have an equilibrium between this ritualistic approach and the demands of personal feeling. In Handel we have personal feeling codified in the interests not of God, but of the God-King or the State. In middle-period Beethoven we have a ferocious conflict to establish a new, revolutionary order: to re-create the past through the assertion of the Will. In Wagner's *Tristan* we have the final subjection of the past, of God and of Society, to the individual's nerves and senses.

But I hope I have also made it clear that no work of art can be 'explained' by reference to its historical connotations. On the contrary, a work of art is itself historical evidence—of a much more inward nature than the documents with which historians usually have to deal. It is true that we cannot fully understand Beethoven without understanding the impulses behind the French Revolution. It is equally true that we cannot fully understand the French Revolution without some insight into Beethoven's music. We can see in his music those elements which are conditioned by his time (for they could not be otherwise) and yet are beyond the topical and local. Beethoven is a part of history. He is also the human spirit making history.

This is fairly obvious in the case of an artist who, like Beethoven, was in conflict with, and wished to change, the world he lived in. It is equally, if less obviously, true of artists who lived in more stable and homogeneous societies. In the sixteenth century there was a common European idiom which we now know as 'Palestrina style.' It was music's common denominator for certain basic assumptions of the Catholic Church and of Renaissance man. Yet it matters to us because it was the framework within which men such as Byrd, Lassus, Victoria, and Palestrina himself expressed very different attitudes to those assumptions. Handel's basic idiom was so universally accepted that he could lift into his own works large sections of other people's music without anyone noticing, or caring if they did notice. Yet what we remember of eighteenth-century baroque is the revivifying experience of truly creative minds. We respond to the profound equilibrium between acceptance and protest, civilization and revolution, lyricism and drama in the music of Haydn and Mozart: while we have forgotten the innumerable symphonic hacks who exploited the small change of rococo style as an easy way of passing the time— and making money. Most of all, perhaps, we see Bach's crucial position in European history in relation to his independence of time. Firmly rooted in what was then present, he philosophically and even technically harked back to a medieval past, while looking forward not merely to nineteenth-century romanticism, but still more to the twentieth century.

So in talking of Music and Society, we should not think we have said anything worth saying in pointing out that there are connections between what has happened in music and what has happened in the external world. That is, or should be, a truism. We should, however, in listening to the music which great and less than great men have created at different times in our past, learn to experience that music as the deepest kind of evidence as to the ways men have thought, felt, and acted. In order to do this, we need an historical sense only because—or in so far as—the past is relevant to the present. In these programmes we want to give some indication of the significance which this 'past' music had when it was still present: and still more to differentiate between those elements of the past which have lost, and those which preserve, a meaning. We want to see, or rather to hear, music as human experience: for if it is not that, it is a game, no more and no less important than ping-pong.

2

Egon Wellesz

THE CLASSICAL HERITAGE:
GREECE AND BYZANTIUM

THE music of western civilization owes its origin to two sources. It has its roots in Hebrew music, in the psalms, in the odes and spiritual songs which early Christianity took over into its services; and in the thought-world of the Greek philosophers which inspired the Fathers of the Church when they stated what kind of music was suitable for the Christian.

There is a fundamental difference between Greek and modern music, namely, the purely melodic structure of Greek music. Harmony (in the modern meaning of the term) was unknown to the Greeks, though they knew occasional concords of higher and lower notes, and also the accompaniment of a melody by an instrument in the higher octave. Music of a purely melodic character demands a different way of listening than that to which we are accustomed (namely, concentration on the flow of the melody, on the characteristic features of the mode). It calls for appreciation of the subtle use of intervals, consisting sometimes of fractions of tones, unheard of in the later music of Europe.

Greek music was both vocal and instrumental. 'Voice and Verse,' however, were not separated in its great epoch. *Mousike* meant music as well as poetry. Chants were partly sung by soloists, partly by a choir in unison, or in octaves, but regularly accompanied by an instrument. Accompanying a song meant either adding a tone from time to time, or playing a variation to the chant. This kind of ornamented playing, by which occasional concords were produced, was called heterophony.

The Greeks had also independent instrumental music, but in Classical times instruments were used singly. Only in the Hellenistic period groups of instruments were introduced. The two main ones were the *kithara*, a stringed instrument, on which sound was produced by plucking the chords, and the *aulos*, a kind of oboe. All sources indicate how much contemporaries admired the skill and even virtuosity exhibited in playing both.

For the Greek, music was a supreme art, aimed at harmonizing body and soul. It had the power of healing by producing a purification of the body, and also of influencing the soul by improving the character. This view is based on the Pythagorean assumption, accepted by Plato, of the existence of a link between the harmony ruling the movements of the universe and the harmony ordering the human soul. The motions of the cosmos were believed to occur according to the same mathematical ratios which produced the musical intervals.

The doctrine of the ethical character of music permeates Greek philosophy as well as Greek musical theory. In the first book of the *Enneads* Plotinus speaks of a path of initiation, enabling the musician whose soul, according to Plato's *Phaedrus*, has kept 'a recollection of those things which it formerly saw when journeying with the Divine,' to rise to the rank of a philosopher, whose soul has a clear vision of 'Absolute Beauty.'

What has come down to us of this music? There are a number of fragments on papyrus but all of them so mutilated that it is hardly possible to reconstruct the music. There are, above all, the two *Hymns to Apollo* carved on marble, from the Treasury of the Athenians at Delphi; the first, dating from about 138 B.C., is the longest piece of Greek music which has come down to us almost undamaged; the second, from about 128 B.C., is only a short fragment, but is also in good condition. Chiselled in stone also is the *Epitaph of Seikilos* for his wife, dating probably from the first century B.C.; it is the only piece of music we possess intact.

From the beginning of the Christian era we possess three hymns, ascribed to Mesomedes, which figure as show-pieces in every history of music. But serious doubts have recently been raised as to their authenticity; they may be of Byzantine origin.

Let us therefore take as examples to illustrate Greek melodies those transmitted on stone which are unquestionably authentic and fairly complete pieces of music. We take first the *Hymn to Apollo* sung at a festival at Delphi in 138 B.C. It is, in fact, a glorification of Delphi, the seat of the Oracle, and of the beauty of Attica.

First Delphi Hymn.   HMV DB 21485 (78 r.p.m.).

B

The second hymn starts likewise with an appeal to the muses to honour Apollo and extols the beauty of Greece. Of this song only the beginning is preserved:

'Come to this slope of Parnassus, which loves the dance, seen from afar with its twin peaks, and lead my song, Muses of Pieria, who dwell on the snow-swept rocks of Helicon; and honour with song and dance the golden-haired god of Pytho, Phoebus. . . .'

Second Delphi Hymn.   HMV DB 21485 (78 r.p.m.).

Finally, there is the short *Epitaph of Seikilos* which was found near Smyrna in Asia Minor. It dates from the first century of our era. It may have been a popular song which Seikilos ordered to be chiselled on the tombstone:

> As long as you live, shine forth and do not grieve at all.
> Life is short, and time claims its tribute in the end.

Epitaph of Seikilos.   HMV DA 2006 (78 r.p.m.).

The *Epitaph of Seikilos* dates from a time when Greece was already a province of the Roman Empire, which in the following centuries expanded in all directions. Constantine the Great began in 324 to rebuild the small city of Byzantium, made it the capital of the Eastern Empire and called it 'New Rome.' Soon after his death the city was called the 'City of Constantine,' Constantinopolis. Constantinople was from the beginning a Christian town. The language of the administration was Latin, that of the people Greek. But the Byzantine Church took over the liturgy of Jerusalem and Antioch and with it the chant of the Syrian churches, which was, in the main, the traditional chant of the Jewish Synagogue. Following the model of the Jewish liturgy, the morning and evening services kept their prominent place in the Eastern Church and were adorned by a great number of chants, hymns, and songs which varied from day to day.

Mass was celebrated frequently, but not daily, and the chants of the Mass had not that variety which one is used to in the western medieval Church. We know nothing about Byzantine Chant in the early days of the Byzantine Empire. The first hymns with musical signs which have come down to us are in manuscript dating from the ninth, or possibly the eighth century.

These signs are, like the tenth-century western musical signs, a kind of *aide-memoire* for the conductor of the choir, or the *precentor* who sings the solos. This early stage of musical signs cannot be called a notation from which one can know the exact pitch. It is only at the end of the twelfth century that the Byzantine musicians develop a system of notation which not only gives the exact pitch, but also all the nuances of expression and the exact rhythmical value of the notes. Indeed, Byzantine musical notation is an admirable instrument for preserving in writing the intention of the composer; it is a much more elaborate system than anything that one finds in the West, and comparable only to our present notation which surrounds the notes with expression marks and other signs.

Byzantine civilization, whose decay lasted more than a thousand years (330–1453), was, in fact, the most brilliant civilization of the Middle Ages. The position is the same for Byzantine Chant, which has only begun to be deciphered during the last twenty-five years. The more we know of it, the more we are impressed by its greatness and beauty.

One may ask how it is possible to trace the authenticity of these melodies back to the early days of the empire? We must remember that from the sixth to the eighth century the greater part of Italy belonged to the Byzantine Empire, and large parts of the population of southern Italy spoke Greek. Thus it happened that Greek chants were introduced into the Roman churches, sung first in Greek, and afterwards to the same melody in Latin. The Roman Church preserved these chants like holy relics in the liturgy of the great feasts. Thus we find in Beneventan manuscripts of the eleventh century—to quote one example only—a bilingual melody, *Ote to stavro—O quando in cruce*, which was sung on Good Friday during the Adoration of the Cross. The melody of the Latin text is of a simple type which speaks for its antiquity. But listen to the melody as it occurs in thirteenth-century manuscripts written in Byzantine monasteries at Constantinople and Mt Athos. One would hardly recognize this richly ornamented melody, yet the two are as alike as the theme of a Beethoven adagio and one of its variations:

(i) *O quando in cruce*; (ii) *Ote to stavro*. HISTORY OF MUSIC IN SOUND, VOL. II. VICTOR LM 6015 (HMV HMS 10, 78 r.p.m.).

Byzantine manuscripts of the eighth century show that the melody of *Ote to stavro* was as simple as that which survives in the Beneventan manuscripts, and that in later manuscripts more and more embellished versions are found.

By extending the investigation to other melodies we come to the following conclusion:

As we have said, Gregorian Chant retains *unchanged* some melodies taken from the old treasury of Byzantine Chant; they are no longer alive, but preserved like relics. Eastern Chant is alive. The work of the composer consists in treating the old treasury of hymn-melodies as an echo of the Divine beauty, as an echo of the chants of the angels. These tunes cannot be replaced by free compositions as happens in the West, but they can be embellished, and the Byzantine composers make use of this privilege by extending the ornamentation until the core of the melodies can hardly be recognized any longer.

We get a completely different picture when we turn from these liturgical chants to the hymn-tune of the so-called *canons*. The canon is a poetical form consisting of nine odes. Each of these nine odes consists of a number of strophes, sung to the melody of the first stanza, the model-stanza.

Canon writing began at the end of the seventh century, and the first great writers in this new *genre* were Andrew of Crete and John Damascene. They lived at the beginning of the great struggle between State and Church which shattered the foundations of the Byzantine Empire; the struggle between Image-worshippers and Image-breakers. The Image-worshippers saw in the pictures and statues of Our Lord, the Virgin, and the Saints earthly representations which deserved veneration; the Image-breakers, or Iconoclasts, basing their belief on the Old Testament's command that no image of God should be made, condemned the adoration of images as idolatry. The struggle lasted for nearly a century, and since the Emperor and the army were on the side of the Image-breakers, it began with the destruction of nearly all statues, images, and books containing pictures of the saints, and led to the destruction of many monasteries, the confiscation of monastic property, and the expulsion of monks and nuns. Defying torture and death, the monks, however, created in these very days of persecution innumerable hymns which, after the victory of Image-worship, were generally introduced into the eastern liturgy.

The melodies of these hymns are from the beginning of the syllabic type, and remained virtually syllabic down to the end of the Empire. This simplicity was necessary because in the canon, consisting of a hundred and more stanzas, every word had to be heard and understood by the congregation. Only at the cadences, occasionally, a few melismas occur.

Let us take as an example the first stanza of the famous *Resurrection Canon* by John Damascene, sung on Easter Day. It runs in J. M. Neale's verse-translation as follows:

'Tis the day of Resurrection: Earth tell it about abroad!
The Passover of Gladness! the Passover of God!
From death to life eternal—From earth unto the sky,
Our Christ has brought us over—With hymns of victory.

Anastaseos Imera. HISTORY OF MUSIC IN SOUND, VOL. II. VICTOR LM 6015 (HMV HMS 10, 78 r.p.m.).

The Greek version of *Glory to God in the Highest* is again a melody of the embellished type, though not as richly ornamented as the Good Friday chant.

Doxa. HISTORY OF MUSIC IN SOUND, VOL. II. VICTOR LM 6015 (HMV HMS 10, 78 r.p.m.).

Byzantine Chant in the great days of the Eastern Church cannot have sounded very differently from Gregorian Chant, a fact which can be proved by an anedote told by a monk of St Gall.

Charlemagne, king of the Franconian realm, received an embassy from Byzantium at his residence at Aix-la-Chapelle. Hidden behind a curtain, he heard Byzantine monks of the retinue of the ambassador celebrating their Service. Charlemagne was so overcome by the beauty of their chants that he ordered his Franconian singers to write down the music without pausing for eating or drinking.

If the music had sounded strange to his ears—I mean, fundamentally different from plain-song to which he was used—Charlemagne would hardly have forced his choristers to write down the music and to make a Latin translation of the words.

APPENDIX

BOOKS

CURT SACHS: *The Rise of Music in the Ancient World.*
EGON WELLESZ: *A History of Byzantine Music and Hymnography.*
H. J. T. TILLYARD: *Byzantine Music and Hymnography.*

3

Alec Robertson

GREGORIAN CHANT

G REGORIAN Chant takes its name, of course, from Gregory I, Pope and saint, who reigned from 590 to 604.[1] Gregory and his advisers codified and reformed a body of chant already existing but which was not the exclusive work of the Western Church. It included, as we shall see, many eastern elements; and one cannot too often stress that the East was the centre of gravity of the early Christian world. The faith itself, its first theology, ritual, music, monasticism, devotion to the Cross, and to the Mother of God, all arose in the East. Gregorian Chant, strictly speaking, is therefore the music proper to the Roman Church, and remains its only official music. Roman sobriety and sense were applied to many pre-existing bodies of chant, and Rome added its distinctive and very important contributions. These, of course, extend beyond Gregory's reign, but I shall be dealing in the main with the golden age of the composition of Gregorian Chant; that is, with the fifth to the eighth centuries, the ages prior to the Western Church's adoption of harmony.

Plain-song is music: but its principles differ, in many ways, from those of figured music. It has melody, but no harmony—organ accompaniment is a concession to human weakness—and its single and supple melodic line has great rhythmic freedom, being in no way constrained by time signatures or bar lines: its rhythm may be called that of fine musical oratory. In its restrained way plain-song covers a wide range of emotion without using any strong dynamic contrasts: and the principal accents of the Latin

---

[1] There is no agreement amongst scholars as to precisely what part Gregory took in development and consolidation of the chant, but it is certain that other Popes before, and half a century after him, contributed to the work.

14

words, far from being treated intensively, are more often than not treated lightly, being put on to high notes that throw them into melodic relief and cause them to shine down on the rest of the word—or phrase—in which they come.

The ends, or cadences, of the phrases are characteristically soft and so are the notes at the top of phrases of climax.[1] This gives an ethereal sound to the music, which seems often to float in the upper air. The compass of the melodies is small, rarely exceeding an octave, and sudden leaps up or down are exceptional. The music has what we call a modal flavour. This is due to the fact that our major and minor scale system was then unknown. There were eight ecclesiastical scales, or modes, derived from Greek scales, each one beginning, in modern parlance, on each white note of the piano and continuing upwards on the white notes only. There was no chromaticism such as the Greeks had, except that B could become B flat to give a softening effect. And so these eight modes have a variety of arrangement of their tones and semitones unknown to our typical major-minor system, which simply transposes the same arrangement of tones and semitones into different keys.

There is a certain correspondence between plain-song and the quiet, simple lines and curves of the columns and arches of the nave of a fifth-century Romanesque basilica: but there is no correspondence between Gothic architecture and plain-song. Gothic architecture is a mass in motion, rather than at rest—its intricate lines and decoration accord rather with the polyphonic music of the period in which it arose. It may also be said here that just as a church is not a beautiful arrangement of stone and glass merely intended to awaken aesthetic admiration but is a building disposed for prayer and praise, so plain-song (or indeed any truly liturgical music) is not merely a pleasing and beautiful arrangement of tones and semitones but music also disposed for prayer and praise.

The earliest church music naturally had to build upon the past, and that meant above all Jewish Bible song. No direct trace of this exists, though age-old traditions are preserved by the more remote Jewish communities. Perhaps, in this connection, we tend to forget that up to A.D. 60, at least, the adherents of the new

---

[1] I speak here of the method followed, and very generally adopted, by the Benedictine monks of the Solesmes Congregation.

faith continued to worship in synagogue and temple. With a measure of poetic licence we could indeed say that the birth of Christian music took place under the shadow of the synagogue, just as the central rite of the Christian faith was instituted at a Jewish Upper Room meeting.

Now the Fathers of the Church, from the first, wanted music to elevate the whole man towards God, and that ideal ran like a golden thread through plain-song. They wanted church music to be different from that heard in the world and they were especially concerned to do battle against the vicious influence of the contemporary theatre: and it *was* a battle.

The Christians in the West ceased to be a persecuted sect by the fourth century, even before Constantine the Great's Edict of Milan. When able to practise their faith openly they received a considerable influx of the rich and learned. Large basilicas were built and it was now possible to begin the shaping of the Liturgy and its music, for the Church went forth singing into the world. Great quantities of melodies were eventually collected for liturgical purposes in the Roman, Milanese, Frankish, and Celtic rites, as well as in the East, which had so strongly influenced the earliest church music of the West. The large churches required that priests addressing their congregations should raise their voices for important pronouncements. This is the simplest kind of plain-song—the inflected monotone used for prayers and Bible readings. A priest with some musical sensibility would be likely to improvise simple embellishments, and by these indicate punctuation. An example is the priest intoning the Epistle for Easter Sunday.

Easter Sunday Mass: Epistle. DGG APM 14017.

A practice originated in Syrian monasteries and churches (and elsewhere) in the fourth century of the singing of successive verses of the psalms by alternating choruses of men and women and children. This singing was called antiphonal from the Greek word *antiphonia*, which means the octave in Greek theory, and may have been so used, because there was a difference of an octave in pitch between the two choruses. Later, a short sentence was added and repeated as a refrain after each verse, or pair of verses, giving rise eventually to that kind of psalm singing we call antiphonal to-day. The early practice is shown in this example:

the canticle *Nunc Dimittis*. The words of the last verse, 'Lumen ad revelationem, gentium,' etc. (To be a light to lighten the Gentiles), are used for the antiphonal refrain before, during, and after the canticle.

Lumen ad revelationem. HISTORY OF MUSIC IN SOUND, VOL. II. VICTOR LM 6015 (HMV HMS 11, 78 r.p.m.).

There were two other kinds of psalmody, both of them a legacy from the synagogue, one called Direct and the other Responsorial. In the first of these, which came also to be called 'Tract,' a whole psalm was sung as a solo. The Tract in the Roman Missal, sung at penitential seasons, is a developed example of this kind of solo psalmody. In the second kind, Responsorial Psalmody, the cantor, as in the Tract, again sang the whole psalm as a solo, but the people responded with a refrain between the verses. Antiphonal and responsorial singing are therefore closely allied.

Antioch and Constantinople were the first centres of another and very popular kind of music making in church—the singing of hymns. St Ambrose, the great Bishop of Milan, was the father of western hymnody, but the music of his hymns has unfortunately not survived. It is thought, from their enormous popularity, that it was of a folksong-like character. The Roman Church for a long time looked on these hymns with some suspicion which she eventually overcame. Her composers imitated the Ambrosian verse metre, tunefulness, and simplicity, and *Te lucis ante terminum* (Before the ending of the day) from the Office of Compline is a familiar example of the Ambrosian type of hymn.

Hymn: *Te lucis ante terminum.* LONDON LLA 14 (DECCA LXT 2708).

By the time St Gregory and his advisers began to undertake the reform of the Roman Chant, it had developed (along with the Liturgy) into the various forms of chants of the Mass we have to-day. These were gathered together into a book called the *Antiphonale Missarum*—Antiphonal of Masses—later known as the *Graduale Romanum*—Roman Gradual.

The Proper of the Mass is so called because it comprises all that material proper to the season or feast being celebrated. First of all the *Introit*. As its name implies—the entering in—it is a processional chant and is of the antiphonal type. It came into the Roman Mass during the fifth century. The Introit for the

*B

third Sunday after Easter, *Jubilate Deo* (Shout with joy to God), has a threefold alleluia at the end of the antiphon.

Introit: *Jubilate Deo.* LONDON LLA 14 (DECCA LXT 2706).

St Gregory's reform worked towards shortening and simplifying the chants. It had been customary for psalms to be sung between readings from the Old Testament and the New Testament, with the people responding with a short interjection. But in Gregory's day these psalms were sung as solos and had become so elaborate that they needed virtuoso singers. These were the gradual psalms—the *gradus* was the step up to the little pulpit from which the gradual was sung, and the music is some of the most difficult and elaborate in Gregorian Chant. One has to remember that it was sung while there was no action at the altar, and everyone was prepared to listen to the singer using his art (though not always!) for the glory of God. The gradual responsory for the Epiphany tells the story of the Wise Men: *Omnes de Saba venient.* The verse 'Surge et illuminare' is particularly fine—the melody rises in great arches of tone at 'illuminare' and 'Gloria Domini.' And you will notice how at the words 'Saba' and 'surge' the accented syllables have only two or three notes, the unaccented ones a whole shower of notes. In this way the accented syllables throw their light over the whole word. *Haec Dies* for Easter Sunday is another splendid gradual. It sings of Christ's resurrection with ardent spiritual rapture—it is one of the finest pieces of Gregorian Chant in the whole repertoire.

Graduals: (i) *Omnes de Saba venient*; (ii) *Haec Dies.* LONDON LLA 14 (DECCA LXT 2706).

After the gradual comes the alleluia, in which the final vowel of the word is vocalized and was known as the *jubilus.* St Augustine has a famous passage in one of his Commentaries on the *jubilus* which he rightly calls, 'a song of joy without words.' Often the music at the end of the verse recapitulates all or part of the alleluia before the latter is sung again. Our last example was the Easter Gradual; here is its complementary alleluia with the verse *Pascha nostrum* which speaks of Christ sacrificing Himself for us. On the accented syllable of the word 'Immolatus' there is a wonderful high-pitched phrase of joy. The alleluia, in this particular case, is not repeated.

Alleluia: *Pascha nostrum.* DGG APM 14017.

The offertory, like the introit, was originally a processional chant, sung as the people came up to make their offerings. It had an antiphon—later much ornamented by the singer—and a psalm. The psalm has now vanished, leaving only the antiphon. The first offertory I have chosen is *Super flumina Babylonis*, a poignant picture of the exiled Jews weeping by the waters of Babylon as they remember Jerusalem. The rising and falling phrases are most expressive.

The second example of the offertory, *Tollite portas* (Lift up your gates, O ye princes), is a joyful piece of welcome to the King of Glory, with a last phrase like a trumpet fanfare.

Offertory: (i) *Super flumina Babylonis*; (ii) *Tollite portas*. LONDON LLA 14 (DECCA LXT 2707).

The Communion chants are also processional as they were sung as the faithful came up to the altar to communicate. They are antiphonal, like the offertory. The psalm verses are no longer sung, and, as in the offertory, only the antiphon, usually a simple melody, remains. There is, however, one exception to this in the Mass for the Dead. In this beautiful chant *Lux aeterna luceat eis Domine*, there is a verse 'Requiem aeternam dona eis Domine,' with the second half of the antiphon repeated after it.

Communion: (i) *Lux aeterna*. DGG APM 14002; (ii) *Pater si non potest*. LONDON LLA 14 (DECCA LXT 2707).

The invariable part of the Mass is called the Ordinary. It consists of *Kyrie, Gloria, Credo, Sanctus*, and *Agnus Dei*; and it is this part, just because it is invariable, that composers have set to music over and over again and still do. Nearly all chants of the Ordinary were composed after the sixth century and so post-date St Gregory. Many of these chants, though by no means all, are too difficult for congregational use. At the same time there is a folksong-like melodiousness and simplicity in some of them, and because no one recognized the existence of folk music or bothered to write it down, we shall never know how much secular music of the time has found its way into them. The chants we have are dated, most of them, from the tenth to the sixteenth century, but the simplest, litany-like chants are undoubtedly much earlier and would have been known to Gregory. Here is the *Kyrie* from one of these, a Mass for days on which there is no feast. It is only in the last *Kyrie* of all that a little elaboration comes in, revealing the hand of the singer-composer.

Kyrie XVII. ENGLISH DECCA LX 3118.

Kyrie eleison had long been a pagan invocation to the Sun God when the Eastern Christians took it over. St Gregory speaks of adding *Christe eleison* to it and repeating each petition a number of times, the people answering the clergy. The number of times was settled in the eighth century at three *Kyries*—three *Christes*—three *Kyries*. So a composer could write a contrasted section of music for the *Christes* and return to the music of the first three *Kyries* for the final ones—or he could provide new music all through.

Let us consider a plain-song setting of a complete Ordinary of the Mass, omitting only the *Credo*. I have chosen one of the most beautiful, No. XI, for Sundays throughout the year. The first *Kyries* in this Mass end with a little up and down phrase (on *eleison*) that the composer liked so much that he brought it into the *Christes* as well—here we have the principle of the motto theme. The last *Kyrie* is slightly elaborated but ends of course with the same motto theme.

The *Gloria*, with no repetition of words and a fairly long text, has, as a rule, simpler music so that it may move more quickly— mostly it follows the rule of one syllable, one note. Here too, to give unity, we find the opening phrase of the *Gloria* is used seven times in its course.

Next comes the *Sanctus*. Notice how the *Hosanna* phrases seem to suggest the obeisance of the people at our Lord's triumphal entry into Jerusalem.

The music of the *Agnus Dei*, the last section of the Ordinary, is beautifully contrived, in this setting, to rise higher in pitch with each of the two repetitions of the words—and here again we have a device that composers in later years were to use extensively to heighten emotional appeal.

Mass XI: *Kyrie, Gloria, Sanctus, Agnus Dei.* LONDON LLA 14 (DECCA LX 3119).

The Divine Office, as we know it to-day, is the great work of St Benedict, the father of western monasticism. He called it *Opus Dei* (God's work) and directed his monks to devote themselves to it before all else. It has an interesting history.

The celebration of the Lord's Supper, the Eucharist, originally held in the evening, was moved to dawn during the times of persecution, and then to the early morning. In a famous letter to the Emperor Trajan, Pliny the Younger described how 'on certain days the Christians get together before sunrise and sing songs to Christ as if he were God.' These vigils, as they were called, were at first limited to Sundays, or rather Saturday night, with the Eucharist celebrated at daybreak on Sunday. Later on the meetings started at dusk when lamps were lit. The psalms and prayers then sung and said are the oldest form of Vespers. Psalm singing was the chief occupation of all at the vigils. We can picture the scene from a report of the conversation of the pilgrims dating from the fifth century—'One of them is astonished by the magnificence and splendour of the ceremonies, another by the vast crowds which they have attracted, a third by the large concourse of bishops. One praises the eloquence of the preachers, another the beauty of the psalmody, another the endurance of the public during the long night office, another the fervour in prayer of the assistants. One recalls the dust, another the stifling heat ... the cries and disputes, the disorder of people getting into each other's way and refusing to give place, each eager to be the first to participate.' [1]

Benedictine communities were established in Rome in the sixth century, civilizing north-western Europe. Not all of the monasteries were true to their high ideals, but Europe owes them an incalculable debt. A by no means uncritical Protestant historian observes that the monks first taught western Europe to work methodically.

The centre of the monks' lives was the singing of the *Opus Dei* from the night office of Mattins through the day offices of Lauds, Prime, Terce, Sext, None, and Vespers to Compline, the 'ending of the day.' In the scriptoria, during the day, some monks and lay assistants would be copying out manuscripts and illuminating them, others would be adapting and composing chants. It required great skill to take the melody of an existing chant and set it to new words, for almost certainly you had to lengthen it or shorten it. There are antiphon 'types' used for over fifty different texts in this way. Sometimes the monks used

[1] *The Legacy of the Middle Ages*, edited by G. C. Crump and E. F. Jacob (Oxford University Press).

a mosaic technique, taking this little group of notes and that one and piecing them together. A snatch of popular song, drifting up from the pilgrims in the courtyard, might go into a bit of chant, or the flight of a bird might suggest a sequence of notes.

Antiphonal psalmody predominates in the Divine Office. The texts of the antiphons are concerned, of course, with the feasts and seasons of the year. They are both preludes and points of meditation, but they also had the practical purpose of setting the pitch and mode of the psalm to follow. The antiphon is so devised as to fit without jar on to the psalm tone following and to join on to the end of it when the psalm was done and the antiphon repeated.

Monotony in the long procession of psalms in the night office was avoided by ringing changes on the eight psalm tones, most of which have also a number of alternate endings. Good chanting goes rhythmically back and forth between the two sides of the choir—like the gentle breaking of waves on the seashore. Here is a typical antiphon and psalm—*Ave Maria*, an antiphon for one of the feasts of Our Lady—and a short psalm of praise, *Laudate Dominum omnes gentes* (Praise the Lord all ye people).

Ave Maria.   London LLA 14 (Decca LXT 2705).

Besides antiphons and psalms each of the canonical hours contains a hymn, and these hymns are among the most tuneful examples of the chant. The verses are metrical but the chant avoids any squareness of treatment. There is a distinctly popular flavour about such hymns as the familiar *Veni Creator Spiritus*.

Veni Creator Spiritus.   London LLA 14 (Decca LXT 2708).

Ave Maris Stella (Hail Star of the Sea) is one of the loveliest of the Marian hymns. Notice the high melody note on the accented syllable of *Stella* which shines down over the whole phrase and hymn.

Hymn: *Ave Maris Stella.*   London LLA 14 (Decca LXT 2708).

The short responsories of the Divine Office are interesting in point of form, for here we have the idea of the rondo prefigured. In the example chosen, *Verbum Caro factum est—Alleluia* (an Easter one), the choir repeat the cantors' words, the cantors continue, the choir repeat the Alleluias, the cantors sing *Gloria*

Patris, the choir repeat *Verbum Caro*, etc., ending with the Alleluias: and so it is a little rondo in being.

Short Responsory: *Verbum Caro factum est.* LONDON LLA 14
(DECCA LXT 2705).

The long responsories are of a different type, and we will take as our example *O vos omnes* (O, all ye who pass by, see if there be any grief like unto My grief). Half of the first section is repeated after the verse, or middle part of the responsory. Notice how the chant underlines the words 'Attendite et videte,' as if calling us to halt before the Cross and meditate on Christ's redeeming love for us.

Quem vidistis pastores is a joyful responsory. It comes from the Mattins of the Nativity and is a dialogue between some village people and the shepherds. 'What did you see, shepherds?' 'We saw one who was born and a choir of angels praising God.'

Both these responsories are, in the restrained way of Gregorian Chant, dramatic pictures—comparable to the early paintings of the scenes they represent.

Responsories: (i) *O vos omnes*; (ii) *Quem vidistis pastores.* LONDON
LLA 14 (DECCA LXT 2708).

At the end of Compline, when the whole monastic family is gathered together before retiring, there is sung one of the three antiphons of Our Lady, of which *Salve Regina* (Hail Holy Queen) is certainly the best known and loved. It has two chants, one simple and one solemn. The solemn (and older) one is especially beautiful and it again emphasizes the complete harmony of word and tone in Gregorian Chant. Notice especially the closing phrases 'O clemens, o pia, o dulcis Virgo Maria,' which are full of the greatest tenderness.

Antiphon: *Salve Regina.* LONDON LLA 14 (DECCA LXT 2705).

The Sequence, the last chant we have to consider, came into being in the first half of the ninth century and thereafter expanded enormously. It grew partly out of a practical consideration. Singers found it hard to remember the long vocalization of the alleluias, and accordingly words were set to them. So began the Sequence—something that follows on, or a succession of notes. Soon sections of the alleluias, given words in this way, became detached from the parent chants as independent compositions. It was a new impetus to invention. *Victimae Paschali*, the Easter

Sequence, has a folksong-like syllabic melody, and is a dramatic dialogue. Mary is asked, after the opening sentences, what she saw at the tomb and she describes the empty tomb, the napkin and linen clothes, and the angels. She hails the risen Christ. It was from such dialogues that the liturgical drama was to come, the birth-place of our modern theatre.

Sequence: *Victimae Paschali laudeo*. LONDON LLA 14 (DECCA LXT 2706).

What impact, it may be asked, did Gregorian Chant make upon the ordinary men and women of the early Middle Ages? They must have picked up and sung or parodied the more popular kind of melodies, but there is all too little evidence as to what part they played in singing at Mass, or what Gregorian Chant meant to them. Much of it was over their heads and trained choirs took over much that was their rightful part. The church was, nevertheless, their concert hall, their library, and their art gallery, and the people must often have been uplifted by what they dimly understood.

In the ninth century the West was able to breathe more freely after the barbarian invasions that had threatened Christianity, and with the Carolingian Renaissance came Charles the Great's determination to develop a Christian culture in an ecclesiastical state with himself as a sort of lay-Pope. It was he, not the reigning Pope, who secured the triumph (in some ways regrettable) of Gregorian Chant over the Gallican and Mozarabic Chants of France and Spain, and it was he who did much to bring about liturgical order with its centre at Rome. But the Popes were determined to be masters in their own home, and after a long struggle became so.

The society of the Middle Ages was not sweetly submissive any more than it was barbarous and ignorant. Its many varieties of religious experience were part of the social structure. Christianity was an inseparable element in men's lives, even if many of them only conformed outwardly, and the Church, whatever scandal some of her ministers gave, was the Ark of Salvation, the teacher of the people. Whatever the failings of the Church of the Middle Ages may have been we can see in its splendid churches, stained glass, illuminated service books, statues, its incomparable architecture, and glorious music a noble expression of the highest ideals of the service and contemplation of God, which called these things forth in unparalleled quantity and richness. And we can be sure that there were in the mass of people thousands of unknown folk, lay and religious, whose lives, inspired by all that is signified by the word Church, were no less beautiful in the sight of God.

APPENDIX

BOOKS

ALEC ROBERTSON: *Sacred Music; The Interpretation of Gregorian Chant.*
WILLI APEL: *Gregorian Chant* (in preparation).
J. S. VAN WAESBERGHE: *Gregorian Chant.*

RECORDS

Most of the examples cited in the chapter were drawn from London LLA 14 (Decca LXT 2704–8). This may be supplemented by the four records London LSA 17 (Decca LX 3118–21) devoted to the Ordinary of the Mass.

Easter Sunday Mass. DECCA ARC 3001 (DGG APM 14017). LONDON LL 1408 (DECCA LXT 5171).
Christmas Vespers. DECCA 7546 (DGG AP 13005).
Good Friday Liturgy. DGG APM 14034.
First Mass for the Dead. DGG APM 14002.
Easter and Christmas Music. ANGEL 35116 (COLUMBIA 33 CX 1193).
Mass of the Day. ENGLISH DECCA LXT 5251.
Solemnis Palmarum Processio. DGG AP 13041.
Ascension and Assumption. ENGLISH DECCA LXT 5227.

4

Denis Stevens

THE TROUBADOURS

AN AIR of mystery pervades the lives of the troubadours, inevitably, for they lived eight or nine hundred years ago, and the passage of time has not always been kind to the rare and precious documents that could tell us about the career and character of each man. It is nevertheless possible to judge their achievements by what has survived of their music, for more than two hundred troubadour melodies have been preserved for us in various manuscripts; some elegantly written and beautifully illuminated, and others very obviously the work of some hasty scribe. Before coming to the melodies, it may be well to see whether the troubadours were alone in their intensive cultivation of song and their strange and subtle code of manners.

The art of the troubadours seems to have grown up in the south of France where the language, in the Middle Ages, was known as Provençal, or *langue d'oc*. '*Oc*' was Provençal for 'yes,' and this type of ending can be seen in countless place names in the troubadour country. In the northern part of France the word for 'yes' was pronounced 'ouil,' almost as it is to-day. So the two main language groups were known as the *langue d'ouil* and the *langue d'oc*. The troubadours were followed by another great generation of poets and singers in the north, and these men, the trouvères, used the French language, which had formed the basis of their life and education. The trouvères were to prove even more prolific; about fourteen hundred of their songs have come down to us.

When we inquire what the motive was behind this new, fine, and sensitive musical culture, we find that the French have a phrase for it: *cherchez la femme*. Indeed, the worship of womankind was in very many instances the idea and the emotion which the troubadour needed in order to create his song. But his adoration had to be a distant worship, a discreet declaration of love, both of these

26

inseparable from a vow of purity, without which the troubadour would be no more than an impostor, a common *jongleur* or juggler. Not that a jongleur was for ever debarred from becoming a troubadour and knight—we have the example of Raimbaut de Vaqueiras, who began life as a minstrel, but was eventually knighted. He fell in love with the prince's sister, but lacked discretion in the manner of his courtship, with the result that malicious tongues began to wag. The Lady Beatrice made it plain that she no longer loved him, and for a long time he was utterly inconsolable. Then suddenly she turned and spoke to him, begging him to compose a song for her. Raimbaut did so at once, taking as his tune one of the *estampies*, or dance tunes, heard earlier in the evening at court. The song is *Kalenda Maya*: 'On the first of May, neither leaf of beech, nor song of bird, nor flower of sword lily pleases me, lady noble and gay, until I receive a speedy messenger from your fair self.'

Raimbaut de Vaqueiras: *Kalenda Maya*. Decca ARC 3002 (alt. Vox PL 8110).

Everybody joins in that song. The phrases are thrown briskly and gaily from one group of singers to the leader, and from the leader back to the group again. That principle of responding to a lead was one of the fundamental features of medieval music in all its aspects. It may well have come originally from the Church —from responsorial plain-song—and the troubadours often took their melodies from Gregorian Chant. They adapted them slightly, but everyone was bound to recognize the contour of the melody. By no means all of the melodies came from a plain-song source; some may have been composed by the troubadour himself, and others have an almost popular lilt which suggests that they belonged originally to the vast repertory of folk-song.

For melodies of the composed type we can do no better than turn to the troubadour, Bernart de Ventadour (*c.* 1145–95). He was the son of a humble servant, but was given both education and encouragement by his master, Count Ebles, himself the son of a poet. When the time came for him to leave his native country of Limousin, he wrote a moving and eloquent song, telling of his love for the Countess of Ventadour and of his need to depart. Legend has it that Bernart, like Raimbaut, was indiscreet in his love. Whatever the reason for his leaving, he must have missed the colourful and fertile valleys of Corrèze. Bernart was inspired by the birds as well as by the scenery around him, as in his song about the lark.

Bernart de Ventadour: *Can vei la lauzeta.* HISTORY OF MUSIC IN SOUND, VOL. II. VICTOR LM 6015 (HMV HMS 14, 78 r.p.m.).

Can vei la lauzeta, like the majority of love-songs by the troubadours and trouvères, was for one voice without accompaniment. But we may ask whether an instrument was ever used to accompany the songs, and if so, did it simply double the melody, or play an introduction and tail-piece? Did it add harmonies in the modern sense of the word? These questions are important, because they are bound up with modern interpretation of the songs, and also with the lives and customs of the troubadours themselves.

The medieval jongleur was a combination of minstrel and juggler. There are often pictures of them in the manuscripts that contain troubadour songs, and they are seen playing instruments like the medieval fiddle or lute, juggling with swords, and even walking the tightrope. The function of the jongleurs was to amuse the audience at courts and castles, acting as a foil to the serious matter of the evening—the troubadour songs themselves—and thus a troubadour and a jongleur often formed what we should nowadays call a 'double act.' The jongleur was capable of playing an instrumental accompaniment to his master's songs, and although not written down, there is no reason to doubt that these accompaniments once existed, if only in the fertile brain of the jongleur. The accompaniments were probably very simple, making much use of drone basses such as one hears from a bagpipe. It is almost certainly wrong to think of troubadour songs as bare melodies, and some editors are imaginative enough to invent accompaniments. An example is *Lancan vei la folha,* also by Bernart de Ventadour. 'When I see the leaves falling from the tree, whoever may grieve or sorrow, I find it much to my taste. Do not think that I want to see either flower or leaf, for she scorns me, she who is the one I most desire.'

Bernart de Ventadour: *Lancan vei la folha.* Vox PL 8110.

In 1155 Bernart paid a visit to England because his patroness, Eleanor of Acquitaine, had recently settled there as the queen of the newly crowned Henry II. Although many English noblemen must have listened entranced to Bernart's wonderful store of songs, there was no apparent desire on the part of the English for a type of art-song similar to Bernart's.

The few secular songs that have come down to us from the twelfth and thirteenth centuries in England bear little relation to the troubadour and trouvère repertoire. The language spoken at the English court was Norman-French; thus rather than foster a local variant of troubadour art, it was easier and more satisfactory to send for one of the troubadours in person. One of the best known of the few English songs that survived is *Worldes blis*, which is sad, even bitter in its sentiments: 'the world's joy lasts no time at all.'

> *Worldes blis.* HISTORY OF MUSIC IN SOUND, VOL. II. VICTOR LM 6015 (HMV HMS 15, 78 r.p.m.).

Bernart did not stay long in England. Eleanor followed him on the long road to Acquitaine, for her relations with Henry II grew steadily worse. Soon she was at Poitiers, holding her fantastic courts of love, where artificial problems were set for lovers, and palms were awarded for excellence in *l'amour courtois*. Troubadours flocked to her court, and some would sing of their brethren absent on the crusades, with no news to tell of their fortunes or whereabouts—as in *Chanterai por mon coraige* by Guiot de Dijon.

> Guiot de Dijon: *Chanterai por mon coraige.* HISTORY OF MUSIC IN SOUND, VOL II. VICTOR LM 6015 (HMV HMS 14, 78 r.p.m.).

There were cheerful moments too, when *ballades* and *rondeaux* were sung and played, and the drums were beaten and the flutes piped merrily. There is the rondeau *Tuit cil qui sunt enamourat* or the ballade *A l'entrada del tens clar*: 'When the fine weather comes to bring back joy again and to annoy the jealous, I wish to show the Queen, for she is so much in love. Away, away, jealous ones, leave us to dance among ourselves.'

> (i) *Tuit cil qui sunt enamourat.* HISTORY OF MUSIC IN SOUND, VOL. II. VICTOR LM 6015 (HMV HMS 14, 78 r.p.m.).
> (ii) *A l'entrada del tens clar.* DECCA ARC 3002.

The rhythm tells us that those songs were meant for dancing, probably a round-dance with a small group of singers and instrumentalists at one side. Dancing was as popular in the Middle Ages as it is to-day, and its influence on troubadour art was very great indeed. I have already mentioned that Raimbaut de Vaquieras based a song on an *estampie*. We may take two further examples of dance music. The first has no text and no special title, but it reminds us of the dance-songs, nevertheless, because there is a refrain which returns at the end of every phrase. The second example is probably English in origin. Right at the end the single line of melody bursts forth into three-part harmony, as if the minstrels had been saving up their *tour de force.*

(i) *La Quarte Estampie Reale*; (ii) *Estampie: 'Spielmannstanz.'* Vox PL 8110.

We must always remember that the tradition of medieval minstrelsy did not exclude participation by men of more exalted rank. Gifted musicians would often take part and would not lose caste by doing so. Some troubadours were noblemen, some were members of a rich family of merchants, others came from a poor family of townsfolk.

In Spain and Italy we find the same diversity of background. By far the largest collection of Spanish songs was made by King Alfonso X of Castile and Léon, and although music was only a small part of his learning, he deserved the nickname of *Alfonoso el Sabio*—Alfonso the Wise. In these Spanish songs love of womankind has already been further sublimated, for it is the Virgin Mary who is praised beyond all measure. The songs are written in a language that is half Spanish, half Portuguese, but the melodies often have a definite Spanish flavour about them.

(i) *Como peden*; (ii) *Quen â Virgen.* HISTORY OF MUSIC IN SOUND, VOL. II.   VICTOR LM 6015 (HMV HMS 15, 78 r.p.m.).

Italy had its troubadour imitators too, though none of their music has come down to us. The spirit of the music survives, however, in the *Laudi Spirituali*, or spiritual hymns sung on pilgrimages throughout Italy during the thirteenth century.

O divina Virgo. HISTORY OF MUSIC IN SOUND, VOL. II.   VICTOR LM 6015 (HMV HMS 15, 78 r.p.m.).

In conclusion, I should mention the field of drama.   In the late thirteenth century a dramatic pastoral called *Le Jeu de Robin et de Marion* was played before the court of Charles d'Anjou at Naples. The author was Adam de la Halle, whose charming tale of shepherds and shepherdesses is matched by equally charming music.

Adam de la Halle: *Le Jeu de Robin et de Marion.* DECCA ARC 3002 (DGG APM 14018).

(APPENDIX: *See* page 72.)

5

Denis Stevens

THE TROUVÈRES AND THE MINNESINGERS

THE trouvères largely followed the ideals of the troubadours, the texts of their songs being in the Norman-
French which is close to the French language spoken
to-day. It is difficult for us to understand fully the nature
and implications of courtly love—*l'amour courtois*—for the popular
love-songs of to-day are not exactly brimming over with courteous
restraint in their adulation of the fair sex. Seven centuries ago
the singer was bound by a strict code of conduct, and often strove
to compose his songs and poems in such a way that their true
meaning should be apparent only to the lady concerned. Others
might hear the song, but would not understand its true import—
or so the theory went. There are certain instances of a seeming
lack of impersonality; Bernart de Ventadour begins a song with
these words: 'Do not be surprised if I sing better than any other
troubadour.' He was not lacking modesty, however; what he
wished to convey was that his love and admiration for his lady
gave him the power to sing better than anyone else.

It was tacitly assumed that a troubadour or trouvère in love was
entirely given up to the fascination of his loved one, and this cult
of adoration was marked by a certain mysticism and a certain
nobility of sentiment. In order to win the favour of his lady, the
singer had to honour her by long service and devotion, and in
accepting this devotion the lady became the sovereign ruler of her
lover's heart and mind. Yet the singer had no right to ask any
reward at first for his service: he was, as it were, entirely at her
mercy; and although he might express his sorrow and regret at
her seeming lack of interest, he had no right to reproach her. The
lady herself was bound to be a paragon of all the virtues. But there
were always malicious gossips, and the singer often refers to their
wicked attempts to damage the reputation of his lady.

Some of the trouvères became so famous that their names were celebrated by great poets who lived many years after them. An example is Gace Brulé, who lived in the twelfth century, for his name was honoured two centuries later by Dante Alighieri in *De Vulgaris Eloquentia*. In Gace Brulé's song *Je ne puis pas si loing fuir* ('I cannot flee so far') words and music go hand in hand to describe the lover's sadness; try as he may, he cannot forget his lady.

Gace Brulé: *Je ne puis pas si loing fuir*. HISTORY OF MUSIC IN SOUND, VOL. II. VICTOR LM 6015 (HMV HMS 14, 78 r.p.m.).

Many singers tried to forget by going off to the crusades. The First Crusade (1096–9) was almost contemporary with the first great phase of troubadour art; three more crusades took place before the first decade of the thirteenth century, and these saw the greatest period in the art of the trouvères. In Europe it was the time when some of the most magnificent of our medieval cathedrals and abbeys were built. Masons and carvers, artists in coloured glass and coloured stone-work were working together to create such unparalleled examples of Gothic art as the cathedrals of Canterbury, Chartres, Mainz, Notre-Dame de Paris, Lincoln, Chichester, and Rheims. With cathedrals being put up, and pagans being put down, there was an opportunity for everyone to rejoice; and that is why so much of the work of the trouvères—in spite of their wonderful love-songs—is full of joy. The form of the *rondeau* is still used, with the alternation between soloist and chorus, and we may take an example by Guillaume d'Amiens; *Prenes-y garde*. A young swain is making amorous advances to an attractive brunette who is trying to keep her mind on the cows she is supposed to be looking after. The chorus chimes in after every verse: 'Keep a look-out! Is anyone watching? If anyone's watching us, give me a shout!'

Guillaume d'Amiens: *Prenes-y garde*. DECCA ARC 3002 (DGG APM 14018).

The songs of Guillaume d'Amiens are to be found in manuscripts in the Bibliothèque Nationale, Paris, and the Vatican Library, Rome. For centuries the songs remained there, unknown and unsung. Medieval songs are found in twenty or more manuscripts scattered throughout the great libraries of Europe, in France, Italy, Spain, and Germany; and there are many more manuscripts which contain just the texts of the songs. Some of the manuscripts are beautifully written and illuminated, ornamented by pictures of the troubadours themselves or their jongleurs, and undoubtedly they were commissioned by some rich nobleman who wished to have the choicest songs of the time enshrined in a vellum manuscript of impeccable workmanship. There are other manuscripts, less sumptuously written, though the texts and music may be quite as accurate. The impression they give is that they must have been used by a minstrel as his day-to-day material.

Each of these manuscript sources has its own character, its own particular repertoire of songs. Sometimes it looks as if each one has its own kind of notation because the musical notes of the Middle Ages assumed many different forms. Most of these apparent differences are due to the personal handwriting of the scribes, but we must remember that musical notation was undergoing great changes during the twelfth and thirteenth centuries. The tendency was to make notation more and more precise so that no loopholes existed in the matter of rhythm and tempo. The actual pitch of the notes—to show this is comparatively straightforward—had been settled for many years.

It is essential to realize that the gradual stabilization of rhythmic signs was not an unmixed blessing. In the old days troubadour songs could be performed in a free manner, with no restrictions about tempo, rhythm, or bar-lines as we know them. When the trouvères were at the height of their achievement the situation was very different; their songs can be, and usually are, transcribed in what is called modal rhythm. This makes use of different note-patterns within a rhythmical framework of triple-time: once the mode has been decided upon, there can be little or no departure from it within the song itself. We may take as an example the gently undulating rhythm of *Quand je voi yver retorner*, attributed to Colin Muset.

Colin Muset: *Quand je voi yver retorner*. HISTORY OF MUSIC IN SOUND, VOL. II. VICTOR LM 6015 (HMV HMS 14, 78 r.p.m.).

The continually repeated phrases at the beginning of this song make it sound almost as though it were based on a folk-song. The text too, with its enumeration of staple foods and delicacies of the table, has an almost goliardic feeling—as though written by one of the wandering scholars. For although the heyday of the medieval Latin lyric was long past, there were still scholars to wander from the newly founded University of Paris to outlying centres of learning, like Padua, Salamanca, and Oxford. Many other scholars besides Peter Abélard must have been musical as well as learned; indeed music was one of the seven liberal arts then taught at all the great universities. The tuition was purely theoretical, but students, then as now, sought to improve their learning by indulging in some practical musical activity.

We may now return to the trouvère ideal, that mystic love which characterized their finest utterances in poetry and in music, and take as an example a song by a trouvère who was also a king: Thibaut IV of Champagne, who was crowned King of Navarre in 1234. Thus we see that the art of song was known to, and practised by, not only the highest rank of the nobility, but even by kings and princes. The melodic contour of Thibaut's *Tuit mi desir* is almost modern in its feeling and tonality; there is more than a hint of what we should call the key of F major. The song is divided into two almost equal halves, and the first half is sung twice in order to accommodate the second pair of verses.

Thibaut IV: *Tuit mi desir*. HISTORY OF MUSIC IN SOUND, VOL. II. VICTOR LM 6015 (HMV HMS 14, 78 r.p.m.).

Even more famous as a trouvère than Thibaut of Navarre was Richard the Lion Heart. The story of his imprisonment in France, and his rescue by his servant Blondel, is a picturesque one, though its authenticity has never been proved. But there is no doubt whatever about Richard's skill as a poet and a singer. His mother, Eleanor of Acquitaine, saw to it that Richard learnt music from the finest of the singers at her courts in France and England. When he grew up he liked to take an active part in the music of the royal chapel, and it is said that he used to help in training the choristers. As an absolutely fearless warrior, Richard was renowned above all his contemporaries, but his daring could lead him into difficulties. At one time during the Third Crusade the bad feeling among factions on both the French and English sides rose to such a pitch that Hugh of Burgundy caused a scurrilous song to be sung up and down the army encampments. Richard replied in kind, and was probably well regarded for doing so. The homeward journey, however, took him across the kingdom of Duke Leopold of Austria, whose standard he had caused to be torn down and besmirched. Leopold

had Richard captured and held for ransom.   During his imprisonment Richard wrote his famous song *Ja nun hons pris*, which has,
unfortunately, not yet been recorded.

In Germany medieval song was practised by the minnesingers,
or singers of love.   They were aristocratic singers, unlike the
troubadours and trouvères, who were often of humble origin, and
they flourished from the middle of the twelfth century until the
end of the fifteenth, to be followed by the mastersingers.   The
music of the mastersingers was not by any means as good, however,
and it is only in the songs of the minnesingers that we find that
freedom from the binding rules of composition which makes for
freshness, charm, and beauty.   Only one complete song by the
earliest important minnesinger has come down to us: *Nu alerst
leb'ich* by Walther von der Vogelweide, a song about the Crusade
of 1228.   'Now at last my life begins for me, since my sinful eyes
behold the Holy Land, the very soil which men hold in honour.
My prayer is answered: I have come to the land where God in
human form set foot.'

Walter von der Vogelweide: *Nu alerst leb'ich*.   Vox PL 8110 (E).

We may take as our next two examples two songs that praise
the beauties of nature.   The first, by a slightly younger contemporary of Vogelweide, Neithart von Reuenthal, is called
May Song.   'May has lifted up many hearts.   He has shown full
well what his sweet joy can do, when he clothes the blackthorn
in white blossoms.'   The accompaniment added there by the
editor is for the psaltery; in the second example, *So schon wir den
Anger nie gesahen* (Never has the green meadow seemed so lovely)
the accompaniment is for viols.

(i) Neithart von Reuenthal: *May Song*; (ii) Anon: *So schon wir den
Anger nie gesahen*.   Vox PL 8110 (E).

One of the outstanding minnesingers of the late thirteenth
century was Heinrich von Meissen.   He was in fact the last of
the old school, and after his death the cult of minnesingers tended
more and more to pass into the domain of city guilds and societies.
He was known to his contemporaries as *Frauenlob* ('Praise of
Ladies'), yet he was not always concerned with courtly love: his
songs in praise of the Virgin Mary are equally typical of his art.

Heinrich von Meissen: *Ey ich sach in dem trone*.   HISTORY OF MUSIC
IN SOUND, VOL. II.   VICTOR LM 6015 (HMV HMS 15, 78 r.p.m.).

Our final example takes our survey up to the fifteenth century. It is again a May song, but with an important difference in the texture; the composer, Oswald von Wolkenstein, has composed his own accompaniment, which is played on the harp. The song is actually an adaptation of a French melody of the fourteenth century; a very tasteful arrangement which preserves all the bird-calls—dove, lark, thrush, nightingale, and cuckoo. The song is an early example of word-painting in music as well as a charming composition in itself.

Oswald von Wolkenstein: *Der May*.   Vox PL 8110 (E).

(APPENDIX: *See* page 72.)

6

Willi Apel

THE BIRTH OF POLYPHONY

D IFFERENT though the song of an Indian warrior, a hymn
to Apollo, and an Alleluia from the Roman liturgy may
be from one another, they have one trait in common:
they consist of nothing but a single melody without
harmonies or other additional elements. Such music is called
monophonic, this being the Greek term for 'one voice.' Compare
with this a symphony by Beethoven, a nocturne by Chopin, a
chorus by Mendelssohn, or a fugue of Bach and you have an entirely different type of music. It may be said to consist of many
simultaneous parts, if we interpret the term 'part' to denote any
additional element, whether produced by the human voice or on
an instrument, whether consisting of chords as in a nocturne by
Chopin or of individual lines as in a fugue by Bach. This, then,
is called polyphonic music. Although polyphony of a more or
less primitive kind occurs in many parts of the world, it was only
in western Europe that its possibilities were systematically
explored in a thousand years' evolution which, we may safely
predict, will continue as long as our civilization exists.

We should remember that it is only in the last fifty years that
musicologists have traced back this marvellous development to its
earlier phases and its very inception. Within my own memory
most music lovers believed that nothing worth knowing or hearing
had been written before Haydn. In the first or second decade
of this century the general public became aware of Bach, and he
now occupies Haydn's place as the 'father of music.' Some music
lovers have a vague notion about a sort of grandfather called
Palestrina, and if you open one of the popular books on music
you may learn that there was something called Gregorian Chant,
created about a thousand years before Palestrina.

These thousand years are a plain vacuum, a long, long period of
'crude beginnings.' The books will tell you that something *did*

happen during this period, but it is so strange that you can hardly believe it.   In the ninth century people made a first crude attempt at performing polyphonic music by singing constantly in fifths. About one hundred and fifty years ago, when this fact was discovered, the verdict was, 'horrible!—impossible!' There was then a rule forbidding successive, or as they are usually called, parallel fifths, and people were shocked to learn that these faulty progressions had once formed the very basis of music. One of the foremost historians of the day, Kiesewetter, actually wrote that such music could not have existed 'because parallel fifths are morally impossible.' Gradually a few more examples of medieval polyphony came to light, but they were full of dissonances no less disagreeable to the ear and no less impossible to the mind than the parallel fifths. In 1841 Kiesewetter published a book in which he reproduced three compositions from the thirteenth century with the inscription, 'Very crude counterpoint.'

About 1920 there emerged for the first time a sufficiently complete picture of the entire development of music during the Middle Ages. It appeared under favourable circumstances. The Middle Ages were no longer looked upon as a period of darkness, ignorance, and barbarism. Not a few of the best minds regarded it as a period of the highest spiritual significance. The musical situation also proved remarkably favourable. There had been a Debussy who scattered handfuls of parallel fifths over each page, and there was a Stravinsky who threw arm-loads of dissonances at his listeners. Some of the leading composers, particularly Hindemith, discovered in medieval music a congeniality of basic tendencies and a remarkable similarity of technical methods.

We may turn now to the birth of polyphony. The place is somewhere in the northern part of the Frankish Empire under the successors of Charlemagne; the time is perhaps about 850; and the crown witness is a monk who recorded the memorable event in a book called *Musica enchiriadis* (*Handbook of Music*). The identity of this monk has not been definitely established, although Hucbald seems at present the most likely candidate. Not only did the author of the *Musica enchiriadis* leave the earliest information about polyphonic music, he also treated his subject with much greater clarity and inner conviction than was done during the subsequent two hundred years. Important additional information is found in the closely related *Scholia Enchiriadis* (*Commentary on the Handbook*), which is a dialogue between master and disciple. Both sources include a considerable number of musical illustrations.

What is this early polyphony? It is not free composition in the proper sense of the word. A pre-existing melody is taken from Gregorian Chant, and to this is added another melody. This principle of creating polyphonic music out of plain-song remained valid for three and more centuries, the pre-existing melody being known as a *cantus firmus*, or 'fixed song.' The earliest method of changing a monophonic melody into a polyphonic piece was to have another singer duplicate the melody at the lower fifth or at the lower fourth. Yet other singers could participate by duplicating either of these parts at the octave, resulting in a sort of three-part or even four-part polyphony. Since all the voices move constantly in parallel motion, this type is known as *parallel organum*—*organum* being the generic term for polyphonic music of the ninth through the twelfth century. This method can be illustrated by taking a commonly employed *cantus firmus* (for example, *Benedicamus Domino*) and hearing it first as a plain-song, then as an organum of the fourth, of the fifth, and as a composite organum with both parts in octave doubling.

Benedicamus Domino (four versions). This was especially recorded for the series by the *Collegium Musicum* of Indiana University.

Nowadays we find the austerity and starkness of such music impressive rather than forbidding—or 'crude' and 'morally impossible.' Another example, actually from the *Musica enchiriadis*, is based on the plain-song: *Sit gloria Domini in saecula: laetabitur Dominus in operibus suis* (May the glory of the Lord abide for ever: the Lord shall rejoice in his works).

Sit gloria Domini. HISTORY OF MUSIC IN SOUND, VOL. II. VICTOR LM 6015 (HMV HMS 16, 78 r.p.m.).

Naturally, parallel organum was too elementary a method to satisfy musicians for very long, and modifications towards greater independence of the voice-parts were bound to follow. Nevertheless, it was used for many centuries because of its very simplicity which made it easily applicable to any chant as an improvised embellishment. When Pope John XXII in 1332 interdicted the use of polyphony in church—polyphony had by then become extremely refined—he made an exception in favour of parallel organum.

The first step away from the rigid parallelism is made in the *Musica enchiriadis* itself. The author describes a modified manner of singing in which the singers of the two parts start and end in unison, using parallel motion for the middle portion of each phrase. This may be called converging organum and is illustrated in the *Musica enchiriadis* by *Rex Coeli*.

> *Rex Coeli*. MASTERPIECES OF MUSIC BEFORE 1750, VOL. I. HAYDN SOCIETY HSL 2071.

The parallel motion here is in fourths, not in fifths. In fact, an organum of the fourth, modified by converging motion, and occasionally interspersed with a fifth or a third, seems to have been the prevailing type of polyphonic music in the tenth and early eleventh centuries. It was not until the second half of the eleventh century that free organum emerged. This is characterized by the gradual abandonment of parallel motion, and by the introduction of various intervals—now an octave, now a fifth, now a fourth, a third, another fifth, etc. Consequently, the parts often move in contrary motion; the added voice moves upwards when the *cantus firmus* moves down, and vice versa. In the old organum the *cantus firmus* was always on top and the additional part was below it. In the free organum the parts frequently cross, so that the Gregorian melody is now above, now below the other part.

There exist a number of treatises in which this novel style is described. One by an unknown author, *Ad organum faciendum* (*How to Make Organum*), is exclusively devoted to polyphonic music, and the author declares it to be much superior to a plain melody. Another author is Johannes Cotto (*c.* 1100), who may have been an Englishman and is therefore often referred to as John Cotton. He recommends careful attention to the variety of motion.

There also exist a number of musical sources, and though most of the compositions cannot be read clearly, five or six pieces can be quite reliably transcribed. Particularly interesting are those in a manuscript from Chartres in northern France. These are not short didactic pieces, but actual compositions of some extension. They indicate the beginning of a later development in which polyphonic composition was applied primarily to the responsorial chants, i.e. the gradual and alleluia. The term 'organum' underwent a certain change of meaning in this connection and came to refer to compositions based on a few special types of chant instead of to a general method of polyphonic treatment. The alleluias from the Chartres manuscript also illustrate an important principle that remained valid throughout the further development of organum: to provide polyphonic treatment only for the soloist sections of the chant, while the choral sections were sung in plain-song. So such a composition consists of an alternation of polyphony and plain-song.

Alleluia Angelus Domini. HISTORY OF MUSIC IN SOUND, VOL. II. VICTOR LM 6015 (HMV HMS 16, 78 r.p.m.).

By far the most extensive source of eleventh-century organa is the manuscript preserved at Corpus Christi College, Cambridge, and known as the *Winchester Troper.* It contains a repertoire of more than one hundred and sixty organal parts. More than one-third of this repertoire of eleventh-century polyphony are alleluias, and the responsories are equally numerous, while graduals are entirely absent. A hundred years later, in the school of Notre-Dame, the graduals occupy an equally important place with the alleluias and the responsories.

The twelfth century is a period of flowering and fulfilment after a long interval of relative stagnation. The feeling of dread that attended the arrival of the year 1000 did not quickly pass, and throughout the eleventh century there prevailed a mood of anxiety. A new enthusiasm for life and activity is only felt at the end of this century and finds its first expression in the First Crusade of 1094. It came to full efflorescence in the twelfth century, which saw the rise of the Gothic cathedrals, the founding of the first universities, the revival of classical Latinity, and the love poetry of the troubadours and trouvères.

Polyphonic music in the twelfth century progresses much more rapidly, and for the first time a centre of activity, or school of music, appears at the monastery of St Martial at Limoges in southern France. From the tenth century on St Martial had contributed monophonic additions to Gregorian Chant, and in the early part of the twelfth century we find the first evidence of polyphonic music there. The novel style that developed at St Martial is called *melismatic organum.* In the earlier types of organum the additional part provided just one note to each note of the *cantus firmus.* We now find a tendency to treat the additional part in a more extended and exuberant fashion, with groups of notes, or shorter or longer melismas, against a single note of the Gregorian

c

melody. While the note-against-note principle still prevails in the St Martial organa, it is often interrupted by a melisma. Whenever it occurs, it means that the singer of the *cantus firmus* part will have to sustain his note until the other singer has arrived at the end of the group of notes. If melismas of ten or twenty notes occur in succession, the single tones of the *cantus firmus* will be drawn out into a series of long sustained notes. So the term 'tenor' was introduced. It derived from the Latin word *tenere*, 'to hold,' and was used to denote a part consisting of long-held notes. This seems more plausible than the explanation usually given; that the tenor is the part that 'holds' the Gregorian melody. Actually it fulfils both functions at the same time.

Our examples of melismatic organum are first an *Agnus Dei* with only a few and short melismas at the beginning, and then two which are based on the *Benedicamus Domino* melody which has already been used as an illustration. This appears as the lower part, and above it the upper part moves in free and quite expressive melismas. In the first *Benedicamus Domino* the melismas do not go beyond groups of six or seven notes, but in the second we find a richly melismatic style, occasionally with twenty notes in a group. Consequently the lower part is considerably drawn out, into a real tenor.

(i) *Agnus Dei*. MASTERPIECES OF MUSIC BEFORE 1750, VOL. I. HAYDN SOCIETY HSL 2071.

(ii) *Benedicamus Domino* (1). INDIANA UNIVERSITY *Collegium Musicum*.

(iii) *Benedicamus Domino* (2). MASTERPIECES OF MUSIC BEFORE 1750, VOL. I. HAYDN SOCIETY HSL 2071.

(APPENDIX: *See* page 72.)

7

Willi Apel

THE NOTRE-DAME SCHOOL

ABOUT the middle of the twelfth century the leadership in music shifted from southern France to its northern part. In secular monophony the troubadours give way to the trouvères, and in polyphonic music the school of St Martial in Limoges is followed by the school of Notre-Dame in Paris. In 1163 the foundation was laid for the cathedral of Notre-Dame, that magnificent testimonial to the greatness of medieval art which was to become one of the most important centres of musical activity. For the first time in the development of polyphony, musical creation steps out of the darkness of anonymity and becomes associated with composers known to us by name: Leoninus and Perotinus. Leoninus flourished in the second half of the twelfth century, Perotinus from about 1180 to 1220.

A good deal of information about these men and their work has been preserved in a treatise generally referred to as *Anonymous IV*. Possibly the nameless writer of this document was a young Englishman who studied at the University of Paris near the end of the thirteenth century and attended lectures on music there. He tells us that Magister Leoninus was a great composer of organa and wrote a number of such compositions which became known as 'The Great Book of Organa.' This book has been preserved in several manuscripts and contains forty-six compositions which form a liturgical cycle. A study of them reveals interesting principles of composition. As in the earlier organa, only the solo sections of the liturgical chants are composed, so that the performance involves an alternation between plain-song and polyphony.

The polyphonic sections are composed in an expansive melismatic style, with melismas of many notes against a single note of the lower part, which thus consists of a succession of long sustained notes, or pedal points (to use the term from organ playing).

43

Occasionally, however, we find passages in which the two parts proceed simultaneously, almost note against note. These two contrasting methods, characteristic of Notre-Dame, are known respectively as organal style and descant style. The difference between the two is outlined for us by an anonymous theorist as early as *c.* 1150. While in the organa of St Martial the two styles are employed more or less haphazardly, in the organa of Notre-Dame they are conditioned by the character of the plain-song melody which forms the basis of the composition. Every gradual or alleluia includes a few words or syllables that are sung to a long group of notes. It is obviously impracticable to compose such a group, a melisma in itself, in a melismatic style, because of the inordinate extension that would result. Leoninus therefore composes such passages in the concise style of *discantus*.

Leoninus has an undeniable claim to fame in the field of rhythm. It is in his works that, for the first time, we find incontestable evidence of strictly measured note values, of regular beats, and of metre. In the descant sections the tenor consists of a succession of notes of exactly equal duration, each to the value of a modern crotchet. To each of these notes correspond two or three notes of the upper part, which subdivide the crotchet into smaller values. Thus was born metrical rhythm, though naturally the rhythm of Leoninus proceeds in very simple patterns, mainly in a constant alternation of a long and of a short value, a crochet and a quaver. Such a combination results in triple metre, and indeed this is invariably employed, not only in the works of Leoninus, but till the end of the thirteenth century. It was considered the perfect metre, being modelled after nature, which in thirteenth-century philosophy always had three parts—beginning, middle, and end.

We may take as an example of the music of Leoninus his organum *Haec Dies*, which consists of an alternation of two-voice polyphony and plain-song. In the opening polyphonic section the upper part traces highly expressive lines above the sustained notes of the lower part. The second polyphonic section, after the plain-song, includes a number of descant passages which represent the modern element in this music. If these are somewhat less impressive, it is because the method is less mature.

Leoninus: *Haec Dies*. INDIANA UNIVERSITY *Collegium Musicum*.

The author of *Anonymous IV* tells us that Leoninus's successor,

Perotinus Magnus, was an even greater composer and excelled as a composer of *discantus*. Abandoning the ecstatic declamations of the older tradition, Perotinus established a style remarkable for its limpid clarity, its rationalistic lucidity, its geometrical rigidity. His most conspicuous contribution to the development of musical style was that he established the principles of writing in three and even in four parts, *organa tripla* and *organa quadrupla*. These are monumental works of great extension, and noteworthy for their organal sections, in which a single note of the tenor is extended into a pedal point of thirty or forty or more measures, while the upper parts move along in regular phrases of four measures and in simple rhythms of an almost dance-like quality. Quite frequently the parts are related to each other by the restatement of short motives, and in the organa of Perotinus we find for the first time in music history evidence of the technique of imitation.

One of Perotinus's *organa tripla* is *Alleluia Nativitas*. It begins with two relatively short pedal points, on F and G, continues with a passage in descant style, and closes with a pedal point on G, and in the last section you will notice what has been called dance-style in Perotinus. (The record contains only the beginning of the *Alleluia*.)

Perotinus: *Alleluia Nativitas*. MASTERPIECES OF MUSIC BEFORE 1750, VOL. I. HAYDN SOCIETY HSL 2071.

The artistic culmination of Perotinus's art is represented by his four-voice organum *Viderunt Omnes*. Its opening section is a sixty-measure pedal point on F over which the three upper parts form a constantly moving superstructure that may perhaps be described as a fluctuating or vibrating F major chord. I would almost compare it to a granitic block emitting sonorous vibrations as if under the impact of a giant's hammer stroke. After the tension built up by the seemingly interminable dwelling on the F major sonority, the sudden change to A minor has a truly dramatic impact, the like of which is hardly found in music for many centuries.

Perotinus's organa stand at the end of the development of this great form of early medieval polyphony. During the thirteenth century two other forms become prominent: the *conductus* and the *motet*. The conductus differs from the organum, first of all, in being an entirely free work of art, both textually and musically.

The organa are invariably based on a Gregorian text and melody, but the conductus are free compositions of Latin poems. These poems are interesting for their variety of subject matter; some give expression to religious feelings, others are contemplative, moralizing, accusing, satirizing, or political. As for the freedom of musical treatment, the famous theorist of the thirteenth century, Franco of Cologne, says: 'He who wants to compose a conductus, must first invent a melody as beautiful as possible. He should then employ this as a tenor to add the other parts.' Perhaps the most striking difference between an organum and a conductus is in their treatment of the text. In an organum practically every syllable of the text is greatly extended, so that the composition consists of a succession of vocalizations. In the conductus the text is treated with just one note to each syllable, and pronounced simultaneously in all the parts, obviously to make the text clearly audible. As an example of the conductus we may take *Veri floris sub figura.*

Conductus: *Veri floris sub figura.* HISTORY OF MUSIC IN SOUND, VOL. II. VICTOR LM 6015 (HMV HMS 18, 78 r.p.m.).

Not all conductus are as simple as that example, and many include more or less extended vocalizations which served as a sort of prelude, interlude, or postlude for the declamation of the text. They were called *caudae* (Latin: 'tail') and were much admired, at least by skilled singers. There are some conductus in which the *caudae* outweigh the passages with text. We may take as an example *De castitatis thalamo*, a conductus that opens and closes with a melisma of moderate extension. 'That pure nuptial chamber, a virgin's womb, is the special place provided by the Father for the Son. In all the world, where could one find the like, that could hold the Son, the equal of the Father.'

Conductus: *De castitatis thalamo.* MASTERPIECES OF MUSIC BEFORE 1750, VOL. I. HAYDN SOCIETY HSL 2071.

The conductus as a musical form appeared in the middle of the twelfth century, and a hundred years later was practically obsolete . . . one of the last examples dates from 1248. The reason for its sudden disappearance is, no doubt, that another form had grown up and was showing possibilities of development that the conductus could not match. In fact, this new form, the motet, was destined to lead a longer life than any other form in the entire history of music; from *c.* 1200 without interruption for more than five hundred years to the time of Bach. It underwent so many changes in its long life that it is practically impossible to find a definition that would be universally valid. Normally it is a sacred composition based on a Latin text, but there are many motets that fill neither requirement.

To observe the motet in its nascent stage we have to turn back to the organa of Leoninus and Perotinus, and to the organal style and descant style used in them. The strictly measured descant sections, based on the melismas of Gregorian Chant, were frequently replaced by new compositions deriving from the melismas, but having different melodies in the upper part or parts. These substitute compositions, known as *clausula*, were soon regarded as independent pieces unconnected with the organum from which they originated. A clausula, therefore, is a short composition in strict triple metre, based on a melisma to a single word of a Gregorian Chant. From beginning to end it is a vocalization. The final step was to abolish the vocalization in the upper part by providing a full text, and the clausula was transformed into the motet. The simplest type of motet is a composition in two parts, in which the lower part, the tenor, is sung to a single syllable or vowel, while the upper part is sung to a full text.

In the earliest stage of the motet the text was a Latin religious poem which provided a commentary on the single word sung by the tenor or to the Gregorian Chant from which this word is taken. The motet provided the opportunity to write new poetry which, however, received liturgical sanction through its connection with the words symbolic of the great thoughts of Christian faith. We may judge how this opportunity filled a need by the fact that soon motets were written in three parts, with each of the two upper parts provided with a text of its own, and the tenor part singing the single word. An example is the motet *O Maria Virgo Davidica*. The tenor has the word *Veritatem* (Verity), which together with the melody is taken from the Gradual for the Feast of the Assumption, *Propter Veritatem*. The two upper parts are a commentary upon the idea of the Assumption. One text pictures Mary, virgin of David's line, as giving her commands in the citadel of heaven. The other speaks of Mary as the hope of sinners and the fountain of pardon.

Motet: *O Maria Virgo Davidica*. HISTORY OF MUSIC IN SOUND, VOL II. VICTOR LM 6015 (HMV HMS 19, 78 r.p.m.).

One of the strangest phenomena in the history of medieval polyphony is that only a few decades after the appearance of the motet we find what are called French motets. In these works the upper part no longer has a Latin religious text, but a French text that has a decidedly secular, and indeed usually amorous, tone. These French motets are not new compositions, for their music is identical with that of one of the Latin motets. There are hundreds of examples. In some there is one Latin text and one French text in the upper parts, but in the later part of the thirteenth century the Latin text tends to be replaced by a second French text. Our example has the tenor *Eius in Oriente*, taken from the Mass for the Epiphany; one upper part sings 'When I see the roses budding . . .' and the other, 'Now in truth, whatever they tell us, Let Robin be my love.'

Motet: *En non diu*. MASTERPIECES OF MUSIC BEFORE 1750, VOL. I. HAYDN SOCIETY HSL 2071.

In these two chapters we have surveyed early polyphony from the ninth to the end of the thirteenth century. Throughout this long period the main development took place in France, but there was musical activity in Spain and England too. England can furnish us with two particularly interesting examples.

The first is the famous *Sumer is icumen in*, the oldest existing canon or round, and the second is one of the few specimens of instrumental music of the thirteenth century that have survived. It is a dance tune written in two parts, and consisting of a number of four-measure phrases arranged in pairs, each pair having the same melody. At the beginning these restated melodies are in the lower part, but later they appear in the upper part where they are more clearly heard.

(i) *Sumer is icumen in*; (ii) *English dance tune*. HISTORY OF MUSIC IN SOUND, VOL. II. VICTOR LM 6015 (HMV HMS 17/18, 78 r.p.m.).

(APPENDIX: *See* page 72.)

8

Denis Stevens

THE *ARS NOVA* IN FRANCE

T HE *Ars Nova*, or new art, of the fourteenth century is so
called after a theoretical treatise by the composer Philippe
de Vitry (1291–1361) which brought about a turning-
point in the development of medieval music and a new
orientation in the art of composition. One of the fundamental
innovations of the new musical art was the liberation of rhythm
from its idealistic fetters. This may be judged by comparing
the rhythmic flow of two pieces of music, one from the thirteenth
century, the other from the fourteenth. The first is a ballade by
the trouvère, Adam de la Halle: *Dieu soit en cette maison.* It is
what we generally call a *chanson de quête*—a song that the children
sing at Christmas when asking for alms. It is not quite a carol,
for a carol has a more popular feeling and style, but the text is
about the birth of Christ, and at the end of each verse there is a
refrain 'May God dwell in this house, and may there be wealth
and joy in plenty.' We should compare the slow, peaceful rhythm
of that ballade with a fourteenth-century ballade by Guillaume de
Machaut: *Je puis trop bien.* It is a short love-lyric for one singer
and two or three instruments. 'I can all too well compare my
lady to the image which Pygmalion made; it was of ivory, so
beautiful, without peer, that he loved it more than Jason did
Medea. Out of his senses, he prayed to it unceasingly, but the
image answered him not. Thus does she treat me who makes
my heart melt, for I pray her ever, and she answers me not.'

(i) Adam de la Halle: *Dieu soit en cette maison.* DECCA ARC 3002
(DGG APM 14018).
(ii) Guillaume de Machaut: *Je puis trop bien.* ANTHOLOGIE SONORE
AS 3 (AS 67, 78 r.p.m.) (alt. DGG APM 14063).

The pulse in Machaut's song is faster and more vital and shows
us that it stems from a different school of musical thought. Adam

de la Halle's rhythms are peaceful, majestic, and self-effacing: Machaut's are clear, concise, with an almost modern lilt.   In fact, his ballade is written in what we should call 6/8 time—two main pulses in a bar, with each pulse divided into three—and this sub-division of the basic time-unit was an important feature of *Ars Nova* style and notation.   The late thirteenth-century motet writers nearly all used triple rhythm, and they were known as exponents of the old art, *Ars Antiqua*.   The new art, first formu-lated and practised by Philippe de Vitry, was warmly supported by many of his friends.   One of them was Jean de Muris, who was a great philospher and mathematician as well as an authority on music, and we may see how the medieval mind looked on these matters from his treatise *Ars Novae Musicae*.   Jean de Muris tells us first about the older fashion of composition, based on triple measure:

That all perfection is implicit in the ternary number follows from many likely conjectures.   For in God, who is most perfect, there is one substance, yet three persons; He is threefold, yet one, and one, yet threefold; very great therefore is the correspondence of unity to trinity. At first, in knowledge, are the separate and the concrete; from these, under the ternary number, the composite is derived.   At first, in celestial bodies, are the thing moving, the thing moved, and time. Three attributes in stars and sun—heat, light, splendour; in elements— action, passion, matter; in individuals—generation, corruption, dis-solution; in all finite time—beginning, middle, end; in all curable diseases—rise, climax, decline . . . every object, if it is ever to stand, has three dimensions.

But de Muris was a member of the group of innovators and he was not content to leave music in the everlasting clutches of triple time.   He continues:

Since the ternary number is everywhere present in some form or other, it may no longer be doubted that it is perfect.   And by the contrary of this proposition, the binary number, since it falls short of the ternary, also since it is thus of lower rank, is left imperfect.

So it came about that the system of notation we know and use to-day was based on the relationship of triple and duple rhythm, and the subdivision of time, which de Muris tells us 'is endlessly divisible to infinity.'   Shorter note-values began to be used, and these gave music the possibility of moving at a quicker pace. We can appreciate this best by listening to the speed and flexibility of the instrumental piece usually called *Le Moulin de Paris*.

Le Moulin de Paris. HISTORY OF MUSIC IN SOUND, VOL III. VICTOR LM 6016 (HMV HMS 20, 78 r.p.m.).

In examining the work of the troubadours and trouvères we saw how closely connected were the twin arts of music and poetry. Indeed, one of the troubadours said that 'verse without music is like a mill without water.' In the fourteenth century there was still a close alliance between the two arts. For example, the practice grew up of interpolating music in long poems called *romans*. It is easy to see why this was done; if the poem was not sung in the manner of certain of the *chansons de geste*, music was needed to bring contrast and relief to the spoken word.

One of the most famous of these poems is *Le Roman de Fauvel*. It is a biting attack on the vices of the times in the form of an allegory; Fauvel, a horse, personifies all the evils inherent in the life of early fourteenth-century France. The letters of the name Flauvel stood for six of these vices: Flattery, Avarice, Usury, Variability, Envy, and Lowness. If we examine part of the text of one of the motets in the poem we can see the vein of thought that runs through it. The first voice sings that forsaken Mother Church sees herself despised by her sons, the sinful clerics. Simultaneously another voice sings 'She who raised on high the children she had nourished, now, scorned, finds by proof that they are impious.' Beneath these two voices is the tenor, an instrumental part, whose melody is taken from a plain-song source. In this case the words of that source, significantly enough, echo the sentiments expressed by the other two voices: 'I have nourished and brought up children, and they have rebelled against me.' While that text from Isaiah would not be heard during the performance of the motet, listeners would recognize the plain-song melody and immediately think of the text that went with it. That particular motet has not been recorded, but another of the 160 pieces from *Le Roman de Fauvel* can be heard. Again there are two supporting texts, but this time all three are sung.

Je vois douleur. ANTHOLOGIE SONORE AS 2.

The cleverness of medieval music is sometimes so great as to discourage us from listening carefully: we know that several different texts are being sung simultaneously, and that remarkable features in form and structure are present, yet we seem powerless to take them all in at once.   In my opinion these many separate elements never were meant to be appreciated all at once, any more than a medieval cathedral was meant to be seen all at once.   All must be studied singly before the complete work assumes its fullest significance.

Sometimes these medieval subtleties are used for expressive means—the device whereby one voice takes up the theme a few beats later, in canon, is used to give the effects of hunters' calls in a lively, anonymous composition of the mid-fourteenth century: *Si je chant main.*

> *Si je chant main.*   HISTORY OF MUSIC IN SOUND, VOL. III.   VICTOR LM 6016 (HMV HMS 20, 78 r.p.m.).

In spite of the individual excellence of many other works, one man dominates French music in the fourteenth century: Guillaume de Machaut.   He was born at the very beginning of the century and lived until 1377, having in the course of a long and varied career been a priest, a secretary of King John of Bohemia, a poet and musician, and finally a canon of Rheims.   Some of Machaut's writings are autobiographical, and we know from these sources that he travelled widely through Italy, Poland, and Bohemia while in the service of King John.   Machaut's contribution to musical history is a great one; he unified the many divergent aspects of the *Ars Nova* style, welding them into a solid and recognizable musical achievement.   His works have only just recently been made available in complete form for the purpose of study and perform-ance, and the task was a difficult one; *Ars Nova* notation is often very complex and the music is scattered throughout many manu-scripts in different countries.

The problems of performance may be illustrated from two different realizations of his great Mass.   The first example is rather fanciful; while instruments did take part in the earliest performances of the Mass, it is a matter for conjecture whether they sounded as brassy as on the first recording.   My own feeling is that the instruments blended more with the voices, rather than standing out apart from them, and the recording of the *Benedictus* is more sober, though none the less interesting.

> Machaut: *Mass of Notre-Dame.*   (i) CONCERT HALL CHS 1107 (complete) (alt. DGG APM 14063); (ii) HISTORY OF MUSIC IN SOUND, VOL III.   VICTOR LM 6016 (Benedictus only) (HMV HMS 21, 78 r.p.m.).

Machaut was one of the first composers to make extensive use of a medieval device known as *isorhythm*, i.e. 'equal rhythm.' An isorhythmic piece is one in which a set rhythmic pattern of notes and rests is repeated at certain fixed intervals throughout the entire work. Sometimes these patterns of notes and rests were restricted to the tenor; occasionally all the voice-parts were isorhythmic, and the composer had to see to it that his rhythmic schemes were faithfully echoed in each part as the composition proceeded. The true subtlety was that each scheme in each voice-part could live its own life, so that the final effect, instead of being one of extreme rigidity, actually sounded varied and full of colour.

Machaut's famous composition based on the plain-song *David* has an isorhythmic tenor of great interest. Above the tenor two independent parts weave a complex web of sound, one taking over from the other with a rapidity and verve which is typical of the *hocket*. This is the name usually given to this form of 'broken music,' for the lines are really broken up and shared between the two voice-parts. Played by instruments (as on the recording), the effect is very striking; sung by voices, it could be much less so, and was even known to goad the higher ecclesiastics into almost frenzied diatribes. Machaut's two hocketing parts are brilliantly contrived; so too is his tenor, which repeats the plain-song three times over an eightfold rhythmic scheme of repetition, following this with a final statement of the melody over a fourfold rhythmic scheme, quite different in outline.

Machaut: *Hoquetus David*. OISEAU-LYRE, OL 3 (78 r.p.m.).

Machaut's genius inevitably brought into being a school of followers, some of whom carried his subtleties and complexities to incredible lengths. Music of the late fourteenth century, such as was heard at the papal court in Avignon and the courts of the Aragon princes (mostly by French composers), is still very little known. It ill deserves neglect, however, for it has a lyrical vein tinged with mysticism, and a charm that is at once fragile and impressive. Something like it may be heard in the totally isorhythmic motet *A vous vierge de doucour* by an anonymous composer. The text of the uppermost voice is in French: 'To you, sweet Virgin, whom I adore, I wish to give my service from now onwards, leaving aside of my own free will all other foolish loves, without delay.' Beneath this, another voice sings in Latin:

'Weeping, I come to Thee, O Virgin, Mother of God, in Thee do I take refuge.'

The instrumental tenor, *Regnum Mundi*, is based on a responsory, and is played on the record by a hurdy-gurdy.

A vous vierge de doucour.   OISEAU-LYRE OL 2 (78 r.p.m.).

Another anonymous piece from the same period, and one very popular then, is truly remarkable for its vivid portrayal of bird songs and the sound of instruments.   The singer calls out to his lady to wake up, for it is sunrise and the lark is chirping away merrily.   It has no isorhythmic structure, nothing that seems in the remotest degree learned.   The piece seems to come to us from the very springtime of music; it makes us realize that the composer, whoever he was, knew the art of writing joyous music, free from care and anxiety, full of life and vigour.   'Now then play up, drums and pipes . . . come on, good fellows, let's go and dance: it's all for you, my lady, whose honour may God increase.'   In between each phrase the singer imitates the sound of the bagpipes, and instruments imitate the singer—an outpouring of medieval *joie de vivre* which is unique among the entire output, wonderful as it is, of the *Ars Nova* composers.

Or sus, vous dormes trop.   OISEAU-LYRE OL 3 (78 r.p.m.).

(APPENDIX: *See* page 72.)

9

Denis Stevens

THE *ARS NOVA* IN ITALY

MUSICAL culture in fourteenth-century Italy was as rich, as varied, and as lively as the literary culture which is prized through the writings of Petrarch and Boccaccio. It had links with French music, but its basic principles of notation, together with its use of forms and styles, was entirely Italian. The starting-point of Italian *Ars Nova* music was in the ideas and examples of Petrus de Cruce rather than Philippe de Vitry, for, though both were Frenchmen, they had widely differing conceptions of musical style and notation.

Petrus de Cruce held that it was possible to divide the breve into two, three, four, five, six, or seven equal parts. Liberty such as this was entirely contrary to the logic of the French, who found all the variety they needed in duple and triple rhythmic combinations. The Italians also welcomed the relatively more simple notation advocated by Petrus de Cruce. At least two dozen Italian composers have left us examples of their music, and if we compare the sound of it with French *Ars Nova* music, we can see immediately how distinctive a personality the Italian composers had.

It has been customary to divide this group of composers into three generations, but it would be incorrect to think of this century's musical culture as beginning in the year 1300 and ending in 1399. There is a slight forward displacement which fits in with other aspects of Italian art and culture, so that we must think of the true *trecento* as extending from about 1325 to 1425. Florence was most responsible for the encouragement of music and poetry, and her name can be heard in connection with many composers of the second, perhaps the greatest of the three groups. Among the earlier men one hears the names of northern cities: Jacopo da Bologna, Grazioso da Padua, Vincenzo da Rimini. The same

55

is true of the third generation, which flourished from about 1390 onwards: Matteo da Perugia, Giovanni da Genoa, Anthonello da Caserta, Bartolomeo da Bologna. Francesco Landini, greatest of them all, heads the brilliant group of composers whose songs filled the villas of the Florentine nobility from the middle of the century until just before its close: Paolo da Firenze, Ghirardello da Firenze, Lorenzo da Firenze, Andrea da Firenze.

We may begin with the *Ars Nova* madrigal, a very different kind of music from the sixteenth-century madrigal. Fundament-ally it is a verse form, with music so arranged to fit into its particular scheme of repetition. We may take as an example the madrigal for two voices only by Jacopo da Bologna: *Non al suo amante*, 'Never did Diana so please her lover, when he was fortunate enough to see her bathing in the cool waters, as the rustic shepherdess pleases me when she washes the white veil which shall protect her fair hair from sun and breeze, so that it made me, now that the sky is fiery, all tremble with the chill of love.'

Jacopo da Bologna: *Non al suo amante*.   OISEAU-LYRE OL 1 (78 r.p.m.).

The sparse, two-part texture is a little hard to get used to at first, but there is no doubt that it gives the voices a chance to shine in a way that they never could in the Renaissance madrigal, with its richly interwoven voice-parts and constant use of imita-tion. The Italian madrigal was a model of clarity and elegance, serving as a vehicle for the sensitive and subtle portrayal of the picture in the poet's mind, as well as for the virtuosity and emo-tional range of the singers. Those florid introductions have more than a faint foretaste of the peculiarly Mediterranean type of singing that we now know as *cante flamenco*.

Not all fourteenth-century madrigals were like *Non al suo amante*. Landini, for example, wrote three madrigals in three-part texture, and each one has a special point of interest. One of them had the two lower voice-parts in canon, and then as the piece moves towards its close, the canon is extended to all three voice-parts. Another madrigal makes use of the French device of isorhythm and is through-composed instead of repetitive. The third has a different text for each voice-part, though the texts all come from the same poem, and they may possibly have been sung in succession, and not simultaneously.

Far more numerous than the madrigals were the *ballate*, easily the most popular musical style and the one always referred to by poets and novelists in their accounts of the social life of the times.

Francesco Landini: *Amar si li alti tuo gentil costum.* HISTORY OF MUSIC IN SOUND, VOL. III. VICTOR LM 6016 (HMV HMS 22, 78 r.p.m.).

There are many references to dances and dance-tunes in the *Decameron*, and some of the tunes have been preserved in a handsomely written manuscript in the British Museum. There are fifteen dances in this manuscript, some being called *istampite*, some *saltarelli*, and one of them a *trotto*. They are written down as single-line melodies, but it is quite possible that they were performed with some accompaniment—a passage in the *Decameron* mentions a lute and a viol being brought out for the performance of dance music.

Saltarello. Vox PL 8110 (E).

To turn now from the kinds of music to the composer, we may consider the life and art of Francesco Landini. The inscription on his tombstone in the church of San Lorenzo, Florence, reads: 'Deprived of the light, Francesco, whom alone Music extols above all others for his great intellect, and his organ music, rests his ashes here, his soul above the stars.' When quite young, Francesco lost his sight as the result of smallpox. By hard work and determination he turned this grave disadvantage into an asset, learning an astonishing amount of music by heart, and developing to an unheard-of degree the art of improvisation. From his childhood up he was surrounded by artists and men of letters and his grand-nephew spoke of Francesco's learning in astrology and philosophy. He studied music with Jacopo da Bologna, spent some time in Verona, participated in a musical competition with another famous composer, Giovanni da Cascia, and in 1346 was commissioned to provide music for the birth of two Visconti princes in Milan. He also travelled to Venice, receiving there from the King of Cyprus a laurel wreath in recognition of his excellent poetry—one member of the jury, incidentally, was Petrarch.

In Florence Francesco was admired and loved by all who knew him. Yet he must often have felt acutely conscious of his lack of sight, for he even mentions it in the text of one of his madrigals, saying that a bird, deprived of light and vision, tends to fly ever higher in search of liberty and heaven. This was true of the composer himself; he explored every known musical and poetic avenue in the endeavour to find the summit of inspiration. So we find that one famous scholar of modern times has called one of his *ballate* 'perhaps the most beautiful work of the century.' This is *Gram piant'agli occhi* : 'Wretched with weeping and heavy with sorrow is he who is about to die, and so, with this bitter and passionate song I call upon death, yet he will not hear me. Even though I live, I never wish to follow anyone but you, my dearest star and sweetest love.'

> Landini: *Gram piant'agli occhi*. DECCA ARC 3003 (DGG APM 14019).

Although Francesco's compositions were undoubtedly popular during his lifetime, it was his organ-playing that was most admired. Many vivid details of his playing are recaptured by the writer Giovanni del Prato. He says that a fascinating experiment with the birds took place one morning when the sun was coming up. Francesco was asked to play a little on his organ to see if the singing of the birds would lessen or increase. As soon as the playing began, many of the birds became silent; then they redoubled their singing, and strange to say, one of the nightingales came and perched on a branch above Francesco's head.

The subject of Landini's texts in his vocal music was not always love; he could be light-hearted when the occasion demanded, as we see from his fishing-song *Cosi pensoso*. This is really a variant of the *caccia*, literally a hunting-song which made use of the device of canon between the two upper voices, the lowest voice being in free style. This *pesca*, or fishing-song, is sung by two tenors with instrumental accompaniment, and tells of the cries of the crawfishers that a lover hears as he walks thoughtfully along the beach.

> Landini: *Cosi pensoso*. DECCA ARC 3003 (DGG APM 14019).

The use of canon, with one voice following another rapidly with the same music and text, helps to make the scene more vivid and the action more vigorous. Only twenty examples of the *caccia* have come down to us, but they nearly all exhibit the same features, though the subjects of their texts differ widely. As well as hunting scenes some depict the noise and bustle of market scenes, and others the excitement of a house catching fire. We may take as an example a regular *caccia* by Ghirardello da Firenze which describes a hunting trip from getting up in the morning to the finding of the quarry and the sounding of the horn.

Ghirardello da Firenze: *Tosto che l'alba.* DECCA ARC 3003 (DGG APM 14019).

Even though the principle of the *caccia* was known and used in France as the *chasse*, even though we ourselves sing in canon and call the result a 'catch,' there is nothing quite like a fourteenth-century Italian *caccia*. It was a frankly descriptive piece of music in which the composer was free to make up his text and his own musical themes, the only proviso being that the two upper voices should sing the same part, slightly out of step. If we find such a readiness to relax in the dance tunes too, it is worth remembering that not all such tunes were frivolous. The opening of *Lamento di Tristano* does indeed sound like a lament, with its solemn yearning tones enhanced by the stringed instrument. Even so, the pace soon becomes more lively and the melodic instruments are joined by a drum. This second section is called *La Rotta* (possibly named after a medieval stringed instrument), and serves as an after-dance to the *Lamento di Tristano* rather as the galliard followed the pavane in the sixteenth century.

Lamento di Tristano. Vox PL 8110 (E).

Very few religious pieces were written by the *Ars Nova* composers, and indeed they were discouraged from writing polyphonic settings of liturgical texts by the Bull of Pope John XXII, issued in Avignon in 1324. Italian composers did not, however, cease altogether in their endeavours to find a new musical vehicle for the liturgy. In the manuscript containing the dance tunes that I have mentioned, there is an anonymous *Gloria* and *Credo* which show quite outstanding if somewhat untraditional artistry. These pieces were undoubtedly meant for performance by a soloist of considerable ability, for they are not easy to sing and call for an amazing degree of perfection in the ensemble. Something very much like it can be heard in the setting of the *Gloria* by Matteo da Perugia, who flourished in the late fourteenth and early fifteenth centuries. The florid writing for the voices and the unusual declamation of the texts comes as a surprise at first, yet we know there is sincerity here.

Matteo da Perugia: *Gloria.* OISEAU-LYRE OL 1 (78 r.p.m.).

Even Landini is known to have written some motets, but unfortunately they have not survived in complete form. The kind of music he would play for the *Kyrie* at his church in Florence may be judged from a recently discovered manuscript containing keyboard music. It includes a set of organ verses for the *Kyrie* which would have been played in alternation with the singing of the plain-song. The composer, whoever he was, kept the plain-song almost intact in the lowest voice and added typically Italian decorative passages for the right hand. Thus this Faenza manuscript may be said to contain the earliest known example of the organ Mass, a style which was not to be practised in Italy again until the time of Cavazzoni in the early sixteenth century.

Jacopo da Bologna, like many of his contemporaries, made use of the madrigal and *caccia* forms even when he wrote liturgical music, not through any spirit of levity, but out of a genuine regard for the need to extend the frontiers of musical art. His motet *Lux purpurata radiis* is for two male voices and one instrument, and, like his madrigal *Non al suo amante*, the texture is clear, interesting, and undeniably Italian.

Jacopo da Bologna: *Lux purpurata radiis*. Oiseau-Lyre OL 2 (78 r.p.m.).

(Appendix: *See* page 72.)

10

Denis Stevens

GUILLAUME DUFAY

UNTIL quite recently the years between Guillaume de Machaut and Guillaume Dufay were an historical no man's land in the otherwise unbroken procession of musicians in France. Those years saw the refinement of musical composition to a degree that has rarely been witnessed before or since, and it engendered the inevitable reaction. The new trend of the fifteenth century was in the direction of simplicity; that is, relative simplicity, for while it would be idle to suggest that the Burgundian court composers could be in any way naïve, they did cultivate what we might call a lighter touch. Certainly the chansons of Dufay and his colleagues (and their religious music to a certain extent) possess a translucent, untrammelled aspect when compared with the works of their immediate forbears. They gained in expressiveness as well as in melodic charm, but they lost almost entirely that vein of mysticism which is peculiar to the immediate followers of Machaut.

A French poet, Martin le Franc, has given us a revealing account of the transition from one style to the other in his poem *Le Champion des Dames*, composed around 1441. He names three of the most famous followers of Machaut and says their music was not 'filled with such goodly melody . . . as Binchois sings or Dufay.' He refers too to 'pleasing concord' and 'the English guise' and music that is 'gay and bright.' It seems that the new style was to some extent an imported one, for the links between French and English music were especially close at the time. The English musicians, conservative in taste, had rejected the over-subtlety of the followers of Machaut and had cultivated their favourite method of descant, smooth and sonorous, easy to compose and ravishing to hear.

Beata Viscera. HISTORY OF MUSIC IN SOUND, VOL. II. VICTOR LM 6015 (HMV HMS 18, 78 r.p.m.).

It was such mellifluous strains that caused the reactions against the mannered complexity of Machaut's successors, and it was just this static, peaceful quality that the early Burgundian composers sought to emulate. Sometimes they did it with an almost self-conscious vigour, setting nearly impossible tasks to be overcome, as when Nicole Grenon takes as the basis for his song *Je ne requier de ma dame* a particularly angular and volatile contratenor from a work by Matteo da Perugia. Grenon looks upon this contratenor as a challenge to his skill in making a song, and so carefully does he add the two remaining voice-parts that the effect is completely placid and far removed from anything rough or angular. The text is a fairly conventional love-lyric, but the music has an entirely personal charm that is heightened when we think of the somewhat awkward melodic basis chosen by the composer.

Nicole Grenon: *Je ne requier de ma dame*. OISEAU-LYRE OL 136 (78 r.p.m.).

An even greater figure than Grenon was Gilles Binchois, a native of Mons in Hainaut. Binchois began life in the army and ended it in the Church; in between whiles he seems to have composed a great quantity of sacred and secular music, much of which is of a very high quality. He served the court of Burgundy for nearly thirty years, and died in 1460. No less a composer than Ockeghem wrote a lamentation on the death of Gilles Binchois. In the text of Ockeghem's work he is called 'the father of joyousness,' and it is not difficult to believe this charming compliment when we listen to his chanson *Filles à marier*.

Gilles Binchois: *Filles à marier*. HISTORY OF MUSIC IN SOUND, VOL. III. VICTOR LM 6016 (HMV HMS 26, 78 r.p.m.).

Like Binchois, the slightly younger composer Hayne van Ghizeghem embraced a military career, and this may partly explain the relatively small amount of music he was able to write. But his music is consistent in style and of fairly even quality. It was in all probability written between 1457 and 1468 when he was studying and was at the same time acting as *valet de chambre* and singer to Charles the Bold. From 1468 onwards his army career seems to have taken up most of his time, and we last hear of him at the disastrous siege of Beauvais in 1472, where he probably perished.

Hayne's songs were used not only for their original purpose, but also for dances and as *cantus firmus* for settings of the Mass. Most of them were for three voices, but he added a fourth to several and so enriched the texture—for instance, *À la audienche*. The complete text has not survived, so it has been recorded as played by instruments. In connection with this song we must also consider *musica ficta*, or 'feigned music.' This device, which composers of the Renaissance used either because they had to or because they wished for a particularly beautiful harmonic effect, was really nothing more than the chromatic alteration of certain important notes. A note written as B flat would be sung as B natural, or a plain F would be sung F sharp. Thus composers were able to achieve an effect of modulation, although they were writing many years before the final codification of our ideas about tonality. *Musica ficta*, however, was largely up to the performer because it was rarely, if ever, set out in the music itself, and many modern editors have misunderstood its function. An example of this misunderstanding may be heard in *À la audienche*; about half-way through there is a loud chord completely off key.

Hayne van Ghizeghem: *À la audienche.* Oiseau-Lyre OL 136 (78 r.p.m.).

When properly used by a modern editor, *musica ficta* can be made to colour a composition and increase its charm and its harmonic appeal. Almost the same is true of the use of instruments which played such an important part in the life at the Burgundian court. These instruments are, for instance, described in the account of the 'Feast of the Pheasant,' a banquet given by Duke Philip the Good of Burgundy in 1454, the purpose being to avenge the fall of Constantinople in the previous year. We learn that there was a castle made entirely of pastry inside which no less than twenty-eight musicians sang and played recorders, rebecs, lutes, horns, bassoons, bagpipes, and cornets. Three choir-boys and a tenor sang a *Benedictus* inside a model church, and there was an organ that played in between the singing. Another group of choir-boys and instrumentalists, again secreted in a pie, sang a motet and a chanson, and when they had finished, the doors of the banqueting hall were thrown open to reveal four trumpeters clad in white who played a fanfare on golden instruments. A white stag followed them in, and on it was seated a beautiful young girl who sang a chanson by Guillaume Dufay. And so the feasting and the music went on until the evening, when another work by

Dufay was performed, a lament for the fallen city of Constantinople. This was preceded by a procession of torch-bearers and musicians with tabors, harps, and lutes.

Guillaume Dufay, whose music was obviously accorded a place of honour at this feast, was born about 1400, not very far from what is now the border between France and Belgium. He was a choir-boy at Cambrai cathedral, but he was hardly out of his teens before he began to travel. We hear of him first in Paris and then in Italy, where he seems to have found a number of commissions to write music for special events. Perhaps Dufay's beautiful setting of the first verse of Petrarch's *Vergine bella* belongs to this period too. 'Beautiful Virgin! clothed with the sun, crowned with the stars, who so pleased the Eternal Sun that he hid his light in thine; love spurs me on to utter speech of thee, and (feeble to commence without thy aid) of him who on thy bosom rests in love.'

Dufay: *Vergine bella.* DECCA ARC 3003 (DGG APM 14019).

After this first Italian visit, Dufay returned home and apparently held some ecclesiastical post at Laon until 1426. By 1427 he was in Bologna and in the following year joined the papal choir in Rome. Later on he served as chaplain and then as director of the chapel to the court of Savoy, but returned once more to Rome and sang in the papal choir. He was, one might say, the composer-laureate of the courts of Burgundy and Rome, the dutiful servant of Church and State, as ready to turn his hand to the composition of a hymn-tune as of a massively proportioned motet in honour of an emperor. Indeed, the demands of occasional music were so deeply ingrained in his mind that it came naturally to him to write a motet to be sung at his own deathbed. This motet was *Ave regina coelorum*, written in 1464—just ten years before his death. Though not sung at the hour of his death, it was performed at his burial. Into the text of the *Ave regina* he inserted a touching prayer for pity on the soul of the dying Dufay.

Dufay: *Ave regina coelorum.* HISTORY OF MUSIC IN SOUND, VOL. III. VICTOR LM 6016 (HMV HMS 25, 78 r.p.m.).

In his *Ecclesiae militantis*, which dates from 1431, Dufay draws attention, not only to Rome as the seat of the Church, but also to a recently settled dispute with the Venetians. Each of these matters is dealt with by a separate voice-part, singing its own text. The third text is in praise of the Pope himself, whose former name, Gabriel, is used in a very subtle way as a foundation for the polyphonic structure. Dufay recalled an antiphon from Gregorian Chant beginning with the word 'Gabriel' and arranged the notes of the plain-song in a regularly disposed rhythmical pattern. This isorhythm is stretched out to serve as one of the supporting voices of the motet. There is yet another supporting part, based on an antiphon with the words 'Ecce nomen domini.' What was important to Dufay was to bring in the name of the Pope and also the figurative acclamation, 'Behold the name of the Lord.' These two supporting parts are interdependent: when one stops, the other starts, and at times they even overlap each other, forming a solid and massive rhythmical framework to the entire piece.

Dufay did not always write in so complex a manner. He was equally ready to pen a light-hearted chanson, such as the rondeau *Pour l'amour de ma doulce amye*. Even the points of imitation seem carefree and gay, and the upper voice ripples along in cadential figures with an unsurpassed charm and vivacity.

Dufay: *Pour l'amour de ma doulce amye*. HISTORY OF MUSIC IN SOUND, VOL. III. VICTOR LM 6016 (HMV HMS 26, 78 r.p.m.).

Dufay also composed many purely liturgical works, including seven complete Masses. One of the most remarkable is the *Missa Caput*. It was only recently that the late Manfred Bukofzer, of the University of California, discovered the meaning of this title. Normally the title of a Mass bears the opening words of the plainsong (or secular song) used as a linear basis for the music. In this case the title derives from the end not the beginning of a text, and it was this fact that made the context so difficult to trace. The *cantus firmus* is taken from the end of an antiphon, *Venit ad Petrum*, whose last word—*caput*—has a long melodic flourish on the first syllable.

Antiphon: *Venit ad Petrum*. OISEAU-LYRE OL 50069.

The nearest plain-song sources to Dufay's theme are found in English liturgical books, in graduals of the Sarum rite. Is it possible that the much-travelled Dufay also visited England? If not, it is difficult to explain how he found this antiphon, and why he took such keen interest in the peculiarly English methods of constructing a cyclic Mass; that is, a Mass which is unified either by a common tenor in all four sections or by a recurring motive at the beginning of each section. Dufay employs both methods in the *Missa Caput,* which shows to the full his expert and sonorous handling of four-part texture.

Dufay: *Missa Caput.* OISEAU-LYRE OL 50069.

(APPENDIX: *See* page 72.)

Denis Stevens

JOHN DUNSTABLE

ONE of the strangest of all phenomena in the history of music is the seemingly sudden appearance of a school of English composers during the first part of the fifteenth century. Power, Jervays, Cooke, Sturgeon, Queldryk, Frye, Smart, Tyes, Troulove, Damett, and many more were active both in England and abroad, composing and singing music which was the envy of all who listened. A school of composers as vigorous as this could hardly arrive without any preparation, but the truth of the matter is that music in fourteenth-century England is very scarce indeed, and even when it is available there is no composer's name to help us assign it to this or that part of the country. England was nevertheless musical, though by no means as productive as France or Italy. Even Chaucer's poor scholar knew a popular religious song of the time:

> And all above there lay a gay sautrye,
> On which he made a-nightes melodye,
> So sweetly that all the chamber rang,
> And *Angelus ad virginem* he sang.

Angelus ad virginem. HISTORY OF MUSIC IN SOUND, VOL. III. VICTOR LM 6016 (HMV HMS 22, 78 r.p.m.).

Angelus ad virginem, both in its solo form and its harmonized form, was well known throughout England in Chaucer's time. It is even found in some manuscripts with an English text; a sure enough proof of the growing use of vernacular. There is something about the style of the music too that arrests our attention. There is an easy flow to the rhythm, and a smooth succession of consonances. English composers liked the kind of sonority produced by what we should now call six-three chords—no matter if they produced a great deal of similar motion. What counted most was the sound.

Other aspects of this sonority and consonance may be heard in the carol, a form which flourished exceedingly in medieval England. Fundamentally processional music, the carol was also an adornment of the liturgy, even though it rarely belonged there. The essence of the carol was in its alternation of solo and chorus, of two-part and three-part texture; and also of its verse and burden.

Carols: (i) *Now wel may we.* HISTORY OF MUSIC IN SOUND, VOL.
III.   VICTOR LM 6016 (HMV HMS 23, 78 r.p.m.);
(ii) *Marvel not, Joseph.* ESOTERIC ES 521.

English carols of that kind enjoy a rare perfection of technique, a rounded smoothness of style, that sets them on a high plane, both musically and liturgically. Strangely enough, some of the works in carol form have non-liturgical texts, whilst others are frankly secular. There is, for example, a drinking-song *O potores exquisiti* which must be the only isorhythmic drinking-song in existence; the wine-bibbers are exquisites, not common roisterers. Side by side with *O potores exquisiti* we find an example of the more popular style: a three-part piece for voices and instruments which would not, perhaps, be entirely beyond the capabilities of a moderately sober group of ale-drinkers.

Tapster drinker. HISTORY OF MUSIC IN SOUND, VOL. III.   VICTOR
LM 6016 (HMV HMS 23, 78 r.p.m.).

Drinking songs, carols, and political songs all went to make up the kind of English life that John Dunstable knew as a lad in the small town in Bedfordshire from which he took his name. He was not an isolated composer in any sense; he built, on a solid bedrock of tradition and technique, his own mighty monument of polyphony, destined to glorify the structural principles of the later Middle Ages as much as to herald the new ideas and sonorities of the Renaissance. He was so famous in his own day that poets, theorists, and musicians vied with each other to sing his praises, yet in the troubled years after his death his music was consigned to silent obscurity. Even at the beginning of the present century only a handful of his compositions were known; now we have sixty-seven works—motets, Mass-sections, songs, and instrumental pieces—found in nearly two hundred versions, scattered throughout Europe. An American scholar, the late Manfred F. Bukofzer, devoted twenty-five years of work to the transcription of these manuscripts, and publication took place in 1953, the quincentenary of Dunstable's death.

We know little, however, about Dunstable's life.   In his youth
he learned to sing, probably at the Chapel Royal, and there he may
have made his first acquaintance with the men and music that were
destined to shape his style.   Dunstable entered the Church and
we find him holding a canonry at Hereford in the years which
preceded his service in the chapel of the Duke of Bedford, brother
to King Henry V.   Henry was himself a musician of no mean
attainments, and the royal encouragement of music could not fail
to have its effect on the quality of the works written especially
for the Chapel Royal.   Some of Dunstable's contemporaries and
colleagues, like Jervays, Byttering, and Power, are represented in
manuscripts found in Italy.   Most of Byttering's music is preserved in the Old Hall manuscript, though there is one item also
found in a York manuscript.   This is a polyphonic antiphon,
which has the original plain-song distributed between the three
voices.   No single voice-part is thus made to retain the somewhat
rigid progression of the plain-song; it is shared out so that all voice-
parts can be equally decorative and melodious.

Byttering: *Nesciens mater*.   HISTORY OF MUSIC IN SOUND, VOL. III.
   VICTOR LM 6016 (HMV HMS 23, 78 r.p.m.).

The Duke of Bedford was regent in France until his death in
1435, and this event seemed to be the signal for the gradual recov-
ery by the French of their native territory.   Soon they regained
Paris, and their victories spread steadily northward.   Yet only a
few years before that songs had been written in praise of the English
exploits at Agincourt.   One of these, *Deo gratias Anglia*, is to be
found in the same manuscript as *Tapster drinker*.

Deo gratias Anglia.   HISTORY OF MUSIC IN SOUND, VOL. III.
   VICTOR LM 6016 (HMV HMS 22, 78 r.p.m.).

In the Bodleian Library at Oxford, along with that manuscript,
is a treatise on astronomy in Dunstable's handwriting, dated April
1438.   By this time he must have returned to England and busied
himself with peaceful and scholarly pursuits; one of his epitaphs
tells us that he was an astronomer and mathematician as well as a
musician.   He died on the day before Christmas, 1453, and was
buried in the church of St Stephen Walbrook, not far from the
Thames at London Bridge.

In the half-century following Dunstable's death at least three
writers give us valuable information about his life and work.   The
Belgian theorist, Johannes Tinctoris, wrote in the latter part of the

fifteenth century that 'the possibilities of our music have been so
marvellously increased that there appears to be a new art, if I may
so call it, whose fount and origin is held to be among the English,
of whom Dunstable stood forth as chief.'   Another writer, John
Hothby, of English birth, spent his later life in Italy and he writes
of Dunstable's music as being 'of recent date.'   He may well have
heard this music in Italy, including the famous song to an Italian
poem, *O rosa bella*, which is usually accepted as being Dunstable's
work.

> Dunstable: *O rosa bella*.   HISTORY OF MUSIC IN SOUND, VOL. III.
>   VICTOR LM 6016 (HMV HMS 25, 78 r.p.m.).

The fact that only a handful of secular works by Dunstable have
come down to us is proof of his devoted adherence to British
traditions, however strongly he may have been attracted by the
music and poetry of other nations.   English composers of the
Middle Ages did not, as a rule, take secular music very seriously.
They were mainly concerned with writing music for the Church,
and especially for the Ordinary of the Mass.   Two recent discoveries of new sources for medieval music consist entirely of
liturgical music.   In between these two sources, and belonging
therefore to Dunstable's own time, is the Old Hall manuscript
which contains nearly one hundred and fifty pieces, most of them
settings of *Gloria, Credo, Sanctus,* and *Agnus Dei*.   The musical
styles range from the simplest to the most complex, and these
individual Mass-sections could be grouped together in thousands
of different combinations.   Any given piece could be used in
conjunction with any other, and even though a mixture of styles
resulted, the composite polyphonic Mass thus formed would
doubtless appeal through its variety of texture and idiom.   As an
example we may take the first part of an anonymous *Credo*, the
plain-song being in the middle voice.

> Anon.: *Credo*.   HISTORY OF MUSIC IN SOUND, VOL. III.   VICTOR
>   LM 6016 (HMV HMS 23, 78 r.p.m.).

In the music of Dunstable we find the same tendency to compose
separate Mass-sections instead of unified cycles.   Only occasionally did he compose two Mass-sections based on the same plain-
song and sharing the same kind of musical style.   Some scholars
go so far as to credit Dunstable with a cyclic Mass, but in fact
certain of the sections are ascribed in one manuscript to Lionel
Power, so that the authorship is rather doubtful.   Power was

easily the most famous of Dunstable's contemporaries, and his three-voice setting of the antiphon *Beata progenies* is not unlike Byttering's *Nesciens mater*. There is a similar willingness to rely on one text for all three voice-parts, just as in the conductus of the earlier Middle Ages. 'Blessed progeny whence Christ was born; how glorious is the Virgin who gave birth to the King of Heaven.'

Power: *Beata progenies*. ESOTERIC ES 521.

Power's *Beata progenies* is entirely characteristic of English style in the late fourteenth and early fifteenth centuries. But there is no doubt that Tinctoris was right in thinking of Dunstable as the fountain-head of the new musical art in England, and he tells us that his music (like that of Binchois and Dufay) possesses a suavity of character that makes it worthy, not only for men and for heroes, but also for the immortal gods. How was this suave floating quality achieved, and how did the texture of the music differ from what was already familiar to fifteenth-century performers and listeners?

In the first place, Dunstable's harmony was smoother and more consonant than that of his predecessors, and he took great pains to avoid unprepared discords, whereas they would think nothing of letting one of the voice-parts leap suddenly upon a note foreign to the triad.

Admittedly, both Dunstable's discords and those of his predecessors resolve in the correct manner; the difference is Dunstable's new method of preparing the ear for the slight shock that is to come, and this is done in so masterly a manner that hardly any shocks are felt at all. There is a similar degree of fluidity in the melodic lines that keep mainly to the smaller intervals favoured by plain-song, especially the interval of a third. In the motet *Sancta Maria* we find clarity of texture, careful declamation, and —a recurring feature of Dunstable's style—a triadic opening that arrests our attention from the outset.

Dunstable: *Sancta Maria*. ESOTERIC ES 521.

One of Dunstable's greatest motets is the four-part *Veni sancte spiritus*. It is an isorhythmic motet and the fixed rhythmic scheme pervades all four voice-parts. It is twice repeated within each of the three sections of the motet, the sections being set off from one another by metrical changes in the tenor, or lowest part. This tenor, almost certainly intended for instrumental performance, is based on part of the hymn *Veni creator spiritus*. On its first appearance the tune is stretched out to such a length that the melody is hardly recognizable as such, but serves as a comparatively static basis for the more rapidly moving upper parts. At the second section of the motet, the notes lose one-third of their value; and in the third section, two-thirds of their value, and the tune at last emerges and can be heard below the intricate flow of the other voices.

An additional feature of interest is the melodic material that Dunstable uses. Although the upper voice sings the entire text of *Veni sancte spiritus*, the melody of this sequence is not used at all. Instead, the melody of the hymn *Veni creator spiritus* (already partly used in the tenor) appears phrase by phrase whenever the tenor is silent for a few bars. This double use of the same plain-song is rare, even amongst the remarkable experiments in thematic integration employed by medieval musicians. One of the other two voices in this motet sings a paraphrase of the sequence *Veni sancte spiritus*, while the other sings the text *Veni creator spiritus* to freely composed music.

Even a brief analysis of a master work of the fifteenth century is bound to seem complex and difficult; art and artifice went hand in hand then. But there will be no difficulty about listening to Dunstable's motet as devotional music, for it is that *par excellence*; its calm and cool sonority can hardly be matched.

> Dunstable: *Veni sancte spiritus*. HISTORY OF MUSIC IN SOUND, VOL. III. VICTOR LM 6016 (HMV HMS 24, 78 r.p.m.).

John Dunstable never allowed tricks of notation to interfere with the real purpose of his music: to place finely spun melody and inspiring harmony at the service of liturgical texts. In the words of his epitaph: *Hic vir erat tua laus, tua lux, tua musica princeps*.

APPENDIX

THE MIDDLE AGES

(CHAPTERS 4–11)

The material—both for reading and listening—available for this period shows an extreme contrast with what is available for later periods, so it has been thought advisable to group the books and records under the general title: *The Middle Ages*.

BOOKS

The most valuable books are two comprehensive works:

GUSTAVE REESE: *Music in the Middle Ages.*
ed. DOM ANSELM HUGHES: *Music in the Early Middle Ages* (Vol. II of the *New Oxford History of Music*).

To these may be added the following volumes:

O. STRUNK: *Source Readings in Music History.*
WILLI APEL: *The Notation of Polyphonic Music—900–1600.*
A. MACHABEY: *Guillaume de Machault.*
L. ELLINWOOD: *The Works of Francesco Landini.*
C. VAN DEN BORREN: *Guillaume Dufay.*
H. BESSELER: *Bourdon and Fauxbourdon.*
MANFRED BUKOFZER: *Studies in Medieval and Renaissance Music*; *John Dunstable: Complete Works.*

RECORDS

Most of the available records of medieval music have been mentioned in the text of the chapters; but the following may be added.

Music of the Twelfth and Thirteenth Centuries.   EMS 201.
Music by Perotinus (and anonymous).   CONCERT HALL 1112.
MACHAUT: *Mass, etc.*   DECCA ARC 3022 (DGG APM 14063).   *Motets, Ballades, etc.*   WESTMINSTER XWN 18166.
DUFAY: *Missa sine nomine.*   HAYDN SOCIETY 9008.   *Secular Works.* EMS 206.   *Missa Caput.*   OISEAU-LYRE OL 50069.
Music of the Middle Ages to the Renaissance.   LONDON INTERNATIONAL W 91116.

12

Paul Henry Lang

THE PASSING OF THE MIDDLE AGES AND
THE COMING OF THE RENAISSANCE

THE Renaissance in music is really a northern flower
suffused with nostalgia for the south. This nostalgia
brought about a meeting, and ultimately an unparalleled
fusion, of the art of north and south. Two waves created
the musical Renaissance; one starting from France in the 1300's,
the other from Flanders in the 1400's, both tending towards
Italy and both reawakening Italian music. The European north
wished to embrace the European south, and from this desire arose
the greatest musical movement the world had known up to that
time.

We have seen that what the *Ars Nova* wanted was worldly,
secular music as long before the troubadours had wanted it, yet
ended up in a quasi-religious poetry and music. The *Ars Nova*
sought after this new secularism in the manner of Petrarch and
Boccaccio; consciously, with determination, with the fervour of
discovery. The same spirit animated the Flemings of the fifteenth
century. 'These men,' wrote a great historian of the last century,
'are veritable children in their curiosity and in the colourfulness
of their imagination; their main desire is to delect their senses,
they play with life as if it were a magic lantern.' The reference
is to the incomparable festivities of the cities of the Duchy of
Burgundy which were adorned by music. This luxurious life
could have led to mere amusement, but the arrival of great musical
poets changed it into the harbinger of a new art for the entire
civilized world.

The great composers of the Low Countries gave this music
wings—almost literally, for between 1400 and 1570 six generations
of them spread all over Europe, a few even reaching the New
World. Thus, Flemish music became French music in France,

Italian music in Italy, and German music in Germany, and its influence was great in Spain and in England. Even the Papal choir in Rome was for a time almost entirely composed of Flemish musicians. Such masters as Isaac and Josquin des Prés composed in several languages other than their own, and we may take as an example an Italian song by Josquin, *The Cricket*.

Josquin des Prés: *El Grillo*. HISTORY OF MUSIC IN SOUND, VOL. III. VICTOR LM 6016 (HMV HMS 28, 78 r.p.m.).

Why should so small a country exhibit such a rich and undisturbed musical development while the surrounding larger nations were comparatively silent? The larger nations were embroiled in endless wars, internal and external; in addition, Germany was visited by the Black Death. But perhaps the most important reason was the collapse of the feudal system which called for the rebuilding of their respective social orders. While the pictorial arts could flourish under these circumstances, music calls for more settled conditions, both psychologically and because of its need for performance. The Low Countries had a well developed and flourishing middle-class civilization, prosperous, free, and art-loving, patronized by the well-to-do burghers.

What were the characteristics of this world-conquering music? First, it will be useful to dispel the long-ingrained notion that all this old music was pure vocal music. Before the impact of humanism on the northerners, these Germanic musicians of French culture did not pay much attention to the text they were setting. All they wanted was a noble melody, and this melody could be presented by voices or by instruments. We can hear a chanson played by instruments as it was performed in the fifteenth and sixteenth centuries. It kept the title of chanson, with the text, or its beginning, indicated, and since the musicians played from the same part-books that the singers used, it is easy to understand how the historians were led astray.

Isaac: *Hélas*. ANTHOLOGIE SONORE AS 4 (AS 43, 78 r.p.m.).

Undoubtedly there is a certain abstract quality in this music. Even such a plaintive and evocative song as Binchois's *Triste plaisir et douleureuse joie* shows this trait because the composer's main endeavour was a beautifully designed melody built on a delicately chiselled and balanced structure. These composers possessed a contrapuntal technique the like of which the world has never known. Furthermore, they liked to illustrate, again in abstract melodic design, the meaning of the words. When the word 'genuflexion' appeared in the text, the melody would imitate the physical motion of bending the knee. Sometimes the composers even hid the exact manner of performance in a riddle that had to be solved before the singers or players could proceed.

This incredible virtuosity prompted the romantic historians to dismiss this art as a sort of musico-mathematical game; but they were wrong, for in the love of the craft there was always a great deal of idealism. By acquiring absolute control and facility in dealing with the craft of composition, these wizards of counterpoint subdued musical matter. This disciplined virtuosity reached its height and its final freedom in the work of the Master of the King's Chapel in Paris, Jean d'Ockeghem (1430–95). His passing was bewailed in words accorded to princes; his thirty-six-part motet was mentioned as one of the musical world's wonders and his contrapuntal technique was held unsurpassable. But this coldly glowing genius summoned his immense musical wizardry to cool his fever and to erect barriers for his passions. He is the last of those in whom the eternal soaring, the mystery, and the heaven-reaching architecture of the Gothic style once more raised their voice against the new humanity of the Renaissance. This Gothic art could not be continued by anyone else, and those who attempted it produced nothing but mannerism.

We may take as an example a sacred work by Ockeghem in which the linear part-writing of the late Middle Ages reaches its apex. This is the *Kyrie* from his Mass *Fors seulement*—so called from the melody which serves as a *cantus firmus* for all three of its surviving movements. And beside this *Kyrie* we may set a chanson that shows that he too was subject to the strong current radiating from Italy. The tremendous melody that opens *Ma maîtresse* has an unmistakably Mediterranean quality, even though the gentle melancholy and the sculptured design are clearly Flemish.

Ockeghem: (i) *Kyrie from the Mass, Fors seulement.* HISTORY
    OF MUSIC IN SOUND, VOL. III. VICTOR LM 6016
    (HMV HMS 26, 78 r.p.m.);
    (ii) *Ma maîtresse.* ANTHOLOGIE SONORE AS 4 (alt.
    OISEAU-LYRE OL 50104).

As more and more Flemish composers go to Italy and become intoxicated with the south, with the lightness, symmetry, and euphony of Italian music, the whole picture will change. The northern pilgrims will teach the Italians complex part-writing, while the Italian light *genres—frottola, villanella, canzona*—will loosen up the formidable constructions of the northerners. The resultant mixture, a truly international musical style, constitutes the advent of the full Renaissance in music.

Anon.: *Three frottole.* ANTHOLOGIE SONORE AS 4.

Already in the music of Jacob Obrecht (*c.* 1430–1505) we feel the warm sun of the Mediterranean; his motets know the colour of the Italian sky and his chansons know the happy and capricious leaps of Italian melody.

Obrecht: *Two chansons.* ANTHOLOGIE SONORE AS 5.

The late medieval composer did not bother much with his text. With the revival of interest in literature, the text acquired new importance and its prosodic requirements could not be ignored. Here begins the history of real vocal music in which the musical line and rhythm follow the natural inflexions and rhythm of the words. Another generation, and in the French Renaissance chanson we have arrived at true *a cappella* choral music. Instruments are still often used, but they are no longer needed, and Erasmus of Rotterdam, the great humanist and disciple of Obrecht, objects to the presence of instruments in church, an objection that would soon be taken up by the Council of Trent.

With Henry Isaac (1450–1527) the Flemish migration was in full swing. He is the first consciously international master who steps out of his Flemish heritage to become a citizen of the world. His Florentine carnival songs are still sounding in the ears of the merrymakers when his great choral frescoes open new ways for the ancient Flemish art of polyphony. Others like Nicholas Gombert went to Madrid; Adrian Willaert went to Venice, Philippe de Monte to Prague—in a word, the Flemish masters are now ensconced in all the centres of music.

In the meantime there appeared a musician in whose art the world mission of the Flemings reached truly universal significance: Josquin des Prés (1450–1521). A disciple of Ockeghem, he subsequently visited Italy, returning to his homeland as a world-famous master at the age of fifty. What was still at times tentative in Obrecht took final shape in Josquin, who found the perfect balance between northern constructive urge and southern radiance.

He is the humanist musician. His melodies are perfectly liquid, yet they declaim. His constructions, complex in his youth, became symmetrical and transparent, and his harmonies are like the colours of the Italian painters of his time. This music is almost Italian, but there hovers over it a slight veil, a northern accent, that demonstrates that we are still dealing with a Flemish composer.

> Josquin des Prés: (i) *Ave Maria.* MASTERPIECES OF MUSIC BEFORE 1750. HAYDN SOCIETY HSL 2071 (alt. DUCRETET THOMSON MEL 194007);
> (ii) *Tribulatio.* HISTORY OF MUSIC IN SOUND, VOL. III. VICTOR LM 6016 (HMV HMS 28, 78 r.p.m.).

The musical Renaissance is, then, an accomplished fact in the first quarter of the sixteenth century. The principal forms that were to dominate the century bore the same names as in the Middle Ages—Mass, motet, chanson, madrigal—but the Renaissance chanson is entirely different from the older Burgundian chanson, and Mass and motet show a new flexibility.

Among the inherited and retained elements the most important was the principle of *cantus firmus* construction. The difference, already present with Dufay and the Burgundians, is that secular melodies are fully as acceptable as sacred ones for the *cantus firmus*. Thus we have Masses written on folk tunes that were known to everyone. The practice signifies that Gregorian Chant, formerly the sole source for such borrowed melodies, had lost its living force. The borrowed melody is now no longer recognizable as such, for it is subjected to the same contrapuntal elaboration as the other parts. But it was a very real constructive element, for it unified all five divisions of the Mass, every one of them being built upon it. We may take as an example part of a Mass composed upon the most famous secular tune of two centuries, *L'Homme armé.*

> Josquin des Prés: *Sanctus from the Mass L'Homme armé.* HISTORY OF MUSIC IN SOUND, VOL. III. VICTOR LM 6016 (HMV HMS 28, 78 r.p.m.).

The presence of these chanson tunes in the Mass is a good example of the spirit of the Renaissance which beckoned to the rich and varied art of the world at large to enter the workshops of the great Church composers. The once stern lines in Mass and motet were mollified by admitting the graceful turns that characterized secular music. The great French historian, Michelet, called the essence of the Renaissance 'the discovery of man.' Somehow this rebirth of the individual has been misinterpreted as 'the man of the Renaissance,' a romantically conceived personality indulging in bold sinfulness.   By extension the whole of the Renaissance came to be considered a brilliant but immoral and godless era.   Yet it was this era that saw the commissioning of thousands of religious pictures and Masses and motets for the churches, and most of these works of art reflect a sincere and devout religious feeling seldom attained in subsequent periods and scarcely known by our painters and composers to-day.   The northerner and the Anglo-Saxon will never entirely understand this animated era because in the end the Renaissance was a triumph of the romantic spirit which reconciled profound seriousness with gay light-heartedness, firm assertion of will with naïve irresponsibility.

The Renaissance did express in music also ideas that purported to echo the sentiments of antiquity.   Closer examination will disclose, however, that here too we are dealing with new weapons forged for new purposes.   Every title-page speaks of 'new means of expression invented by the author,' while at the same time they were convinced that they were drinking from the fountain of antiquity.   This new pride, tone, and consciousness was greatly supported and disseminated by the invention of music printing in Venice at the opening of the sixteenth century, and within a few decades, as other printing establishments appeared in Paris, Rome, Antwerp, and Nuremberg, a world distribution of music became possible.

(APPENDIX: *See* page 86.)

13

Paul Henry Lang

LASSUS AND THE FLEMISH SCHOOL

WE have seen how shortly after the opening of the sixteenth century Flemish musicians began to appear in all the musical centres of Europe. Since for two hundred years they were the undisputed leaders in music, it is logical and necessary to follow their long reign to its very end before we can deal with the other aspects of the Renaissance. However, it stands to reason that this unique domination could not have been one-sided, that the northern visitors received more than mere stimuli in Italy and France.

As a matter of fact, the French influence was constant, for the simple reason that while these Flemish composers were racially Germanic, with few exceptions their culture was French. They were the 'Latins of the North.' Therefore the destinies of French literature, under the full impact of humanism, would inevitably influence the art of the musicians, the secular phase of which was based on French texts. Flemish composers started and ended the development of the French polyphonic chanson, while Frenchmen ruled its middle period.

In Italy the earnest and learned northerners watched the carefree art of the popular forms with condescension, but also with unconcealed wonder and envy. They never imagined that music could be so light and effervescent. By combining the much more artistic manner of the chanson with the *frottola*, they created the flower of Renaissance secular music, the madrigal. And finally, by incorporating the suppleness and transparency thus gained in their Masses and motets, they set the tone and technique for a new type of 'learned music' that gained universal acceptance.

Without exception the originators of all these new styles, forms, and manners were Flemings, but all their innovations took place on foreign soil and were eventually taken over by the native composer.

In France Josquin des Prés and Pierre de la Rue, a Fleming in spite of his French name, stand at the beginning of the development of the chanson.   This chanson is no longer the old Burgundian love-song, sung by one singer while the other parts were taken by instruments, but a choral piece.   Based on elegant and sophisticated French verse, it was intimate, conversational, fresh, and full of irony.   The setting likes to tarry on significant words that permit pictorial and imitative sounds.

Josquin des Prés: *Je ne me puis tenir*.   HISTORY OF MUSIC IN SOUND,
    VOL. III.   VICTOR LM 6016 (HMV HMS 28, 78 r.p.m.).

Immediately after this generation the French composers entered the field, although there were still Flemings among them.   But the final period of the chanson is again under Flemish auspices, as we shall see when we reach Roland de Lassus.

Jacob Obrecht closes the fifteenth century and is among the first great masters of the north to show the Mediterranean influence to a considerable degree.   His sovereign contrapuntal ability, the pure design of his imitative part-writing, and his *cantus firmus* technique (outstanding even among the Netherlanders) unite with a fine feeling for rounded form and for rich harmony. There is too a certain robust quality about his music.

Obrecht: MOTETS: (i) *Si oblitus fuero*. HISTORY OF MUSIC IN
            SOUND, VOL. III.   VICTOR LM 6016 (HMV
            HMS 27, 78 r.p.m.);
        (ii) *Parce, Domine*. MASTERPIECES OF MUSIC
            BEFORE 1750, VOL. I.   HAYDN SOCIETY HSL
            2071.

Henry Isaac, although not younger than Obrecht, already represents the embodiment of the international and infinitely versatile Flemish musician, surpassed among the later composers only by Lassus.   He writes in any style with absolute ease and can match and surpass Italians and Germans on their own grounds.   But like a sorcerer he can take these various styles and mix their ingredients to create new forms and new styles.   We may take as examples three instrumental pieces, played by a consort of viols, all of which probably originated as vocal compositions.

Isaac: (i) *Chanson*; (ii) *La la hö hö*; (iii) *Innsbruck, ich muss dich
    lassen*. HISTORY OF MUSIC IN SOUND, VOL. III.   VICTOR LM
    6016 (HMV HMS 31, 78 r.p.m.).

In 1527 one of the Flemish pilgrims, Adrian Willaert (1490–1562), arrived in Venice, where he was to spend the rest of his life

*D

as the admired music master of St Mark's cathedral. This revolutionary made Venice into a great *avant-garde* musical metropolis for the rest of the century, and the famous Venetian painters actually shared their contemporary renown with musicians who were every inch as great and bold. Willaert wanted nothing less than a thorough and complete revision of music-making. His selection of Venice was a providentially proper one. The tradition-bound Romans would not have accepted boldness, but the colourful city-republic on the Adriatic, revelling in an eternal carnival, wanted to be surprised. Unfortunately, none of the larger pieces by Willaert has been recorded, but his essential boldness is well reflected in his smaller works.

Willaert: *Three Madrigals*. ANTHOLOGIE SONORE AS 5.

St Mark's in Venice, an old Byzantine-style structure, had two choir-lofts with an organ in each. By using the double choir-loft, Willaert created a new style. Music virtually multiplied itself in such works as his *Vespers* for double choirs; there were new sonorities and new dimensions, new colours and new groupings. Here the choirs disputed one another, there they united in tremendous ensembles in eight parts. But the colour was not only external, the new choral sound. Internally it appeared in the form of new harmonies, notably in the gradual gain of chromaticism which was to lead to the demise of the old ecclesiastical modes. Venice received this new music with jubilation, and disciples flocked to Master Adrian—the first generation once more consisting largely of his own compatriots—and Willaert became one of the greatest teachers in the history of music.

Among his disciples was Cipriano de Rore, the creator of the classic madrigal. The name should not deceive us; despite its Italian sound, he was a native of Antwerp. His madrigals are real chamber music for the delectation of musical gourmets, but their dreamy quality again shows them to be the work of a son of the Lowlands. There were many others who followed in the wake of Josquin and Willaert, but the greatest, and the one who closes the long reign of the Netherlands composers was Roland de Lassus, also known as Orlando di Lasso (1532–94).

Lassus was twenty-four years old when he became choir-master to the Duke of Bavaria in Munich. Yet he had already served a long apprenticeship in Milan, Naples, and Rome, and had

had a trip to France, a stay in Antwerp, and possibly a trip to England.   Thus, when he went to Munich he brought with him not only what he had inherited but also what he had learned: Flemish motet, Italian madrigal, and French chanson.   Now he added to all this German song.   By 1570 Lassus was the prince of European musicians, and Pope, emperor, and king received him like a royal personage.   Lassus was a child of Renaissance and humanism. When at the age of sixty-three he died—in 1594, the same year that Palestrina died and Florentine opera was born—his life-work rose over him like a great cap-stone.   It was both the boundary mark of Flemish musical influence and the monument over the tomb of humanism.

Lassus composed twelve hundred motets, hundreds of Masses, psalm settings, madrigals, chansons, and German choral songs. In his church music he penetrates into depths unknown since Josquin; his *Pentitential Psalms* show a man shaking and crying 'mea culpa.'   Yet his chansons are even more Gallic and frivolous than those of French composers, and some of the wittiest and most elegant of them cannot be sung to-day because of the audacity of their texts.   His madrigals are suave and sensitive, while his German songs reflect the somewhat clumsy humour of his adopted country.   Whatever the *genre* he cultivated, it was always in perfect idiomatic style, and yet his own personality is everywhere unmistakable.

Lassus: *Matona, mia cara.*   Epic 3LC 3045 (alt. DGG APM 4055).

Then Lassus, who so much enjoyed life, denounced his earlier conduct and his secular works, and after recovering from a deep mental disturbance dedicated the rest of his life to church music only.   After Lassus, the ambassadors of Flemish music had to choose between two courses.   Philippe de Monte, who went to Prague, associated himself with the spirit of southern humanism, composing well over a thousand madrigals.   On the other hand, Jacobus de Kerle (*c.* 1531–91) joined the imperial Counter-Reformation body and soul.   But Lassus attempted the impossible; he thought that the Counter-Reformation could be incorporated in humanism.   That was the reason for his temporary collapse; the universal master of music could not deny his nature.   The classic reconciliation of the two tendencies, though on Church territory, was effected by Palestrina and Victoria.   Lassus did not become the 'priest of music,' the musical warrior for the Church, but he became the embodiment of the universal musical genius of the times.

We may take as examples of his sacred music two motets and a Mass-section. The first motet takes its text from Ecclesiastes and is for two choirs: 'To everything there is a season . . . a time to be born and a time to die.' The second motet is in four parts: *Scio enim.* (For I know that my Redeemer liveth.) And our third example is the *Benedictus* and *Hosanna* from his Mass, based on a song by another composer, *Puisque j'ai perdu mes amours.*

> Lassus: Motets: (i) *Omnia tempus habent.* Anthologie Sonore AS
> 6 (AS 104, 78 r.p.m.).
> (ii) *Scio enim*; (iii) *Benedictus and Hosanna.* History
> of Music in Sound, Vol. IV. Victor LM
> 6029 (HMV HMS 36, 78 r.p.m.).

If we look back on this incomparable period of Netherlands music, we behold an extended, logical, and uninterrupted stylistic development. The rather forbidding architectural severity of the Gothic gave way to the mellow and slightly melancholy art of the Burgundians. With Ockeghem and his school the ingrained love of the Germanic artist for 'construction' returns in a sort of neo-Gothic. With Josquin des Prés the Renaissance is upon us, but he did not found a school and after his death a consolidation took place. The archaic elements of Ockeghem's polyphony were minimized, while the flexibility and articulation gained from chanson and madrigal were incorporated in the motet style. The resultant polished, balanced, and flowing choral style was carried to such perfection by the middle of the sixteenth century that neither Lassus nor Palestrina could add to it anything—beyond, of course, a great many masterpieces.

By the time we reach the sixteenth century instrumental music was well on its way to independent existence. Lute, harpsichord, organ, various viols, and all sorts of wind instruments were in use and we should not think of these as primitive, hard-to-play instruments. Dances, fantasias, and serious contrapuntal works called *ricercars* were written for them in increasing numbers, and they are full of a particular grace that is characteristic of the instrumental medium. Each and every one of these new types of instrumental works became a prototype of the fantasies, fugues, suites, and other well-known later *genres*, though the pioneering composers

of the sixteenth century should be regarded, not as mere forerunners, but as bold innovators.

Willaert: *Ricercar*. HISTORY OF MUSIC IN SOUND, VOL. IV.
   VICTOR LM 6029 (HMV HMS 41, 78 r.p.m.).

It may be asked: What was the secret of the Netherlanders'
incomparable skill? While such a question cannot be answered
briefly, their musical education undoubtedly had a great deal to
do with it. The cathedral choir schools of Flanders and northern
France taught not only the art of singing but the technique of
composition too. Every youngster grew up a learned musician,
and even the lesser talents could proceed with formal security
and had been invested with a high aesthetic sense. No wonder
that Flemish choir singers were sought after by every chapel,
ecclesiastic or princely.

A fascinating chapter still remains to be written about the role
of the Flemish musicians in the colonization of the New World.
We do know that the first of them, a Franciscan friar, Pedro de
Gante, arrived in Vera Cruz in 1523—only six years after Willaert
settled in Venice! He apparently taught the Indians the great
polyphonic art of his homeland, and two magnificently illuminated
scores in the National Museum of Mexico testify to his success.

But the Flemings were not particularly liked abroad, though
held in awe and respect. The Italians learned from them assidu-
ously, though perhaps with some envy, and as the sixteenth century
advances we begin to perceive the tremendous struggle for the
southern traditions; the disciple will overwhelm his master and
take his place. Roman classicism, the madrigal, and Venetian
choir music were all inaugurated by Flemings and consummated
by Italians. The first begins with Josquin and is capped by
Palestrina; the second owes its inception to Verdelot and de Rore
and ends in Marenzio; the third starts with Willaert and is consummated in the two Gabrielis. But before one dynasty passed
and was succeeded by another there was an idyllic interval when
there reigned a compromise between north and south, polyphony
and melody; one of the rarest and greatest historical confluences
in which the predecessor and successor unite, with all their forces,
in a common focus for a short period.

APPENDIX

(CHAPTERS 12 and 13)

BOOKS

Studies of Renaissance composers and national schools in English are much fewer than might be supposed. The most valuable book for study in conjunction with the chapters on the Renaissance is:

GUSTAVE REESE: *Music in the Renaissance.*

Other books that deserve mention here are:

M. BUKOFZER: *Studies in Mediaeval and Renaissance Music.*
G. S. BEDBROOK: *Keyboard Music from the Middle Ages to the Beginnings of the Baroque.*
R. O. MORRIS: *Contrapuntal Technique in the Sixteenth Century.*
KNUD JEPPESEN: *The Style of Palestrina and the Dissonance.*

Three books on the Flemish composers should be mentioned:

ERNST KRENEK: *Johannes Ockeghem.*
C. VAN DEN BORREN: *Roland de Lassus.*
E. R. SOLLITT: *Dufay to Sweelinck.*

RECORDS

Anthology of Renaissance Vocal Music. PERIOD SPLP 535 and 597.
Motets of the Fifteenth and Sixteenth Centuries. LYRICHORD LL 52.
Pre-Baroque Sacred Music. FESTIVAL FLP 70–202. CAMBRIDGE CR 101.
Russian, Polish, English, and Spanish Music. ANTHOLOGIE SONORE AS 10.
Flemish Choral Music. EPIC 3 LC 3045.
Flemish Organ Music RENAISSANCE 39. (NIXA PLP 239).
OCKEGHEM: *Missa Prolationum.* KINGSWAY 221.
ISAAK: *Missa Carminum.* WESTMINSTER WL 5215.
ISAAK AND GALLUS: *Choral Works.* WESTMINSTER WL 5347.
JOSQUIN DES PRÉS: *Secular Works.* EMS 213.
LASSUS: *De Profundis; Lamentations.* CONCERT HALL 47. *Penitential Psalms.* CONCERT HALL 1196. *Mass: Puisque j'ay perdu.* UNICORN 1013. *Neue Teutsche Lieder; Chansons.* DGG APM 14055.
JOSQUIN DES PRÉS: *Miserere—Motet.* ARGO RG 90.
MANCHICOURT: *Mass.* ARGO RG 90.
ANON.: *Emendemus in melius—Motet.* ARGO RG 90.

14

Paul Henry Lang

THE FRENCH RENAISSANCE SCHOOL

THE sixteenth century represents a wholly new period in French history. In the Middle Ages there was no political unity in the land; every province was a more or less sovereign state. In Francis I the country had a real and powerful monarch, and the court became the undisputed centre of political, economic, and artistic life, from which everyone took his cue. There grew up a large and powerful aristocracy which imitated and echoed everything done at the court of Paris. There was also a growing and very influential middle class of rich citizens, and the great change in the general orientation of French music in the sixteenth century, from sacred to secular, is directly attributable to their influence. It stands to reason that the secular world, now considerably more independent of the Church, would want to assert itself in artistic matters, and indeed in music it demanded more for its own use.

From the Gallic bards to the modern Parisian café, the French have been singing chansons. In every type of this truly French form of music, whether highly artistic or merely street songs, their characteristic humour, sensibility, mischief, and prudence are unfailingly expressed. This is understandable; the French are a very articulate and discursive people, they like to talk and to argue, and they dislike everything that has no clear and arguable meaning. It is for this reason that if one speaks of French culture, it is literature that comes first to mind. And for the same reason they have always been partial to music that either accompanies a text or, as in programme music, attempts to represent something that can be expressed in words.

The French military expeditions to Italy acquainted French musicians with the popular music of Renaissance Italy. It was again the *frottola* that served as a catalyst between the older

Flemish chanson and the French Renaissance chanson. In 1515, when Francis I opened the gates to Italian artists and musicians, the spirit of humanism simply poured into the country. Beginning in 1528 enormous numbers of chansons were printed. But the French, being what they are, always fastidious and refined, the harmless doggerel of the *frottola* did not suit them, and they used for texts the elegant and piquant poetry of the times.

The *Ars Nova* had already recognized and demanded respect for the poet's needs; the *frottola* went further as it demanded an easily understood setting for the words. The popular side avoided complications because of its very nature; the courtly avoided them because of its wish to demonstrate its transparent lightness and elegance. Therefore, both emphasized the power of the word, the language, realizing what the aesthetics of the era demanded of music: 'to pour spirit into the words.'

The change is a very significant one, for from now on we are dealing with sung poetry, and not with music accompanied by a text. Actually, by 1536, one encounters indignant strictures aimed at the 'barbarous' mishandling of the text by older composers. We therefore see ourselves in the presence of a real Renaissance movement because this respect for, and understanding of, poetry is obviously the result of the rebirth of arts and letters.

Since the French musicians possessed a superior technique, the result of the long association with the Burgundian-Flemish chanson, this new type of Renaissance music was created in an astonishingly short time. The very first printed edition of secular music which appeared in 1501 in Venice contained a multitude of French chansons: these were the old Flemish chansons of the fifteenth century. Twenty-seven years later a similar milestone in the art of music-printing was reached in France, and again it was a collection of chansons. Just what happened in the intervening quarter of a century is not known, but these were the fully developed Renaissance chansons.

Chansons: (i) Guillaume Costeley: *Allons au vert bocage*; (ii) Claudin de Sermisy: *Quant que vivray*; (iii) Passereau: *Il est bel et bon.* HISTORY OF MUSIC IN SOUND, VOL. IV. VICTOR LM 2609 (HMV HMS 34, 78 r.p.m.).

These Renaissance chansons no longer sang of the Platonic love of the aristocratic chansons of the fifteenth century, but glorified earthly love, and were often unsparing in their use of rather saucy details. They defy comparison in their freshness of invention, true vocalism, and fine lyricism. Another striking feature is the superbly rounded form; in the first part logically setting forth the purpose of the song, developing the material in the middle, and ending with a little recapitulation. Their emotional range is nowhere so wide as that of the Italian madrigal, but they are always delightful because of their frothy delicacy and elegance. They fascinate with their rhythm and with their wonderful musical declamation, which is precise yet light. The individual parts are independent and graceful, yet they do follow a remarkable, if unobtrusive, polyphonic technique. Nothing is left of the old fifteenth-century chanson, for this, its Renaissance cousin, has become a descriptive story-telling art. It is satirical, naughty, yet intimate and often echoing delicate and refined sentiment, and it is full of melodic invention, some of it astonishingly modern. But above all, it is the words that dominate the music, and here begins the path which French music has followed ever since.

Among the first great masters of the form was a soldier of fortune who served as court musician to knights, princes, and cardinals: Clément Jannequin. One glance at his chansons and we realize that we are dealing with a full-blooded French composer in a Flemish-dominated musical world. Jannequin composed veritable musical murals that have an outspoken pictorial quality, the very rhythm of life. He cast his military memories in a large chanson in which one can hear the sound of battle: the trumpet calls, the charging horses, and the clashing of arms. He did the same in his music for the hunt, for the chattering of Parisian housewives, the medley of street vendors' cries as they ply their trades. Perhaps the most engaging, and virtuoso, piece is the chanson entitled *The Song of the Birds*. Jannequin is able to re-create the chirping and singing of the birds and give a true musical impression of the morning's delightful sounds in the woods.

Jannequin: *Le chant des oiseaux*. ANTHOLOGIE SONORE AS 6 (AS 7, 78 r.p.m.).

The new vivacity, the pictorial element, the faithful musical declamation, and the everyday tone characteristic of the new chanson became immensely popular, and Paris once more became a world centre of music. Jannequin's chanson *The Battle* set a fashion that even penetrated into church music, and finally the highest Church authorities had to prohibit what they called 'battle music in church.'

Other notable chanson composers from among the many are Guillaume Costeley (1531–1606), Claudin de Sermisy (c. 1490–1562) and Claude Le Jeune (1528–c. 1600). Their chansons are not so pictorial or extended as Jannequin's, but show an even more delicately sophisticated choral technique. All of them are characterized by a very modern concept of vocal writing and harmony. With this music we no longer need special historical conditioning; it is so modern that we can listen to it as we do to Schubert.

> (i) Costeley: *Mignonne. Allons gay*; (ii) Garnier: *Reveillez-moi*; (iii) Sermisy: *En entrant en ung jardin*. ANTHOLOGIE SONORE AS 6 (AS 45, AS 15, 78 r.p.m.) (alt. BRUNSWICK AXTL 1048: DUCRETET THOMSON HEL 194007).

The great popularity of chanson and madrigal during the Renaissance signified not only a tremendous growth in music-making, but also a reorientation in the concept of musical creation. The chanson remained within the orbit of contrapuntal music, but it no longer depended upon the *cantus firmus*. Every bit of such a piece was freely invented by the composer. Another trend must be noted. Whereas formerly the pivotal part was in the tenor, which contained the borrowed melody, there is a definite tendency now to assign the leading part to the uppermost voice. The fact that some of the chansons recorded are performed by one voice, with the accompanying instrument(s) taking the others, illustrates the new concept. This is clearly a tendency towards the accompanied solo music which appears with the early baroque.

Later in the sixteenth century, under the influence of the courtly, humanistic poets, Ronsard and Baïf, the chanson becomes a vehicle of Renaissance thought. The enthusiastic humanists, proceeding from ancient theories, declared music and poetry twin sisters who could not be separated, and Antoine de Baïf declared the oneness of the French language with classical Latin and proposed to apply antique metres to French verse. This led to the so-called 'measured verse.' In reality this was a gentle fraud, because French is not a quantitative but an accented language. But these learned poets managed to arrange lines that followed classical metre, and this procedure, which eliminated the bar-line, resulted in infinitely subtle rhythmic shading and called forth remarkable musical compositions.

It might be thought that the excessive zeal of the poet would thus force the musician within intolerably restrictive barriers, but there is no trace of coercion in these melodically fresh and rhythmically varied pieces, nor are they pedantic.   The influence of measured verse was lasting, and one glance at some of Monteverdi's works will show that this influence was not restricted to France.   This new measured chanson was no longer addressed to everyone from king to shopkeeper—only to 'the rarest of cultivated minds'— yet nevertheless it too became very popular.

The late Renaissance chanson, which became more sophisticated and refined by the day, accustomed musicianly ears to constructions that no longer knew a central accent or symmetrically divided phrases.   The outcome, the *air de cour*, or court air, was a lyric song, rather melancholy in character.   Their melodies are usually well written, often beautiful, but their chief characteristic is their free rhythm, which constantly alternates between $3/4$, $4/4$, $2/4$, and $6/4$.   Very soon the four-part setting of the *air de cour* in which the uppermost part dominated developed into a solo song, the three lowest parts played on the lute.   So again we are on the road towards the solo music of the baroque.

   (i) Claudin de Sermisy: *Vivray-je*. HISTORY OF MUSIC IN SOUND,
      VOL. IV. VICTOR LM 2609 (HMV HMS 40, 78 r.p.m.);
   (ii) Nicholas de la Grotte: *Je suis amour*. ANTHOLOGIE SONORE AS
      6 (AS 36, 78 r.p.m.).

In the meantime the chanson reached its apex in the hands of Roland de Lassus.   Thus the circle closes; the Flemish-born *genre* again passes from French into Flemish hands.   This is understandable if we consider the great Netherlander's qualities. He was a man of the world with a considerable literary culture, and French was virtually his mother tongue.   Although of a profound nature he was also spirited, full of witty invention and easily drawn into that rapidly moving conversational tone which exudes from the chanson.

French church music remained outside the orbit of the chanson which so completely transformed secular music.   On the whole Mass and motet remained faithful to the principles established by Josquin des Prés.   The Flemish domination in the field of church music was so strong that it seems that all the native inventiveness went into the production of chansons and related types.   In the sacred music of sixteenth-century France we search in vain for the seraphic mysticism of the Italians, the passionate fervour of the Spaniards, or the profound devotion of the Flemings. This is a rather worldly, elegant art, even though by no means lacking in some sincerely dedicated compositions. It seems as if the great chanson composers, some of whom held Church appointments, wrote church music to discharge their statutory obligations rather than from conviction or a natural bent.

There was, however, one significant exception. The Reformation attracted some of the finest musical minds in France, and they turned to the Psalms, translated into French by Protestant poets. Many of these settings were very simple but others vied with the greatest Catholic motets. The greatest composer of such polyphonic psalms was Claude Goudimel (c. 1510–72), tragically killed in the Massacre of St Bartholomew. Both Goudimel and Le Jeune, also a Huguenot, exhibit in these works a profound conviction and devotion to the cause which rings in their music.

> Goudimel: (i) *Psalm 25* (two settings); (ii) *Psalm 19*. Le Jeune: (iii) *Psalm 42*; (iv) *Psalm 69*. ANTHOLOGIE SONORE AS 6 (AS 12, 78 r.p.m.).

With the very beginning of the printing of music in France, we encounter much instrumental music, and that testifies to its popularity. Many a famous chanson was transcribed for lute or harpsichord, but it was the French liking for dance rhythms that produced the original music for these instruments. Original it was only in its spirit, and this literature cannot compare with that of the Italians or the Flemish, but it did prepare the ground for the great French lute and harpsichord schools of the seventeenth century.

Towards the end of the sixteenth century this love of dance music resulted in a movement that we usually ascribe wholly to Italian incentive: the preparation for the dramatic stage which opened the next century. Actually, the French were more experienced than the Italians in the organization of ceremonies and spectacles because of the central importance of the court in Paris. Thus arose the dramatic ballet, performed with means of unprecedented lavishness. This 'court ballet' was not just danced to musical accompaniment; it represented a most artistic combination of the various elements—measured verse, songs, recitation, and dance-pantomine. The age was entirely convinced that this was a virtual re-creation of the 'universal' art of classical antiquity, and while this was as little true as the claims advanced a quarter of a century later by the Italians for their opera, there can be little doubt that the French actually made the decisive step towards the lyric stage considerably ahead of the Italians.

As the sixteenth century closes, we behold a rich harvest of French music from which the chanson detaches itself as the most significant artistic contribution of French genius.   But everything seems to have run its course, and what we see is a beehive of activity, of experiment, of popularization—that is, the typical picture of a transition period which leads to the world-conquering style of the seventeenth century.

APPENDIX

Records

French Renaissance Vocal Music.   DECCA 9629 (BRUNSWICK AXTL 1048).
French Renaissance Music.   ANTHOLOGIE SONORE AS 41.
Parisian Songs of the Sixteenth Century.   OISEAU-LYRE OL 50027.
French Solo Songs of the Sixteenth and Seventeenth Centuries.   WESTMINSTER WL 5085 (NIXA WLP 5085).
JANNEQUIN: *Chansons.*   DECCA ARC 3034 (DGG APM 14042).

15

Paul Henry Lang

THE GERMAN RENAISSANCE SCHOOL

I N Germany the influence of Renaissance ideas and ideals was
far greater in the arts than in letters or in the general pattern
of culture. Great painters such as Grunewald, Dürer, and
Holbein arose, and great musicians joined them, but their fate,
like the fate of the German Renaissance, was settled by Martin
Luther and the Reformation. There are important points in
which Renaissance and Reformation agree, and humanism had a
far more important share in leading Luther to the Bible than is
usually conceded, but on the other hand the two movements do
not run parallel.

The Reformation had a popular character; the Renaissance is
courtly, artistic, learned, and exclusive. Luther represented a
middle-class civilization, whereas the Renaissance was aristocratic.
The middle class had its own standards of ethics, and accepted from
the Renaissance only such elements as it could use for its own
purposes. Everything had significance only to the extent to which
it could support the *idea*; a very Germanic concept that will
return with a vengeance in Wagner. In Luther's particular case,
the reformer ceaselessly fought for practical-moral aims to which
everything was tied, and this created a cheerlessly sober, earth-
bound, and circumscribed world of arts and letters, best exemplified by the meistersingers. In Germany the Renaissance
remained an uncompleted movement.

Up to the time of the Enlightenment the German Evangelical
Church was the focal point of artistic life. The German towns
in the Protestant north had independent municipal governments,
a fact which contributed considerably to the Protestant movement.
Musicians were employed in the towns' churches and schools,
and their work used for civic and other solemnities. This patronage soon created a respectable body of cantors, organists, and

teachers who were all members of the citizen class. Thus this
northern Protestant music was served by citizen-burghers for,
and in the interest of, their fellow burghers, whereas in the clerical
chapel choirs in the south the musicians represented the unbroken
tradition of centuries of medieval culture directed by the Church
and the aristocracy. These musicians in the north who learned
a great deal from the Flemings, and later the Italians, nevertheless
remained German, because the school and Church for which they
worked provided them with ample occupation.

The German artist of the fifteenth century, whether a painter
or a musician, still employed all his technical and formal means to
express feelings and moods. In contemporary Italy art was a
source of joy for its own sake, but to the Germans it was merely
a means of expression. Unlike the Italians the Germans did not
value absolute beauty. Throughout the fifteenth century German
music was dominated by a growing polyphonic literature, the
cantus firmi of which were taken from courtly lyrics or folk-song.
In the music of the Netherlanders and the French we did not find
such a preponderance of secular popular elements. German folk-
song was a powerful element in the spiritual life of the nation and
more than anywhere else moulded their music. One of the principal monuments of it is the so-called Lochamer song book, which
dates from about 1450; others were the Glogau and Munich
collections from about 1480. The instrumentalists of the era
were very important too, such as Conrad Paumann, the blind
organist, and the lute players. Our example of the music of
Paumann is an organ work based on a song from the *Lochamer
liederbuch*.

Paumann: *Mit gauczem Willen*. HISTORY OF MUSIC IN SOUND, VOL.
III. VICTOR LM 6016 (HMV HMS 30, 78 r.p.m.).

In the field of polyphonic church music the German composers
of the fifteenth century are only minor masters, but by the turn
of the century we encounter interesting and independent composers. Adam of Fulda (*c.* 1445–1505) must be regarded as the
first significant master of the first generation of German composers;
he joined Obrecht and Isaac, then the leading international masters.
None of his music is available on records, but we can sample the
music of the time in two anonymous songs of the fifteenth
century. The first is 'Once I saw the morning star'; the second
begins: 'The wood is bare of leaves in this cold winter. I am bare

of joy and memories make me old. I have to avoid the one I love because of the envy and cunning of gossips.'

Anon.: (i) *Ich sachs eins mals*; (ii) *Der wallt hat sich eutlawbet.* ANTHO-
LOGIE SONORE AS 7.

Heinrich Finck (*c.* 1445–1527), the much travelled contemporary of Adam of Fulda, lived to a ripe old age. He was a spirited and learned composer whose style contemporaries found 'unusual'— a sure indication of an independent mind. Indeed, if we compare his style to Obrecht's lovely and intimate music, Finck's is bold and powerfully expressive. His Masses and motets are very important, and so are his songs that saw many printed editions in the sixteenth century. We may take two of Finck's songs as examples. The first opens: 'Wake up, my treasure, I hear the sentry's call from the battlements. Day shines in the firmament and night is turning.' The text of the second song may be summarized thus: 'O dear heart, recognize my pain. I have no peace. Your face has captured my heart. On my oath, there shall never be anyone more beloved than you. You are my comfort on earth. While I live, I shall not regret any service.'

Finck: (i) *Wach auf*; (ii) *Ach herzigs herz.* ANTHOLOGIE SONORE
AS 7 (AS 51, 78 r.p.m.).

Paul Hofhaimer (1459–1537) was the greatest organist of his age, the first famous German instrumentalist and the teacher of a host of excellent musicians of the next generation. But beyond that he was certainly the most talented and engaging composer of German polyphonic song between the generation of Adam of Fulda and the early Protestant composers. His songs have a noble melodic line, pleasing harmonies and, above all, a savour of their very own. We may take as an example a short organ piece by one of Hofhaimer's pupils, Hans Buchner, based on what we would call a nonsense song.

Buchner: *Es gieng ein Mann.* HISTORY OF MUSIC IN SOUND, VOL.
III. VICTOR LM 6016 (HMV HMS 30, 78 r.p.m.).

As we proceed further into the sixteenth century we encounter not only greater composers but definite indications of the spread of the spirit of the Renaissance among German musicians. They were all connected in one way or another with Henry Isaac the great Netherlander. He was stationed in Innsbruck and Constance and taught many of the German composers, who admired his music unreservedly. Among them was Thomas Stoltzer (*c.* 1475–1526), whose works contain a great variety of German and Latin compositions in a style that grew from the spirit of the late German Gothic, yet his polyphonic constructions disclose a remarkably personal imagination. He deals freely with the *cantus firmus* and sets against it fantastic and expressive counterpoints. In his psalm settings towards the end of his life he shows a seemingly inexplicable change in style, but there can be little doubt that what happened was that Stoltzer became acquainted with Josquin's music and was suddenly enveloped by the full radiance of the Renaissance. His music becomes light and transparent, his declamation clear, his harmonies simple, and his form beautifully rounded.

Isaac's most distinguished personal pupil was Ludwig Senfl (*c.* 1489–1543). Born in Zürich, he studied in Vienna with Isaac and succeeded him at the imperial chapel in 1517. Eventually he settled in Munich in 1530. He corresponded with Luther and other Protestant leaders and apparently exhibited enough sympathy with the movement to make his position in the Catholic court untenable, even though he did not break with the Church.

Senfl was the greatest German composer of his time, recognized as 'the prince of all Germanic music from Scandinavia to the Alps.' He was a worthy predecessor of Lassus, who occupied the same post in Munich in the next generation. Like Lassus, Senfl was a profound musical poet and wonderfully many-sided; he severely observed the traditions of the Josquin school, but he did also break new paths with bold reforms towards freer, more subjective, and more passionate lyricism. He was the greatest master of German choral song and the founder of German Mass and motet style based on the Netherlands precepts. Senfl's polyphonic part-songs are often characterized by a robust sense of humour and they strike a peculiar, partly erotic, partly demonic tone of lyricism. All in all, he was the Dürer of German music, though perhaps we come still nearer his status if we call him the Josquin of Renaissance music in Germany.

We may take as examples of his music a six-part motet: 'This day is so sacred that nobody can praise it enough. Because the true Son of God subdued hell and banished the devil there'; and then a bell song, *Kling, klang.*

Senfl: (i) *Also heilig ist der tag*; (ii) *Kling, klang.* ANTHOLOGIE SONORE AS 7 (AS 51, 78 r.p.m.).

It was fortunate for the future of music that, unlike the Swiss and Scottish reformers who demolished organs and burned missals, Martin Luther took over everything from the Roman rite that he could adapt to his own Church's usage. It must be remembered that there was an ancient tradition in Germany of so-called 'spiritual songs' in the vernacular, and also in a curious mixed German-Latin. The reformers themselves often declared that they built upon a vast existing treasure, and the new Lutheran Church song, the chorale or hymn, raised the folk-song to immense artistic and religious power. To this newly acquired eminence much was added by the spirit of the times. The populace was deeply excited and provoked by religious problems, and folk-song must have taken on all the religious fervour of the day. Still, the decisive step was that the reformers made this new song an integral part of the divine service. Even Luther and his musical helpers were surprised at the impact this innovation had upon the congregation. This hymn singing became so general that one might say that by the end of the sixteenth century in Protestant Germany the church song had taken the place of folk-song, and would keep its place for a century and a half. Two other sources were Gregorian Chant and original hymns, expressly composed for the Church.

It was not so much in style as in the use of the vernacular that Protestant church music of the sixteenth century differed from the Catholic, though the use of the vernacular did gradually endow Protestant music with accents and inflexions that it did not know in the Latin world. Actually, the great rhythmic variety of the old spiritual folk-song was not suited for congregational singing until methodically simplified. This killed the wonderful rhythm of the old song, but also made the chorale a truly popular religious expression of Protestantism, the perfect counterpart of Gregorian Chant. Towards the end of the sixteenth century the settings are simple four-part harmony, with the tune moved up from the tenor to the treble, where it became instantly comprehensible to the congregation.

The generation of composers that followed those who actually witnessed the great religious upheaval could not close their ears to the blandishments emanating from the Mediterranean. This was also the time when Flemish and Italian musicians took up residence in the principal German centres, and the most influential of the visitors was Lassus, who understood German, sympathized with the native composers, and proved to be a congenial teacher.

Hans Leo Hassler (1564–1612) was one of the first German composers to follow in the footsteps of such painters as Dürer and go to study in Italy. Hassler went to Venice, where his teacher was the elder Gabrieli, and he became perhaps the most engaging musical personality among the 'Italianized' composers. His melodic invention is fresh and his tunes are amazingly durable. Canzonet and madrigal taught him formal roundness and elegance while the Venetian polychoral works imparted to him a mural-like pomp and colour, a radiance that was as new in German music as was the madrigalesque animation. Yet Hassler remained a German musician, and the expressive style he initiated became the foundation of the great musical literature of the following century. We may take as an example a piece that begins in the learned motet style, but ends in the simpler style of the chorale: 'My hour is come and I shall be on my way. So be my guide, Lord Jesus Christ. You will not leave me. At the end I commend my soul into your hands. You will preserve it.'

Hassler: *Wenn mein Stündlein*. ANTHOLOGIE SONORE AS 7 (AS 72, 78 r.p.m.) (alt. DGG APM 14010).

Some of the greatest musicians of the age presided over the imperial, ducal, and electoral chapel choirs—Lassus in Munich, de Monte in Prague, and Scandello in Dresden. A typical German representative is Jacob Handl, known also as Gallus (1550–91). He was one of the finest German practitioners of the Venetian polychoral style and a master of Flemish polyphony.

Handl (Gallus): *Mirabile mysterium*. HISTORY OF MUSIC IN SOUND, VOL. IV. VICTOR LM 6029 (HMV HMS 36, 78 r.p.m.).

The influence of humanism considerably enlarged the intellectual horizon of German composers, which was still entirely medieval at the close of the fifteenth century. A large instruction literature was written for use in the schools, and in the person of Conrad Celtes the Germans had their equivalent of Baïf and his French measured music. The sixteenth century closes then on this tone. On the one hand, German Protestantism accepted music as an element in its worship commensurate in importance with Holy Writ; while on the other hand, the secular musicians were immersed in the severe beauties of classical versification which they hoped to restore into their music. Between the two extremes was German choral song that was beginning to be touched by outside influences. Soon the full flood of the Italian baroque would force all parties to pause and take stock, for the world of music was about to change all over again.

APPENDIX

The German Renaissance composers are rather poorly represented on records. There is a selection from the song books on one recorded anthology of Renaissance music:

Music of the Renaissance.   Vox PL 8120 (E).

Also:

Music of the Fifteenth and Sixteenth Centuries.   Oiseau-Lyre OL 50104.

Hassler: *Teutsch Gesang.*   DGG APM 14010.

Lechner: *Teutsche Lieder.*   DGG APM 14010.

16

Paul Henry Lang

THE SPANISH RENAISSANCE SCHOOL

THERE is something exotic in the character of Spanish culture which sharply separates Spain from her sister nations France and Italy. The harsh asceticism, the severe cult of traditional ideals, the hypnotic stubbornness with which Spaniards cling, not only to their religion, but to everything connected with it in no matter how tenuous a fashion—these are some of the traits responsible for the peculiar Spanish soul. The noble pathos of the feudal chivalric world was imbedded in this soul, and therefore the culture of the Spaniards always retained a certain aristocratic quality; a quality present in the refinement of speech, in the poetic *élan* of everything Spanish, in the pomp and circumstance of their functions, public and private, and in the very moral values they believed in. Unlike Italy or France, where the middle classes always exerted considerable influence on cultural trends, Spain knew only the knights in silk and brocade and the rabble in rags, and they lived side by side without mingling.

The Moorish invaders also exerted a tremendous influence on Spanish music. They were not a horde of barbarians, but a nation with a brilliant culture whose capital city, Cordoba, was as much an artistic centre as any city in Europe. Just how strong and how lasting was the oriental influence on music is not yet determined.

All we can say in a general summary introduction is that the basic tone of Spanish music is a fantastic mysticism which is expressed in prickly national rhythms as well as in passionate abandon. The Spaniard's melody is far more severe than the Italian's, his comic sense more cunning, and his pathos more dangerous.

Proceeding on the basis of the known characteristics of Spanish cultural history, we shall not be surprised to find in the thirteenth century a fine song literature that is religious and aristocratic in spirit.   These *cantigas* follow in the tradition of the troubadours, a lively Spanish branch whose art existed in the twelfth century. A magnificent collection of over four hundred *cantigas* is now available for study and performance.

(i) *Quen â Virgen*; (ii) *Como poden per sas culpas*.   HISTORY OF MUSIC IN SOUND, VOL. II.   VICTOR LM 6015 (HMV HMS 15, 78 r.p.m.).

Beside the *cantigas*, mention should be made of the musical mystery play.   Nowhere in Europe were mystery plays as much liked and practised as in Spain, a fact that must have vastly contributed to the rise of the splendid Spanish theatre of the baroque.

Then during the fifteenth century there began a movement of consolidation.   This resulted in the gathering and publication of literary-musical collections called *cancioneros*, i.e. song-books. These are artistic documents of the first magnitude, presenting not only contemporary music, sacred and secular, but also the older troubadour literature.   Once more we witness the familiar dichotomy, the opposing techniques of learned polyphony and the Mediterranean preference for homophony and precise rhythm. What the *frottola* was for the Italians, the *cantarcillo* was for the Spaniards; a popular, instrumentally accompanied piece, largely devoid of the complicated artistic apparatus of the polyphonic forms.   And the Spanish musician was far more faithful to the text than his northern contemporary.

The *cancioneros* contained romances and so-called *villancicos* which occupy a position in Spanish music analogous to that of the madrigal in Italy.   Even though many of these *villancicos* were written by learned composers, they remained simple and largely syllabic in order to safeguard the correct prosody of the text.   The most remarkable collection of these songs is the *Cancionero de Palacio*, and the most representative composer who figures in it is Juan del Encina (1468–1529).   Curiously enough, the madrigal which conquered all other countries made no headway in Spain.   The *villancico* remained entirely Spanish, and even when it used more nearly madrigalesque counterpoints it was unmistakably Spanish in tone.

For examples of the vocal music of this period we may take the anonymous carol, *Salute me, sons of Eve*; and a carol by Juan Vasquez, *Dark-haired one, give me a kiss*.

(i) Anon.: *Dadme albricias, hijos de Eva*; (ii) Juan Vasquez: *Morenica, dame un beso*.   ANGEL 35257 (COLUMBIA 33 CX 1308).

The romance was a ballad of great antiquity.   Undoubtedly
descended from the old epics of chivalry, these ballads had traditional melodies which were still respected by Renaissance composers and were immensely popular in all strata of Spanish society.
Many of the romance tunes were used by instrumental composers,
who built variations, *differencias*, upon them.   Furthermore,
their cultivation led to an entirely new literature: the solo song
with lute accompaniment.

Spanish instrumental music and the accompanied song are
entirely original types of music that far outstripped the rest of
Europe at this stage of the Renaissance.   The principal plucked
instrument was the *vihuela de mano*, a cross between a lute and
guitar.   The Spanish lute composers were legion, and their music
was varied, original, enchanting, and is now undeservedly neglected.   We may take two examples from the work of Alonzo
de Mudarra: the first is a setting of David's lament for Absalom and
the second is a pavan for lute.

Alonzo de Mudarra: (i) *Triste estaba*; (ii) *Pavan*.   WESTMINSTER WL
  5059 (NIXA WLP 5059).

Among the great practitioners of lute music were Don Luis Milan
(*c.* 1500–*c.* 1561) and his contemporary, Miguel de Fuenllana
Their music is chamber music in the true sense of the word; everything is on a small scale of sonority, but invention, texture, form,
and expression are all exquisite and written in the highest artistic
terms.   These fantasias are real instrumental poems, idiomatic
and virtuoso, and the songs are true lyricism that is as fresh to-day
as it was in the sixteenth century.

Milan: (i) *Sospiro*; (ii) *Pavanas*.   WESTMINSTER WL 5059 (NIXA
  WLP 5059).
    (iii) *Toda mi vida os amé*.   HISTORY OF MUSIC IN SOUND,
  VOL. IV.   VICTOR LM 6029 (HMV HMS 40, 78 r.p.m.).

Spanish keyboard music was equally original and advanced.
It can be epitomized in the work of the great organist and harpsichordist Antonio de Cabezón (1510–66), court musician to Charles
V and to Philip II, whom he accompanied to England and Flanders.
Like Fuenllana, Cabezón was blind from childhood, but this
affliction did not deter him from becoming one of the most
significant composers of the century.   His originality is really
stunning, whether seen in his variation technique or in his bold
chromatic fugues.

Spanish church music of the Renaissance is in the realm of drama. There is nothing else like this in Renaissance music. At the end of its development are three great musical personalities: Morales, Guerrero, and Victoria. Apparently all three are the product of Italian spirit and Netherlands technique, and two of them, Morales and Victoria, lived and worked in Rome and are truly apostles of the art of Palestrina. Yet all this is only in appearance; these Spaniards are not Romans, or even Italians —they are unassimilable. Morales's *Responsoria*, Guerrero's *Passions*, and Victoria's *Hymns* do not teach the Italian harmony of faith; there is a dark glow in them, a feverish ecstasy and a consuming melancholy. These composers never even wanted to be confused with the more temperate sons of Italy.

Cristobal Morales (*c.* 1500–53) shows a consummate knowledge of the Franco-Flemish polyphonic style. Such a finely polished style cannot be created overnight, and it is safe to assume that the Flemish migration must have occurred rather early in Spain. However, even without true knowledge of the history of Spanish music immediately before the sixteenth century, we are surprised by a curious fact. The principal centre of Spanish church music of the sixteenth century was not Madrid, but Rome. This is doubly curious because the chapel choir in Madrid was Flemish, and must have had the greatest of reputations. Yet the archives tell us that almost all significant Spanish composers were at one time or another in Rome. The reason is that the Spanish composers wanted to go to the Eternal City, not for glamour or for lucrative employment, but because Rome was the hallowed centre of the Church.

At the age of twenty-three Morales became a member of the Pontifical chapel, and he stayed in Rome for over ten years. Though his is the international Flemish polyphonic style, it is Spanish in every fibre, which means a dramatic tone, contrasts, and pathos. His motets, perhaps his finest works, show an interesting technique that at all times serves his dramatic imagination. In a five-part setting he would use one voice with a different text so as to bring out the dramatic contrast. As our example of the music of Morales we may take *Puer natus est nobis*.

Morales: *Puer natus est nobis*.   ANGEL 35257 (COLUMBIA 33 CX 1308).

Perhaps the most engaging instance of the pious Spanish mind can be found in the life and work of Francisco Guerrero (1528–1599).   He spent most of his time as choirmaster in the cathedrals of Seville and Malaga, but all his life he dreamed about the Holy Land.   Finally in 1588 he made the journey which resulted in a document as moving as it is extraordinary.   This travel diary, *Voyage to Jerusalem*, saw ten printings in a century and a half, so great was its popularity.   'One of the main obligations of my service,' wrote Guerrero, 'was to compose annually new *villancicos* for Christmas, and each time I encountered the word "Bethlehem," I felt my desire grow to visit that sacred place and to perform my music there in the company of the angels and shepherds who attended the first ceremony.'   These Christmas compositions were real dramatic pieces, free of any strictness of style, and they show how long the medieval mystery play survived in Spain.

Tomas Luis de Victoria was born towards the middle of the century and was probably a chorister in the cathedral of Avila until his departure for Rome in 1565 to prepare for the priesthood.   It is possible that he studied with Palestrina, and it is certainly more than a mere coincidence that he followed Palestrina in the chair of music at the *Collegium Romanum* in 1571.   In 1575 he was ordained a priest.   He must have spent considerable time in musical study during these ten years because his technique was phenomenally secure and developed.   Soon after his ordination he resigned his post at the college to become a parish priest, and his church was that of one of the greatest spiritual figures of Christendom, Philip Neri.   For five years he and Victoria lived in daily contact, and surely this friendship must have contributed to their religious experience.

One more important circumstance must be recorded in order to understand this remarkable and saintly man.   Victoria was born in Avila, the birth-place and centre of activity of St Teresa, the embodiment of the Spanish religious spirit.   We do not know whether Victoria met St Teresa, but he could not have lived his youth in Avila without coming under the influence of this ardent and vigorous woman.   This may explain why Victoria never composed anything but sacred music.   He was a priest of the Church and a priest of music who never even used a *cantus firmus* of secular origin.

Victoria's Masses are among the most accomplished *a cappella*

E

works in the entire history of music. It was in his motets, however, that he rose to heights where few, if any, ordinary mortals
can follow him. Here, where the constantly changing texts fired
his creative fantasy with constantly changing imagery, he exhibits
an inexhaustible inventiveness, warmth of feeling, and poignancy
of expression. The contrapuntal lines are liquid and impeccably
drawn; it is customary to ascribe this to Palestrina's influence,
which is probably true. But the profoundly passionate style that
belies the order and sobriety of the technique of composition is
entirely his own and entirely Spanish. We may take three of his
motets as examples: the six-part *O Domine Jesu*; *O quam gloriosum*; and the Christmas motet, *O magnum mysterium*.

> Victoria: (i) *O Domine Jesu*. HISTORY OF MUSIC IN SOUND, VOL. IV.
> VICTOR LM 6029 (HMV HMS 34, 78 r.p.m.);
> (ii) *O quam gloriosum*. LYRICHORD LL 35;
> (iii) *O magnum mysterium*. ANGEL 35257 (COLUMBIA 33 CX
> 1308).

Returning from Rome, Victoria became chaplain to the Empress
Mother Maria, sister of Philip II, and choir-master to the convent
where she lived. Upon her death, Victoria composed a Requiem
Mass for six voices—his last work, for he died in 1611—and there is
nothing in the *a cappella* literature that can equal its glowing dark
colour and its passionate lamentation.

> Victoria: *Officium defunctorum (Missa pro defunctis)*. Vox PL 8930
> (E).

The God of the Spaniards of the sixteenth century demanded
the whole man, his whole soul with all its passions and most intimate dreams. The more profound this man's spiritual life, the
more he invoked the ascetic principles of the Church to guard
against the wild instincts of the flesh. In literature this conflict
was side-stepped, and instead of passions the Spanish poets dealt
with ornaments. But in music Spanish religious idealism found
its most congenial medium—as in the next century it was to find
it in painting—and the concentration was so intense that the love
of heaven acquired a passionately sensuous force that no secular
music or poetry could equal. This is what disturbs people beyond
the Pyrenees, but the Spanish composer of the Renaissance,
enchanting or ribald in his songs, offered to God love as a sacrifice,
as the whole of life. Like the Spanish theatre and Spanish painting, Victoria's music carries us into the dramatic, visionary,
passionate world of the baroque.

APPENDIX

BOOKS

G. CHASE: *The Music of Spain.*
J. B. TREND: *The Music of Spanish History to 1600; Luis Milan and the Vihuelistas.*
H. COLLET: *Victoria.*

RECORDS

MORALES: *Lamentabatur Jacob.*   NRLP 219 EMS 219.
VICTORIA: Masses: *O Magnum Mysterium; O Quam Gloriosum.*
   LYRICHORD LL 46.   *Selected Works.*   PERIOD 706.
Spanish Music, c. 1500.   EMS 219.
Five Centuries of Spanish Song.   HMV ALP 1393.

17

Gustave Reese

RENAISSANCE ITALY:
MADRIGALS AND ROMAN CHURCH MUSIC

I F the Netherlands and France jointly constituted one of the
two principal regions that moulded the central musical
language of the Renaissance, Italy provided the other. This
she did not only through the genius of her native musicians,
but also through that of her poets and through the civilized taste
that prevailed in the courts of her nobles and of her princes of the
Church. This taste drew to the peninsula from the north-west
many of the leading musicians of the fifteenth and sixteenth
centuries. Not only did they travel south on their own initiative,
attracted by the prospect of lucrative posts, but occasionally they
were recruited by emissaries sent by Italian patrons. At times
the foreigners quite overshadowed their Italian colleagues but,
whatever northern features they may have retained in their music,
they were greatly influenced by the taste of the host nation, so
that in many instances their works belong more to the music of
Italy than to that of their own countries.

The beginning of the influx about the year 1425 was partly the
result of a decline in native musical creation after the brilliant
flowering of Italian music in the fourteenth century and the early
fifteenth. By the middle of the latter century manuscript collections copied out in Italy itself were likely to contain more music
by Frenchmen and Netherlanders than by Italians, and for several
decades thereafter northerners were favoured by the wealthier
courts. But as the fifteenth century drew to a close Italian composers were once more coming to the fore. To be sure, their
compositions were mostly modest little pieces, but they had a
distinctive character. Isabella d'Este, Marchioness of Mantua,
probably the most amiable Renaissance patroness of the arts, to
whom homage was paid by Titian, Leonardo da Vinci, and Ariosto,

gave particular encouragement to these native musicians at her small but brilliant court. The kind of pieces that they produced are written in one or another of several forms, most of them fairly rigid. One of these is called *frottola*, and, rather confusingly, the term is also applied generically to all the forms as a group. More interesting than the simple and repetitious patterns represented in these forms is the nature of their content. The Italian love of directness and clarity is fully evident. The texture is mostly chordal rather than polyphonic; complexity is absent. As a rule, the melody in the highest voice is definitely the main one. Sometimes a *frottola* has many stanzas and the short musical setting is sung over and over for each stanza.

The *frottola* literature was developed mainly at Mantua, but Florence produced a counterpart in its repertoire of carnival songs, less rigid in form but similar in texture. The latter feature may be illustrated by a piece from this repertoire. In Florence there was not only pre-Lenten revelry, but a period of festivity that extended through May and much of June. Torchlight processions with decorated cars of masqueraders were the main feature of the carnivals. The carnival songs of the guilds had texts of a local and topical nature, and there were songs of the tailors and perfumers, of the millers and the beggars, and of the young wives with old husbands. In the anonymous song of the widows, the *Canto delle vedove*, we learn that the ladies are no angels, but for this, they say, the men are more to blame than they. Since it is carnival time, they call upon the men to dress as Turks, devils, and hermits, and join their company.

Anon.: *Canto delle vedove.* Vox PL 8120 (E).

It is partly out of antecedents such as the *frottola* and the carnival song that there finally emerged that most typically Italian contribution to the music of the late Renaissance—the sixteenth-century madrigal. Its development was an intricate process, affected by the French chanson, which was itself likewise affected by the *frottola*. When the madrigal actually began to take shape its musical aspect was, as a result of Italian influence, much less complicated than typical Franco-Netherlandish polyphony, but as a result of Franco-Netherlandish influence, more complex than the typical *frottola*. In short, the madrigal provided a common meeting ground for the two streams of influence. Early

in the sixteenth century the foreign musicians were more prominent in madrigal composition than the Italians, who made their
contributions more in the realms of poetry and social background.
The poems might be of fourteenth-century origin, and Petrarch
was a great favourite of the madrigalists throughout the sixteenth
century, but the new madrigal is not at all a continuation of the
madrigal that had figured prominently in the fourteenth-century
music of the Italian *Ars Nova*. The madrigalists in the main
chose their texts with great seriousness and set them with the
utmost care. They felt obligated to supply each individual line
with a suitable musical parallel. In the true madrigal, therefore, if
the text has more than one stanza, each is newly set. This is a
cardinal principle. In the earlier part of the century the settings
tended to have a certain musical self-sufficiency. But, as the
century progressed, the music became more and more illustrative
of the poem. It is clear then that the madrigal is not, strictly
speaking, a form, since there is nothing even approximately
constant about its shape; it is, rather, a type—one in which elegant
but not over-complex vocal polyphony is used to express the
content of a poem.

In the 1530's the leading madrigalists were Philippe Verdelot,
a Frenchman; Costanzo Festa, a native Italian; and Jacques
Arcadelt, a Netherlander. Since they belong to the early phase
of the sixteenth-century madrigal it is to be expected that their
characteristic contributions will express the mood of the poems,
but that the music will have a considerable amount of independent
artistic validity. We may take one example by each composer,
and in each instance the setting will be found to have a song-like
character differing from the declamatory nature of the later
madrigals.

The first is Arcadelt's celebrated *Il bianco e dolce cigno*. 'The
white and gentle swan dies singing, while I, with tears, approach
the end of life.' The second composition is more jolly: Festa's
Quando ritrovo la mia pastorella. The piece is recorded in an
English translation, and that makes it sound very much as though
it were a genuine English madrigal. However, we must remember
that the Italian madrigal repertoire came first. The resemblance
emphasizes how much the English madrigal was indebted to the
Italian, not how much the Italian was indebted to the English.
The third example is *Con lagrime e sospir*, originally written by

Verdelot for four voices. Like many of the other early madrigals, however, it is so song-like that it lends itself to performance by a single voice, singing the highest part to instrumental accompaniment, and was so arranged for voice and lute by Adrian Willaert. This is the version listed. The text begins: 'Refusing with sighs and tears, my lady nonetheless grants the desired kisses to my heart.'

(i) Arcadelt: *Il bianco e dolce cigno.* Victor M 535 (78 r.p.m.).
(ii) Festa: *Down in a flow'ry vale.* Parlophone R 372 (78 r.p.m.).
(iii) Verdelot: *Con lagrime e sospir.* Westminster WL 5059 (Nixa WLP 5059).

In the latter part of the sixteenth century the chief perpetuator of the song-like madrigal was Palestrina. He produced examples of great elegance, but they did not open up new paths. Orlando di Lasso—to use the Italianized form of this Netherlander's name —also wrote madrigals that are closely related in spirit and technique to those of the early part of the century. The range of expression is quite wide; at one extreme, madrigals that are deeply and genuinely melancholy, and at the other extreme, light and joyous, not strictly madrigalian pieces which were later derivations from the Mantuan *frottole* and Florentine carnival songs. A fine example of Lasso's lighter compositions is the *villanella*, or country song, that begins *O la, o che bon eccho.* This is a playful little echo piece in which one four-part choir answers another from beginning to end. It illustrates in a sportive way the descriptive effects that were favoured in late sixteenth-century Italian secular vocal polyphony, whether serious or light.

Lasso: *O la, o che bon eccho.* Victor LM 136 (alt. DGG APM 4055).

The highly prolific Philippe de Monte has left us more than a thousand madrigals. He is another late sixteenth-century Netherlander who wrote Italian madrigals in a conservative vein. If Palestrina, Lasso, and Monte continued the tradition of the early sixteenth-century madrigal into the latter part of the century, a revolution in madrigal writing had been produced at about its mid-point by the boldly original Cipriano de Rore.

Although a Netherlander, and although capable of writing with distinction in the older song-like style, Rore gave the madrigal the direction which was to be especially cultivated by the native Italians. This led the madrigal to become essentially a dramatic and declamatory composition, intimately tied up not only with the spirit of its text but also with the sound and meaning of individual words.   Indeed, many a later madrigal may be called a piece of highly inflected polyphonic recitative.

Giaches de Wert was in many ways a closely related successor to Rore.   In *Ah, dolente partita* (Ah, this parting will slay me) he provides a deeply impassioned setting for a poem taken from a famous pastoral drama of the time.   Madrigals were frequently settings of extracts from plays or epics, and those associated with plays might on occasion be included in full stage performances. The melodic interest of Wert's composition is too great to permit it to be classified purely as polyphonic recitative, but the piece is nevertheless a far cry from the earlier song-like madrigals.

Wert: *Ah, dolente partita.*   CONCERT HALL CHC 36.

It was in the latter part of the century that the native Italians took over the madrigal and made it, in every sense, their own.   Having found in the dramatic declamatory variety a medium admirably suited to their artistic impulses and desire for expression, they produced examples of the type in great profusion.   The leading masters among these madrigalists were Luca Marenzio, Carlo Gesualdo, Orazio Vecchi, and Claudio Monteverdi.

Marenzio, generally regarded as the most elegant of the madrigalists, had an astonishing gift for illustrating words and yet preserving musical values.   Even though every mention of flying, of a bird's song, or of other sounds of nature, brings forth descriptive music, Marenzio manages to have each passage intrinsically valuable as music and to make all the passages unite into a coherent composition.   His charming *Strider faceva le zampogne a l'aura* (At dawn the shepherd made his bagpipes screech in the air for Phyllis or for Neera) represents the drone of the bagpipe and the singing of birds.   Attractive as a composition like this may be, one would hardly apply the term song-like to it in the same sense as one might to the Verdelot or Arcadelt pieces.

Marenzio: *Strider faceva le zampogne a l'aura.*   ANTHOLOGIE SONORE 120 (78 r.p.m.) (alt. DGG APM 14045).

Of all the Italian madrigalists, undoubtedly the one least interested in songfulness and most concerned with emotional utterance is Carlo Gesualdo, Prince of Venosa.   The turbulence sometimes expressed in his music was part of his life.   Having discovered the unfaithfulness of his first wife he murdered her, her lover, and an infant whose paternity he doubted.   Gesualdo often produced

musical effects which even to-day seem violent.   These resulted
from his daring use of chromaticism and dissonance, both of which
are evident in *Resta di darmi noia*.   The text may be rendered
as follows:

> Stay thee from giving me torment,
> Cruel and deluding thought:
> That which is never to be is that which gives thee pleasure.
> Death to me is happiness;
> Wherefore I refrain not from hoping
> At last to find contentment.

Gesualdo: *Resta di darmi noia*.   PARLOPHONE B 77028 (R 1022,
78 r.p.m.).

The Italian flair for dramatic expression found a distinctive
outlet in the madrigal comedies of Orazio Vecchi.   They are
definitely not intended to be acted but they do consist of dialogue
that has at least abstract dramatic significance.   The music
characterizes the various persons but through polyphony; in
other words, a single character may be presented as singing in
five parts.   The most famous of the madrigal comedies is *L'Amfiparnaso*, or *Round About Parnassus*, which deals with the standard
characters in the traditional *commedia dell'arte*.

Vecchi: *L'Amfiparnaso*.   CETRA 50066.

Another choral dramatist of great ability is Adriano Banchieri,
well known for his *Festino*, which deals with merry-making before
Lent.   Among his other works is *La Pazzia Servile*, or *The Folly
of Old Age*, which, like a typical madrigal comedy, combines serious
passages with the gayer ones.   One of the gayer ones is *Tre
villanelle vezzose e belle*, which is supposed to be sung by three
young girls who say 'Three charming and beautiful country girls
are we, my lords, who dance a *balletto* to give you pleasure.   A
golden slipper makes her dance well, and a black one makes me fall
in love.   Fa la la.'   This little piece is actually an abbreviated
balletto.   The *balletti* are characterized mainly by their *fa la la*
refrains which were taken over into the later English form known
as the ballet.

Banchieri: *Tre villanelle vezzose e belle*.   ALLEGRO 3029.

Our last madrigalist is one of the greatest: Claudio Monteverdi.
It was impossible for the madrigal, within its small bounds, to
develop any further in expressiveness than it did at his hands.

*E

In his use of dissonance he is as daring as Gesualdo, but more masterly. Concentrating less on the madrigal than Marenzio, he nevertheless competes with him seriously in that field. The first opera composer of authentic genius, Monteverdi included in his output *Arianna*. Most of the music has been lost, but Ariadné's lament is included in what survives. *Arianna* was so successful that Monteverdi recast portions of it into madrigal form, including the lament, *Lasciatemi morire*. 'Let me die, let me die. And what do you wish, you who would comfort me in such a dire plight and in such cruel martyrdom? Let me die, let me die.'

   Monteverdi: *Lasciatemi morire*. Victor LM 136 or Vox PL 6670
     (alt. DGG APM 14020).

All the composers whom we have discussed as madrigalists were also writers of sacred music. Such music flourished mainly at two centres, Rome and Venice, each of which may be said to have had its musical dependencies. The Roman school was a brilliantly vigorous one with many representatives. But, in perspective, all earlier figures seem to be preparing the way for Giovanni Pierluigi da Palestrina and all later ones to be following in his footsteps. His style is a remarkably disciplined one, every detail being treated with such care and taste that his music is generally regarded as the classical model of sixteenth-century contrapuntal writing. One of the most brilliant aspects of his art is the skill with which he takes a pre-existent composition—often his own—and elaborates it into a long and imposing Mass setting. Of his one hundred and five known surviving Masses, no less than fifty-two elaborate pre-existent polyphonic models. The reworking of basic material, not once only but many times in the course of a complete Mass, is often accomplished with consummate technical dexterity in combination with spiritual loftiness and poetic imagination. One of Palestrina's greatest motets is his six-part *Assumpta est Maria*, and on this he constructed one of his finest Masses. The motet is in two *partes*, or movements, and the *Benedictus* of the Mass is based on the second of them. Whether or not one follows the skill with which Palestrina varies his material in the *Benedictus*, one can hardly fail to be powerfully moved by the sheer majesty of the music.

   Palestrina: (i) *Assumpta est Maria*. Concert Hall CHC 44.
      (ii) *Benedictus: Missa Assumpta est Maria*. Concert
     Hall CHS 1231.

(Appendix: *See* page 122.)

18
Gustave Reese

RENAISSANCE ITALY:
INSTRUMENTAL MUSIC AND VENETIAN
CHURCH MUSIC

ITALY, the traditional land of song, has left us one of the most important bodies of instrumental music produced by the Renaissance. It is in Italy that we find our earliest datable sources of lute music. Strangely enough, the oldest of these bears a date as late as 1507, although it is obvious that much lute music existed well before that time, even if it does not survive. Evidence, in both literature and the visual arts, makes it clear that the lute was used in Europe in the Middle Ages and early Renaissance. Numerous carved and painted lute-playing angels help to make the medieval and Renaissance heaven a place of celestial bliss. Fiesole, just outside of Florence, is made a place of earthly bliss, almost at the very beginning of the *Decameron* of Boccaccio, partly through the lute-playing of Dioneo, who was definitely *not* an angel. Moreover, the lute music that reaches us is so highly developed that it must have been preceded by a strong line of forerunners.

In 1507 and 1508 four books of lute music were printed in Venice by Ottaviano dei Petrucci, who is one of the greatest figures in the history of music printing. The first two contain music arranged or composed by Francesco Spinaccino, of whom very little is known. Many of the arrangements are adaptations for lute of well-known Franco-Netherlandish secular polyphonic works for voices, but the books also include music specifically written for the instrument. We may take a *ricercar* from Spinaccino's Book II as an example. The term *ricercar*, to most of us, denotes a contrapuntally intricate instrumental work, characterized by fugal passages of some complexity. However, the word came to mean this only at a later date. In Spinaccino's time it was the designation for a very short piece consisting mainly of runs and block chords.   Our example will show that the early *ricercar*, by virtue of these runs and chords, was very definitely instrumental in character.

Spinaccino: *Ricercar*.   ALLEGRO AL 93.

Petrucci's fourth lute book, devoted to music by Joanambrosio Dalza, also includes some *ricercari*.   But even more interesting are the sets of dance pieces in it which may be regarded as the early forerunners of such later dance sets as the *French Suites* of Bach. Dalza will at one time illustrate the principle of thematic relationship between the various dances, and at another time the principle of thematic contrast.   One of Dalza's sets is entitled *Pavana alla ferrarese* and consists of three dances—a *pavana*, *saltarello*, and *piva*.   A standard pavan consisted of three strains, each immediately repeated.   But a pavan for performance by a virtuoso could differ from one intended for dancing in much the same way as a concert waltz by Chopin could later differ from a waltz for dancing by Johann Strauss.   Dalza's pavan begins with the AABBCC pattern, but then indulges in pleasant variations on the preceding material.   Like a normal *saltarello*, Dalza's is a sprightly dance, and it contrasts agreeably with the more dignified pavan. *Piva* is one of the Italian words for 'bagpipe,' and Dalza's dance is characteristically provided with a drone.

Dalza: *Pavana alla ferrarese*.   PERIOD SPL 577.

In this particular Dalza set there is no obvious thematic relationship between the dances.   But pairs of thematically related dances—the first one slow and the second fast—were greatly favoured throughout the Renaissance.   In our example the first piece is, in modern terminology, in 4/4 time and the second in 6/8, but the melodic and harmonic resemblances are so close that one can hardly fail to note them.   This pair, a *Passamezzo* and a *Padoana*, comes from a lute book printed in Venice in 1561.

Jacomo Gorzanis: *Passamezzo and Padoana*.   PERIOD SPL 577.

The *passamezzo* at this time is generally (though not in our example) built on one of two formulas called the *passamezzo antico* and the *passamezzo moderno*.   These are usually referred to as *melodic* formulas but—since they are normally placed in the bass where they are not clearly heard as melodies but do have an effect on the harmony—it would accord better with what the listener perceives to call them *harmonic* formulas.   Other formulas include the *romanesca* and the *folia*, the latter to become the basis of Corelli's famous *La Folia*. There is a very large literature of compositions on these formulas, not only for the lute but also for other instrumental media.

Our concluding example of lute music takes us back somewhat in time. It is from a book published in 1547 in Venice, devoted to works by Francesco da Milano, who was so much admired that he was sometimes called *Il Divino* ('the divine one'). The piece is a fantasia—that is, a composition with a rather free structure, but fairly contrapuntal in nature.

> Francesco da Milano: *Fantasia*. ALLEGRO AL 93 (alt. OISEAU-LYRE OL 50102).

There was a host of lutenists in Italy, and a list of them, even if it were limited to the important names, would be very long. It is perhaps of special interest, however, that one of the outstanding lutenists in the latter part of the century was Vincenzo Galilei, the father of the astronomer Galileo Galilei.

Even more impressive than Italy's music for lute was her music for keyboard, and examples of it survive from as far back as the *Ars Nova* period. However, we are here concerned with music of a much later time. The first sixteenth-century keyboard print of real importance appeared in 1523 and was the work of Marc' Antonio Cavazzoni, a musician of Pope Leo X's private chapel. His son, Girolamo Cavazzoni, wrote the next known extensive Italian keyboard collection, which was published in 1542, and among its contents are settings of Gregorian hymn melodies. It had been an established practice to have alternate stanzas of a plain-song hymn sung by the choir, and to represent the stanzas that the choir did *not* sing by settings played on the organ. These instrumental sections made use of the melody belonging to the hymn, sometimes rather faithfully, but sometimes with very much liberty. Both kinds of treatment are applied by Girolamo to a hymn melody to-day sung to the text *Nunc Sancte nobis Spiritus*, but in his time to the text *Ad coenam agni providi*, later revised to *Ad regias agni dapes*.

> Girolamo Cavazzoni: *Ad coenam agni providi*. PERIOD SPL 586.

Music was cultivated with particular splendour and solemnity at St Mark's in Venice, where there were two choir lofts and two organs, and the organists included many of the greatest musicians of the century—Annibale Padovano, Claudio Merulo, Andrea and Giovanni Gabrieli, and Gioseffo Guami. Andrea Gabrieli became an organist at the cathedral in 1564, and first organist in 1585. He was so celebrated that his pupils included not only Italians—among them his nephew, Giovanni—but also musicians attracted from abroad, such as the German, Hans Leo Hassler. At the hands of Andrea the fantasia is a highly developed composition, based on one theme, which is modified by ornamentation, inversion, and other devices. Andrea's *Fantasia allegra* gives the impression of being based on three themes; but what seems to be the second theme, usually presented in abbreviated form, is a decorated inversion of the real basic theme; and what seems to be the third theme is just another variant.

Andrea Gabrieli: *Fantasia allegra.*   Vox PL 8470.

Claudio Merulo was not only an organist at St Mark's and a composer, but also an organ builder and even a music printer. His historically most important contribution to keyboard literature is in the field of the *toccata*. Such a piece in his period was a considerable expansion of the type of composition which the *ricercar* had originally been—that is, a piece made up mainly of running scale passages and of chordal passages.

With Giovanni Gabrieli the Venetian school reaches a peak in its development. It would seem, however, that he was not so remarkable an organist as he was a composer, for he never officially attained the position of regular first organist at St Mark's. But in 1585 he did become second organist. Whatever his skill at the keyboard, he is a versatile genius as a composer, able, like Monteverdi, both to function with distinction as a writer of Renaissance music and to forge new paths as a writer of baroque music. His keyboard works include not only *ricercari* of the later polyphonic type—works in which he sometimes comes surprisingly close to producing a fugue—but also compositions of other kinds, for instance, this organ toccata which, quite typically, avoids thematic development and instead makes impressive use of cascading scale passages and of block chords.

Giovanni Gabrieli: *Toccata.*   Vox PL 8470.

Naturally the organ was not the only keyboard instrument the Italians used in the sixteenth century. Stringed keyboard instruments were favoured also, especially the harpsichord. Compositions of the more polyphonic type, such as the later motet-like *ricercari*, could be played not only by a soloist on a keyboard instrument, but also by instrumental ensembles—for example, by groups playing on viols or recorders.

The Flemish Adrian Willaert, who belongs not to the line of organists at St Mark's, but to the line of choir directors, was a man of extraordinary versatility. With him we are turning back in time from the Gabrielis, for he became *maestro di cappella* as early as 1527; he spent no less than thirty-five years in that capacity. His influence as a teacher was far reaching. Several important musicians of the next generation were his students, among them Cipriano de Rore, Andrea Gabrieli, Gioseffo Zarlino, and Nicolò Vicentino. Rore was actually to become Willaert's successor as *maestro di cappella* at St Mark's, and Zarlino—one of the most important theorists in the history of music—was in turn to succeed Rore. Willaert, as a composer, produced French chansons, Italian madrigals, Masses, and motets, and also instrumental music of great distinction. Our example, a three-part polyphonic *ricercar*, bears some marked resemblances to vocal motet style, but reveals aspects of chamber-music style also. Andrea Gabrieli was among the composers of *ricercari* that give the impression of having been written with the capacities of an instrumental ensemble more specifically in mind, and we may set one of his *ricercari*—a sparkling piece, particularly delightful for its unexpected changes in rhythmic pulse—beside the *ricercar* by Willaert.

(i) Willaert: *Ricercar*. HISTORY OF MUSIC IN SOUND, VOL. IV. VICTOR LM 6029 (HMV HMS 41, 78 r.p.m.).

(ii) A. Gabrieli: *Ricercar* (No. 2 of three). COLUMBIA 70366 D (78 r.p.m.).

Renaissance part-books that appear to be intended for use in ensemble performance do not normally specify particular instruments for the individual parts. Actually it would seem that a part might be played by any instrument having a suitable technical capacity for it. However, Giovanni Gabrieli, in one of his most celebrated compositions, does indicate the instrumentation precisely. This is his *Sonata Pian' e Forte*, which has the added distinction of being one of the earliest pieces to contain indications for *piano* and *forte* performance. Here the term *sonata* simply means a piece to be sounded by instruments rather than to be sung. Gabrieli's *Sonata* is written for two four-part instrumental choirs. In each of these the three lowest parts are indicated as being for trombones. In the first choir the top part is for *cornetto* (not the equivalent of our modern cornet, though on the record represented by a trumpet), but a gentle wood-wind instrument. In the second choir the top part is for *violino*, by which is meant an instrument more like the modern viola than the violin. By using the two choirs antiphonally, Gabrieli obtains impressive colour contrasts, and still another colour effect is obtained by combining them.

> G. Gabrieli: *Sonata Pian' e Forte*. ESOTERIC ES 503 (alt. ENGLISH DECCA LX 3102).

An instrumental *canzon* of this period differs from a *ricercar* in several respects; it is less polyphonic in character, and it is more likely to consist of a chain of well-defined sections with clear cadences. One section or another may recur from time to time, and an occasional *canzon* may consequently make one think ahead to the structure of the later *rondo*. More often than not a *canzon* will open with a long note and two notes of half its length; this is true of our example, Giovanni Gabrieli's spirited *Canzon in the Ninth Tone*. At the beginning of its history the *canzon* was an instrumental transcription of a French chanson. It is interesting that while the Italians sometimes made transcription of Italian madrigals they preferred to transcribe French chansons. Indeed, they often called a *canzon* a *canzona francese*. The music of Italian madrigals was likely to reflect the text in such detail that the words were an indispensable part of the complete art work. The music of the French chanson, on the other hand, was more self-sufficient and therefore lent itself better to transcription for instruments. The *Canzon in the Ninth Tone*, however, appears to be a wholly original work and is again for two four-part choirs that play antiphonally and sometimes combine. No specific instruments are called for. Where this happens, it seems reasonably clear that brass instruments were sometimes used in the performance of ensemble pieces, and that is the procedure followed on the record.

> G. Gabrieli: *Canzon in the Ninth Tone*. ESOTERIC ES 503.

While instrumental music was fostered at all the great Italian cultural centres—Rome, Florence, Ferrara, Mantua, Milan—the wealth of Venice, 'the Queen of the Adriatic,' made her an ideal patroness of the arts. Naturally vocal music received its share of attention too, and Willaert, both the Gabrielis, and other members of the Venetian school were excellent madrigalists. But it was in her sacred polyphony that Venice made her most distinctive contribution to the vocal repertoire. This was largely because St Mark's—with its two choir lofts as well as its two organs—was especially suitable for the performance of antiphonal compositions. Undoubtedly related also in some way is the antiphonal writing in polyphonic compositions which, like the *canzon*, have no ecclesiastical function. The Venetians simply came to like antiphony and developed it into a characteristic of their style. They also wrote normal sacred polyphony for a single chorus. A good example of such music is the short motet, *Sancti et Justi*, by Claudio Merulo. As an excellent writer of sacred vocal polyphony he was only one of a numerous and distinguished company belonging to the Venetian school or to its musical dependencies. The text of this motet is adapted from the first part of the psalm that begins 'Rejoice in the Lord, O ye righteous,' and *Alleluias* are added with charming effect.

Merulo: *Sancti et Justi*. Vox PL 8030 (E).

Sometimes at St Mark's the performance of sacred polyphony was given added colour and magnificence by the combination of voices and various kinds of instruments. This was eventually to lead to the full blossoming of the early baroque at Venice after Monteverdi became *maestro di cappella* in 1613 and produced his most distinguished church music in the newer style. Giovanni Gabrieli's *Jubilate Deo*, although printed as early as 1597, shows the trend towards the baroque well under way. Two four-part choruses sing antiphonally, reinforced by instruments, and the work displays a jubilant brilliance that leads one to imagine that the music is being performed by all the inhabitants of the Serene Republic.

G. Gabrieli: *Jubilate Deo*. CAMBRIDGE CRS 201 (alt. ENGLISH COLUMBIA DX 1863, 78 r.p.m.).

APPENDIX
(CHAPTERS 17 and 18)

BOOKS

HENRY COATES: *Palestrina.*

ALFRED EINSTEIN: *The Italian Madrigal,* 3 vols.

CECIL GRAY AND PHILIP HESELTINE: *Carlo Gesualdo, Prince of Venosa, Musician and Murderer.*

FRANCESCO CAFFI: *Storia della musica sacra nella già Cappella Ducale di S. Marco in Venezia dal 1318 al 1797,* 2 vols.

LIONEL DE LA LAURENCIE: *Les Luthistes.*

ANDRE PIRRO: *Les Clavecinistes.*

RECORDS

MARENZIO AND MONTEVERDI: *Madrigals on texts from Il Pastor Fido.* WESTMINSTER 105.

GESUALDO: *Italian Madrigals.*   SUNSET 600.

GESUALDO AND MONTEVERDI: *Italian Madrigals.*   WESTMINSTER WL 5171.

GESUALDO AND MARENZIO: *Madrigals.*   DGG APM 14045.

BANCHIERI: *Festino.*   ESOTERIC ES 516.

The Italian Madrigal at the end of the Renaissance. ANTHOLOGIE SONORE AS 8.

PALESTRINA: *Magnificat, etc.*   PERIOD 513 (NIXA PLP 513).*   *Twelve Motets.*   RENAISSANCE X 55.   *Missa Iste Confessor; Missa sine nomine (Je suis déshéritée).*   LYRICHORD 49 (ALLEGRO ALX 3016).   *Missa Papae Marcelli, etc.*   EPIC LC 3045 (PHILIPS NBR 5803).   *Missa Veni Sponsa Christi.*   UNICORN 1013.   *Missa Brevis; Missa Ascendo ad Patrem.*   ALLEGRO 3097.

A. GABRIELI: *Missa Pater peccavi, etc.*   VOX PL 8370 (E).

Motets of the Venetian School, Vol. II.   VOX PL 8610 (E).

19

Gustave Reese

ENGLAND UNDER THE TUDORS: VOCAL MUSIC

THE outpouring of English music that helped to bring the reign of the earlier Queen Elizabeth to a glorious close placed England in the front rank of musical nations. This achievement, however, was a gradual process spread over the reigns of all five Tudors. After England, under Dunstable, had attained the leadership of western music in the first half of the fifteenth century, she was temporarily overshadowed by developments on the Continent, where that leadership passed into the undisputed possession of the great Franco-Netherlanders. English music isolated itself from the newer trends of the late fifteenth century. Among the older types of music still cultivated at the dawn of the Tudor period was the carol, in the strict sense, a form indigenous to England herself. It was of popular origin, but could be inserted into the liturgy, and many carols had to do with specific seasons. But it was their form, and not their function, that made them carols, and their distinctive feature is the burden, a self-contained formal and metrical unit. The burden is meant to be sung at the beginning and after each stanza of the carol so that it acts in the manner of a refrain.

In pre-Reformation England, as elsewhere, sacred music for normal church use consisted mainly of Masses and motets. Robert Fayrfax was perhaps the most representative early Tudor church composer, and his surviving works include both forms. John Taverner, the greatest English composer of the next generation, has left us a larger number of Masses and motets—among them an especially fine Mass based on the folk melody *Western Wynde* and a Mass *Gloria tibi Trinitas* that was to make musical history. The latter work is based on the plain-chant after which it is named, a melody that reappears frequently against new counter-melodies. At the point in the *Benedictus* where the text reads

In Nomine Domini, there occurs a musical passage that aroused the deepest admiration. It became the point of departure for a whole species of compositions, called *In Nomines*, that are built upon the same plain-chant.

Taverner: *Mass: Gloria tibi Trinitas (Benedictus).* HISTORY OF MUSIC IN SOUND, VOL. III.   VICTOR LM 6016 (HMV HMS 30, 78 r.p.m.).

The formal break between England and the Papacy came in 1534 and, naturally, had a profound influence on sacred music, though for many years Latin was retained in the liturgy along with the growing use of English.   As a result it is often impossible to tell whether a certain piece of music was originally intended for Roman or Anglican use, especially since musicians who had composed for the old rite later composed for the new one—or both. Among the men belonging to this group are Christopher Tye, Thomas Tallis, and Tallis's pupil, William Byrd.   By Tye we have some twenty Latin motets and four Masses, including compositions of great excellence.   Tallis's work is highly diversified.   An imposing motet by him, *Spem in alium*, is for as many as forty voices. On the other hand he could be eloquent also in pieces that are both short and written for a normal number of parts, for example, his hymn *O nata lux de lumine*, in which the five voices set the text in simple chord-like writing.

Thomas Tallis: *Hymn: O nata lux de lumine.*   VANGUARD BG 551 (alt. ENGLISH COLUMBIA LX 1283, 78 r.p.m.).

Byrd, by all odds the best English writer of Latin church music of the period, was perhaps the greatest composer England has ever produced.   Our present example will be *Ego sum panis vivus* (I am the Living Bread) which closes with an *Alleluia* section rich in rhythmical variety.

William Byrd: *Ego sum panis vivus.*   MASTERPIECES OF MUSIC BEFORE 1750, VOL. II.   HAYDN SOCIETY HSL 2072.

Among the many other composers of Latin church music were Thomas Morley, Richard Deering, and Peter Philips.   The men who contributed to this literature were so numerous and so gifted that, notwithstanding the gradual elimination of the Latin language from the Anglican Church, the English contribution to Latin church music figures among the most important ones of the Renaissance.

After the English language was introduced into the service,

Archbishop Cranmer issued the Litany in English in 1544. The text was set to the traditional chant according to the principle that there should be only one note to a syllable. In 1550 John Merbecke issued his *Book of Common Praier Noted*, in which he set the text to chant-like melodies that were partly original and partly adapted from the Gregorian repertoire. In his setting of 'Postcommunion IX,' *If ye shall abide in me*, the text is simply but eloquently underscored by the music.

> Merbecke: *If ye shall abide in me.* ENGLISH COLUMBIA LX 1379 (78 r.p.m.).

Naturally, not a great deal of music was ready at hand especially suitable for the Anglican service. So Latin polyphonic works were sometimes taken over bodily and simply supplied with new English texts; Taverner's famous *In Nomine* passage is one example of music that was so adapted.

The continuing growth of Protestantism eventually gave Britain equivalents of the Psalters that had already appeared on the Continent. In these books, containing metrical translations of the psalms, various melodies might be treated in different settings and an individual melody or setting thereof be fitted to several different psalms. A tune known as *Windsor*, extracted from Tye's composition, *The Acts of the Apostles*, was treated by many composers. Our example presents the settings of Richard Alison, Thomas Ravenscroft, and William Damon (each taken from a different Psalter), but with the texts they used replaced by various stanzas of the metrical version of Psalm 116, found in the *Bay Psalm Book* of 1640—the first book printed in what was to become the United States of America.

> *Early American Psalmody.* NRLP 2007.

Although William Byrd remained a Catholic, he produced excellent music for Anglican use, including many anthems and several services. The *Great Service*, a composition of large proportions and extraordinary brilliance, is surely one of the towering achievements of Tudor music.

> Byrd: *Great Service.* VANGUARD VRS 453.

Thomas Morley, Thomas Weelkes, and John Bull are among the remaining principal composers of the time who wrote sacred music to English words. But even more important in this field was Orlando Gibbons, whom we can call a Tudor composer only by stretching a point; born in 1583, he pursued his career primarily under James I.   But a large part of his output belongs to the Tudor tradition, and he brought the old polyphonic style to one of the last high points it was to reach in England.

> Orlando Gibbons: *Hosanna to the Son of David.*   ENGLISH COLUMBIA D 40120 (78 r.p.m.) or WESTMINSTER XWN 18165 (alt. ARGO RG 80).

If Tudor church music was remarkable, it is the secular forms of English music—the madrigal, ayre, virginal music, and fancies for viols—that embody most richly the spirit of the English Renaissance.   The most brilliant variety of Tudor secular vocal music is the madrigal, but this bold nationalization of an Italian style did not take place in a void.

Under Henry VIII the window towards the Continent opened again and, among the secular songs appearing in English manuscript sources from about 1480 to about 1520, a number were borrowed from across the Channel.   The style of English secular part-songs during Henry's reign often seems like that of Ockeghem.   It is surely a misnomer to refer to them as madrigals, for the term 'English Madrigal' should be reserved for later works written in original imitation—if that is not too paradoxical an expression—of what had first appeared in Italy.   It is more suitable simply to call these earlier compositions 'English part-songs.' One of the best writers of such compositions was William Cornysh, among whose examples is a three-part setting of Sir Thomas Wyatt's poem, *Hey, Robyn, Joly Robyn, tell me how thy lady doth.* It is wholly likely that, when Shakespeare had the Clown sing the beginning of this poem in Act IV of *Twelfth Night*, he intended the actor playing the role to sing one of the three parts of Cornysh's composition.

The native tradition, deriving from the part-song, maintained its independence throughout the later vogue for Italianate music, and we find the part-song style in almost all the secular works of Byrd.   His first secular publication (1588) includes the exquisite *Though Amaryllis dance in green.*   This combines the equivalents of 3/4 time and 6/8 time successively and simultaneously, with results that are utterly enchanting.   That it is not a true, Italianate madrigal is shown (to mention only one point) by its having two stanzas sung to the same music.

> Byrd: *Though Amaryllis dance in green.*   HMV C 3739 (78 r.p.m.).

The tradition of the English part-song continued to be fruitful at the same time as the Italianate madrigal was cultivated, and we find the old style still alive in some of the distinguished part-songs of so late a composer as Orlando Gibbons.

In the last decades of the sixteenth century, however, many English composers became fascinated by the knowingness and wealth of Italian music. The rise of the madrigal in England expresses one characteristic aspect of Elizabethan life, its eager emulation and appropriation of foreign culture. It parallels in time the literary Italianization and was a relatively small but brilliant aftermath of the madrigal tradition on the Continent. Three things distinguished the English madrigal from its forerunner. First, it was a more popular development. We hear in England of no professional madrigal singers employed by the nobility, as in Italy. Instead the madrigals were designed for the private use of the new gentry and the rising middle class. Second, it was not a literary development to nearly the same extent as the Italian madrigal. Last, the English composer relied less than the Italian upon external features such as word-painting, and this helped to make it possible for the English madrigal to maintain more of what we might call a 'songful character.'

Much Italian music had been circulating in England from about 1560, and by 1588 it had become profitable to publish a large anthology of Italian madrigals with translations, under the title *Musica transalpina*. Among the composers represented was Marenzio, who was destined to have a strong influence on the English madrigalists. Similar collections followed, and soon English composers began to publish collections of their own. Thomas Morley, the founder of the English madrigal school, was the most prolific, popular, and influential, as well as the most Italianate master. He was very fond of the *balletto* (or 'ballet' in English), one of the lighter, not strictly madrigalian Italian forms. He retained its structural features, that is, two or more stanzas all sung to the same music, the music being divided into two sections, each immediately repeated, the *fa-la-la* refrain at section endings being highly characteristic.

Thomas Morley: *Sing we and chant it*. ESOTERIC ES 520.

Thomas Weelkes is the boldest and most individual of the English madrigalists, even though, like Morley, he was strongly

influenced by the Italians, particularly Marenzio. But Weelkes
was able to capture the most impressive qualities of Marenzio
which escaped Morley—especially the ability to paint and design
on the grand scale, giving to some of his works the broad strokes
that distinguish the late Italian madrigal. His *O care, thou wilt
despatch me* represents the extreme in harmonic experiment in
the English madrigal and, though the work is not a ballet, it makes
wonderful use of the conventional ballet refrain. The pathetic
quality of the text is mirrored by touches of chromaticism and
impressive chordal relations.

> Thomas Weelkes: *O care, thou wilt despatch me.* VANGUARD BG
> 553 (alt. NIXA WLP 6212).

John Wilbye, notwithstanding the small size of his output, is
generally regarded as the finest English madrigalist, though
Weelkes should undoubtedly be considered a serious rival.
Wilbye is perhaps the only Elizabethan composer to comprehend
fully the work of Marenzio, but he has a very clear musical
personality of his own—melancholy, poetic, and extremely
sensitive—and he is equally adept at light madrigals, which
overshadow Morley's, and serious compositions, which stand
beside those of Weelkes.

> John Wilbye: *Adieu, sweet Amaryllis.* VANGUARD BG 554, or WEST-
> MINSTER WL 5221 (alt. NIXA WLP 6212).

The English madrigal began to decline at the turn of the century,
and the printed output ended in 1627. However, other types of
vocal composition came off the presses, such as fantasias based on
London street cries and secular songs designed for the pleasure of
people not skilled enough for madrigals. Ballads were especially
popular and often new ballad-texts were printed as broadsides
with the directions 'To be sung to the tune of'—say, *Greensleeves.*
Still another type of vocal music was the ayre. Usually the
ayre was deliberately planned so that either all the parts could
be sung or the highest part could be sung and the lower ones turned
into an instrumental accompaniment, both alternative versions
being fully worked out by the composer. There was little con-
sistency, apparently, in the choice of instruments to accompany
the ayre. The lute, orpharion, and viola da gamba were usually
mentioned in the titles of the song-books, but in various combinations. The lute seems to have been the standard instrument
of accompaniment, and the bass viol was normally used in

conjunction with it. As an example of the ayre we may take John Bartlet's *Of all the birds that I do know* in the four-part version and in the version for voice and lute.

John Bartlet: *Of all the birds that I do know.* VANGUARD BG 553 (four-part version); VANGUARD BG 539 (solo voice and lute).

The best composers of ayres include Morley, Robert Jones, Francis Pilkington, and the poet Thomas Campion. But the greatest was John Dowland, partly because he most fully realized the expressive possibilities of the solo song with instrumental accompaniment. His part-versions, however, are of high quality also. He was himself one of the greatest lutenists of the time. Our example will be the most famous of all his ayres, *Flow my tears*, known also as *Lachrymae*.

John Dowland: *Flow my tears.* HMV DB 5270 (78 r.p.m.), or DECCA ARC 3004 (alt. NIXA WLP 5085).

(APPENDIX: *See* page 136.)

20

Gustave Reese

ENGLAND UNDER THE TUDORS:
INSTRUMENTAL MUSIC

ENGLAND under the Tudors cultivated instrumental music with at least as much brilliance as she did vocal music, and with perhaps even greater originality, and the fostering of music for instruments was limited to no one social class. The waits—that is, the bands of musicians maintained by the towns—not only sang for their fellow-townsmen, but also performed on instruments. There was instrumental playing in the great manor houses of the English countryside, and at the royal court instrumental music was supported with particular enthusiasm and lavishness.

The music that was played consisted mainly of compositions for keyboard instruments, for lute, or for instrumental ensemble. Stringed keyboard instruments may be traced back to at least the fourteenth century in England, and the organ much farther back than that. But there is a total lack of compositions dating from earlier than the sixteenth century that are known with certainty to be both English in origin and intended for keyboard instruments. Generous compensation is made for this lack when the Tudor period is reached.

The English virginal—on which Elizabeth I was herself a fine performer—was a modest little instrument with neither pedals nor stops. It did not have the splendour of the harpsichord, nor was it possible to sustain a tone on it, as one could on the organ, or to produce gradations in volume. However, the illusion of a sustained tone could be created by the addition of ornamentation, a marked characteristic of virginal music, while the illusion of greater volume could be produced by the use of fuller chords. Much of the keyboard music that comes down to us could be played on either the virginal or the organ, but some of it is clearly intended for one instrument or the other.

A large body of keyboard compositions is based on pre-existent music either sacred or secular, including Gregorian melodies. It was a common practice in England, as elsewhere, to sing alternate stanzas of a plain-song hymn and to have the other stanzas represented by organ settings of the hymn melody. But it seems to have been an English speciality to base the organ sections occasionally not upon the plain-song melody itself, but upon a countermelody that had been written against it according to certain principles, the plain-song itself being actually excluded from these sections. The countermelody was called the faburden. An example is *O lux on the faburden* by John Redford, based on a countermelody written against the chant *O lux beata Trinitas*. Perhaps of greater interest, however, in relation to specifically instrumental composition, is the strikingly characteristic keyboard figuration.

John Redford: *O lux on the faburden*. HISTORY OF MUSIC IN SOUND, VOL. III. VICTOR LM 6016 (HMV HMS 30, 78 r.p.m.).

An especially imposing body of instrumental pieces based on a chant melody is the group of *In Nomines* which were written for lute or for instrumental ensemble as well as for keyboard. That the *In Nomine* as a species orginated from a passage in Taverner's Mass *Gloria tibi Trinitas* (itself based on a chant melody) has already been mentioned, and some of these instrumental pieces make a bow to Taverner by quoting or paraphrasing part of his composition at the outset. John Bull, a famous virtuoso as well as a brilliant composer, wrote two *In Nomine* settings, and in the one that is our example the plain-song is rather forcefully hammered out at the beginning.

John Bull: *In Nomine*. EMS 236.

Another group of keyboard pieces based on pre-existent music consists of transcriptions or other reworkings, sometimes quite elaborate, of favourite polyphonic vocal compositions of the period. For example, the *Fitzwilliam Virginal Book*—the largest English source of keyboard music of the time—contains an arrangement by Peter Philips of the much admired *Margot labourez les vignes* by Lassus.

The English produced especially happy results in writing instrumental pieces based on popular or folk melodies, some of these being dance tunes. Such pieces often took the form of a set of variations on the borrowed melody.   William Byrd has left us several compositions of this type, and an especially charming little example is *Wolsey's Wilde*.   English composers treated the variation form in a particularly interesting manner.   They did *not*, as was usual later, begin with a simple preliminary statement of the theme.   Instead they broke up the melody into sections and immediately followed each statement of a section by a variation; after that the composer might add as many further variations as he wished.   This is the general plan of *Wolsey's Wilde*, the section containing the additional variations being a rather short one.

Byrd: *Wolsey's Wilde*.   Victor 1424A (HMV DA 1014, 78 r.p.m.).

Even if composers sometimes incorporated popular melodies into their pieces in dance forms, they often preferred to write entirely original works.   As on the Continent, two dances— whether produced by one method or the other—not infrequently created a pair in a way that foreshadowed the coming birth of the suite.   Particularly favoured were pairs made up of a pavan and a galliard.   The normal English pavan followed the international pattern in consisting of three strains, each immediately repeated, variations being applied to the repetitions if the composer so wished.   The galliard, a somewhat gayer dance, but similar in form, might, like its continental counterpart, be thematically related to the preceding pavan.   Byrd's *Pavana Bray* and *Galliarda Bray* illustrate all these structural points, though the thematic relationship between the two pieces is rather fleeting.

Byrd: *Pavana Bray* and *Galliarda Bray*.   London LL 713 (Decca LXT 2795), also Decca AX 546 (78 r.p.m.).

The keyboard repertoire also included regular programmatic compositions with descriptive effects, like John Bull's *The King's Hunt*.   This rollicking piece happens to present us with a rather elaborate series of variations at the same time as it invokes the spirit of the chase.

Bull: *The King's Hunt*.   English Columbia 5713 (78 r.p.m.), or London LL 713 (Decca LXT 2795).

One may perhaps regard as a subcategory of the descriptive works a group of little *genre* pieces that seem to foreshadow by more than two centuries the intimate *Characterstücke* of Robert Schumann.   These are usually delicate and give the impression of being quite introspective.   Good examples are *The Fall of the*

Leafe by Martin Peerson and *A Toye* by Giles Farnaby—the word 'toye' signified a light *genre* composition.

(i) Peerson: *The Fall of the Leafe.* ANTHOLOGIE SONORE AS 13, or EMS 236 (alt. DECCA X 550, 78 r.p.m.).
(ii) Farnaby: *A Toye.* ANTHOLOGIE SONORE, AS 13 (alt. DECCA X 551, 78 r.p.m.).

Also important in the keyboard repertoire were examples of the fantasia, a type concerning which we shall have more to say when we reach instrumental ensemble music.

If we turn from keyboard instruments to the lute, we find that it too was highly favoured by the English, though England was late in producing great performers on the instrument. None of the surviving lute-solo works can be dated with assurance earlier than the mid century. Lute music tends to resemble virginal music so far as forms and types are concerned. The main difference is in texture and was brought about, of course, by the attempt to write for the instrument idiomatically. In this body of music we again find *In Nomine* pieces—no fewer than one hundred and fifty of them—and transcriptions of pre-existent polyphonic vocal works. John Dowland's *Flow my tears* has already been introduced as an example in its version as an ayre for solo voice and lute. There are arrangements of it under the title *Lachrymae* for virginal, but even more of them for lute. Compositions based on popular tunes are numerous in the lute repertoire. Among various settings of *Greensleeves* there is one by Francis Cutting that treats it with remarkable liberty, and one may be able to recognize the grand old tune only if one knows in advance that it is there. Another great favourite of the period was *Goe from my window goe*, and a charming anonymous variation setting of it is our second lute example.

(i) *Greensleeves*, set by Francis Cutting; (ii) *Goe from my window goe*, anonymous setting. ALLEGRO AL 93.

Particularly characteristic of the lute repertoire are the numerous dance pieces, such as pavans, galliards, allemandes, courantes, jigs, etc. We may take as examples two compositions by John Dowland, by all odds the greatest of the English lutenists. The first—a quite jolly piece—is called in one continental source *Chorea Anglicana Doolandi* (meaning Dowland's English Dance) and in another *Allemanda englessa* (meaning English Allemande). The second is *The King of Denmark's Galliard*, possibly written

at Elsinore, for Dowland was at one period in the service of King
Christian IV of Denmark.

Dowland: (i) *English Allemande*; (ii) *The King of Denmark's Galliard.*
    PERIOD SPL 577.

One interesting feature of the surviving English lute music is
that much of it comes down to us in teaching manuals.   These
contain text matter, explaining how to play the instrument and
also how to read the special kind of notation in which the music was
written.   Then they proceed to supply a little repertoire of pieces.
By having much of its literature set forth in this form, English
lute music resembles lute music on the Continent but differs from
English virginal music.   There are also text-books and a quantity
of music for related instruments—the cittern, pandore, and
orpharion.   The cittern was standard barber-shop furniture, a toy
with which the waiting customer could amuse himself, and was
mainly for unskilled players.   All three, as well as the nobler lute,
were drawn upon in the playing of ensemble music.

The places where instruments were used included, of course,
the theatre.   In the public theatres music was likely regarded as a
stage property, much as were costumes and machines.   When a
king entered or left the stage, trumpets played a flourish.   During
banquet scenes, 'hoboyes' sounded.   The beating of a drum
denoted a marching army, and for each phase of a battle there was
special music.   It is quite evident that the musical formulas for
certain dramatic situations were taken from real-life practices
in Elizabethan England.   Trumpets and kettledrums, for instance,
were the signs apparent of Elizabeth and her nobility, heralding
the monarch on all state occasions.   The technical terms for
trumpet and drum usage found in the military treatises of the time
were also theatre terms.   The band of musicians attached to the
theatre also sometimes engaged in *entr'acte* music and here, it may
be assumed, the music might take on the nature of a self-sufficient
ensemble composition, such as was performed outside the theatre.

If an ensemble, regardless of the scene of its activity, consisted
of instruments of different types, it was known as a broken consort.
If it consisted of instruments of one type—viols, for example, or
recorders—it was called a whole consort.   A considerable number
of instrumental ensemble compositions come down to us without
any indication that they are intended for a particular kind of group.
It seems reasonably clear that such works were presented, like

their counterparts on the Continent, on any instruments upon which they could be performed. But there can be little doubt that the whole consort of viols was the type of ensemble that enjoyed the greatest popularity. Inventories of the royal court and of less exalted households list a rather large number of chests of viols—that is, sets of viols in various sizes. These sets are in some ways analogous to the group of four instruments used in our string quartet. Indeed, English instrumental ensemble music reveals important prefigurations of the string quartet of the future and is among the most original and historically significant contributions made by England to the art of music. In this repertoire we again encounter the usual types—*In Nomines*, pavans, galliards, etc.—but especially distinctive are the fantasias. While splendid examples of the fantasia are included in the keyboard and lute repertoires, it is likely that, when we finally come to know all the English instrumental music of the period, we shall find the fantasias for instrumental ensemble to be the most impressive ones.

Among the ensemble pieces of Thomas Weelkes there is one that might well be called a fantasia, even though it bears in the source only this superscription: 'for 2 basses Tho. Weelkes.' It is in reality for six parts, and the inscription merely refers to the fact that two of them are bass parts. Short as it is, this rich and noble composition creates an impression of great breadth and stateliness.

Weelkes: *Piece for viols*. ENGLISH COLUMBIA 5714 (78 r.p.m.).

That most charming and readable of all English theorists, Thomas Morley, adds to Part I of his manual an appendix which consists of a group of wordless compositions. While such pieces are not necessarily outside the pale of vocal performance, and Morley's text indicates this fact, it is clear that they may be performed by instruments likewise. The last composition in the appendix is a smiling, Italianate little piece, simply entitled *Aria*.

Morley: *Aria*. VANGUARD BG 539.

It would be quite mistaken to conclude from what has been said that the instruments desired for ensemble music are never plainly indicated. On the contrary, Morley himself in 1599 brought out a collection in which he specifically called for treble and bass viols, cittern, pandore, recorder, and lute. There are several other English collections of the time in which particular instruments are clearly designated.

Orlando Gibbons seems to be the finest composer of the first great flowering of English instrumental ensemble music, which spanned the late Tudor and early Stuart periods. No survey of that flowering—even if the emphasis is on Tudor music and Gibbons was essentially a Stuart composer—could rightly be brought to a close without including an illustration of his brilliant writing. Our last example will be a splendid four-part fantasia in which Gibbons toys with fugal imitation, rhythmic variety, and all kinds of interesting devices.

Orlando Gibbons: *Fantasia* (second on the record). BARTÓK BR 913 (alt. OISEAU-LYRE OL 50131).

APPENDIX
(CHAPTERS 19 and 20)

BOOKS

MORRISON C. BOYD: *Elizabethan Music and Musical Criticism.*
E. H. FELLOWES: *The English Madrigal Composers; William Byrd.*
W. H. GRATTAN FLOOD: *Early Tudor Composers.*
BRUCE PATTISON: *Music and Poetry of the English Renaissance.*
PETER WARLOCK: *The English Ayre.*
MARGARET GLYN: *About Elizabethan Virginal Music and its Composers.*
DENIS STEVENS: *The Mulliner Book: A Commentary.*
C. VAN DEN BORREN: *The Sources of Keyboard Music in England.*

RECORDS

An Evening of Elizabethan Verse and its Music. COLUMBIA ML 5051.
A Treasury of Madrigals. COLUMBIA ML 4517.
English Lutenist Songs. OISEAU-LYRE OL 50102.
Shakespeare Songs and Lute Solos. HMV ALP 1265.
English Songs. ENGLISH DECCA LW 5243.
FARNABY: *Canzonets and Virginal Music.* EMS 5.
Dowland and his Contemporaries. EMS 11.
DOWLAND: *The First Book of Ayres.* PERIOD SPL 727. *Lachrimae, etc.* EMS 12.
Elizabethan Love Songs and Harpsichord pieces. NIXA LLP 8037.
Old English Organ Masters. PERIOD SPL 578.
Masters of Early English Keyboard Music. OISEAU-LYRE OL 5075–6.

21

J. A. Westrup

FROM RENAISSANCE TO BAROQUE

THE word 'baroque' has been borrowed by musical historians from historians of the other arts, particularly architecture. Originally it meant 'irregular' or 'strange' and was used as a term of contempt. But it has become generally respectable and is used to indicate the style of a particular period. It would be a waste of time to discuss whether 'baroque' means the same in music as it does in architecture. We need only accept the fact that it is in common use to-day to describe a period reaching roughly from 1600 to 1750—or, from the beginning of opera to the death of J. S. Bach.

What are the outstanding characteristics of baroque music? They can be concisely summed up in three words—splendour, clarity, and pathetic expression. We are inclined to-day to associate splendour particularly with opera; but even when it became a public spectacle after 1637, seventeenth-century opera often achieved its splendour more by scenic extravagance than by elaborate musical resources. The one place above all others where large-scale performances were possible was in church. At St Mark's, Venice, Giovanni Gabrieli (1557–1612) specified exactly what instruments he required and used them both in combination with the voices and as a contrast to them. His motet *In Ecclesiis*, a hymn of praise to God, is a splendid example of the style. There are contrasts between solo voice and chorus, and between voices and instruments, and also contrasts between a more traditional style of intricate part-writing and massive blocks of harmony designed to echo round the church in which the music was sung.

Giovanni Gabrieli: *In Ecclesiis*. HISTORY OF MUSIC IN SOUND, VOL. IV. VICTOR LM 6029 (HMV HMS 39, 78 r.p.m.).

Once this style was established it spread to other countries as well, and we find it in Germany in the work of Michael Praetorius (1571–1621) and Heinrich Schütz (1585–1672).

When Gabrieli was alive there was no such thing as an orchestra as we understand it. The modern orchestra grew out of two necessities. One was the obvious need for increasing the number of string-players in an ensemble where the performance was to be given in a large building. The other was the advisability of having something like a standard organization so that works which had first been performed in one city could be performed again elsewhere. It was the development of opera as a public spectacle that made these requirements urgent. Once the orchestra was recognized as a normal medium, it was adopted in royal and princely establishments as well. They already had a supply of good wind-players, including trumpets and also timpani, which were primarily used for military and ceremonial occasions. The seventeenth-century cult of splendour and massive sonority encouraged composers attached to courts to use all these resources. By the end of the century the orchestra was well established as a medium for independent instrumental music in addition to its earlier functions in the theatre, the church, and the royal palace.

In writing for the orchestra composers did not merely aim at splendour. They realized that one of the principal virtues of the string ensemble was its capacity for clear and precise expression. They also saw that it could be used to suggest pathetic emotions, by using forms of expression already familiar in vocal music. Development of this kind went hand in hand with the growth of a new kind of chamber music. The character of the violin was partly responsible for this. It is perhaps difficult for us to realize how brilliant and penetrating this instrument sounded to seventeenth-century ears by comparison with the viol, which had been the favoured instrument for chamber music in the sixteenth century. The violin also had a wider range of expression. All this, together with a desire for more clearly defined rhythms, led to a cultivation of the clarity which I mentioned as the second of the outstanding characteristics of the baroque period. Dance music, of course, had always had a clearly defined rhythm, and it was only natural that such rhythm should continue to be used in the instrumental music of the seventeenth century, whether it was in a definite dance-form or not. But the most striking change occurred in music which was contrapuntal in character—that is to say, music in which the parts had a good deal of melodic independence and indulged in imitation. In the early part of the sixteenth century instrumental music of this kind was modelled very closely on vocal music. As time went on it acquired a character of its own. Instruments have a much wider range than voices, and this was freely exploited. It was also realized that they had much more flexibility. So a truly instrumental style of writing grew up with a much more clear-cut structure and a harmonic development as precise as in dance music. Earlier instrumental music had employed contrasts similar to those in the madrigal or motet, where the words would obviously suggest a change of mood. In course of time these contrasts came to be more clearly defined by a change of rhythm, so that an instrumental piece might fall into two or more sections. In the seventeenth century these sections became independent movements. Thus the suite, or series of dance movements, and the sonata developed side by side and became in fact closely interrelated.

In keyboard music there were other developments as well. The tradition of writing variations continued, and in the Lutheran Church we find composers still following the ancient practice of building music on a pre-existent theme by writing pieces on the melodies of hymn tunes. But here too the new type of contrapuntal writing made itself felt, with its use of clear-cut and sharply rhythmical melodic phrases and of harmonic development organized into definite patterns. For our example we turn to Girolamo Frescobaldi (1583-1643), who was for many years organist of St Peter's, Rome. This *Capriccio* illustrates not only the keyboard music of this period, but also many of the characteristics of chamber music as well. The piece has seven clearly defined sections, differing in character one from another. The theme of the first section is precise and strongly rhythmical and is developed by means of imitation. The same theme is used in the remaining sections, but so transformed in rhythm that the contrasts between the sections are strongly defined.

Frescobaldi: *Capriccio*. HISTORY OF MUSIC IN SOUND, VOL. IV.
    VICTOR LM 6029 (HMV HMS 42, 78 r.p.m.).

In vocal music the change of style is most marked. Throughout the sixteenth century protests were made against the way in which words were set in the madrigal: that too much attention was paid to illustrating the meaning of individual words, and that it was impossible to hear the words when a poem was sung by several voices and imitation was employed. These are objections which would naturally occur to literary men, but musicians also took notice of them. Some of the later madrigalists were well aware of the difficulty of hearing the words and in particularly expressive passages took care to avoid imitation. There was, however, the further objection that in a composition for several voices there could be no real freedom in the setting or the performance. The natural rhythm of the words was subordinated to musical rhythm, which had to be exact if the voices were to keep together. This difficulty still existed when madrigals were performed by one voice with instruments playing the other parts, and even when sung to lute accompaniment, since the accompaniment was a transcription of the vocal parts.

A great deal of original music for solo voice and lute accompaniment was composed during the sixteenth century. But even here there was not the complete independence which progressive minds were looking for. The accompaniment in such cases was very often modelled on the kind of part-writing to be found in the madrigal, or else the piece was cast in a simple dance rhythm which was attractive as music but did not allow scope for the intense personal expression which was one of the characteristics of Renaissance art. If we want an example of solo singing cast in a traditional form we may look at the anthems of Orlando Gibbons, who was organist of the Chapel Royal and Westminster Abbey and died at the age of forty-two in 1625. The sections for solo voice are accompanied by strings and organ, but the accompaniment is highly contrapuntal and might almost equally well have been written for supporting voices.

Gibbons: *Behold Thou hast made my days as it were a span long.*
HISTORY OF MUSIC IN SOUND, VOL. IV. VICTOR LM 6029 (HMV HMS 38, 78 r.p.m.).

There are two reasons why Gibbons's writing for solo voice is on traditional lines. First, it is in the nature of church music to be conservative; even Monteverdi, perhaps the most original composer of the period, wrote some church music in a thoroughly old-fashioned style. And secondly, the development of music in England lagged behind the changes that had occurred on the Continent.

This new style of solo song was an attempt to answer all the

objections that had been raised against vocal music by subordin-
ating the accompaniment to the solo voice. To do this effectively
it was necessary that the bass should move only when a change
of harmony was required, and that the harmony itself should be
free of any melodic movement in inner parts which would restrict
the freedom of the singer. The Italian word *recitar* (to recite)
had been used at least as far back as the beginning of the sixteenth
century to mean the singing of words by a solo voice. But it
now came to have a much more specialized meaning. It meant, in
fact, to recite in song as one would recite in speaking, keeping the
rhythm of the words and letting the voice rise or fall in accordance
with the sentiments which were being expressed. The new style
became known as recitative.

Four important points emerge from the study of this style as we
find it in the works of such early practitioners as Giulio Caccini
and Jacopo Peri, who were themselves singers. First, the singer
was left entirely free to adjust the time to suit himself. The
notation was only a rough indication of the relative note values.
The accompanist therefore had to follow the singer and act
merely as a harmonic support. Secondly, since the chords of the
accompaniment formed a harmonic progression independent
of any individual movement of separate parts, the sequence of
harmonies could exist in its own right and could even dictate the
notes which the soloist was to sing. Thirdly, the traditions of
madrigal writing had familiarized composers with the use of
cadences for the sake of punctuation. These cadences were
transferred bodily to the new recitative and were a great help in
emphasizing the structure of sentences. In addition, certain
melodic formulas which had been used by the madrigalists—
particularly those used for the expression of passionate emotion—
found their way into recitative quite naturally and became incorporated into the new style. Fourthly, the tradition of vocal
ornamentation, which had been applied to the upper part of a
madrigal, continued to survive in the new form. In some cases
the ornamentation was fully written out by the composer; in
others it was left to the singer to improvise.

It follows that the new style of recitative was not quite so simple
and monotonous as it may appear in the printed texts. Its
performance combined the arts of the singer and the actor, and it
is quite clear that the practice did not entirely correspond to the

theory. If the principal aim was to let the music serve the words, the introduction of ornamentation was indefensible. What was new and significant was the freedom of rhythm allowed to the singer.

Recitative did not kill lyrical song. Both forms flourished side by side. In lyrical movements in a regular rhythm composers found that they could achieve enchanting effects of colour and contrasts by using instruments, either to provide interludes between the singing or to play counterpoints to the vocal line. The word *concerto*, which originally meant any kind of ensemble, came to be used particularly for mixed combinations of this kind.

There developed a more intimate relationship between recitative and song. Composers would sometimes break into a few bars of lyrical melody in the course of a recitative, and it was not long before such interruptions became substantial enough to become complete sections. The solo cantata was a favourite field for this form of association. Recitative and song would alternate in accordance with changing emotions of the text. As a good example of the contrast between rhythmical song, or aria, and recitative, I have chosen a substantial part of a cantata by Luigi Rossi (1598–1653). The singer expresses his admiration for the eyes of the beloved, ending with the plea, 'Pity me at least, if you do not love me.'

Rossi: *Occhi Belli*. HISTORY OF MUSIC IN SOUND, VOL. VI.
VICTOR LM 6031 (HMV HMS 58, 78 r.p.m.).

The cultivation of recitative suggests something very different from the new style of instrumental music, where the emphasis was on clarity and sharply defined rhythm. If in recitative there was no rhythm other than the words, it does not follow that it was formless. The use of regular cadences was a safeguard against that, and the earliest composers would often create a logical structure by repeating the bass with variations of the melody above it. In the aria too a favourite device was to repeat a sequence of bass notes—a *basso ostinato*, or obstinate bass—as the foundation of a song. This device was also fruitful in instrumental music.

In general, musicians of the baroque period, with all their enthusiasm for brilliant display and intense emotional expression, never lost sight of the fact that music has its own laws.

APPENDIX

BOOKS

MANFRED BUKOFZER: *Music in the Baroque Era.*
ERNEST WALKER: *A History of Music in England.*
E. H. FELLOWES: *English Cathedral Music; Orlando Gibbons.*

RECORDS

Baroque Organ Music. RENAISSANCE SX 202 (NIXA PLP 224).
French Baroque Organ Music. CLASSIC EDITIONS 1008.
BENEVOLI: *Festival Mass.* EPIC 5LC 3035 (PHILIPS ABR 4015–16).
CARISSIMI: *Jepthe.* DECCA ARC 3005 (DGG APM 14020).
FRESCOBALDI: *Fiori Musicale.* ALLEGRO 111. *Organ Music.* VOX PL 8780 (E).
A. SCARLATTI: *St John Passion.* OVERTONE 1. *Cantata: Su le Sponde del Tebro.* DECCA ARC 3008 (DGG APM 14024).
LECLAIR: *Flute Sonatas.* OISEAU-LYRE OL 50050–1. *Violin Sonatas.* OISEAU-LYRE OL 50087–8.
GIBBONS: *Church Music.* WESTMINSTER XWN 18165. *Anthems, Madrigals, etc.* DGG APM 14056. *Anthems, etc.* ARGO RG 80.

22

J. A. Westrup

MONTEVERDI

MONTEVERDI was the most distinguished opera composer of the early seventeenth century. He also excelled in the composition of madrigals of widely different kinds and wrote a considerable amount of church music.

He had a long life and a comparatively uneventful one, though it was not entirely happy. He was born in 1567, the son of a doctor, and at the age of twenty-three he entered the service of the Duke of Mantua as a string player. In 1602 he was promoted to the post of director of music and remained in Mantua for a further ten years until his patron died. For the next thirty years until his death in 1643 he was director of music at St Mark's, Venice. These seem to have been his happiest years, for at Mantua he was poorly paid and overworked and he became a widower at the age of forty. Many of his letters have survived and these combine to reveal much about his personality. Composition was not a routine job for him, but an intense effort, and from the letters we also learn of his profound interest in human beings— an interest which no doubt inclined him strongly towards the composition of opera. We know too that he had the good fortune to live in a highly cultured society: Tasso and Rubens were among those to be found at the Mantuan court.

Monteverdi composed eight books of madrigals. The first was published in 1587 and the last in 1638, five years before his death. A ninth book of miscellaneous pieces was issued posthumously. This material covers practically the whole of his working life, and inevitably we shall find changes of style; the most noticeable being the abandonment of the traditional conception of the madrigal which first became decisive after Monteverdi's migration to Venice.

The early madrigals are remarkable for their very expressive use of dissonance, their capacity for dramatizing a story, and the skill with which a picturesque background is translated into music. A good example is *Ecco mormorar l'onde* from Book II (1590), composed before Monteverdi went to Mantua. The poem describes the dawn, and the morning breeze brings a rare refreshment to hearts in anguish. Notice the sombre beginning for the lower voices, and the skilful way in which the first fluttering of dawn is suggested in the music. Notice also the gay suggestion of the breeze, set in a popular style, and the splendidly tranquil ending.

Monteverdi: *Ecco mormorar l'onde.*   HMV DB 5042 (78 r.p.m.).

Monteverdi's first opera was composed in 1607, but it is evident that before this he had become interested in the new form of declamatory solo song. There are examples in the third and fourth books of madrigals (1592 and 1603). The more personal the words, the more the composer felt compelled to adopt an individual style of expression. To emphasize the text, Monteverdi also exploited new resources of harmony, and drew on himself sharp criticism. When he published his fifth book he made a brief comment on this criticism in the preface, which ended with these significant words: 'The modern composer builds on the foundations of truth.' His brother, Giulio Cesare, considerably elaborated his views in a commentary printed in 1607. Giulio Cesare wrote: 'My brother's intention has been to make the words the mistress of the music and not the slave.' These two statements are the key to Monteverdi's work. The words dictate the expression, and in the pursuit of that expression truth is what matters, not any convention. Hence any audacities of harmony are justified if they serve as a faithful expression of the words. This does not mean that Monteverdi consistently uses dissonance, and there is much in his harmony that is so extremely simple that it may even seem naïve to sophisticated minds. But he realizes that at times the utmost simplicity is more moving than any self-conscious attack on the emotions.

In the fifth book of madrigals there are many examples of a declamatory style, and he goes further and adds a *basso continuo* or thorough-bass part for the harpsichord or lute. The idea of writing accompanied madrigals was not new, but the fact that

*F

Monteverdi adopted it is a significant development of his style. In the sixth book (1614) an accompaniment is indispensable to six of the madrigals, though it also contains two cycles which do not require an instrumental bass.   One of these cycles, *Lasciatemi morire*, is an arrangement for five voices of a lament sung in recitative by Ariadne in the opera *Arianna*.   The fact that solo recitative could be arranged as a madrigal shows how close his madrigal technique had become to the style of writing adopted in opera.   The general plan of the accompanied madrigals is that passages for one or more voices with instruments are contrasted with others for all five voices in the earlier style.   The solo passages often demand considerable virtuosity.

In Book VII (1619) the change of style is complete.   It contains nothing in the older style and is in fact a very mixed collection. Most of the pieces are duets, trios, and quartets with instrumental accompaniment, and an example from the duets will illustrate the passionate intensity that Monteverdi could devote to words of a sentimental character—a poet lamenting that all he desires is taken from him.

Monteverdi: *Ohime dov'e il mio ben*.   HMV DB 5040 (78 r.p.m.).

Another example, also from Book VII, is a catalogue of the charms of the loved one, the sprightly character of the music being emphasized by vivacious *ritornelli* for two violins.

Monteverdi: *Chiome d'oro*.   HMV DB 5040 (78 r.p.m.).

The eighth book of madrigals (1638) is even more varied.   It is divided into two parts, madrigals of war and madrigals of love, though the distinction between them is not so marked as might be expected.   War is considered as a metaphorical state of love. Instruments are used in the more elaborate pieces and the style ranges from a charming frivolity to intense emotional expression. The title-page tells us that some of the works are in dramatic style, and these are contrasted with the songs without action.   An exceptionally beautiful example of the former is the *Nymph's Lament*. A short trio for male voices describes how she wandered hopelessly through the meadow, and then follows the actual lament, built on a simple sequence of four descending notes in the bass, repeated as an ostinato throughout.   The lower voices support the solo intermittently with a commentary and expressions of sympathy.

Monteverdi: *Pianto della Ninfa*.   HMV DB 5042 (78 r.p.m.).

Each section of Book VIII also includes a substantial dramatic work. In the war section it is *Il Combattimento di Tancredi e Clorinda*, or *The Fight between Tancred and Clorinda*. In the love section it is *Il Ballo dell' Ingrate, The Ballet of the Hard-hearted Ladies*. Both these works had actually been written many years earlier.

Il Combattimento is a kind of mixture of opera and secular oratorio to a text by Tasso. The story is told by a narrator. Other soloists represent Tancred and Clorinda and sing the words assigned to them in the poem. The two characters appear in costume on stage and fairly detailed instructions are given for the performance. To illustrate the combat a string ensemble is used to play rapid scale passages, violent tremolandos, and aggressive pizzicatos. Monteverdi's output contains nothing as directly exciting as the descriptive passages of this work.

Il Ballo is a kind of masque, designed for dancing as well as singing. Ladies who have been hard-hearted to their lovers have been consigned to Hades. But they are let out for a brief spell to enjoy the pure air of the earth and also to impress on the ladies in the audience how grievous a sin it is to reject love. The subject is highly fanciful and might be amusing if it were not that Monteverdi has charged it with a pathos that makes a direct appeal to our emotions.

It is this capacity for entering into the joys and sorrows of human beings that makes Monteverdi the greatest opera composer of his time. He wrote more than a dozen operas but only three survive complete. A fourth, *Arianna*, is represented only by a fragment, the heroine's lament. The first of the complete operas, *Orfeo*, was performed in 1607 and published two years later. The other two, *Il Ritorno d' Ulisse in Patria* and *L' Incoronazione di Poppea*, date from the last years of his life and are preserved in manuscript.

Orfeo was Monteverdi's first attempt at opera, and it is obvious that he had made a very close study of the new style of recitative, which he handles in masterly fashion. But there is far more in the work than recitative: an extended pastoral scene and choruses which reflect the madrigal and motet style of the sixteenth century, for instance. Contrast between instrumental resources is carefully observed. The keyboard instrument accompanying the recitative changes according to situation and character; strings are used for the scenes on earth and wind instruments for those in Hades. If there is an astonishing variety of treatment there is no feeling of incongruity, and all kinds of structural devices are used to give the work coherence. We are so accustomed to large-scale works to-day that it is not easy for us to realize the problems facing composers whose experience was based entirely on relatively short movements.

We may take as our example of *Orfeo* an extract from Act IV. Pluto has just relented and agreed to let Eurydice follow Orpheus back to earth, but on the condition that he does not turn and look at her. Orpheus celebrates their announced departure with an aria introduced by a *ritornello* for violins, and this leads into an anguished recitative that reflects his doubts. When he hears a noise he turns to see if Eurydice is following him. A spirit tells him that he has failed to observe Pluto's condition, and Eurydice takes a piteous farewell of him. Orpheus would follow her back to Hades, but he cannot, and in a frenzy of horror he finds himself being led towards the upper world which means nothing to him any more. A solemn symphony for wind instruments concludes the scene.

Monteverdi: *Orfeo, excerpt from Act IV*. HISTORY OF MUSIC IN SOUND, VOL. IV. VICTOR LM 6030 (HMV HMS 44, 78 r.p. m.).

The consideration of Monteverdi's other two completed operas is best deferred to the next chapter, but his church music must be considered in conclusion. There is no evidence that, despite his long service at St Mark's and his entry into the priesthood in 1632, he was particularly drawn towards church works. They offered him little opportunity for human characterization. When we look at the Masses and motets he had to write to fulfil his duties, we find that some of the music is in so traditional a style that it makes nonsense of any view that Monteverdi was a completely revolutionary composer. No doubt the reason is that church music is always inclined to be conservative in character. But there is a considerable amount of church music similar in style to the later madrigals, with instruments participating on equal terms with the voices, including the Vespers of 1610. This includes psalm settings, a *Magnificat*, and independent pieces. The treatment is often so rich and varied that it is not at all easy to detect the plain-song. In this field, no less than in madrigals and opera, Monteverdi was a master of his craft.

Monteverdi: *Vespro Della Beata Vergine* (1610). OISEAU-LYRE 50021–2.

APPENDIX

Books

H. F. REDLICH: *Claudio Monteverdi.*
L. SCHRADE: *Monteverdi, Creator of Modern Music.*

Records

MONTEVERDI: *Madrigals.* HAYDN SOCIETY HSL O/9004–5, DECCA 9627 (BRUNSWICK AXTL 1051). *Mass for Four Voices.* CONCERT HALL 1196. *Works by Monteverdi.* VOX PL 8560. *Vespro della Beata Vergine.* VOX PL 7902, OISEAU-LYRE OL 50021–2. *Ora pro nobis, etc.* DGG AMP 14020.

23

J. A. Westrup

THE RISE OF OPERA IN ITALY

RECITATIVE figured largely in early opera, and this was only natural. There was no older model for extended solo singing, and since the intention was to re-create the spirit of Greek drama, composers turned as a matter of course to a form of vocal writing which came near to speech. As time went on it was inevitable that musicians should feel that there was a certain monotony in continuous recitative, particularly as it offered few opportunities for using characteristically musical resources. This was perhaps even more obvious in the solo cantata than in opera, where attention would be focused on the action. But lyrical sections—known as *aria* or *arietta*—were so attractive to the ear that they came more and more to dominate opera. In consequence recitative was more and more restricted to those parts of the libretto which were essential to the action and became more and more conventional. It came into its own again when composers revived Monteverdi's experiment of using the orchestra to intensify a dramatic situation. Recitative accompanied by instruments became a staple element of eighteenth-century opera and oratorio.

The earliest operas that have survived complete are settings of the same libretto by the two pioneers in recitative, Jacopo Peri and Giulio Caccini. The subject they took was the story of Orpheus and Eurydice, later to be used by Monteverdi in his *Orfeo*. Peri's *Euridice* was performed in Florence in 1600 and published the next year. Caccini's setting was published in 1600, but not performed until 1602. In each case the story is told for the most part in recitative, but there are also lyrical sections and choruses for shepherds.

Peri explained his intention in a preface. He accepted the view that Greek tragedy was sung throughout and used recitative as a modern equivalent. Neither he nor Caccini were aware that they were inaugurating a new musical form, and it was only gradually that works of this kind came to acquire the name *opera in musica*, that is to say, 'a musical work.' Music came to exist in its own right, and people went to the opera to enjoy fine singing, as well as to admire a spectacle. The inclusion in Monteverdi's *Orfeo* of a quite substantial number of ensemble pieces for voices and instrumental movements shows that it took over a good deal of the function that music had enjoyed when it was used in the form of interludes in spoken drama in the sixteenth century.

It is quite possible that opera would have remained a brief experiment if it had not been taken up in Rome. In the theatre of the Barberini family there were opportunities for far more elaborate productions than the performances at Florence and Mantua. We find extensive use of the chorus and a growing inclination to break up the recitative with arias, and one composer, Mazzochi, actually wrote in 1626 that he introduced *arioso* sections 'to break the tediousness of the recitative.' Another feature of the Roman operas is the introduction of scenes of a lighter character, some of which are pure comedy. In Stefano Landi's *La Morte d'Orfeo* (1619) the ferryman Charon sings a jovial song in which he invites Orpheus to drink from the waters of Lethe which bring forgetfulness.

Landi: *La Morte d'Orfeo: Bevi, bevi.* HISTORY OF MUSIC IN SOUND, VOL. IV. VICTOR LM 6029 (HMV HMS 44, 78 r.p.m.).

Although opera was so vigorously cultivated in Rome, it remained very much a court entertainment. The decisive change came in 1637 when the first opera house was opened in Venice, and opera became a commercial entertainment. This did not necessarily mean any lowering of musical standards, but it did mean some reduction of resources. The managers could hardly afford to spend so much on chorus and orchestra as the princely patrons in Rome, particularly as they still had to provide a lavish stage spectacle to attract an audience. Hence we find that the chorus plays only a minor role in the Venetian operas, and the orchestra generally consists merely of strings and harpsichord.

It was for Venice that Monteverdi wrote his last two operas— *Il Ritorno d'Ulisse in patria* (1641) and *L'incoronazione di Poppea* (1642). The return of Ulysses to his native Ithaca deals with exactly the kind of human relationships which were to figure so largely in eighteenth-century opera—Penelope's obstinate attachment to her absent husband, the ardent determination of the suitors to win her hand, and the triumphant reunion of Ulysses with his wife.   The same is true of *L'incoronazione di Poppea*, which deals with incidents in the life of the Emperor Nero.   His passion for Poppaea leads him to sweep aside all opposition, including his old teacher Seneca, and finally to make her his empress.

Both these works follow the lead of Roman opera by introducing scenes of light relief.   In *Poppea* we have the charming love-scene between a page and a maidservant, which is entirely irrelevant to the plot but serves to throw into strong relief the stoicism of Seneca and Nero's unbridled passion.   In *Ulisse* Iros, the court buffoon, is a comic character.   At the end of the second act Ulysses destroys the suitors.   The third act opens with Iros lamenting the end of his patrons; where is he to turn now for food and drink?

Monteverdi: *Il Ritorno d'Ulisse in patria: O dolor, o martir.*   CONCERT HALL CHS 1085 (NIXA CLP 1085).

This very amusing scene is a combination of recitative and *arioso*, which may be defined as a passage in regular rhythm which emerges from the recitative but is quite distinct from it in style. With the development of the aria as a vehicle for fine singing and for summing up a dramatic situation, *arioso* passages tended to disappear from the recitative.   The aria which is our example is sung by Arnalta, Poppaea's nurse, and is in the form of a lullaby, with a contrasting section at the end.

Monteverdi: *L'incoronazione di Poppea: Arnalta's lullaby.*   CONCERT HALL CHS 1184.

Francesco Cavalli (1602–76) who was a singer in St Mark's choir under Monteverdi, wrote more than forty operas, not all of which have survived.   He must have come under Monteverdi's influence, but he may well have influenced his master in turn. Very similar types of music occur in the operas of both composers. There are frequent examples in Cavalli and Monteverdi of *arioso* and of complete arias, and both used the ground bass as a foundation for a vocal piece.   In Cavalli's *Egisto* (1643) there is a superb example of a solo on a chromatic ground bass, like that used by Purcell in the heroine's lament in *Dido and Aeneas* and by Bach in the *Crucifixus* of his *Mass in B minor*.   For an example of the flowing melody of which Cavalli was a master we may examine the passage from *Egisto* in which two lovers hail the dawn.   This is not in the strict sense a duet, but the sections for the two singers show parallels in the music as well as in the text.

Cavalli: *Egisto: Musici della selva.* HISTORY OF MUSIC IN SOUND, VOL. V.   VICTOR LM 6030 (HMV HMS 45, 78 r.p.m.).

Cavalli was not only a master of song but also had a vivid sense of drama and could use the orchestra to create atmosphere.   His younger contemporary, Cesti (1623–69), had the same gifts.   The most famous of his works was *Il Pomo d'Oro* (*The Golden Apple*), composed for a state occasion in Vienna and produced there in the winter of 1666–7.   No expense was spared in the lavish production. The opera opens, appropriately, with a stately prologue making reference to the Emperor's dominions, and the action proper does not begin until the opening of the first act.   In the underworld Proserpine sings of the horrors of Pluto's kingdom.   The orchestra, used mainly in alternation with the singer, consists solely of wind instruments—two *cornetti*, three trombones, and a bassoon; we may recall the similar ensemble used by Monteverdi for the infernal scenes of *Orfeo*.   The *cornetti* (a now obsolete instrument replaced in the recording by clarinets) are used to provide treble parts to blend with the trombones.   The keyboard instrument is a reed organ, which Monteverdi too had used for the supernatural scenes in his opera.   The total effect is to emphasize the fact that we are in a world remote from all human associations.

Cesti: *Il Pomo d'Oro: E dove t'aggiri.* HISTORY OF MUSIC IN SOUND, VOL. V.   VICTOR LM 6030 (HMV HMS 45, 78 r.p.m.).

As the aria established itself more and more firmly as an indispensable element, composers were bound to consider ways of organizing it into a coherent shape.   So long as it was merely a pastoral ditty there was little difficulty, but once it outgrew this stage there were problems for which the older traditions of strophic song provided no solution.   One method was to organize the vocal melody above a ground bass, though this method could not be used for every aria without the risk of intolerable monotony. The new method which became most popular was simply to repeat at the end of the song the material which had been used at the beginning, a structure which may be represented by the formula ABA.   We find a miniature example in Monteverdi's *Orfeo*, and later on we come across more extended examples.   They came to be called *da capo* arias, because the singer went back to the head, or beginning, of the song.

By the time of Stradella (*c.* 1645–82) the aria was well established as the most important part of an opera.   The two *da capo*
arias of our next example make much use of a figure in the bass
which recurs frequently as a foundation and may also appear in the
voice part.   This is not quite the same as a ground bass because there
is no regular repetition of a formula, but it shows how the principle
could be adapted to give coherence to an aria of another kind.

> Stradella: *Floridoro: Stelle ingrate* and *Dimmi amor.* HISTORY OF
> MUSIC IN SOUND, VOL. V. VICTOR LM 6030 (HMV HMS 46,
> 78 r.p.m.).

Fine singing and splendid staging remained the principal
ingredients of later seventeenth-century opera in Italy.   Singers
came to be idolized, not least the *castrati* or male sopranos.   By
all accounts their voices were capable not only of great sweetness,
but also of a virile intensity.   In love duets male and female
soprano voices could intertwine at the same level, and duets were
the staple form of these operas.   The operatic ensemble as we
understand it to-day was virtually non-existent outside comedy.
But in Alessandro Scarlatti's opera *Tito Sempronio Gracco* (1720)
we find a rare example of a quartet in a serious opera, though it
does not give us the simultaneous characterization of four different
people.   Scarlatti called it an aria for four singers—which in fact
is what it is.   It is in *da capo* form and the rhythm is that of the
siciliana, familiar to us from the *Pastoral Symphony* and 'He shall
feed His flock' from *Messiah*.   The singers are three sopranos
and a tenor.

> Alessandro Scarlatti: *Tito Sempronio Gracco: Idolo del cor mio.*
> HISTORY OF MUSIC IN SOUND, VOL. V. VICTOR LM 6030 (HMV
> HMS 46, 78 r.p.m.).

APPENDIX
BOOKS

D. J. GROUT: *A Short History of Opera.*
E. WELLESZ: *Essays on Opera.*
S. TOWNELEY WORSTHORNE: *Venetian Opera in the Seventeenth
Century.*

RECORDS

CAVALLI: *Il Guidizio Universale* (oratorio).   COLOSSEUM 1032.
MONTEVERDI: *Orfeo.* DECCA ARC 3035–6 (DGG APM 14057–8).   *Il
Ballo delle Ingrate.* HAYDN SOCIETY 30001 Vox PL 8090 (E).   *Il
Combattimento.* ANTHOLOGIE SONORE AS 9 Vox PL 8560 (E).
A. SCARLATTI: *Il Trionfo dell'Onore.* CETRA 1223.

24

Denis Stevens

ITALIAN INSTRUMENTAL MUSIC IN THE SEVENTEENTH CENTURY

ITALIAN operas in the seventeenth century were rarely published, unlike church and chamber music, which appeared frequently and brought out all the best in Italian composers between the time of Gabrieli and that of Geminiani. Purely instrumental music could be divided into two main groups, concertos and sonatas, and both were common to church music and chamber music. You could hear a sonata, played by violins, cello, and organ in many a church in the days when that kind of music was not only allowed, but actively encouraged: in fact, the pieces were actually called *sonate da chiesa*—church sonatas. In the larger churches you could hear a concerto played by groups of string and wind instruments, now alternating their contrasting tone-colours, now combining them, and always with an organ accompaniment. At first these pieces were published at the end of sets of part-books containing motets, settings of the Mass, and other liturgical music, so that when the singers had finished their part of the service they could pass the books over to the instrumentalists. Later composers and publishers began to issue complete books of instrumental pieces.

Giovanni Gabrieli was one of the earliest composers to make use of the term 'concerto.' The true meaning of the word is still much debated, but fortunately most scholars agree that the result —in terms of instrumental sonorities—is contrast. This contrast may have taken place between a loud group of instruments and a soft-toned group, or between groups of similar timbre but different range. An example of the latter kind can be heard in this *Canzona* for double string orchestra by Giovanni Gabrieli.

Giovanni Gabrieli: *Canzona No. 1.* LONDON LS 686 (DECCA LX 3102).

The texture is still essentially polyphonic—the kind of music

155

that one would find in double-choir motets of the same period—
yet there are unmistakably instrumental touches in the individual
lines.   The essence of the concerto form is there.   Two bodies
of instruments are playing, first one, then the other, and at a climax
point they join forces.

Sometimes the Italians spelt '*concerto*' with a 'c' in the middle
of the word; sometimes they spelt it with an 's'—'*conserto*.'   In
the first case the Latin root would be '*concertare*'—'to fight side
by side, to compete as brothers in arms.'   But in the second case
it would be '*conserere*'—'to congregate, to join together.'   Just to
confuse things even further, some composers used the word
'*concento*,' with the obvious implication that the musicians gathered
together in a circle.   Rather than worry about these derivations
and meanings we should consider how best to reproduce what the
composer wrote.   Shall it be done with a huge body of strings,
drowning out the faint twanging of an insufficient harpsichord, or
with a smaller group like those we can see in drawings and paintings
of baroque concerts ?

Two famous theoretical writers, Agazzari and Gasperini, at
each end of the seventeenth century, can help us.   In his treatise
published in 1607 Agazzari makes an important distinction between
continuo instruments and their corresponding function.   The
correct instrument to support a large orchestra is the organ, and
that is why the bass part in any given set of books is usually
labelled '*organo*.'   We find Gasperini saying the same thing in a
treatise published in 1708.   He even goes so far as to distinguish
between different ways of treating discords, depending on whether
an organ or harpsichord is being used.   Sometimes both instruments were used, for in the *concerto grosso* no single instrument
had the dynamic range to support the delicate tones of the soloists
and to add body to the passages where everybody joined in.

The effectiveness of the harpsichord in a small group may be
gauged from the closing section of a sonata by Gabrieli, for oboe,
violins, and continuo.

Giovanni Gabrieli: *Sonata a tre.* DUCRETET-THOMSON DTL
    93046.

A ready and effective substitute for the harpsichord was the
lute, and there is obviously room for the plucked string instrument
in modern performances of music of the baroque era.   Just as the
lute was used as an alternative to the harpsichord, so the *cornet*

(pronounced 'cor*net*', and not to be confused with our *cor*net) was brought in by way of substitute for the violin. It was made of wood, though sometimes covered with leather, and it was played with a mouthpiece similar to that of a French horn. It is difficult to play, and its tone is not easy to describe, but we have now a successful modern recording in which two cornets are joined by two violins, gamba, organ, and three trombones. The music is the opening of Monteverdi's *Sonata sopra Sancta Maria*.

Monteverdi: *Sonata sopra Sancta Maria* (*Vespers of 1610*). DECCA ARC 3005 (DGG APM 14020).

The place of the cornet was soon ousted, however, by the more brilliant and versatile trumpet, and the trumpet seems to have had a great vogue in the town of Bologna, where such composers as Perti, Cazzati, and Torelli wrote brilliant sonatas and concertos for one or two solo trumpets and strings. Solo instruments are often grouped in pairs. In chamber music the same tendency can be seen in the trio sonata which dominated the Italian scene for the latter half of the seventeenth century and far beyond, influencing French, German, and English composers towards its further development. The trio sonata belies its name, for there are four instruments: two violins, cello, and harpsichord. The cello and harpsichord play from the same music and are considered as an entity; their respective functions are to strengthen the bass line and to provide an interesting improvised middle to the texture. Similarly a continuo instrument or instruments is implied in a sonata for solo violin in Italian music of this period.

The Italian organists of the seventeenth century were of slighter stature than the French and Germans, but their contribution was no mean one. In the works of the greatest of them, Girolamo Frescobaldi, a touch of the concerto principle may be sensed, even though modern recordings make no effort to reproduce it. His *Fiori Musicale* contains music for the organist to play at Mass; it is solo music, but it is not intended to be played continuously. In the *Kyrie* the organist was supposed to provide verses to alternate with the chanting of the choir. The nine invocations of the *Kyrie* would be divided alternately between choir and organ. Thus a system of contrasting tone-colours and dynamics would be set up, and the effect would be that of a concerto with the organ as soloist and the voices as *concerto grosso*.

Frescobaldi: *Kyrie*. PERIOD 586 (NIXA PLP 586).

The theatrical contribution to the development of Italian instrumental music is more direct and definite than that of church music. Theatre orchestras, which were not very large, not only accompanied the singers, but also introduced the drama and linked the scenes together with short instrumental pieces called *sinfonie*. The opening *sinfonia avanti l'opera*, or symphony before the opera, had the utilitarian purpose of indicating that the opera was about to begin.

It was due to Alessandro Scarlatti that this overture became a work of artistic importance rather than a purely functional call to order in a crowded opera-house. He helped to develop this new form into the symphony, linking his own product with the contemporary *concerti grossi* which were enjoying such a vogue. He called his collection of twelve symphonies *Sinfonie di Concerto Grosso*, thus stressing their dual nature. The first two sections of his *Symphony in D minor* demonstrate Scarlatti's method of securing the maximum contrast in spite of slender resources— only flutes, strings, and continuo. Very often the violins play in thirds; they are echoed by the two flutes also playing in thirds, and this is a legacy from the trio sonata. Scarlatti's slow movement starts as if with a flute solo, accompanied by strings and harpsichord; but soon the second flute joins in as if to underline the *concerto grosso* part of the original title.

Alessandro Scarlatti: *Symphony No. 5 in D minor.* ANGEL 35141
(COLUMBIA 33 CX 1171).

The *concerto grosso* proper did not as a rule include wood-wind instruments, but was essentially an interplay between small and large forces of strings. The small group consisted at first of two violins and continuo, though later some composers added a viola to the group. It comprised the best three players from the orchestra, plus the most brilliant and imaginative harpsichord player, and he was freer than his orchestral-continuo colleague because he was unfettered by figures in the cello part. He could contribute much bold and inventive figuration as well as fill the gap in compass between the two solo violins and cello.

The name of Arcangelo Corelli will always be of prime importance in the history of the *concerto grosso*, but others—Alessandro Stradella, Giuseppe Torelli, and Tomasso Albinoni, for example— made important contributions too. The *concerto grosso* was taken up in France by Leclair, in Germany by Telemann, and in England

by William Boyce and Handel. There was another memorable
Italian, Francesco Geminiani, who had studied with Scarlatti and
Corelli and ultimately lost his place in the Naples opera orchestra
because no one could follow his excessive rubato and changes of
tempo. He later settled in Dublin, taught and gave concerts and
published a treatise on violin playing. He wrote violin sonatas
and several sets of *concerti grossi*, and many of them are of the very
first rank. The E minor *Concerto Grosso*, Opus. 3, No. 3, is a fine
example of Geminiani's understanding of the sonorities of a
string orchestra.

Geminiani: *Concerto Grosso in E minor, Op. 3, No. 3.* Vox PL 8290
(E) or Westminster 18002.

Apart from the understandable ascendancy of the stringed
instruments, the oboe and bassoon gradually emerged as solo
instruments rather than as mere orchestral effects. When the
German flautist, Quantz, tried to interest Scarlatti in the flute,
the Italian maintained that all wood-wind instruments played
out of tune, though later he relented and wrote some flute pieces
for Quantz. What Scarlatti did for the flute, Vivaldi did for the
oboe and bassoon, and his finales show the agility he expected
of his bassoon player.

Vivaldi: *Bassoon Concerto in D minor.* London LS 591 (Decca LX
3100).

Vivaldi also wrote numerous oboe concertos, although many
were originally violin concertos which he authorized to be played
on the oboe. His contemporary, the Venetian nobleman Tomasso
Albinoni, wrote solo oboe concertos of great beauty and deep feeling, and these works probably did more than any others to bring
the oboe to the forefront as a solo instrument at the beginning of
the eighteenth century. They have melody, charm, and display
in equal measure.

Albinoni: *Oboe Concertos, Op. 7.* Oiseau-Lyre OL 50041.

APPENDIX

Books

M. Pincherle: *Antonio Vivaldi et la musique instrumentale.*
C. Sartori: *Bibliografia della Musica Strumentale Italiana.*

RECORDS

ALBINONI: *Sonata in G Minor*. DECCA 9572 (BRUNSWICK AXTL 1004).

ARIOSTI: *Lesson V.* DECCA ARC 3008 (DGG AMP 14024).

BARSANTI: *Concerti Grossi*. OISEAU-LYRE OL 50008.

CORELLI: *Concerti Grossi, Op. 6.* VOX PL 7893.

LEO: *Concerto in D.* ANGEL 35254 (COLUMBIA 33 CX 1276).

LOCATELLI: *Concerto Grosso*. WESTMINSTER WL 5030.

MANFREDINI: *Concerto Grosso*. DUCRETET-THOMSON EL 93042.

TARTINI: *Concerto in F.* ANGEL 35255 (COLUMBIA 33 CX 1277).

VIVALDI: *Concerti for Orchestra*. OISEAU-LYRE OL 50073. *L'Estro Armonico, Op. 3.* VOX PL 7423 (E). *La Tempesta di Mare, etc.* HMV ALP 1439.

25

Denis Stevens

THE ITALIAN VIOLIN SCHOOL

NOBODY knows for certain who invented the violin, or where it was invented, but the earliest days of the instrument and its music have been associated with Italy. There have been many romantic, and almost certainly inaccurate, ways of accounting for this; some saying that the best kind of wood for violins was found only in Italy, others saying that Italian makers alone held the secret of the varnish which was applied to the body and neck of the instrument after its multitude of parts had been glued together and allowed to dry. It is not impossible that the climate of certain Italian towns, in particular Cremona, was especially suitable for the process of careful drying.

The violin is—or should be—a perfect marriage of two kinds of beauty: beauty of form and beauty of tone. In the hands of a master, a violin can be the most eloquent and expressive of all instruments, at the same time the most brilliant and the most soulful. In spite of its range of effects, the violin is above all an instrument that sings, and so the Italian people gained a reputation not only for making violins, but for composing violin music. The instrument was developed steadily throughout the sixteenth century, though it did not have an immediate success because it was less suited to playing the music then popular. Music and instruments are inseparably bound together: the development and cultivation of the one will lead to new ideas for the other.

Later on the harpsichord held out against the piano in the same way that the viol held out against the violin. When we hear sixteenth-century consort music played on modern stringed instruments, somehow the sounds are all wrong: polyphony needs evenness of tone and great suavity. Solo music, on the other hand, requires great brilliance and power of tone. The earliest violins, however, were not as brilliant and powerful as ours. A desire for greater brilliance led musicians to adopt higher and higher tuning pitches, and standard pitch has moved up a tone or even a tone and a half since the time of Bach. This has meant that many of the fine old violins have had to be altered by the substitution of thicker bass-bars, longer necks, and tighter strings than they were ever meant to support. In some instances these changes have altered the whole character of the instruments, and the wonder is that they still sound so well. It is still possible to find some violins that have not been mutilated in the interests of higher pitch and bigger tone, and on records we can hear one made orginally in 1793 and restored to its pristine form.

Corelli: *La Follia*. Decca ARC 3008 (DGG APM 14024).

Arcangelo Corelli (1653–1713) was one of the greatest of the seventeenth-century violinists and composers. Little is known of his early life. He travelled a good deal, and he was first attached to the court at Munich; he then went to Paris, but the brevity of his visit was said to be due to the jealousy of Lully. About 1685 Corelli returned to Italy, settling in Rome, where he enjoyed the favour and protection of Cardinal Ottoboni and composed music for the weekly concerts at the palace. He seems to have been a man of modest and amiable disposition. As a composer in the Italian style, Corelli had few rivals, and his sonatas for solo violin and continuo have enjoyed an almost constant vogue since the day of their first publication. Their variety and effectiveness is splendidly shown by Corelli's variations on the old ground bass theme, *La Follia*.

Corelli: *La Follia*. Decca ARC 3008 (DGG APM 14024).

Corelli had many predecessors in the field of violin composition, and though few of the names are well known their role in the development of the Italian violin school was an important one. We have some evidence of their renown as early as 1610, not in Italy but in England, where a young composer named John Cooper thought fit to change his name to Giovanni Coperario after a brief period of study in Italy. Some of his solo sonatas and trio sonatas are excellent works, judged by any standards, and the same can be said for many of the sonatas and suites composed by the Italian Biagio Marini. Other noteworthy writers for the violin were Quagliatti, Farina, Merula, Fontana, and Uccellini, and it was due to them that the compass of the violin was extended. Uccellini makes use of some remarkably high notes which seem never to have appeared in violin music before; while Merula is often said to be the first to make extensive use of the G string.   Farina's contribution appears to be a frivolous one; the imitation on the violin of the mewing of cats, the barking of dogs, the cackling of hens, and the fifes and drums of the military.

During the second part of the century the two main centres of music printing and publishing were Venice and Bologna.   New firms joined old-established family businesses, and there were other publishers in Rome.   Without suggesting that this activity was of the type known as feverish, it is perfectly clear that composers had a good deal to contend with when once their manuscripts had been consigned to the printer.   Notational misprints, which are by no means infrequent in normal publications, often take on horrifying proportions in complex works involving *scordatura*, a method of tuning that was capable of extending the technical possibilities of string instruments.   Rests are often miscounted and misprinted, and since no scores were available, the musicians had to do the best they could with the part-books, beginning a bar earlier or later until the result seemed to fit reasonably well.

All this, however, was part of the game, and musicians were usually good enough to make up for any defects in the material they had to use.   It was owing to the outstanding richness of the vein that the pure gold of Corelli's workmanship eventually came to light.   Without the lesser masters, the greater men would never have achieved the success that they did.   Giuseppe Torelli —as far as the history books are concerned—is a lesser master when compared with Corelli, but there is more than a mere spark of genius in the way he uses two solo violins in his concerto for Christmas Eve.

Torelli: *Concerto in G minor* (*Grave/Vivace*).   DECCA 9649.

Torelli went to Bologna from Verona and settled down to a life of teaching and playing.   Several of his most important published works have survived, and many unpublished ones are preserved in the archives of the Collegiate Church of San Petronio in Bologna, where he was an instrumentalist.   His concertos influenced those of Vivaldi, as much in form as in texture, and eventually this influence was felt by J. S. Bach, who copied down many concertos by Italian masters, rearranging them and reworking them as he thought fit.

Another lesser master who is gradually coming into his own is Tomasso Albinoni. He was primarily a dramatic composer, and it is said that he wrote more than forty operas. Nowadays it is his violin music that attracts the attention of scholars and performers. Even if the writing for the solo violin does not match Torelli and Vivaldi at their most brilliant, it is nevertheless finely turned and idiomatically set forth.

Albinoni: *Violin Concerto No. 7 in D.* Decca 9598 (Brunswick AXTL 1023).

Like Torelli and Vivaldi, Albinoni also served as source material for Bach's inquiring mind. Spitta tells us that Bach 'must have had an especial liking for Albinoni's compositions. Even in his later years he was accustomed to use Albinoni's bass parts for practice in figured bass.' Vivaldi, however, often composed so quickly that he rarely troubled to figure the bass at all. Once he added a few figures to the bass part with the remark: 'These are for the dimwits.'

Strange and improbable stories still surround the name of Antonio Vivaldi, and they at least point to the fact that he was a very remarkable and colourful personality. Just as Corelli had his orchestra in Rome, so Vivaldi had his at Venice, at the *Ospedale della Pietà*, a home for waifs and strays. An English traveller who visited Venice in 1720 affirms that 'Every Sunday and Holiday there is a performance of music in the chapels of these hospitals, vocal and instrumental, performed by the young women of the place: who are set in a gallery above, and . . . are hid from any distinct view of those below, by a lattice of ironwork. The organ parts, as well as those of other instruments, are all performed by the young women.'

Not all of Vivaldi's two hundred or so violin concertos date from his Venetian period; some were composed when he served the princely courts of Mantua and Vienna. But the brilliant young violinists of the *Pietà* must have inspired Vivaldi to combine grace and purity with an ample measure of display. Vivaldi had an outlook upon violin playing which united all the common-sense things that the violin, by its very nature, was most capable of expressing. He was an Italian, and singing was in his veins. For him the four strings of the violin were soprano, contralto, tenor, and bass; each had its characteristic timbre, each had its own range of artistic possibilities. Equal in importance to the solo part in Vivaldi's estimation was the accompanying body of strings which, together with the continuo instruments, made up the orchestral part in his larger concertos. The orchestral accompaniment to a solo concerto called for careful planning on the composer's part. Vivaldi ensured variety of colour by many different means, not the least of which was the implied use of two keyboard instruments; a large harpsichord or chamber organ would be used for the full passages, and a small harpsichord for the solos.

Vivaldi's best known work, both in the eighteenth century and now, is *The Four Seasons*, a series of four descriptive concertos which constitute the first third of his Opus 8. Each concerto is prefixed by a poem, describing the general character and events of spring, summer, autumn, and winter. Vivaldi illustrates the poems by primarily musical descriptive passages, and not (as was the case with Farina) the distortion of musical elements to make for a poor copy of nature.

Vivaldi: *The Four Seasons*. VICTOR LHMV 26 (HMV ALP 1234).

Many Italian composers for the violin attempted to emulate Vivaldi, but few succeeded. The one way ahead lay in a complete re-evaluation of technical problems, even to the extent of altering the violin bow and so changing the tone of the instrument. Guiseppe Tartini (1692–1770) made various experiments of this nature, and his school of violin playing at Padua was perhaps the last of the really great Italian schools. His name is inseparably connected with a sonata that is not really one of his best works: the *Devil's Trill*. It is in his sonata in G minor, sometimes called *Didone Abbandonata* (*Dido Forsaken*) that we hear the swan-song of the great Italian.

Tartini: *Sonata in G Minor; 'Didone Abbandonata.'* ENGLISH DECCA LX 3137.

APPENDIX
BOOKS

M. PINCHERLE: *Corelli.*
D. B. BOYDEN: *Francesco Geminiani: The Art of Playing on the Violin.*
R. GIAZOTTO: *Tommaso Albinoni.*

RECORDS

CORELLI: *Violin Sonatas.* ALLEGRO ALX 109.
PERGOLESI: *Sonata for Violin and Strings, etc.* ANGEL 3538–B (COLUMBIA 33 CX 1307).
TARTINI: *Violin Concerto in E.* DECCA 9572 (BRUNSWICK AXTL 1004).

26

A. K. Holland

PURCELL AND ENGLISH SEVENTEENTH-CENTURY MUSIC

THE English are said to be conservative in their artistic tastes and it has even been unkindly suggested that they usually begin to get enthusiastic about new things at the moment when other countries are about to give them up. Some of the things which were most characteristic of English music in the seventeenth century began to take shape in the sixteenth, for example the formation of a self-contained instrumental style. Roughly, the period we are concerned with may be divided into three phases: the post-Elizabethan, the Commonwealth or Puritan phase, and the Restoration. This last is much the most important for our purpose, for it was Purcell's own period. His dates are 1659–95.

Now the music of the seventeenth century was everywhere influenced by the example of Italy, that 'Great Academy' of artistic teaching since the Renaissance. It was from Italy that the chief innovations of the period came: the invention of what came to be known as opera, the development of the cantata for solo voice or chorus with instrumental accompaniment, and the growth of self-contained instrumental music. But the English were conservative and they proceeded slowly, though not more so than other countries such as France and Germany. They had their own instrumental music, those *fantazias* or Fancies, as they called them, for the viols which, incidentally, were not primitive violins but different instruments tuned and strung differently. Enormous quantities of music were written for these instruments in the first quarter of the century and they lingered on in England long after they had practically been given up elsewhere. As we shall hear, Purcell composed some of the very latest examples, though whether for viols or violins is not quite certain, for by his time the violin, as they said, had largely put the viol out!

Purcell: *Fantasias for Strings*. DECCA ARC 3007 (DGG APM 14027).

166

We must remember that in England the seventeenth century was a period of great political and religious upheaval. The Puritans have often been blamed for destroying the English musical tradition, but in point of fact the Puritans were not in the least hostile to music as such. They were opposed to elaborate church music, and there is plenty of evidence that the extremists carried their hatred of church music to the lengths of destroying a number of church organs and music books. On the other hand most of the leading Puritans were musically minded. Cromwell had an organ set up at Hampton Court—he had borrowed it (shall we say ?) from one of the Oxford Colleges. And he ran State concerts and entertained musicians. Music publishing made its first great strides during the period, and many famous collections such as Playford's *English Dancing Master* appeared on the scene. Roger North, the old chronicler of the times, tells us that there was a great deal of amateur practice in country houses. Not exactly a picture of a country bereft of all musical activity!

At the same time there is no doubt that Puritanism brought about a great rift in the minds of Englishmen, a cleavage expressed not merely in the violence of the Civil War, but in the way of thinking about life and art. The most significant change of the Commonwealth period was the steady secularization of music and the growth of the professional spirit. Driven out of their posts in the church and deprived of the patronage of the Royal Chapel, musicians took to teaching and to giving public concerts. Actually, we hear of public concerts for the first time during the Commonwealth period. It was during this period also that the first English operas began to appear uneasily upon the stage, careful as they had to be to avoid the imputation of being stage plays, which were forbidden.

The new Italian style of singing which took the form of recitative, the declamatory style which formed the basis of the early Italian operas, had been slowly percolating into England through the medium of the most characteristic English form of entertainment, the Court Masque.

The masque was an aristocratic entertainment, consisting of poetry, allegory, song, dialogue, dancing, and, above all, splendid and costly scenery. In fact, the English addiction to masques and masquerades probably explains why opera as the Italians understood it was slow in making headway here. We have a sort of transitional stage in Shirley's masque of *Cupid and Death* with music by Matthew Locke and Christopher Gibbons which shows music beginning to take a major role; and in Blow's *Venus and Adonis*, although it is still called a masque, we have actually a small chamber opera of which every word is sung. The importance of Blow's work lies in the fact that it seems to have been the model on which Purcell's only real opera, *Dido and Aeneas*, was based.

John Blow: *Venus and Adonis*. OISEAU-LYRE OL 50004.

We are now in a position to approach Purcell more directly. Next to the recitative, the chief formal innovation of the period is the development of a new type of concerted music. The old fantasies treated each of the parts as of equal importance. The parts imitated each other in the manner of a fugue but none took precedence. Purcell's *fantazias* were written in his twenty-first year. It is in the first set of sonatas two years later that he makes open acknowledgment to Italian influences. These are written for two violins, bass viol, and harpsichord. There is still a good deal of independent part-writing, but the tendency is for the keyboard instrument to assert harmonic rights, and with that there is a much more clearly defined sense of key. The movements, four or more in number, alternating between slow and quick, usually contain a movement called *Canzona* in the fugal style. Purcell's sonatas belong to the so-called *chiesa*, or church, type, by reason of their more serious nature, as compared with the *sonata da camera*, or chamber sonata, which consisted of dance movements and ultimately crystallized in the suite, whereas the church type was the forerunner of the modern sonata. They were none the less secular in tendency for all their gravity and a certain clinging to the older methods of composing concerted music.

Purcell: *Trio Sonatas*. PERIOD 572 (alt. ARGO RG 84–5).

These were the things that Purcell wrote presumably for private use rather than public performance. But as the leading composer of his age, his main work lay in other directions. He grew up under King Charles II. His father and his uncle were both gentlemen of the Chapel Royal, that is, singers in the King's private chapel. He quickly showed signs of precociousness, began composing at an early age and entered the Chapel choir. Later on, when his voice broke, he became assistant to the tuner of the King's wind-instruments, a very valuable training for a boy of his talent. Purcell's voice, by the way, turned into that of a high counter-tenor or male alto and we have records of his ability as a singer and of what were called the 'incredible graces' that he introduced into his singing. A great deal of Purcell's more spectacular vocal writing was intended for this particular voice.

Purcell: *Music for a while.* HMV C 3890 (78 r.p.m.).

Purcell's next post was that of organ-tuner at Westminster Abbey, where he came under the influence of the great Dr Blow, and when Blow retired Purcell succeeded him as organist at the age of twenty. From then on all paths were open to him.

Charles II had returned from France with a taste for everything French. He is said to have detested the old English music and those solemn fantasies which had left their mark on Purcell. His band of violins played in the Royal Chapel when he attended service, and the type of anthem he encouraged consisted of long instrumental passages and 'verses,' that is, interludes of a declamatory nature for one or more voices. These 'verse' anthems, of which Purcell composed many, besides the so-called 'full' anthems in the more traditional style, were an excellent training for an all-round composer with duties as Court Musician. Almost every year Purcell produced a Royal Ode. The words were often the merest doggerel written in a vein of adulation that we should nowadays regard as too much savouring of toadyism. But that was the convention of the time.

We know as little of his life or his politics as we know of Shakespeare's. That he was a convivial soul we must infer from the number of catches and rounds, often with somewhat Rabelaisian words, which he wrote. At the same time we have a very clear account of his activities as a composer. He was one of the first, if not actually *the* first, to write odes for the annual celebration of the feast of St Cecilia. These celebrations seem to have been instituted in England in the year 1683 and Purcell wrote no less than three odes round about this time and others in later years. The form of the odes is very similar to that of the Chapel Royal anthems with its verses for alto, tenor, and bass, its full choruses and instrumental interludes. The ode for 1692, *Hail, Bright Cecilia*, is one of his finest, and the poem is not as flat-footed as some of the verses Purcell was forced to accept for royal occasions.

G

Conventional it may be, but it is rich in the kind of verbal images that Purcell loved to illustrate; not merely, as one would expect, images relating to the art of music, but images of motion, of contrast, and vivid suggestion which Purcell caught up and embodied in his favourite devices of repetition and word-painting. The chief solos are for counter-tenor and one—the fantastic aria *'Tis Nature's Voice*, with its incredible runs and florid passages—was sung by Purcell himself. The whole scheme of the work is finely planned in its balance and contrast of keys and the instrumentation for flutes, oboes, trumpets, strings, and drums with harpsichord and organ is in his most brilliant style.

The chorus, *Soul of the World*, is a great invocation to music, one of his most memorable pages. The words are by Dr Nicholas Brady, and if they are not great poetry, they are very serviceable verse.

> Soul of the World, inspired by thee
> The jarring seeds of matter did agree.
> Thou didst the scattered atoms bind
> Which by the laws of true proportion joined
> Made up of various parts one perfect harmony.

Purcell: *Ode for St Cecilia's Day* (1692): *Soul of the World*. HMV DB 21273 (78 r.p.m.).

Now before coming to consider the dramatic music which is Purcell's crowning glory and yet in another sense his gravest hostage to fortune, let us turn aside for a moment to consider what were the main characteristics of this art, this baroque art, which he practised. Baroque is a term, borrowed from architecture, which has been applied to the whole period of which the beginnings were marked by the Florentine operas, the middle by the age of Lully and Purcell, and the culmination by the art of Bach. It denotes, in very general terms, the use of florid ornament, motives of marked and sometimes exaggerated contrast, discontinuity of treatment emphasized in music by sectional construction and key contrast, emphatic changes of mood, tempo, metre, and texture (for instance, chordal passages contrasted with others of contrapuntal part-writing), and generally a certain restless use of decoration. It is not in its application a term of reproach, but is intended, like the word Gothic in other connections, to represent a definite style and phase in the history of music.

It is clear that the first reaction that ensued after the Puritan regime had collapsed and the monarchy had been restored was in the direction of theatrical shows. The stage directions of some of these musical entertainments can still fill us with amazement, with their flying witches, gods and goddesses descending in a machine (or car) drawn by peacocks, their ornate columns, their rocks and clouds, their painted backcloths, and all the apparatus of pantomime, only more so. They called it opera, though in fact it was a mixture of drama, singing, and dancing in which the tradition of the spoken play was employed to produce something that was supposed to resemble the Italian model. The English prejudice against works that were wholly sung kept the result from being opera in the genuine sense. Another feature of these semi-operas is that the principal characters do not sing, and the principal singers do not speak. The English tradition of reserving music for scenes of ritual, magic, or the supernatural descended from Shakespeare's time. It explains the numerous temple scenes, incantation scenes, the witches, and the deities to be found in Purcell's works. The other more or less consistent element is the pastoral scenes.

Dryden was associated with Purcell in one of his finest works for the stage, *King Arthur*. It is a very complicated mixture of legend and fantasy all designed to build up a great patriotic spectacle in praise of England. An even more fantastic hotch-potch was *The Fairy Queen*, which is an adaptation of Shakespeare's *Midsummer Night's Dream*. It was one of the most lavish productions of its time. It follows Shakespeare more or less, but although the music is more extensive than in most of Purcell's stage works he set no single line of Shakespeare. Here too the most extended music belongs to the masques which occur at the end of the acts. Titania summons a fairy-masque for the entertainment of Bottom, there is a masque of the Four Seasons, and finally a Masque of Hymen for the lovers which includes for no reason at all a Chinese scene in which various dances are executed by Chinamen, and six monkeys perform a comic dance. In short it is just a pantomime with Shakespeare as a pretext.

Purcell: *The Fairy Queen (excerpts)*. OISEAU-LYRE OL 50029 or ALLEGRO 3077.

Finally we come to the work by which Purcell will be remembered as long as music lives. Every schoolgirl has heard of *Dido and Aeneas* or at least every schoolgirl ought to have done, because

it was written for a girls' school and for girls to perform.   It is
Purcell's one and only real opera.   It plays for little more than
an hour, but it is a true masterpiece of music drama.   Of course
we have the usual Restoration witches to give colour to the scene
and a chance for magic incantation.   There is a hunting scene, a
thunderstorm, a racy quayside scene, and, finally, Dido sings the
great Lament which is one of the things that time cannot stale.
It is based on the device in which Purcell excelled and of which
he made so light, as if it were an easy thing for anyone to do—
namely, the recurrent or ground bass.   Dido dies of a broken
heart and a chorus rounds off the work.   The short recitative
which introduces the aria has been called the most wonderful in
the English language and German critics have described the whole
work as 'Shakespearian' though nothing is less Shakespearian
than the text of the poet, Nahum Tate.   The real poet, the real
Shakespeare, is Purcell.

Purcell: *Dido and Aeneas*.   VICTOR LHMV 1007 (HMV ALP 1026).

APPENDIX

BOOKS

GERALD R. HAYES: *Musical Instruments and their Music 1500–1750*,
 Vols. I and II.
E. H. MEYER: *English Chamber Music*.
E. J. DENT: *Foundations of English Opera*.
ROGER NORTH: *The Musical Grammarian*.
J. A. WESTRUP: *Purcell*.
H. CART DE LAFONTAINE: *The King's Musick*.
H. C. COLLES: *Voice and Verse*.

RECORDS

PURCELL: *Come Ye Sons of Art*.   OISEAU-LYRE OL 53004.   *Harpsichord
 Suites*.   OISEAU-LYRE OL 50011.   *Three Divine Hymns*.   HALL-
 MARK RS 1.   *Instrumental and Vocal Pieces*.   ESOTERIC 519 and 535.
 Vocal Music.   DGG AMP 14059.
VARIOUS: *String Music of Purcell, Gibbons, and Locke*.   BARTÓK 913.
 Music of Purcell, Jenkins, and Locke.   BACH GUILD 547.

Church works by Purcell and his contemporaries are included in the
four series of 78 r.p.m. records issued by English Columbia under the
title *English Church Music*.

27

H. Wiley Hitchcock

THE FRENCH SCHOOL:
LULLY AND CHARPENTIER

SELDOM has a nation's art been so closely identified with politics as was the music of seventeenth-century France. The two great French kings of the era were both vitally interested in music; Louis XIII was actually a composer of sorts, and the deep personal concern for music of Louis XIV was evidenced in numberless ways in the music written for his court. At Versailles there were no less than eight distinct musical groups permanently employed by the Sun King. Music of every imaginable sort was to be heard: opera, ballet, hunting music, mealtime concerts, music for *soirées* and dances, chamber music for the Sunday concerts, and church music for the royal chapel.

The history of seventeenth-century French music is essentially the history of music at court. The composer who could gain the ear of the king wielded immense power over the fortunes of other composers. He could force another composer into types of music not of his own choosing. He could prevent other composers from studying where they wished. He could monopolize whole areas of the musical life of France.

Politics affected music in another way too. An important power behind the throne was the Italian Mazarin, and, in a conscious effort to persuade French taste to the pleasures of Italian music, Mazarin imported musicians, set-designers, and whole opera companies from Italy. Immediately factions hostile to Mazarin politically aligned themselves against Italian music as well— specifically against the novel Italian vocal style of the opera. For almost a century arguments raged over whether the French should try to create an opera in imitation of the Italians, or whether French music should not be altogether a different thing from Italian music.

Two great composers whose works reflected the divided opinion of the French on the relative merits of the French and Italian styles were Jean-Baptiste Lully and Marc-Antoine Charpentier. During their lifetimes—and they were exact contemporaries—Lully had all the chips on his side of the table.   Shrewd, well-versed in the devious arts of courtly intrigue, he wielded an incalculable influence on the trends and emphases of music at court. Lully was Italian by birth, but he realized that the anti-Italian sentiment of a large part of the court could be parleyed into personal success for him.   He officially changed the Italian form of his name; he parodied the Italian vocal style in some works; and he prevented the young composer Desmarets from going to Italy to study.   His talent as a conductor was so obvious that he was able to persuade the king to give him an orchestra of his own: it was called 'the little violins,' to distinguish it from the famous band of 'twenty-four violins of the king,' established under Louis XIII as the first permanent orchestra in history.

For more than half a century ballet had been the most popular kind of musical entertainment on the grand scale that the court had known.   And so long as ballet remained popular, Lully wrote ballets.   New triumphs for him came when he joined forces with the respected and witty Molière; together, they created the so-called comedy-ballet.   The moment it seemed that French opera might appeal to the king and the court circle, Lully contrived to acquire a monopoly over it.   In 1673 he produced his first opera, or as he called it, 'lyric tragedy,' with libretto by Philippe Quinault.   According to the terms of the royal privilege which gave Lully sole charge of opera in Paris, it was impossible for anyone else to mount a musical drama there.

From 1673 until his death in 1687, Lully and Quinault produced about one new opera every year.   Almost single-handed Lully created French opera, defined its nature, and gave later composers models that were followed for generations.   He was a clever man and a good musician.   He realized that the French had the best ballet in Europe and the greatest love for it.   And so he made sure to include in his operas sections that would grant Parisians some of the same pleasures they had come to expect from the ballet; feasts for the eye and ear quite apart from the drama itself. For these ballet-scenes, and for gigantic choral episodes accompanied by full orchestra, Lully wrote some of his most powerful music, such as the big chaconne from *Cadmus and Hermione* of 1673.

Lully: *Chaconne: Cadmus et Hermione*. ANTHOLOGIE SONORE AS 114 (78 r.p.m.).

It has been said that the pomp and brilliance of the French court are perfectly reflected in the overtures to Lully's operas. Certainly the opening measures are a 'kingly' music—properly dignified, solemn, and (let us admit) a bit pompous. And certainly the dance section that follows is as carefully designed and as stylized as the gardens of Versailles; and the pseudo-counterpoint in which the dance rhythms are presented is as pretentious—and perhaps as hollow—as the daily ritual attending the waking of the king. We must add, however, that the Lully overture became all the rage. The opening of Handel's *Messiah* is a Lullian overture; and so is the carefully named *French Overture* for harpsichord by J. S. Bach.

Lully: *Overture: Armide*. MASTERPIECES OF MUSIC BEFORE 1750. HAYDN SOCIETY HSL 2072.

Lully's approach to the subject-matter and to the musical style of his operas was both shrewd and wise. Not only did the French have the best ballet in Europe, they also had the best drama. It was the era of Corneille and Racine and of classical French tragedy at its best. Lully set out to make his operas essentially classical tragedies, intensified by music, but not distorted or obscured by it. The words of the drama were not to be made unintelligible by the music. The course of the drama was not to be interrupted by lengthy arias in the Italian manner, no matter how beautiful the music. It was obvious to Lully that the French were simply too rational-minded and too much oriented to drama itself to accept otherwise.

And so, after carefully studying the exaggerated style of declamation at the *Comédie française*, Lully intensified the texts given him by Quinault with just enough music to heighten the effect, and yet not enough to let the music itself claim all the attention. He cautioned that 'my recitative is made solely for speaking.' As for arias, they were few and hardly different in style from the recitative. They were most like the formal, unemotional court airs that had been heard off the stage in France for more than a century.

Perhaps one must be a little bit French to like Lully's airs.

Certainly they will seem somwhat monochromatic and lack-
lustre to persons who view opera in the Italian way—that is, as
essentially a 'concert in costume'—rather than in the French way,
as a musically intensified drama.

Lully: *Bois épais: Armide.*   COLUMBIA M 578 (78 r.p.m.).

During his lifetime, and even afterwards, Lully had things his
own way.   He ruthlessly eliminated other composers when they
threatened to compete for the favour of the king; he monopolized
the most spectacular of musical productions, the operas; he carefully altered his emphasis and his principles to fit the changing
tastes of his king.   At his death in 1687 the name Lully was
virtually equated with French music; many Frenchmen judged
the music of other composers by the degree to which it approxi-
mated Lully's style.

The composer whose very name bespoke bad music in some
circles was a representative of the pro-Italian, anti-Lully camp.
Marc-Antoine Charpentier, trained in Rome under the great
oratorio composer, Giacomo Carissimi, returned to Paris in the
1650's to find a musical dictator in full sway.   What a paradox!
The 'French' music of the Italian-born Lully was set against the
'Italian' music of the Parisian, Charpentier.   Charpentier turned
to the periphery of the court: the musical retinue of a wealthy and
pious noblewoman, the Duchesse de Guise.   For her he composed
numerous motets and cantatas in the Italian style and several small
oratorios.   He first came to the attention of a wider audience when
he wrote larger motets, oratorios, and sacred operas for the most
important Jesuit church in Paris and for the Jesuit college of
Clermont.

There is seldom a possibility of monotony in Charpentier's
vocal style, as there is in Lully's.   The Roman-trained Frenchman had learned well the lessons of Carissimi: that all music
deserves gracefully curved melodies; that church music can be as
dramatic and intense as opera; and that vocal music must be
interesting *as music* regardless of the importance of the text.   His
motet *Oculi omnium* is like a little moralistic drama.   A small
band of hungry supplicants call upon the Lord for help.   He
invites them to the heavenly table.   A chorus of angels, already
appeased by the Lord, sing His praises ecstatically.   For a time
the supplicants look on wistfully from a distance.   Finally,

however, they join the chorus and identify themselves with the blessed.

Charpentier: *Oculi omnium.*   HAYDN SOCIETY 2065.

A composer of these capabilities could hardly escape the notice of influential persons.   Indeed, after Lully violated an agreement with Molière and turned to writing operas, Molière chose Charpentier to collaborate in his comedy-ballets.   Unfortunately, the playwright died after *Le Malade imaginaire,* for which Charpentier wrote the songs and incidental music.   Charpentier produced no real *tragédie lyrique* until late in his life.   *Medea* was first presented in 1693, and even then the baleful shadow of Lully's influence prevented Charpentier from the real success he deserved.   As one contemporary put it, 'cabals of the envious and ignorant' hissed the opera into quick obscurity.

Charpentier, potentially a much greater composer than Lully, retired once again to the less conspicuous realm of sacred music. More than five hundred religious compositions came from his pen. Official and public recognition finally came in 1698, when he was past sixty.   He was appointed Master of Music of the *Sainte-Chapelle,* that Gothic palace of stained glass and carved stone on the Île de la Cité.   He had a choir of perhaps sixty voices, and the royal instrumentalists too were often at his disposal.   Some of his most brilliant and powerful compositions date from this period; huge oratorios, mighty motets and *Te Deums* for two or three choruses, soloists, and full orchestra, rich and colourful settings of the Mass.

Certainly one of his most successful works was a Mass to be sung at midnight on Christmas Eve.   To the solemn words of the Mass he set music of skipping jubilance.   As French organists had done before him, Charpentier based most of this Christmas music on old favourite French carols.   The gentle, solemn prayer of the *Agnus Dei* is set to tripping minuet rhythms, based on the carol *At midnight an alarm was given.*

Charpentier: *Midnight Mass.*   WESTMINSTER WL 5287 (DUCRETET-THOMSON EL 93006).

By the turn of the eighteenth century the controversy of French versus Italian musical style had died down.   French composers had begun to write music in forms long popular with the more progressive Italians.   One such form was the *cantata*—known in

*G

Italy for almost a century, but introduced into France only in the era of Charpentier. If the French opera reflected the grandiloquence and sober stylization of court life under the Sun King, the cantata reflected quite another aspect of French manners. Basically the cantata is a tiny work of dramatic music. In a solo cantata one singer sings both the narrative passages and the monologues or dialogue passages. There is no real action and cantatas are never staged. Composers like André Campra treated the cantata as an opportunity to write charming, if trifling, music on pastoral themes. The traditional delight of French composers in almost pictorial representation of the pleasures of nature is often displayed in these works. 'Nature,' it need hardly be said, was *always* mild; the same Nature that the courtiers enjoyed amid the plane-trees and the thickets of the Versailles gardens—far enough from the palace to let them imagine they were living the simple, natural life; close enough to it that they still felt secure and sheltered.

Campra's solo cantata, *The Butterfly*, is for tenor voice with flute, violin, cello, and harpsichord accompaniment. 'Precious' is certainly the word for the text. The first part is sung in declamatory style, and an *air* follows. Whenever the words 'je vole'— 'I fly'—appear, Campra literally makes the words 'fly' in long coloraturas up and down.

Campra: *Cantata: Le Papillon*. ANTHOLOGIE SONORE AS 96 (78 r.p.m.).

The cantata by Campra tells how French artistic taste was changing at the beginning of the eighteenth century. A new delight in sheer 'prettiness,' in decorative details, rather than profundity or complexity, is obvious. The impending rococo style of the era of Louis XV is already apparent. The age of the rather frigid splendour of Lully's music and of the warm but sober brilliance of Charpentier's music was past. French music was approaching a new era—that of Couperin and Rameau.

(APPENDIX: *See* page 185.)

28

H. Wiley Hitchcock

THE FRENCH SCHOOL:
COUPERIN AND RAMEAU

THE last twenty years of the reign of Louis XIV were nowhere nearly so splendid as the earlier years. The ageing king grew melancholy and increasingly pious. Thus the greatest composer of the court circle did not follow Lully in composing ballets and operas. François Couperin was called upon to write intimate, quiet music—music designed perhaps more to soothe than to stimulate, music to provide a harmonious background to courtly banquets, music to edify and inspire within the arched and vaulted walls of the Versailles chapel.

François Couperin was born on 10th November 1668, the only child of a church organist and violinist in the king's band. Only eleven when his father died, Couperin succeeded him as organist of the church of St Gervais. In 1693 he became organist of the Chapel Royal at Versailles. By 1710 he was already known as 'Couperin le grand,' both because of his excellence as a performer and composer and because there were a confusing number of other past and present Couperins who were also musicians.

Not only did Couperin write church music and play the organ at St Gervais and Versailles, he was also a favourite harpsichordist of the court circle during the regency of the young Louis XV, and he directed the chamber music concerts that took place almost every Sunday at court. After an uncomplicated, essentially serene and successful life, Couperin died in 1733. Unlike Marc-Antoine Charpentier, he was by no means unknown outside France; nor was he forgotten after his death. Bach knew his music well: in fact, the great Saxon organist and the great Parisian keyboard player had a long correspondence. Bach copied out some of Couperin's harpsichord music, and Couperin's style is reflected in some of Bach's most lovely keyboard music.

The 'musical world' created by Couperin seems to reflect perfectly—in microcosmic form, to be sure—the *real* world from which it sprang. First of all, his music is completely French in spirit. In common with other French music and art from the twelfth century to the twentieth, it is sophisticated, witty, brilliant but not ponderous, often humorous, translucent. It is deceptively simple and clear. It is frequently terse, epigrammatic, understated. All these adjectives might apply to other great French artists—to La Fontaine, for example. Couperin knew the works of La Fontaine well, and he set to music one of his poems, called *Epitaph for a Lazy Man*.

> John came and went without a penny's gain;
> Interest and principal went sliding down the drain,
> For he considered worldly goods a matter for disdain.
> Using up his time for John was no great strain:
> Two halves he made of it, and used to make a test
> Of sleeping one half, of resting all the rest.

Couperin sets this as a duet—partly, perhaps, so that he can make a musical pun at the words 'Deux parts en fit' ('Two halves he made of it') by omitting the accompaniment and letting the two voices represent the two divisions of the lazy man's time. The spirit of the music is so artless that we hardly realize that it is strictly contrapuntal almost throughout.

Couperin: *Epitaphe d'un paresseux*.   Vox PL 6380.

If Couperin could mirror in his music the sophisticated artlessness of La Fontaine, he could also find inspiration in the sights and sounds of a bustling Paris: soldiers marching through the streets, birds twittering in the gardens of the Louvre, milkmaids on their daily rounds, strolling players, gipsies, and dancing bears, the Italian comedians. It is especially in his harpsichord music that Couperin captured these and virtually every other phase of the society of his time. But Couperin was no second-rate composer-naturalist, content to rely on pictorialism to make his point. We need not know the titles or the source of the inspiration to enjoy the *clavecin* music. Such knowledge can sometimes be fascinating, though, especially if it can help illuminate the range of Couperin's experience and interest and point up his wit and humour.

We may take as an example the rather large work which is the high light of the eleventh suite for harpsichord, first published in 1717. The original title reads: *The Record of the Grand and Ancient Order of* . . . but the last word is unreadable; it is spelt *Mxnxstrandxsx*. To Couperin's audience this puzzle was easily solved; the word was *Ménestrandise*. This was the name of the musicians' guild, essentially a trade union of unskilled workers, which had tried several times to create 'closed shop' regulations in France. The guild hoped to force the musicians of the court and the aristocracy to join the more plebeian players of dance and tavern music in paying annual dues. Couperin joined several other composers in protesting to the king, and this composition may have been one of Couperin's musical contributions to the propaganda war.

Couperin called the five parts of the work 'acts,' and it is a little drama. *Act I : The Officers and the Jury of Union Members.* They apparently stride into the hearing-room. The atmosphere is somewhat solemn, but not without a certain ludicrous tinge. Couperin's music combines the sobriety of the seventeenth-century harpsichord composers with the *graces* (as trills and other ornaments were suggestively called) of the early eighteenth century.

Act II presents the complaints of the barrel-organ players and the musical beggars. They apparently know only one tune. The hurdy-gurdy men play it slowly; the beggars pep it up a bit. But the same tired old bass drones on and on.

Act III. On to the scene come the jugglers, tumblers, and clowns, accompanied by trained bears and monkeys. As befits their trade, the tired little tune is taken at breakneck speed, leaping and cavorting in a diabolical dance.

Act IV. Couperin portrays *les invalides*, worn-out popular minstrels, crippled in the service of their guild. The music sounds bitterly sympathetic.

Act V. Disruption and Rout of the Whole Troupe, caused by Drunkards, Monkeys, and Bears. Amid the confusion and the comic fife-and-drum effects, we still seem to hear the little popular tune. And we come to realize that there are subtle interrelationships between the individual movements that unify the entire work.

Couperin: *Les Fastes de la grande et ancienne Ménestrandise.* LYRI-CHORD LL 12 or MGM E 538 (alt. OISEAU-LYRE OL 50060).

We have all seen examples of the French pastoral tradition of the seventeenth and eighteenth centuries in the paintings and poems of the period. The 'return to nature' philosophy of Rousseau was a late expression of the pastoral convention, as was Marie Antoinette's *Le Hameau*, that charming imitation of a peasant cottage, in which the court ladies played at the 'simple life' on the edge of the Versailles gardens. Couperin reflected the pastoral convention in several works, among them the exquisitely simple but artful love-song called *Musette* after the bagpipe-like background.

Couperin: *Musète*. Vox PL 6380.

At its best the art of Couperin sublimates subject-matter of outward simplicity, even ridiculousness, into 'something rich and strange.' This art is the musical parallel to Watteau's painting: trifling subjects are somehow lent great gravity. Compare the two artists' versions of Harlequin, traditionally the comic hero of the Italian comedy. Watteau's portrait of Gilles, called *Dans le goût burlesque*, is well known; Couperin's *Arlequine* for harpsichord has, I think, the same combination of half-comic simplicity and surprisingly sober, almost tragic effect.

Couperin: *L'Arlequine*. LYRICHORD LP 12 (alt. OISEAU-LYRE OL 50065).

By the time of Couperin's death in 1733, another man had acquired fame—or notoriety—in the French musical world: Jean-Philippe Rameau. A real intellectual, with a great interest in musical theory, Rameau had published in 1722 his *Treatise on Harmony*. Despite the fact that this ingenious work was to provide the foundations of musical science up to the twentieth century, it was awkwardly written and its author was misunderstood and found himself the target of bitter criticism from musicians and scientists throughout France. But more, and fiercer, controversy surged up when in 1733 Rameau produced his first opera, *Hippolyte et Aricie*. He was attacked as faithless to the Lully tradition of French opera. From our vantage point it seems like a tempest in a teapot; Rameau revered Lully above all French musicians, and certainly *Hippolyte* and more than twenty other operas show him to be very much in the main stream of French operatic tradition. Two facts must really have been at the base of the hostility towards the fifty-year-old genius. First, he never found a librettist to match his talents. Second, his operas were full of strange and daring instrumental effects. To us they are ravishing; to Rameau's contemporaries they seemed harsh, radical, and subversive—subversive in the sense that the orchestra seemed at times more important than the singers, or the text, or the drama itself. One of Rameau's listeners claimed that 'for three hours the musicians have not even the time to sneeze.' The closing air of *Hippolyte*, addressed to the nightingales of an enchanted forest by a shepherdess, may suggest Rameau's imaginative use of instruments.

Rameau: *Rossignols amoureux: Hippolyte et Aricie.* DECCA DL 9683 (BRUNSWICK AXTL 1053).

Besides serious operas, or lyric tragedies, Rameau also composed opera-ballets. This kind of work combines a maximum of ballet with a minimum of opera, a maximum of sheer visual spectacle with a minimum of plot. The most exotically colourful scenes and situations are strung loosely together in a series of so-called entrées. Unlike modern ballet, though, singers are utilized, as are large singing choruses.

The opera-ballet *The Festivities of Hebe*, first produced in 1739, opens with the appearance of various gods and goddesses who have gathered for a celebration in honour of Hebe, goddess of youth. The goddess of love announces that the festivities will take place on the banks of the Seine, and she and Hebe exhort the others to follow them to the river's edge. Amor sings the principal music of the duet alone at first. Then in a characteristic, utterly rationalistic way, Rameau goes on to compose a perfectly balanced 'rondeau with two couplets.' This simply means that the duet theme is heard three times; between its first and second statements, and between its second and third statements, are heard 'couplets,' or episodes, based on different musical material. Each couplet is for a single voice rather than duet, the tempo is slower, and the vocal style is much more declamatory. The whole piece is perfectly symmetrical, the duet opening and closing the passage and furnishing, moreover, a central axis. Thus are science and art intermingled in the precise musical thought of Rameau.

Rameau: *Volons sur les bordes de la Seine: Les Fêtes d'Hébé.* DECCA DL 9683 (BRUNSWICK AXTL 1053).

Rameau's main contributions to musical theory were in the field of harmony. He was preoccupied with different chords and with their interrelationships, and his concern with such matters

shows up frequently in his works.   One such example is the very
well-known harpsichord piece called *The Hen*.   If we allow ourselves to be concerned only with the theme—and it never changes
—we will come away from the work with little but a tired, bored
reaction.   The real musical point is rather the exploration of
various keys and harmonies; the same melody, in other words, is
seen from several different points of reference.   One difference
between Rameau and Couperin as harpsichord composers—and
between mid eighteenth-century and early eighteenth-century
musical thought in general—is this preoccupation with harmony
rather than with melody and counterpoint.

Rameau: *La poule*.   MGM E 538 (alt. Oiseau-Lyre OL 50082).

If any portion of Rameau's work is destined to live on through
changing eras, it is the music he wrote for the numerous ballet-
sequences of the operas.   The aesthetics of opera has changed so
completely since Rameau's time that there is little hope of reviving
his operas as such.   But as long as we have orchestras, and provided we have adventurous conductors, Rameau's orchestral music
will continue to attract and enchant; for example, two *entr'actes*,
rich in exotic guitar-effects and kaleidoscopic changes of instrumental colours, from an almost unknown opera, *Acanthe et
Céphise*.

Rameau: *Entr'actes: Acanthe et Céphise*.   Decca DL 9683 (Brunswick AXTL 1053).

Perhaps no better statement about Rameau's particular gifts,
and his position in musical history, can be found than that made
by Debussy, emphasizing his own roots in the specifically *French*
thought of Rameau:

We have . . . in Rameau's work a pure French tradition full of
charming and tender delicacy, well balanced, strictly declamatory in
recitative and without any affectation of German profundity or over-
emphasis or impatient explanation. . . .   We may regret that French
music should so long have followed a course treacherously leading away
from that clarity of expression, that terse and condensed form, which
is the peculiar and significant quality of the French genius.

APPENDIX
(CHAPTERS 27 and 28)

BOOKS

The only important work on French classic music, written in English is:
WILFRID MELLERS: *François Couperin and the French Classical Tradition*.
In French, the following are to be recommended:
HENRY PRUNIÈRES: *Lully*.
CLAUDE CRUSSARD: *Marc-Antoine Charpentier*.
PAUL-MARIE MASSON: *L'Opéra de Rameau*.

RECORDS

LULLY: *Operatic Arias*. LYRICHORD 16. *Miserere*. OISEAU-LYRE
OL 53003. *Ballet Music*. ANGEL 35255 (COLUMBIA 33 CX 1277).
Le Bourgeois Gentilhomme. ENGLISH DECCA LXT 5211–13. *Marches,
etc.* LONDON INTERNATIONAL TWV 91092.

CHARPENTIER: *Mass: Assumpta est Maria*. VOX PL 8440. Excerpts
from *Medée*. DECCA 9678 (BRUNSWICK AXTL 1049). *Magnificat,
etc.* HAYDN SOCIETY HSL 102.

COUPERIN: *Motets*. OISEAU-LYRE OL 50079. *Harpsichord Music*
(complete). OISEAU-LYRE OL 50052–67. *Concert Royal No. 3*.
OISEAU-LYRE OL 50031.

RAMEAU: *Cantatas*. LYRICHORD 44. *Hippolyte et Aricie*. OISEAU-
LYRE OL 50034. *Instrumental Music* (complete). OISEAU-LYRE OL
50080–4. *Harpsichord Music* (complete). WESTMINSTER WN 3303.
Two Suites for Haprsichord. NIXA WLP 5128.

29

Arthur Hutchings

NORTHERN EUROPE BEFORE BACH

I N my boyhood the small English town where I lived had its
German band of five players which played at cattle shows,
flower shows, harvest homes, municipal banquets, and civic
ceremonies. In later years, when I came to study music, I
found that in Germany itself these town bands, or *Stadtpfeiffer*,
existed in the period under study here. And they played on just
the same occasions, and at weddings and funerals too. They
were a relic of the medieval waits or minstrels, but the regular
combination of these particular instruments belonged especially
to Germany, and so did some of the music they played.

The *Stadtpfeiffer* were organized with typical German thorough-
ness; each player had apprentices, and they were expected to reach
a high technical standard before being recommended for a place
in the band of another city. That is why, later on, Bach could
write such difficult high trumpet parts for players who from boyhood had specialized in the upper register of the instrument called
the *clarino*. Bach could have secured such players in almost any
court orchestra or in the music loft of the principal church of any
thriving city. Because the *Stadtpfeiffer* could play the music of
Johann Petzold (or Pezel) so well in 1621, Bach could demand,
and get, the kind of trumpet playing he did in 1721 in the last
movement of his second Brandenburg Concerto.

(i) Pezel: *Gigue*. ANTHOLOGIE SONORE AS 8 (78 r.p.m.).
(ii) J. S. Bach: *Brandenburg Concerto, No. 2*. ENGLISH COLUMBIA
 LX 440 (78 r.p.m.) (alt. DECCA LX 3029).

Until the seventeenth century no *great* German music is
immediately associated with Germany, recognized as obviously
German. We think of such German-born composers as Isaac
and Gallus as belonging to the sixteenth-century Flemish school,
and we associate Hassler, of a later generation, with the sumptuous

Venice of Gabrieli. But the town band music was German *of* Germany, and we can notice two features of it which will be well worth tracing in far more ambitious German music. First, a four-square tune, characteristically German. Second, the treatment of that tune by German elaboration—the adding to the tune of counterparts or counterpoints which display certain devices. For instance, in an *intrada* by Pezel, the inversion of the tune half-way through the dance, a device found in some of Bach's gigues.

Pezel: *Intrada*.   ANTHOLOGIE SONORE AS 7 (78 r.p.m.).

Bach himself liked such a bluff, four-square melody; an example is the *quodlibet* at the end of the *Goldberg Variations*.   One or two melodies of much the same regular shape come in Mozart's German operas and again in the most German of all operas, Weber's *Der Freischütz*. They can be found in student songs and still heard in village beer gardens.

The second feature is the method of accompanying the melody, not with plain, regular chords but by lines with their own independent rhythms. One German who loved this process was Martin Luther, and he wrote in 1542: 'When music is polished by art, one sees with wonder the great wisdom of God; for while one voice takes a simple part, around it go three or four other parts, leaping and springing, and marvellously adorning the simple part, like a square dance in heaven.'   Luther is describing what he found in his favourite composer, Josquin des Prés, and it would have given him greater delight still to have heard his own countrymen putting counterpoint to the hymn tunes or chorales of his German Church. They also were simple tunes which gradually took on a square German shape.

We must never suppose that Luther wanted only congregational music. He believed that music was a foretaste of heaven, and that it was therefore (even as an entertainment) the most godly occupation people could have on earth.   The churches were to sound with the music of as many orchestral instruments and as many well-trained voices as could be provided, and even a congregational chorale might be treated as Michael Praetorius treats the epiphany hymn *How brightly shines the morning star*. He sets it with contrapuntal parts and, by contrast, with plain broad harmonies.

Praetorius: *How brightly shines the morning star*.   HISTORY OF MUSIC IN SOUND, VOL. IV.   VICTOR LM 6029 (HMV HMS 38, 78 r.p.m.).

We have seen how the town bands and the *Kantorei*—the establishment of voices and instruments of the Lutheran church gallery—have put a simple tune into relief by sounding it with elaborate counterparts. We must now examine the process in organ pieces. Germany had produced the most famous organs and organists of Europe long before Luther's day, and we may be sure that the Reformation organists practised the art of setting chorales with counterpoints. Naturally they studied the artifice where it was most brilliantly demonstrated, and they were drawn to two main training grounds. Some went to Venice, which was nearer Germany than Rome was, and more advanced musically too. But most of the organists went to study under Sweelinck, organist of the Old Church in Amsterdam.

Sweelinck was not only an organist; he was a renowned harpsichord player, a friend of Dr John Bull, and a prolific composer of secular part-songs and instrumental pieces, including fully developed fugues. But we may take an example of the kind of music that made men call him 'the maker of German organists.' It is a series of variations on a chorale, and it is very easy to follow because the chorale goes plainly on one keyboard, while a single line of counterpoint goes on another.

Sweelinck: *Chorale variations: Ach Gott, von Himmel*. HISTORY OF MUSIC IN SOUND, VOL. IV. VICTOR LM 6029 (HMV HMS 43, 78 r.p.m.).

Lutheran organists were expected to compose such pieces, not just as voluntaries, but as part of the service, so they often composed for solo organ pieces of similar design to those they composed for choir and orchestra. This organ music made wonderful progress in the three generations after Luther; that is, from Sweelinck, who died in the same year as Praetorius, 1621, up to the North German organists who were famous in Bach's boyhood—Reinken, Pachelbel, Böhm, and Buxtehude.

The greatest of them was undoubtedly Buxtehude, whose evening concerts were so famous that young Bach walked two hundred and fifty miles to hear them. Dietrich Buxtehude was a Dane, and he settled in the part of Germany nearest to Denmark. He was appointed to St Mary's Church in Lübeck, and he was nothing less than an outstanding genius of the organ. While his treatment of the Christmas carol *In dulci jubilo* sounds easy, it is a more elaborate piece than the Sweelinck chorale variations because

Buxtehude has a habit of altering the melody itself, which is in the topmost part.

> Buxtehude: *Chorale prelude: In dulci jubilo.* HISTORY OF MUSIC IN SOUND, VOL. VI. VICTOR LM 6031 (HMV HMS 61, 78 r.p.m.).

Beside Buxtehude's chorale prelude we should set one of Bach's superbly clever treatments of the same carol.   Bach also puts the melody in the topmost part, but he makes it go in canon; it follows in the tenor, which is played by the feet.   The left hand puts a bass below this pedal part which has the tune, and the left-hand bass is itself in canon with the alto.   So the whole piece is a texture of four parts, called a canon four-in-two; soprano and tenor the same melody chasing itself, bass and alto the same music chasing itself.

> Bach: *In dulci jubilo.* HISTORY OF MUSIC IN SOUND, VOL. VI. VICTOR LM 6031 (HMV HMS 61, 78 r.p.m.).

The greatest German musician of the century before Bach and Handel remained thoroughly German in his expression, despite his admiration of Italy and the ideas he imported from that country.   Heinrich Schütz was well-educated, gentle, dignified, of fine appearance and character, greatly beloved by other musicians.   He went to Venice twice for a long stay, and the prefaces and dedications of his works declare his admiration for his master there, Giovanni Gabrieli, and then for Monteverdi, who was at St Mark's when Schütz undertook his second journey to Italy. But Schütz was a thoroughly German musician long before Germany was a nation at all.

Our classics are the German classics, and their music has something in common which we do not find until Germany had found her musical voice.   We still do not always find it in Latin music. We cannot call this quality mysticism, for music can be mystical when it is clear, sunny, radiant, even entertaining.   But we are safe in saying that in the greatest German music there is a vein of individual sentiment which tells us something about the composer's philosophic outlook, a matter which the French or Italian artist often hides. German listeners regard a composer's personal communication with religious reverence, and because Schütz is one of the first German composers in whom we recognize Teutonic *Individualismus,* we put him first in the line of German classics.

One of his most impressive and individual pieces comes from the *Symphoniae Sacrae,* published in 1650.   It needs double choir,

six soloists, organ, and strings.   Schütz could have let the soloists
and the various instruments show off in turn; the Italians he
admired would certainly have done so.   But he always subordin-
ates the part to the whole, and he is here dealing with St Paul's
conversion in his own uniquely concentrated way.   He focuses
his expression upon one idea—the voice of conscience insisting,
penetrating, and echoing in the apostle's mind.   The words
'Saul, Saul, why persecutest thou me?' obsess the whole being
of St Paul in Schütz's expression.   The design of the piece is a
crescendo from the opening bass voice onwards.   It spreads and
reverberates with all the arts taught by the Italians until the final
echoes of the word 'Saul' are the last thing we hear.

  Schütz: *Saul, Saul*.   HISTORY OF MUSIC IN SOUND, VOL. V.   VIC-
    TOR LM 6030 (HMV HMS 53, 78 r.p.m.).

  Schütz represents the educated Lutheran, whom we may contrast with the type which went straight from the choir school to
apprenticeship in the organ loft.   Schütz was an organist, but he
left no pieces for the organ.   I think it is significant that he
composed at least one opera, *Dafne*, though we have not found a
copy; and it is also significant that he was concerned only with the
Dresden court and its chapel, not with parish music.   He occasionally uses the words of a chorale, but it is not his habit to use chorale
melodies at all.   His outlook is highly stylized and liturgical, and
his motets and settings of the Passion, and his love of the old
modes, are all part of his fondness for formality and austere
grandeur.

  Much of Schütz's music is to Latin words, despite the fact that
he set German as wonderfully as Purcell set English, and his music
seems as if it could serve the Roman rite as well as the Lutheran.
Some of the other seventeenth-century Lutheran music is unlike
most of the Protestant music with which we are most familiar.
There are settings of *Kyrie* and *Gloria* in Greek and Latin, called
Messen; there are Latin *Magnificats*, and brilliantly scored church
concertos and symphonies, or cantatas.   When no orchestra is
used, they are called motets, a word we associate with the Catholic
usage.   Lutheran music before Bach's death was very different
from Lutheran music of later times when the rationalist and pietist
movements had turned the orchestras out of the churches, turned
the choir schools into ordinary day schools, and reduced music
largely to hymns.   Before the pietist movement, the high point of

orthodox Lutheran worship was the most brilliant piece of music; and it was usually called the *Hauptmusik* (chief music or head music), the Concerto, or the *Stück* (*the* piece, *the* work).   Its rehearsal and performance was in itself an offering to God, and the composer had a considerable choice of words—scripture, or a paraphrase of scripture, or the words of a chorale, or verse and prose composed by a local writer.

Schütz nearly always chose a strictly liturgical or scriptural text, and this is one of the points which show a more refined, more sophisticated taste than that of the average parish cantor—even than of Bach himself.   We do not disparage Bach when we say that some of his music is naïve in expression, even when it is more masterly than any before or since.   Schütz's refined taste was unique.   Bach at the height of his powers was at his most florid and ebullient, and he took his words from writers whose models were opera libretti; they wanted church music to have the emotional appeal of opera.   Schütz commanded the range of emotional appeal—that was the fruit of his Italian journeys—but at the height of *his* powers he became deliberately reticent, economical, even austere.   He sometimes composed as if he renounced all means of expression except those used by Palestrina a whole century before him.   But his reticence suggests enormous suppressed power.

We may illustrate this supreme quality from his last works. *The Story of God's Birth*, usually called *The Christmas Story*, uses only just enough instruments to illuminate the scenes delicately, as on some early frescoes.

Schütz: *The Christmas Story*.   Oiseau-Lyre OL 50020.

The Christmas Story dates from 1664.   Two years later comes downright austerity.   For his settings of the Passion, Schütz dispensed with all instruments except the voice.   Even the recitative, without accompaniment, is less florid than most medieval narrative chant.   True, there are graphic touches—the shouts of the angry crowd, the crowing of the cock and Peter's bitter weeping, the last loud cry of Jesus from the Cross, but they are all toned down to produce an effect of awful intensity.

Schütz: *The Passion According to St Matthew*.   Renaissance X 49 (Nixa PLP 203).*

APPENDIX

Books

ADAM CARSE: *The Orchestra in the Eighteenth Century.*
MAX GRAF: *Composer and Critic.*
ROBERT M. STEVENSON: *Patterns of Protestant Church Music.*

Records

BÖHM: *Organ Music.*   HAYDN SOCIETY 3006 (DGG APM 14043).
BUXTEHUDE: *Organ Music.*   WESTMINSTER 18117/18149/18193/18221.
VARIOUS: *Organ pieces.*   PHILIPS ABL 3110/3066.   *Cantatas.*   VOX PL
   7330/7430/7620 (E) OVERTONE 6.
PACHELBEL and WALTHER: *Organ Music.*   OVERTONE 8.
PEZEL: *Brass Music.*   PERIOD 526 EMS 7.
South German Organ Music.   VOX DL 223.
SCHEIDT: *Tabulatura Nova.*   OVERTONE 3.
SCHÜTZ: *Funeral Music.*   DECCA ARC 3006 (DGG APM 14023) REB
   9.   *Seven Words from the Cross.*   VOX PL 6860 (E).   *Symphoniae
   Sacrae.*   WESTMINSTER 5043.
SWEELINCK: *Harpsichord Music.*   VOX PL 9270.

30

Arthur Hutchings

J. S. BACH

LONG after Bach's death, indeed after Beethoven's, a sober historian could have declared that Bach's influence upon music and western man was almost negligible. We can trace very few of his ways of musical thinking in his two most famous sons, Carl Philip Emanuel and Johann Christian, who were his most gifted pupils. Those other musicians who admired him in his lifetime, such as Gerber, Krebs, Agricola, Goldberg, Altnikol, and Kittel, can hardly be blamed for being poor missionaries. They were not rich and influential, and they were not in a position to sponsor publication and performance of music which most audiences found distasteful even after 1829. That was the year in which Mendelssohn gave his much altered and truncated performance of the *St Matthew Passion*—an event which is usually taken to mark the beginning of the Bach revival. I want to show how the resurrection of Bach's music depended upon its apparent death with the flesh of its creator; what fascinates us about his most characteristic expression is exactly what prevented it from fascinating any contemporary listeners unless they had been born and bred in the orthodox Lutheran culture of Bach's own district.

Books tell us that the Bachs had long been famous musicians before the birth of Johann Sebastian. So they were, but only in the rather unexciting country of Thuringia, which is some hundred miles broad and fifty miles long. The great Bach did not travel far beyond its borders, and neither did his fame, except as an organist. As a lad he walked north to hear Buxtehude, and he finally settled in Leipzig just over the border of Saxony; and then late in life he travelled farther east and north to Berlin. His reputation had gone that far because, as soon as he arrived, Frederick the Great wanted him to play and extemporize.

We do not in the least disparage Bach when we recognize his

work as the enrichment by study, and by sheer genius, of the solid but elaborate musical dialect of Thuringia and its organists. Handel could have recognized the genius and not just the dialect, because he came from the part of Saxony that just touches the Bach country, and had been trained in the sort of music that a Thuringian cantor was expected to compose and perform. A young German musician regarded appointment as a Cantor or *Kapellmeister* as the goal of his ambitions. The Cantor was director of music to a municipality and its churches; the *Kapellmeister* musical director to the establishment of a prince or nobleman, including his orchestra, opera-house, and chapel. A *Kapellmeister* was not only better paid and better dressed than a Cantor; he had far more chance of advertising his abilities. To be an eligible candidate for the post of *Kapellmeister* a musician had to travel—to Italy, to the opera-houses and to concerts like those given by Vivaldi with his huge orchestra in Venice. That is what Handel did. It is true that he risked going freelance, but he made the venture while he could fall safely back upon an appointment as *Kapellmeister*. To notice how Bach deliberately resigned a good post as *Kapellmeister* to become Cantor at Leipzig, and to examine his reasons for doing it is the most important part of this essay.

First we should compare Cantor's music with *Kapellmeister*'s; the polite, international, chiefly Italian style, and the north German church style. The style of the *Kapellmeister* and opera composer at its most mellifluous may be judged from the love duet from Act II of Handel's *Sosarme*.

Handel: *Duet: Sosarme Act II.*   OISEAU-LYRE OL 50093.

This music is easy on our ears, and it seeks no more than the enchantment of the ears. Handel's genius makes conventions glow with life and beauty; Bach's genius enriches and transcends by its sheer imagination the local organists' styles, having already absorbed all it needs from Italian and French music. Bach's duet, *Et in unum*, from the Mass in B minor will also be easy on our ears, but if our ears take it too easily they are going to miss a good deal.

Bach has reached that part of the Creed which deals with the doctrine called the Eternal Purpose. The words assert that Christ was begotten of God the Father before all ages, and that always

He must be regarded as *consubstantialis*, of one substance, or divine nature, with the Father. Hence the chain of phrases affirming belief in God *of* God, Light *of* Light, Very God *of* Very God. To illustrate this, Bach puts the voices into a free canon. The one melody common to the two voices represents the one Godhead common to the two Persons of the Holy Trinity so far acknowledged in the articles of the *Credo*; and in order that neither shall be regarded as the greater, the voices take turns to be leader and follower in the canon.

Bach: *Et in unum: Mass in B minor*. ANGEL 3500C or WESTMINSTER WAL 301 (COLUMBIA 33 CX 11213 or NIXA WLP 6301).

The marvel about this music is not just the devising of the canon, but its sheer facility and ease. We do not admire Bach just for his technical feats, but for the expressive significance with which he invests them, and the grace with which he crowns their demonstration. Canons are far harder to maintain gracefully than fugues; the difficulty is to keep the melody and the harmony interesting without stopping the follow-my-leader, and the difficulty increases, especially at changes of key, when the follower comes *soon* after the leader. Every third piece in the *Goldberg Variations* is a canon. In Number 18 the two upper parts maintain canon at the sixth, with the follower coming at the distance of a minim, a mere unit of the time signature. Number 19 is just a free invention, but if we did not know this, should we imagine the first piece to be any less free than the second?

Bach: *Goldberg Variations* (*Nos. 18 and 19*). VICTOR LM 1080 (HMV ALP 1139).

In the eighteenth century neither variation would have been thought easy on the ears, and this was not just the opinion of fools. Let us take a comment on Bach's music written by Johann Adolf Scheibe, Bach's junior by some twenty years. Scheibe had the advantage of a university education and foreign travel, and he edited one of the first musical magazines, *Der Critische Musikus*, which may be called *The Musician of Taste*. In the issue for 14th May 1737 appeared these words:

This gentleman [meaning Bach] is an extraordinary artist both on keyboard instruments and on the organ . . . we are astonished at his technique. We wonder how it is possible for him to move his fingers and his feet so fast without entangling them, or how he can cover the widest leaps without producing a single wrong note. This great man would be universally admired if he were more pleasing and did not banish naturalness from his composition by pedantic and intricate devices, by obscuring beauty with over-elaborate artifice.

His works are hard to perform because he expects singers and players to accomplish with their throats and instruments what he can bring off at the keyboard. That is, of course, impossible. All the ornaments are written out in full . . . the melody is unrecognizable. All the parts are made to strive with each other; all are equally important, so that it's impossible to pick out the principal part. In short, Bach is to music what Lohenstein is to poetry. With both of them one admires the laborious effort and the exceptional workmanship, vainly pursued because they do not conform to reason.

Some ardent admirers of Bach have called Scheibe's article an attack, but we have only to think of Swift or Pope to regard the article as perfectly calm and serious, and without venom. At Leipzig University Scheibe had come under the influence of the ideas of Boileau and the taste of the French academicians, with their watchwords—Reason, Nature, Clarity, Noble Simplicity. Scheibe was, too, a competent musician, and in a later issue of his paper he singled out one work of Bach for special and generous praise. Significantly enough that work was the *Italian Concerto*. Scheibe would hardly have known the music that Bach wrote as *Kapellmeister*, such as the Brandenburg Concertos. Admittedly, some of their slow movements display the elaborate counterpoint of Thuringian organists, and even when Bach is being simple and entertaining he cannot resist a canon—for instance, in the fourth movement of the First Brandenburg Concerto. But that minuet is surely as easy on the ear as most movements in *concerti grossi* of the times. And would Scheibe have thought the sunny finale to the Fourth Brandenburg Concerto to be at all pedantic or obscure, just because it is really a disguised fugue?

Bach: *Brandenburg Concertos*. DECCA LXT 5198–9.

Perhaps the Bach concerto movement which comes nearest to pure lyricism and clarity of an Italian kind is the slow movement of the Concerto for Two Violins. It is almost unweighted by what Scheibe's school of thought would have called excessive ornament and untasteful rivalry of voices.

Bach: *Concerto for two violins in D minor*. HMV DB 1718 (alt. HMV BLP 1046).

The very scoring and structure of each of the Brandenburg Concertos was humorously surprising, and they are one further proof that Bach *could* have become a famous *Kapellmeister*, or perhaps an opera composer of international fame—another Handel. At no period were his circumstances more happy than when he was *Kapellmeister* at Cöthen. He made good friends with his musical colleagues, and he served a prince and a court who were prepared to meet special demands rather than lose him. His salary was raised more than once.

Yet he deliberately left the friends, the salary, the good living accommodation, the honour, and the status. He became a Cantor, and the Leipzig Cantor was regarded by Lutherans as Anglicans regard the organist in one of their famous cathedrals; several fine musicians had preceded Bach in the post. He managed to bring up a large family, to give his sons the advanced education that he himself missed, and to get engraved at his own expense the compendious schemes of ideal music—the *Catechism Preludes* and the *Art of Fugue*, for example—which he surely knew would have no great immediate sale. But the great Bach was less regarded than the local school headmaster. *Apparently*, that is what he chose to do, but I don't think he did.

I am certain that Bach hoped to raise the whole status of Cantor by raising the whole status of church music. He did not sign himself 'Cantor', but 'Director of Music and Court Composer,' and I do not think this was merely a proud gesture. I believe that Bach cherished an ideal for notable centres of orthodoxy like Leipzig. He wanted them to have a musical establishment with singers and players not inferior to those of ducal and royal orchestras and operas. The Cantor himself in this school would be the equivalent of *Kapellmeister*, free to develop his genius, to compose and direct final rehearsals of music that had been prepared by his assistants.

The help from good town trumpeters and the extra singers and players from the university enabled Bach in his first few years at Leipzig to show just what was possible if the school and the city wanted to realize this ideal. In those first few years he composed some of his most brilliant church music. Leipzig heard the magnificence of princely concert and opera blended with the chorale treatments, the contrapuntal elaboration, and the musical symbolism of the church tradition.

Bach: *Cantata No. 51: Jauchzet Gott*. RENAISSANCE X 35 (NIXA PLP 235) or LONDON LL 993 (DECCA LXT 2926) or COLUMBIA ML 4792 or BACH GUILD 546.

It is ridiculous to suppose that Bach went to Leipzig because he liked the organ.   There was no need for him to have composed five sets of *Hauptmusik*, two or three hundred works for five years of Sundays and week-day festivals, with oratorios, Passions, Masses, and motets as well.   There must have been hundreds of such pieces lying ready composed and copied.   The favoured texts for cantatas were modelled on opera libretti, so that the kind of music that moved people's feelings in the theatre should also move them to piety in church.   Only a musician capable of being a great opera composer could have set those texts as Bach did. But neither town council nor school authorities grasped Bach's ideal.   If only Luther could have come to life and ordered its realization!   And therefore, as Bach aged, his ideal became a dream, realized only on paper in those collections we now treasure such as the *Catechism Preludes*.

So he who was despised for his German-ness, his local dialect, has been gradually hailed as one of the most universal artists. And so he is.   When friends wanted to compliment Bach in versified greetings, they made play with his name.   The word *Bach* means 'brook,' 'fountain,' or 'source.'   What was once a complimentary metaphor is no longer fanciful: for Bach is the source to which most modern composers trace their biggest technical advances; he is the fountain to which amateurs go for their most lasting musical refreshment; and even when we are especially fond of another composer, we turn aside to drink again and again at this ever-satisfying brook.   Why at this one especially?

The answer, I am sure, is a philosophic and religious one. Bach's music sometimes demands strenuous work, but if it is ever disquieting or depressing, then it is wrongly played and mis-interpreted; as it is when it is made to sound unctuous or senti-mental.   It does not speak of transient beauty, of the beauty of Mozart's most touching lyricism or even Handel's.   If ever it illustrates sorrow or the transience of worldly beauty and happi-ness, Bach is showing the sorrow as the price of sin.   Not all listeners hold that theological doctrine, but they are forced to do so temporarily while listening to Bach.   Always there follows the assurance of strong faith; always we feel the utter sanity of a man either so wholly deceived or so wholly fortified by his belief that he conveys comfort—in the literal meaning, becomes a *fort*, a stronghold, and we feel this even in mere dance movements. This is exactly what Bach would have wished.

APPENDIX

BOOKS

C. SANFORD TERRY: *Bach: A Biography.*
ALBERT SCHWEITZER: *J. S. Bach.*
CECIL GRAY: *The Forty-Eight Preludes and Fugues.*
H. DAVID and M. MENDEL: *The Bach Reader.*
HARVEY GRACE: *The Organ Works of Bach.*

RECORDS

The music of J. S. Bach is well represented in the current catalogues with generous selections of his cantatas, orchestral works, chamber music, and music for solo instruments. The LP record has also brought us generally much more authentic performances. Attention may be drawn to the following records among the many available:

St Matthew Passion. WESTMINSTER 401 (NIXA WLP 6401).
Cantata No. 140, 'Wachet auf.' WESTMINSTER WL 5122 (NIXA WLP 5122) or BACH GUILD 511 (NIXA BLP 311).
The Organ Music.
Comprehensive sets from Decca (Archive series DGG) and from Westminster (now being released). Also selections by Albert Schweitzer on English Columbia 33 CX 1074/1081/1084/1249.
Italian Concerto: Chromatic Fantasia and Fugue. LONDON LD 9187 (DECCA LW 5170).
The Well-tempered Clavier. VICTOR (six records) BRUNSWICK AXTL 1036–41 (piano).
Goldberg Variations. VICTOR LM 1080 (HMV ALP 1139).
The Musical Offering. LONDON LL 1181 (DECCA LXT 5036).
The Art of Fugue. WESTMINSTER WAL 220 or ENGLISH DECCA LXT 2503–5.

31

Anthony Lewis

HANDEL

MUSIC has often been called the universal language, and in its long history there has been no figure that better illustrated this universality than Georg Friedrich Handel. German by birth, Italian by spirit, and English by naturalization, he was the true eighteenth-century cosmopolitan, adapting himself with extraordinary skill to the demands of the society in which he lived at any particular time. After many years of residence in Great Britain his enemies might still mock at his strange use of the English tongue, but his mastery of the country's musical language was evident in one of the very first works he wrote there, the *Te Deum* composed to celebrate the Peace of Utrecht.

Born in Halle in 1685, Handel received his first systematic musical education at the age of eight under Zachau, one of the most distinguished German musicians of the day. Zachau's scheme of instruction was comprehensive, and the child Handel received a thorough grounding in counterpoint and harmony and in playing the organ, harpsichord, violin, and oboe. All the instruments which Zachau taught him were to leave a lasting mark on Handel's career. He became one of the greatest virtuosi in Europe on the harpsichord; his skill on the organ has a permanent memorial in his wonderful series of organ concertos, unique of their kind and a sensational novelty when first introduced to the English public of his day. As a violinist he became also very proficient, and on one occasion snatched a violin out of the hands of the eminent Corelli to show him how to play a difficult passage. There is no account of him as an oboist, but his oboe concertos and his use of the instrument in the orchestra show an exceptional sympathy with its character and potentialities.

Handel's father, a barber-surgeon, was not so dazzled by the

tempting offers which the extraordinary gifts of his son aroused
to be moved from his conviction that he should have a sound
general education. This culminated in the university at Halle
which Handel left in 1703, having completed the course in law.
Even this subject may have had its influence on future artistic
events. Handel was an able business man and a shrewd negotiator,
and the survival of the Italian opera in London was as much due to
these qualities in him as to his creative genius.

Handel's next significant move was to Hamburg, where he
joined the staff of the famous opera-house, then under the direction of Reinhard Keiser. Though it appears that Handel did
not always get on well with Keiser, nevertheless he was again very
fortunate in his association with one of the leading figures of
German music whose place in the history of music is a secure and
honourable one. Both as violinist and harpsichordist Handel
learnt much at Hamburg that was to stand him in good stead as a
composer. The fruits of this experience were his first two operas,
Almira and *Nero*, both produced in 1705. Handel is not usually
thought of as a precocious composer, but this achievement at the
age of twenty finds few rivals elsewhere.

His success in opera fired him with a desire to visit its home,
Italy, and in 1706 he left Hamburg *en route* for the south.
Whether he realized it or not his visit to Italy was to be one of the
most important periods in his life, very largely determining its
future course from the artistic point of view. With all his precocious gifts, when he left Hamburg he was in many respects still
rather a raw apprentice; the impact of Italy was to transform him
into an accomplished young master, equipped with all the refinement of technique and polish of manner that its sophisticated
society had to offer.

We may imagine Handel's dismay when, on arrival in Rome,
he found that all opera was forbidden by papal edict. This might
well have seemed the end of his ambitions, had not the Romans
resolved that in no circumstances would they be deprived of their
favourite entertainment. The great patrons of the art accordingly
gave musical parties in their palaces at which so-called cantatas
were performed. Many of them were in fact short dramatic
scenes set to music of the same type and style as is found in the
contemporary opera. Handel himself wrote many cantatas of
this kind, and the finest of them is *Apollo e Dafne*. It is one of

H

the most important achievements of his early maturity, and it stands in much the same relationship to his later career as *Die Entführung aus dem Serail* does to Mozart's. The libretto is based on the classical legend of the god Apollo who sees Daphne, a nymph dedicated to the service of Diana, as she worships the goddess in her grove. Fired with love for her, Apollo tries to persuade Daphne to yield to him. She repulses him angrily and tries to escape in flight. Apollo gives chase, but just as he thinks he has caught Daphne, she is transformed into a laurel.

To accompany the two characters of this dramatic cantata Handel used only a small orchestra by our standards—a flute, two oboes, bassoon, strings, and continuo—but it is so disposed as to obtain the maximum effectiveness and variety. Particularly noteworthy is the accompaniment to Daphne's first aria. There is a long and most beautiful obbligato for oboe, and this is supported by strings playing *pizzicato*; the first violins in octaves with the violas, the second violins in octaves with the cellos, and the double basses (*arco*) holding the fundamental bass line. It is a unique lay-out which produces a most delicate and transparent effect.

Apollo pleads with Daphne in an aria of great lyrical power, *Come rosa*. Below the unison of the violins Handel takes the unusual step of writing a part for solo cello, leaving the bass in the hands of the continuo. Handel never believed in squandering his resources, and when he wrote something he thought especially good he saw that it was not wasted. So we find the material of this aria appearing in various guises in later works, and indeed the whole of the music of the Italian period became for him a veritable storehouse of ideas.

The chase is delightfully characterized by Handel in a scene in which the solo violin represents Daphne and the solo bassoon Apollo. In a noble concluding aria, Apollo declares, brokenhearted, that if he may not love Daphne in human form, a wreath of her laurel leaves shall for ever adorn his brow. The composer's handling of the final dramatic situation is most impressive as the torrent of semiquavers in the orchestra that symbolizes the chase gives way to bewildered recitative over the bare continuo.

Handel: *Apollo e Dafne.* Oiseau-Lyre OL 50038.

Outside Rome opera was not subject to papal restrictions, and

Handel enjoyed great success with his operas *Rodrigo*, produced in Florence, and *Agrippina*, given in Venice. Fresh from these triumphs he returned to Germany and left again almost at once for England, where he arrived in 1710. The sophisticated society of the court of Queen Anne had been much attracted by what they had seen of Italian opera, but there was no native composer at the time who could master the style. Thus when Handel produced his *Rinaldo* in 1711 the circumstances were very favourable to its success. It was his finest operatic achievement to that date, despite the fact that it was written in only fourteen days, and it immediately established his reputation. It was the first of a long series of operas produced in London which were to comprise Handel's main creative activity for the next thirty years.

The favourite type of Italian opera of Handel's day was known as *opera seria* and its general characteristics had been established by Alessandro Scarlatti. The libretto was usually based on some classical or medieval legend and cast in such a form that the main burden of the performance could be maintained by a small group of solo singers. There was little choral or ensemble writing, but sometimes there would be opportunities for ballet or for descriptive music, although generally the purely orchestral contribution was confined to the overture and appropriate introductory music elsewhere. The main substance of the action was carried on in *secco* recitative, that is, speech-rhythm declamation with only continuo accompaniment; for moments of special dramatic or emotional interest the orchestra would be added in support. The arias were mostly of the *da capo* type and were commentaries on the action, summing up the emotional situation stage by stage. It is perhaps the reflective nature of the *da capo* aria that has given modern producers most difficulty, for these arias are essentially static and will not respond to a doctrine of constant activity. When it is realized that Handel's operas are pyschological music dramas in which the chief vehicle of expression is the human voice, we can hope for a sympathetic approach to these fine works so long neglected. One of the richest musically is *Sosarme*, which was produced in 1732, and we can hear it on records.

Handel: *Sosarme*. OISEAU-LYRE OL 50091–3.

Not long after his first successes in London as an opera composer, Handel took up an appointment which was to lead indirectly towards the form with which he eventually superseded opera, namely oratorio. For in 1718 he became chapel master to the Duke of Chandos and in the duke's service wrote not only the famous series of Chandos anthems and the pastoral *Acis and Galatea*, but also the masque *Haman and Mordecai*. It was this masque that Handel adapted some twelve years later to become his first oratorio, *Esther*.

Despite the constant artistic success of his operas, amid jealous rivalry and financial difficulty, there came a time when the man of the world saw that the English public wanted a change of medium. He rightly judged what elements in the *opera seria* his London audience would like to see preserved in the oratorio and what fresh elements should be introduced. Thus he maintained the dramatic basis, but cut down the *secco* recitatives, while keeping the arias; and recognizing the English interest in choral singing, he made the chorus a protagonist in the action and an important and essential part of the musical design.

The first oratorios were written while he was still mainly concerned with opera, but by the time *Saul* and *Israel in Egypt* were reached his attention was becoming more and more concentrated on the new form which, after *Messiah* in 1742, was to claim his chief energies for the rest of his life. It may seem paradoxical to say so, but there is little doubt that the universal popularity of Handel's great masterpiece *Messiah* has obscured the true nature of his genius. For *Messiah* of all the oratorios is the only one that is not avowedly dramatic in treatment, though often highly dramatic in style. All the other oratorios are either sacred music dramas or virtually operas in English. They maintain the essentially dramatic core of Handel's musical character that runs through all his music from his youthful days in the Hamburg opera-house and his early triumphs in Italy to the Italian operas in London and finally the oratorios. As Bach's artistic home was the church, so was Handel's the theatre, and unless his oratorios are regarded from that point of view they will be misunderstood. A good example is *Semele*, a setting of a libretto by Congreve, that was first performed in 1744 at Covent Garden Theatre, where most of the oratorios were produced. Those who say that early English opera died with Purcell would do well to consider the claims of *Semele*, which has been revived with success on the English stage.

Handel: *Semele*. OISEAU-LYRE OL 50098–60000.

My emphasis has been on Handel's dramatic work, since that was central to his genius, but he had many other fields of activity. For instance, his splendid keyboard fugues use that musical resource in a different way from Bach, with impressive results. Again, it is likely that more music lovers are acquainted with Bach's Brandenberg Concertos than know Handel's superb set of twelve *Concerti Grossi*, Opus 6, which equally represent a peak in the orchestral music of this period. Then also the trio sonatas are virtually unknown to the musical public. They require for their performance an ensemble of two violins, cello, and harpsichord which is no longer a viable economic unit, and the consequence is that the great chamber music of this period, on a level with the string quartets of Haydn, is now rarely heard.

What are the qualities that have given Handel his place among the greatest masters of the art? So versatile was he, so prolific and so universal in his appeal, that it is hard to urge the claims of one aspect rather than another. For some it will be his sturdy rhythm that carries the listener on with irresistible impetus, and gives the joyous exhilaration of choruses like *Now love, that everlasting boy* from *Semele*. For others it will be the emotional intensity of the great accompanied recitatives such as those in *Semele* and *Jephthah*, or the brilliant handling of the powerful dramatic scenes in *Samson* or *Belshazzar*. Many, I fancy, will feel that one of his most attractive musical traits is the exquisite purity of his melody. But perhaps to the majority the overwhelming impression of Handel is of titanic strength, strength that is the more majestic for its capacity to be gentle without weakness, expressive without loss of sinew. Breadth and fundamental power are of its very essence, and it has the enduring quality of the truly monumental. As the superb architecture of the *Hallelujah* chorus reveals itself, one feels that if the word 'classical' has any meaning, it must belong to the music of Handel.

APPENDIX

BOOKS

EDWARD J. DENT: *Handel.*
ed. GERALD ABRAHAM: *Handel: A Symposium.*
O. E. DEUTSCH: *Handel: A Documentary Biography.*

RECORDS

Messiah. LONDON LLA 19 (DECCA LXT 2921–4) or WESTMINSTER WAL 308 (NIXA NLP 907).
Te Deum for the Peace of Utrecht. HAYDN SOCIETY 2046.
Concerti Grossi, Op. 6. LONDON LLA 21 (DECCA LXT 5041–3) or WESTMINSTER WAL 403.
Organ Concertos. VOX PL 7132/7202/7802 (E).
Violin Sonatas. COLUMBIA ML 4787 or LONDON LL 652 (DECCA LXT 2751).
Water Music. DECCA ARC 3010 (DGG APM 14006).

32

Lionel Salter

EIGHTEENTH-CENTURY KEYBOARD MUSIC

EVERYTHING about keyboard music underwent a complete transformation in the eighteenth century. The idiom changed from the so-called 'learned style' to the '*galant*' and thence to what we now know as the 'Viennese classical': the kind of works written changed entirely, ranging from fugues and chorale variations at one end of the century to rondos and sonatas at the other; and perhaps most striking of all, there was a revolution in the actual instruments themselves—which was to have considerable influence on keyboard technique and on the relation between the keyboard instrument and others in concerted music. The gulf in style in the twentieth century between, say, Debussy and Skalkottas is not as wide, seen dispassionately, as that between the cool formality of Böhm at the beginning of the eighteenth century and the fiery subjectivity of Beethoven at the end of the century.

(i) Böhm: *Gelobet seist du, Jesu Christ*. TELEFUNKEN LGX 66009.
(ii) Beethoven: *Sonata in C minor, Op. 13* (*Allegro molto*). WEST-MINSTER WL 5184 (alt. HMV ALP 1062).

The favourite instruments of the time were the harpsichord and the organ. The harpsichord produced its incisive, clean-cut tone by a key mechanism which caused small tongues of quill or leather to pluck the strings: the player could not, by altering the weight or speed of his finger touch, affect the tone at all, and in order to obtain variety he had to bring into operation different stops which caused the strings to be plucked at another point or which acted on upper or lower octaves of the strings. As there was no time to change stops while the fingers were busy playing, any changes had to be left to the ends of sections of a work, so that the effect was of what is called 'terraces' of tone—sudden contrasts of volume or tone colour. Similarly, on the organ, crescendos and diminuendos were out of the question (the swell-box, an English invention, was relatively late to be adopted), and changes of timbre were introduced only at structural divisions of

the work.   In a fugue the growing complexity of the music provided all the heightening of tension necessary, without any addition
of colour or greater volume.

The eighteenth-century organ was smaller and shriller in tone
than our present-day instrument, worked on light wind pressure,
abounded in bright mutation stops, and, except in northern
Germany, possessed but a rudimentary pedal-board.   Bach had
more extensive instruments at his disposal, and he revelled in his
pedal-board.   That emotional appeal was not ignored, despite
the formal periods of his music, is shown by Bach's predilection
for a tremolo stop in his organ specifications: this would approxi-
mate to the human voice, whose effect Bach often seems to have
had in mind when writing for instruments.

A recent progressive step had been the introduction of equal
temperament, a system of tuning keyboard instruments by dividing
the octave equally into twelve semitones.   Before this, the 'mean-
tone' system had meant that it was only possible to work satis-
factorily in about five or six nearly related keys: modulation outside these either meant being out of tune or involved cumbersome
keyboard complications to provide all the necessary accidentals.
Rameau and Bach were ardent champions of the system; indeed
Bach's *Forty-eight Preludes and Fugues* and other compositions
could not have been conceived without it; and they paved the
way for a freer harmonic language.

Bach: *Chromatic Fantasia*.   Victor LCT 1137 (alt. Nixa LLP 8047).

Nevertheless it took a long time for equal temperament to be
universally accepted.   Sarti contemptuously dismissed Mozart as
'only a clavier player with a depraved ear, a sectary of the false system
that divides the octave into twelve semitones'; and as late as 1850
some organs were still being tuned in mean-tone temperament.

In France descriptive music had always been popular, and
Couperin, whose *ordres* are delightful series of miniatures (not meant
to be played continuously), wrote in the preface to his 1713 volume:
'I have always had some plan in composing these pieces, and the
titles illustrate the ideas I have had.'   Many of these pieces are
cast in the binary mould of the dances of the eighteenth-century
suite, though with pastoral or character titles; others are pure
programme music.   Much the same might be said of Rameau,
though he is more harmonic, less linear in thought than Couperin.

Both also made significant contributions to the new instrumental forms that were beginning to take shape; Rameau by his feeling for key-relationships (his *rondeau Les Cyclopes*, for example, has elements of sonata form) and Couperin with such works as his great B minor *Passacaille* in rondo form—a piece of an astonishingly passionate nature.

Couperin: *Passacaille from 8me Ordre*.   HMV DB 4944 (alt. OISEAU-LYRE OL 50058).

An interesting forerunner of the sonata form which was eventually to emerge in the latter part of the eighteenth century came from an unexpected and remote source—from Spain.   Domenico Scarlatti was a brilliant harpsichord virtuoso, and the 550 odd sonatas that he wrote for his own use at the Spanish court—apparently all after he had passed the age of fifty—form one of the most dazzling chapters in the history of the development of keyboard technique.   Every aspect of harpsichord virtuosity is to be found here—rapid repeated notes, flying leaps exploiting the full extent of the keyboard, cascading runs and arpeggios, passages for crossed hands.   Being himself a lively Neapolitan, a true son of the people, Scarlatti was fascinated by the folk music of the Spanish peasants he heard around him: its characteristic harmonies and rhythms found their way into his compositions.   The clashing dissonances heard in so many of his harpsichord pieces are the strummings of the Spanish guitar; the rattling repeated notes in which he delighted are representations of the castanets; and where other composers were writing gavottes and minuets, Scarlatti was introducing the whirl of the *jota*.

D. Scarlatti: *Sonata in A, L 428*.   WESTMINSTER WL 5359.

Even during Bach's lifetime tastes were changing.   The religious sect of Pietism inspired a swing of feeling away from artifice and strict doctrine towards homely simplicity and sensibility: this exactly suited the rapidly increasing bourgeois class, who may not have possessed much learning, but who were insistent on their capacity to feel emotions just as keenly as their social betters. Expressiveness became the new cult in Germany.   The harpsichord was altogether too impersonal an instrument to satisfy this outburst of (frequently lachrymose) feeling: it lacked the human voice's ability to swell its tone according to the emotional intensity of a phrase, and singing quality from an instrument was exactly what was now demanded.

*H

The ideal instrument to which personal feelings and whispered confidences could be entrusted was the clavichord. Touching its keys caused small blades or 'tangents' of brass to press against the strings, emitting a faint, sweet tone. More important, the simplicity and responsiveness of its action were such that the volume of tone could be varied by differences of finger touch, so that within rather narrow limits some flexibility of dynamics was possible. Moreover, a kind of vibrato could be obtained, comparable to that on a stringed instrument or to the natural pulsation of the human voice. Its flexibility of tone encouraged a different kind of playing, expressive in intention, but easily becoming free, even sloppy, in rhythm. But the clavichord remained the favourite of most composers, who admired its sweetness, its sensitivity, and its half-tints of shading.

Bach: *Fugue in G minor* (on the clavichord). HISTORY OF MUSIC IN SOUND, VOL. VI. VICTOR LM 6031 (HMV HMS 59, 78 r.p.m.).

The clavichord's modesty of utterance prevented it from being of much value in larger surroundings or in combination with other instruments, and outside Germany it had little popularity. As far back as the beginning of the eighteenth century experiments had been made with harpsichords whose strings were struck by hammers instead of being plucked. The attraction of a hammer instrument to a public that was finding the harpsichord deficient in expression was that the hammers could be thrown against the strings at different speeds, controlled by the player's fingers, and thus cause louder or softer tone. These new 'soft-louds' or pianofortes were frail affairs, judged by modern standards, with wooden frames, and thin single strings tuned to a range of five octaves struck by light leather-covered hammers. Their sound was small—actually less in volume than the harpsichord—and at first players found great difficulty in cultivating the kind of touch necessary to produce controlled graded tone. How the pianoforte compared with the harpsichord in timbre and volume can be heard in the double concerto for the two together by Carl Philip Emanuel Bach.

C. P. E. Bach: *Double Concerto in E flat.* PARLOPHONE PMA 1009.

We first hear of the pianoforte being played in public as late as 1767 in London, although it had been known for some years previously in private homes. The light touch and small resonance of the pianoforte encouraged a new, more transparent style of writing which exploited runs, broken-chord figurations, and other fluent elegances. The pianoforte superseded the harpsichord both for solo use and in concerted music; when Haydn directed his symphonies in London in 1791, he did so from the pianoforte. When Mozart composed a concert aria for Nancy Storace, to whom he was deeply attracted, he wrote it with an important part for the pianoforte, which he himself played. Into this he poured all his feelings, the voice and piano carrying on an intimate and tender dialogue so that the work sounds, as Einstein has well said, 'like a declaration of love in music, the transfiguration of a relation that could not be realized except in this ideal sphere.'

Mozart: *Ch'io mi scordi di te.* Vox PL 7370 (alt. NIXA WLP 5179).

The principal figure in the development of pianoforte style and technique was Carl Philip Emanuel Bach, to whom Mozart paid tribute. Bach had written the most celebrated keyboard tutor, his *Essay on the Correct Way to Play the Clavier*, in 1753; but it was as a composer for the instrument that he was even more important. His contemporaries all remarked on the amazing fertility of his invention, and if any one person can be called the father of the sonata it is he. His numerous examples reveal a remarkable feeling for design—a living, not by any means static, design—and an elegance of expression. His rondos too show an attractive vein of fantasy.

C. P. E. Bach: *Rondo in G.* OISEAU-LYRE OL 50097.

Though a keyboard instrument had been essential at all concerted music-making since the seventeenth century, it was only rarely that it attained solo status, compared with, say, the violin or the oboe. The first harpsichord concerto was Bach's Fifth Brandenberg (*c.* 1721), and during the next decade or so he produced several other works which featured the harpsichord. In all these, however, the instrument is merely first among equals, and even when it was used quite virtuosically only contributed one particular element of colour in the unfolding of the design. The difference that fifty years brought may be seen by comparing one of Bach's concertos with one of Mozart's.

(i) Bach: *Concerto in F.* PARLOPHONE SW 8147 (78 r.p.m.) (alt. NIXA PLP 547).

(ii) Mozart: *Concerto in A, K 414.* DECCA ARC 3012 (DGG AP 13021).

The style of writing has changed from a close-knit contrapuntal texture to an easier, more fluent homophonic idiom with grace-fully balanced phrases; the pianist is now a star personality either the equal or the superior of the orchestra; and the form of the movement is different so as to ensure that the soloist is given all the important thematic material.   Indeed, as a principal character in the drama, the piano now has to make an entrance as it were; and the pattern evolved by Mozart was to have the orchestra expound the chief themes of the movement on its own and then for the piano to present them all over again, though usually with some decorative modification.   Towards the end of the movement, too, the orchestra would pull up while the soloist played a highly ornamented cadence, or *cadenza*, introducing all kinds of virtuoso passage work and free meditation on the themes of the movement.

So far as solo pianoforte music was concerned, the man who represented the link between the generations of C. P. E. Bach and Beethoven was Haydn.   His earliest sonatas were based on C. P. E. Bach's style, with its characteristic ornamentation, wide range, and chordal treatment; but gradually they developed in individuality and in power.   A new seriousness, even a nobility, is often felt beneath the elegant surface; a sense of poetry in slow movements quite unlike anything that had gone before; and from the point of view of form they frequently possess an astonishing unity.

Haydn: *Sonata No. 34 in E minor.*   OISEAU-LYRE OL 50078.

In his later piano works, such as the *Variations in F minor*, Haydn achieves a passionate utterance akin to that associated with his pupil Beethoven.   Even limiting our view to those of Beet-hoven's works which fall in the eighteenth century there is a new drama, energy, and intensity about them, and a troubling pro-fundity of emotion in the slow movements.   There is the impres-sion that this vital personality is about to break through the bounds both of existing instrumental capabilities and of current musical language.   And so of course he was.

APPENDIX

BOOKS

A. DOLMETSCH: *The Interpretation of the Music of the Seventeenth and Eighteenth Centuries.*

A. J. HIPKINS: *History of the Pianoforte.*

C. P. E. BACH: *Essay on the Correct Way to Play the Clavier.*

W. L. Sumner: *The Organ: its evolution, principles of construction, and use.*
A. Loesser; *Men, Women, and Pianos.*
Ralph Kirkpatrick: *Domenico Scarlatti.*

Records

Many records of eighteenth-century keyboard music will be found listed in other chapters. But attention should be drawn to Ralph Kirkpatrick's records of sixty sonatas by Domenico Scarlatti that he edited for publication: Columbia SL 221. Another recording of all the D. Scarlatti sonatas is in progress on a series of Westminster (Nixa) disks of which more than a dozen are now released.

The following collections of keyboard music should be mentioned:

French Masters of the Keyboard. Oiseau-Lyre OL 50028 Lyri-chord LL 19.
Spanish Keyboard Music. Westminster 5312 (Nixa WLP 5312).
Spanish and Portuguese Keyboard Music. Oiseau-Lyre OL 50032.
Italian and German Harpsichord Music. Oiseau-Lyre OL 50043.
The Art of the Organ. Columbia KSL 219 (Philips ABL 3066/3110).

(This last set contains a selection of baroque music played on a variety of European organs.)

33

Karl Geiringer

BACH'S SONS AND THE MANNHEIM SCHOOL

IN the eighteenth century the triumphant rise of natural science brought about a complete change in man's general outlook and conception of the universe. The earlier uncritical acceptance of doctrines handed down by the writers of antiquity had been replaced by empirical observation, and this had led to the revolutionary discoveries of Galileo, Newton, and Kepler. Before long scientific methods were not confined to the domain of science. All manifestations of life were subordinated to Reason and even the Muses were expected to follow its dictates closely.

A certain trend towards naturalism may be observed in the rococo style that originated early in the eighteenth century. Shepherds and shepherdesses became the fashion both in poetry and in painting; for they displayed the simplicity, charm, and impudent gaiety which people of the rococo era cherished. In music this spirit produced the so-called *style galant*. Baroque contrapuntal art was forsworn as too pompous and powerful and, most of all, as contrary to reason; a monodic style became the goal. As Mattheson, the great composer and writer, claimed: 'The ear often derives more satisfaction from a single well-ordered voice developing a clear-cut melody in all its natural freedom than from twenty-four parts which, in order to share the melody, tear it to such an extent that it becomes incomprehensible.' As for the emotional content, the aim professed by the song-writer Valentin Görner is typical: 'We are trying to write engaging, charming, jocular, graceful, amorous, and gay tunes.'

It is interesting to note that the new rococo style in music grew up at the very time that baroque music reached its climax. Even before Bach's *St Matthew Passion* and *Mass in B minor* or Handel's *Israel in Egypt* were written, a strong reaction had set in against the style of the great old masters of baroque music. As Paul

Henry Lang points out: 'The essence of the new artistic creed was an urge for liberty: liberation from the rules that had become stereotyped, from the stylistic conventions that had become rigid, from the artistic forms that had become immutable.' The new rococo period tried to supplant majestic splendour by graceful delicacy. Whereas baroque art had striven towards a powerful unity of form, the rococo artists preferred variety. Music had changed the buskins of pomposity for the dancing slippers of the *style galant.*

A good example of the rococo style is a little minuet from a Quintet in F major by Alessandro Scarlatti (1659–1725). This Italian master was one of the greatest opera composers of the early eighteenth century, and he also composed delightful works in other fields. This minuet for flute, oboe, violin, bassoon, and harpsichord conjures up a picture of society ladies with powdered hair, costumed as shepherdesses, gracefully dancing and curtseying to their partners.

A. Scarlatti: *Quintet in F.* HAYDN SOCIETY HSL 117.

The *style galant* did not remain unchallenged. The delicate and carefree artistic idiom which had conquered southern and western Europe was replaced, particularly in northern Germany, by a more solid musical language in which emphasis was laid on expressive power and sensibility. 'It is the business of music,' declared Daniel Webb, 'to express passions in the way they rise out of the soul.' Another writer exhorted his fellow artists with this axiom: 'A musician cannot move others unless he himself is moved.' This impulse came to music from outside. The slogan 'back to nature,' which implied a return to sincerity of feeling, originated with Jean Jacques Rousseau, and German literature and music accepted it eagerly. Goethe wrote his *Sorrows of Young Werther*, and its unrestrained emotionalism moved people all over the world to tears and even to suicide.

The work of the sons of Johann Sebastian Bach was determined by these different trends and at the same time contributed greatly to shaping them. The eldest son, Wilhelm Friedemann, was born in 1710 and received his musical training mainly from his father. He was an inspired organ virtuoso whose improvisations, as a contemporary reported, 'filled listeners with awe and reverence.' Friedemann served at first as organist in Dresden and later as church music director in Halle. He resigned from this

position before securing another and spent the last years of his
life rather unhappily as a freelance composer.   He died at the age
of seventy-four in straitened circumstances in Berlin.

More than any other Bach son Friedemann was under the influence of his father, whose favourite he was.   He tried to use the
strict forms cultivated by Johann Sebastian, but imbued them with
a modern spirit.   A good example is the Overture in D minor for
two flutes and strings which he used as an introduction to a cantata
written in 1758 in honour of King Frederick the Great of Prussia.
It starts with a poignant slow introduction, filled with grieving
sighs and heart-felt exclamations by the wind instruments.   This
is followed by an energetic four-part fugue, entrusted solely to
the strings, which is full of vitality and excitement, despite the use
of a form considered old-fashioned at that time.

W. F. Bach: *Overture in D minor*.   Concert Hall 1251.

Friedemann's younger brother, Carl Philipp Emanuel, was born
in 1714 and trained in music by his father alone.   He served first
as court accompanist to King Frederick the Great and subsequently as church music director in Hamburg, where he died in
1788.   He enjoyed great fame both as a performer and as a composer; fame far exceeding the reputation won by his father.
Emanuel was the foremost exponent of the style of sensibility in
music and the passionate subjectivism of his compositions made
a deep impression on later composers, particularly on Haydn
and Beethoven.   His favourite instrument was the clavichord.
Emanuel's performances on this instrument were greatly admired,
and a contemporary thus described his playing of the clavichord:
'His soul seemed absent from the earth.   His eyes swam as though
in some delicious dream.'

Emanuel wrote a character-piece entitled *Farewell to my
Silbermann Clavichord* in 1781 in the form of a rondo.   He gave a
clavichord from his collection to a pupil, an instrument constructed
by Gottfried Silbermann, a great organ-builder and friend of the
Bachs.   The artist sent with his instrument a composition expressing his sadness at the loss of a cherished possession.   This is a
stirring piece that grows out of a single subject stated at the
beginning.

C. P. E. Bach: *Farewell to my Silbermann Clavichord*.   Anthologie
Sonore AS 28 (78 r.p.m.).

It would be wrong, however, to regard Emanuel Bach as a one-sided composer, merely concerned with sentimental music. A Symphony in C that he wrote in 1780, together with three other symphonies, will prove that his music could convey the most various moods. The symphony is scored for two oboes, two horns, strings, and harpsichord. The tender and graceful *andante* reveals Emanuel's art of imbuing the light rococo idiom with depth and warmth, thus paving the way for later developments. This *andante* is followed by a sparkling and jolly *allegro* finale that displays his sense of humour in the use of sudden contrasts and surprise effects.

> C. P. E. Bach: *Symphony in C.* Concert Hall 1251 (alt. Nixa WLP 5040).

Johann Sebastian's youngest son, Johann Christian, an offspring from his union with Anna Magdalena Wilcken, was born in 1735. His life was very different from that of the other Bachs, who all sedately served in Germany and refrained from long journeys. Christian, however, after studying with his half-brother Emanuel in Berlin, went to Italy, where he won great success as an operatic composer. In 1762 he was called to London as a *maestro* of the King's Theatre and was appointed music teacher to the queen. He stayed in London, where he enjoyed tremendous prestige as a composer, performer, and teacher, but died prematurely in 1782.

Christian's music is graceful and highly polished, yet tender, and he contributed decisively towards infusing classical poise and beauty into the *style galant*. These qualities of Christian's music fostered similar trends in the creative output of young Mozart. There were few contemporary artists for whom the Salzburg composer felt so much love and admiration. Mozart's loyalty to Christian did not waver from their first meeting in London in 1764, when the boy of eight played duets with the music master to the British queen, to their reunion in Paris fourteen years later, and finally to the day in 1782 when Mozart wrote to his father: 'I suppose you have heard that the English Bach is dead. What a loss to the musical world!'

Two examples should illustrate for us the style of Christian Bach's music; first an Allegro in D for flute, oboe, violin, viola, and cello. This was written in the 1770's and is a finely wrought gem, every delightful detail of which is planned with supreme competence. It prompts us to agree with what Mozart's father once wrote about Christian Bach's chamber music: 'The small is great, when it is composed in a natural, fluent, and easy manner and is worked out soundly. Has Bach debased himself by composing such works? By no means! The solid texture and structure, the continuity: these distinguish the master from the bungler.'

One of Christian Bach's achievements was that he greatly helped to promote the new pianoforte, and he was also one of the first to play piano duets. A good example is the Sonata in G for piano, four hands, whose minuet is somewhat like the Scarlatti minuet mentioned earlier, though more appealing and heart-felt.

> J. C. Bach: (i) *Allegro in D*. ANTHOLOGIE SONORE AS 115 (78 r.p.m.); (ii) *Sonata in G for piano duet*. WESTMINSTER 18025 (alt. NIXA WLP 5069).

Christian Bach enjoyed a great reputation outside England too, and it is significant that he was twice commissioned to compose an opera for Mannheim, capital of the German Palatinate, which boasted one of the best orchestras to be found in the eighteenth century. The Elector of Mannheim, a passionate friend of music, had assembled at his court a number of outstanding musicians who were pioneers in producing dynamic shadings in the orchestral sounds such as had never been heard before. A contemporary writer described the effect of the playing of the Mannheim orchestra in these poetical phrases: 'Its *forte* is thunder; its *crescendo* a waterfall; its *diminuendo* a crystal-clear brook murmuring in the distance; its *pianissimo* a breath of spring.'

So eminent a group of performers was bound to stimulate creative work, and there is a whole school of composers who wrote for the Mannheim orchestra and contributed significantly to the evolution of the classical symphony. The majority were of Austrian or Bohemian origin, including Christian Cannabich, Ignaz Holzbauer, Franz Xaver Richter, and Anton Filtz. Most important, however, was the Stamitz family, which contributed three distinguished composers. The eldest, Johann W. A. Stamitz (1717–57), exercised a decisive influence on the growth of symphonic music. Among the many pupils he trained, his brilliant son, Karl Stamitz (1746–1801), was particularly successful. The merry and brilliant rondo allegro from Karl's *Symphonie Concertante* for seven solo instruments and orchestra may illustrate the exquisite sense for tonal colours and the delightful freshness of melodic inspiration displayed by this important representative of the Mannheim school.

Karl Stamitz: *Symphonie Concertante*. WESTMINSTER 5017.

APPENDIX

BOOKS

KARL GEIRINGER: *The Bach Family*.
C. SANFORD TERRY: *Johann Christian Bach*.

RECORDS

C. P. E. BACH: *Chamber Music*. OISEAU-LYRE OL 50017. *Magnificat*. BACH GUILD 552. *Symphonies*. BACH GUILD 504. *Symphonies in C and D; Clavier Concerto*. NIXA WLP 5040.
J. C. BACH: *Chamber Music*. OISEAU-LYRE OL 50046. *Orchestral Music*. COLUMBIA ML 4869.
THE MANNHEIM SCHOOL: *Wind Music*. CLASSIC EDITIONS 2010.
KARL STAMITZ: *Flute Concertos*. OISEAU-LYRE OL 50035. *Violin Concerto in D*. VOX PL 7540.
KARL STAMITZ AND RICHTER: *String Quartets*. BARTÓK 915.

34

Karl Geiringer

EIGHTEENTH-CENTURY OPERA

MAKE-BELIEVE and pretence were part of the spiritual equipment of the baroque period. People wanted to appear glamorous and more than life-sized. The rich decorated the walls of their houses with paintings simulating vistas of wide colonnades and formal gardens; while clouds painted on the ceilings of ball-rooms and even vestibules seemed to lead the glance right into heaven. The men's formal, full-bottomed wig with curls and the women's pompous crinolines were both intended to add dignity to the appearance of the wearers. Opera, in which heroes of divine character and powers enacted stories of mythological origin to the accompaniment of stirring music, seemed to be the best vehicle to express the artistic ideal of the time; and Italy, the home of *bel canto*, was the country where opera had originated and where it flourished for a long time.

At the beginning of the seventeenth century the dramatic element in opera seemed of paramount importance. Gradually, however, the Italians' sensual pleasure in the beauty and refinement of the human voice led to significant changes. It became the main purpose of opera composers to satisfy the ambition of the *prima donna* and the *primo uomo*. The audiences came to hear a great *castrato* or a famous woman soprano deliver endless arias with all the ornaments and trimmings they were capable of providing. The form of opera thus developed in Italy, and especially in Naples, became the model for composers all over Europe.

A good example of what was fashionable and most pleased audiences is Cleopatra's aria *Da tempeste il legno* from Handel's *Giulio Cesare*, composed in 1723 and first performed in London in February 1724. The text expresses strong emotions, but it is not easy to recognize the mood of deliverance from pain through love in this rather conventional *da capo* aria. (Incidentally, Handel's operatic music was often on a much higher level.)

Handel: *Giulio Cesare* (*Da tempeste il legno*).　Vox PL 8012 (E).

Composers of less imposing stature than Handel were even more under the domination of star singers who resisted any attempt by a *maestro* to deprive them of their technical fireworks in order to achieve dramatic expression. An excerpt from a contemporary book illustrates the situation. In 1720 there appeared a satire entitled *Teatro alla moda* by the distinguished composer Benedetto Marcello. Although the caricature is somewhat exaggerated, we have the impression that the author's trenchant remarks are the result of bitter experience:

The composer will hurry or slow down the pace of an aria, according to the caprices of the singers, and will conceal the displeasure which their insolence causes him by the reflection that his reputation, his solvency, and all his interests are in their hands. . . . The director will see that all the best songs go to the *prima donna*, and if it becomes necessary to shorten the opera, he will never allow her arias to be cut, but rather other entire scenes. If a singer has a scene with another actor, whom he is supposed to address when singing an air, he will take care to pay no attention to him, but will bow to the spectators in the loges, smile at the orchestra and the other players in order that the audience may clearly understand that he is the Signor Alipi Forconi, *Musico*, and not the Prince Zoroaster, whom he is representing. . . .

If [a singer] has a role in a new opera, she will at the first possible moment take all her arias (which in order to save time she has had copied without the bass part) to her *Maestro* Crica so that he may write in the passages, the variations, the beautiful ornaments, etc., and the *Maestro* Crica, without knowing the first thing about the intentions of the composer either with regard to the tempo of the arias, or the harmonies, or the instrumentation, will write down everything he can think of, and in very great quantity, so that the virtuosa may be able to sing her aria in a different way at every performance . . . and if her variations have nothing in common with the bass part, with the violins which are to play in unison with her, or with the concertizing instruments, even if they are not in the same key, that will be of no consequence, since it is understood that the modern opera director is both deaf and dumb.[1]

A twofold reaction set in against this strange type of opera: composers either ridiculed it or they tried to improve it. Let us consider each attempt in turn. It became the custom to insert in the intermissions of the three-act serious opera short musical comedies, called *Intermezzi*. Here the mythological heroes were

---

[1] Cf. Donald Grout: *A Short History of Opera*, New York, Columbia University Press, 1947, pp. 190–2.

replaced by common people of the eighteenth century who sang simple, folksong-like melodies, accompanied by a handful of instruments.   The deeds of valour and the pompous diction of serious opera gave way to unassuming farces often presented in dialect.   One such comic opera is *La Serva Padrona* (*The Maid as Mistress*), composed in 1733 by Giovanni Battista Pergolesi (1710–36), which marks a milestone in the history of opera.   In one aria, *Sempre in Contrasti*, a grumpy old bachelor complains to his servant about the discomforts she inflicts on him.

> There's always upheaval,
> Wherever you are
> It's here and there,
> It's up and down,
> It's yes and no.
> But now enough.
> It will be stopped.
> What do you say?
> Isn't it so?
> Ah . . . what . . . no!
> But so it goes!
> There is always upheaval, etc.

Pergolesi: *La Serva Padrona* (*Sempre in Contrasti*).   CETRA 50036 or ANGEL 35279 (COLUMBIA 33 LX 1340).

Among the many composers of serious opera who tried to increase the dignity and dramatic truth of the form, the German, Christoph Willibald von Gluck (1714–87), was the most outstanding.   He laid down his principles in the famous introduction to his opera *Alceste*:

I resolved to avoid all those abuses which had crept into Italian opera through the mistaken vanity of singers and the unwise compliance of composers, and which had rendered it wearisome and ridiculous. . . . I endeavoured to reduce music to its proper function, that of seconding poetry by enforcing the expression of the sentiment, and the interest of the situations, without interrupting the action, or weakening it by superfluous ornament. . . .   In fact, my object was to put an end to abuses against which good taste and good sense have long protested in vain. . . .   I also thought that my chief endeavour should be to attain a grand simplicity, and consequently I have avoided making a parade of difficulties at the cost of clarity.

As an example of Gluck's method, we may take the beginning

of the second act of his *Orfeo ed Euridice*, first performed in Vienna on 5th October 1762. Orpheus, the great singer of Greek mythology, has lost his wife, Euridice, who was bitten by a snake; and he descends to the underworld to claim her back. As the act opens, the furies of Hades perform a weird dance and sing a threatening chorus. Orpheus (sung in the original by a *castrato* and in our day by a woman contralto) entreats them to give him access to Hades, but the answer is an implacable 'no.' Gluck achieves a most dramatic contrast between the chorus of furies, accompanied by trombones, and the heart-stirring plea of Orpheus, singing to the sound of a harp which is meant to conjure up the sounds of the ancient Greek lyre.

> Gluck: *Orfeo ed Euridice*. URANIA URLP 223 (NIXA ULP 2923)*
> (alt. HMV ALP 1357).

The greatest opera composer of the eighteenth century was undoubtedly Wolfgang Amadeus Mozart (1756–91). His mature operatic masterpieces draw the conclusion from the developments of the era before him. Like Shakespeare's plays they combine serious and comic elements to provide a picture of life in all its aspects. In Mozart's operas we find the most forceful drama, but at the same time they are unsurpassed in sheer melodic beauty. Any example mentioned in this short essay seems to be completely inadequate when we bear in mind the abundance of superb pieces that must go unmentioned. Yet the three examples will at least serve to illustrate the inexhaustible variety and inspiration displayed in Mozart's operas.

Among the dazzling array of musical gems in *The Marriage of Figaro* the aria *Non più andrai* placed at the end of Act I was the favourite with Mozart's contemporaries. Here the clever barber and valet Figaro makes fun of the young page Cherubino, who has so far mainly been interested in flirting with young ladies but is now forced to join the army. Mozart's use of trumpets and horns is inspired by Figaro's teasing reference to the victories that Cherubino is going to win on the battlefield.

In the duet *La ci darem la mano* from *Don Giovanni* we notice Mozart's art of psychological characterization. Don Giovanni sings a caressing tune to the peasant girl Zerlina whose love he tries to win. She is strongly attracted to the glamorous nobleman, yet she hesitates, for she is engaged to an honest peasant. At the end, however, she is swept off her feet, and the duet concludes jubilantly as they express their intention to hurry to Don Giovanni's castle.

Mozart: (i) *The Marriage of Figaro* (*Non più andrai*).
       (ii) *Don Giovanni* (*La ci darem la mano*).

Mozart's last opera, composed to a German text, shows a further development of his artistic idiom. In *The Magic Flute*, first performed in Vienna on 30th September 1791, Mozart deals with an enchanting fairy-tale whose content is given depth through the inclusion of symbolism derived from the free masonic ritual. The bass aria *In diesen heil'gen Hallen* (*Within these sacred halls*) is sung by the high priest Sarastro, who proclaims in it Mozart's own ethical message:

We know no thought of vengeance, within these temple walls,
Where love leads back to duty, Whoever from duty falls.
By friendship's kindly hand held fast, He finds the land of light at last.
Here each to ev'ry other, by mental love is bound,
Where every wrong finds pardon, no traitor ever is found.
Those whom this bond cannot unite, are all unworthy of the light.

Mozart's music displays the utmost seriousness and dignity, but at the same time a simplicity and directness which almost reminds us of a folk-song. This is the least complicated but at the same time possibly the most impressive kind of music Mozart wrote.

Mozart: *The Magic Flute* (*In diesen heil'gen Hallen*).

We have only to compare the unadorned simplicity and heart-stirring beauty of Mozart's operatic music with the over-ornate and stilted aria from Handel's *Giulio Cesare* to evaluate the tremendous development that eighteenth-century opera underwent in six decades. Men like Pergolesi, Gluck, and, most of all, Mozart were responsible for this splendid evolution which led to a climax of artistic achievement but rarely found in the whole history of music.

APPENDIX

Books

A. Einstein: *Gluck.*
E. J. Dent: *Mozart's Operas.*

Records

Gluck: *Alceste.*   Oceanic 304.   English Decca LXT 5273–6.   *Iphigenia in Tauris.*   Vox PL 7822.
Cimarosa: *The Secret Marriage.*   Angel 3549 C/L or Vox PL 8450.
Mozart: *The Abduction from the Harem.*   Decca DX 133 (DGG DGM 18184–5).   *Idomeneo.*   Haydn Society 2020 (Nixa HLP 2020).*
The Marriage of Figaro.   London XLLA 35 (Decca LXT 5088–91).
Don Giovanni.   Victor LCT 6102 (HMV ALP 1199–1201).   *Cosi fan tutte.*   Angel 3522 C (Columbia 33 CX 1262–4).   *The Magic Flute.*   Decca DX 134 (DGG DGM 18267–9).

35

Karl Geiringer

HAYDN

THE various stylistic trends of the post-baroque music of the eighteenth century are all to be found in the work of one of the greatest masters of the time, Joseph Haydn. The light and playful grace of rococo music and the passion and warmth of the style of sensibility were the foundations on which Haydn built. In conjunction with Mozart he developed the musical idiom which we have come to designate as Viennese classical music.

Haydn may be described as a self-made musician. He received but little theoretical instruction and owed most of what he knew to his keen interest in the music of the past and the compositions of his own time. His artistic development was slow indeed, and he wrote his greatest masterpieces when he was over sixty. As he grew in artistic stature, his fame gradually spread throughout the civilized world, and he finally enjoyed an unprecedented reputation.

Haydn was born in 1732 in the eastern part of Austria, a section inhabited by Germans, Hungarians, and Croatians, and we have reason to assume that all three races were represented among Haydn's ancestry. His father was a wheelwright, and being unable to provide an education for the gifted boy, he entrusted the five-year-old Joseph to a cousin who served as schoolmaster and director of church music in a small town. From then on Haydn was on his own and he never received financial support from his parents. For nine years he worked as a choir-boy at St Stephen's in Vienna, the most important cathedral in the Austrian Empire. He had to leave St Stephen's at the age of seventeen, when his voice broke, and thereafter he supported himself through a variety of musical jobs until in 1760 he entered the service of the Hungarian Prince Esterházy. He quickly advanced to the rank of conductor and maintained his connection with this powerful aristocratic family until his death in 1809. During the first thirty years he served in the castles of Eisenstadt and Esterház in Hungary. After 1790, however, he was frequently granted leave of absence, and his duties decreased in proportion as his fame increased. In the years 1791–2 and 1794–5 he paid two extremely successful visits to London, and these were high lights of a rather uneventful life.

Among the earliest of Haydn's works is an entertaining Organ Concerto in C, written in 1756. He wrote organ works only in the early phases of his career, and the gaily prancing finale of this concerto is certainly experimental in character. The manner in which the young composer employs the dignified church instrument to fulfil the tenets of the *style galant* may seem rather startling to us, and indeed Haydn later realized that this merry piece might be more suited to the harpsichord, and so catalogued it as a harpsichord concerto.

Haydn: *Organ Concerto in C* (1756). HAYDN SOCIETY HSLP 1043 (NIXA HLP 1043).

Our next example was composed fifteen years later and is of quite a different character; rococo gaiety is replaced by an ardent, strongly emotional language. Haydn had succumbed to the influence of Carl Philip Emanuel Bach, and many of his works composed about 1770 reflect in their pathos and stirring subjectivism the impact of the Hamburg Bach's style. The Twentieth Piano Sonata in C minor is the only one by Haydn in that passionate key; the first movement is full of poignant music with unexpected pauses and sudden contrasts.

Haydn: *Sonata No. 20 in C minor*. HAYDN SOCIETY HSLP 3013 (NIXA HLPY 3013)* (alt. DECCA LXT 5144).

While piano and especially organ works were on the periphery of Haydn's creative output, the string quartet was particularly close to his heart and occupied him from early youth to the end of his career. He wrote more than eighty quartets, and has been justifiably called the father of the string quartet. The Quartet in C major, Opus 33, No. 3, gives a good idea of the classical perfection of style that Haydn had achieved by about 1780. By then both the frills of the rococo style and the strong emotionalism of the era of sensibility had been overcome, although they had left their imprint on Haydn's music. Out of the combination of these earlier artistic trends grew the classical style of his full maturity.

In this context the word 'classical' may best be explained as well-balanced. In classical music we find a perfect blend of the work of the mind and the work of the heart; inspiration is as important as the action of the intellect. Classical works seem to be born out of the fundamental qualities of the instruments or voices for which they were written. All technical problems are completely solved, and the musical ideas fit the musical form to perfection.

Haydn had by this time developed the method of thematic development; he dissected the subjects of the exposition and reassembled the fragments in the most various ways. Even the accompanying parts were often based on motives derived from the main subjects, and thus in his string quartets all four instruments were given an important share in the thematic elaboration. In the finale of the Quartet, Opus 33, No. 3, known as the 'Bird' Quartet, since different bird calls may be discerned in its movements, the call of the cuckoo supplies the basis of the first subject. The merry cuckoo call appears not only in the leading violins, but just as frequently in the viola and cello. The second subject, which is closely related to the first, has the character of Hungarian gipsy music. Such episodes appear frequently in Haydn's works. They may have been inspired by childhood impressions as well as by his protracted residence in Hungarian castles.

Haydn: *String Quartet in C, Op. 33, No. 3.* HAYDN SOCIETY HSQ
20 (alt. COLUMBIA 33 CX 1383).

The symphony, like the string quartet, occupied Haydn throughout his life. One hundred and four symphonies may be attributed to him with certainty, and recent research tends to enlarge this figure. His creative achievement in this form reached its climax in the twelve symphonies that he wrote for London. Here he managed (in the words of Paul Henry Lang) 'to achieve the ideal balance of homophony and a specific modern polyphony. What a fantastic cavorting of melodies, rhythms, syncopations, dynamic contrasts, general pauses, hesitations, sudden pauses, distortions!' A remarkable feature of these symphonies, written by a man over sixty, is that they occasionally seem experimental. Haydn tends to try out new devices, even at the sacrifice of the poise of former years. Fundamentally Haydn remained a classical composer, but again and again episodes are to be found in which expressiveness and passionate feeling break through the classical composure. Here we discern the first indications of romanticism.

A characteristic example of this tendency towards experimentation is the second movement of the Symphony No. 100 in G major, usually referred to as the 'Military.' The nickname is due to the employment of military instruments such as triangle, cymbals, and big bass drum in the second and last movements. The melody of the *allegretto*, taken from the French romance *La gentille et jeune Lisette*, was an old favourite of Haydn's. The combination of the sweet, graceful tune with the powerful percussion instruments is decidedly a bold experiment which also shows Haydn's sense of humour. Even bolder is the trumpet fanfare that sounds near the end of the movement; this is followed by a drum roll that rises from a mysterious *pianissimo* to a thunderous *fortissimo*. The ending seems to suggest some kind of programme for the music, and in this respect, too, Haydn prepared the way for later composers, including Beethoven.

Haydn: *Symphony No. 100 in G, 'Military.'* WESTMINSTER 5045 (NIXA WLP 5045).

While in London Haydn had been among the audience of the great Handel Festival of 1791 at which he found a whole nation aroused by monumental performances. Compared with the scale of these concerts, his own efforts to entertain a small group of music lovers at the Esterhazy castles must have seemed almost insignificant. Haydn intensely desired to write works that were meant for a whole nation. The results of this desire were the two great oratorios he composed after his return to Vienna: *The Creation* and *The Seasons*. In these works the deeply religious Haydn had an opportunity to express his love for all things created and his delight in the beauties of nature. Two prominent features of his oratorios should be mentioned: his musical interpretation of visual impressions and the epic fervour of his choral style. They can be illustrated in the recitative and chorus that close Part One of *The Creation*. In the recitative Haydn describes first the sunrise, then its full splendour, and after a pause the magically soft moonlight and the twinkling stars. The ensuing chorus alternates with three solo voices and presents the angels' jubilation over the achievements of the third day of creation.

Haydn: *The Creation*. HAYDN SOCIETY 2005 (NIXA HLP 2005) (alt. DGG DGM 18254–6).

To conclude, a final example of Haydn's wide-open mind.   At the age of sixty-four he became acquainted with a newly invented instrument, the so-called keyed trumpet with finger holes closed by keys.   Later generations discarded this instrument as its tone qualities were by no means equal to those of the valve trumpet. In Haydn's time, however, the keyed trumpet was considered a revolutionary innovation, and Haydn decided to try out the instrument by writing a concerto for it.   The result is a work cherished up to our own time by all trumpeters as one of the most effective compositions in their repertoire, and the dazzling finale is a high light in the concerto literature of the eighteenth century.

Haydn: *Trumpet Concerto*.   Haydn Society HSLP 1038 (Nixa HLP 1038).

APPENDIX

Books

Karl Geiringer: *Haydn*.
Rosemary Hughes: *Haydn*.

Records

Haydn is well represented on records.   The Haydn Society (of Boston) is in the process of making all the string quartets available; many of these records have already been released (Nixa).   The piano sonatas are represented by a fair sampling and so are the symphonies; the later symphonies are available in a number of different versions.   But some aspects of Hadyn's work might be overlooked, and this short list may serve to draw attention to them.

Cantata: Arianna a Naxos.   Haydn Society 2051.
English Songs.   HMV DLP 1121.
The Seasons.   Decca DX 123.
Opera: Orfeo ed Euridice.   Haydn Society 2029 (Nixa HLP 2029).*
Missa Sancti Bernardi de Offida.   Haydn Society 2048.   Parlophone PMA 1010.
Missa Solemnis in D minor.   Vanguard 470.
Seven Last Words of Our Saviour (string quartet version).   Haydn Society HSQ 39 Nixa WLP 6202.

36

Karl Geiringer

MOZART

WOLFGANG AMADEUS MOZART was Haydn's dearest friend and, as a creative genius, was his equal or possibly even superior to him. Mozart's whole existence took place in Haydn's lifetime, but it was barely half as long; the Salzburg composer was born twenty-four years after the great master of Esterház and he died eighteen years before him. In many respects the creative output of the two great classical composers displays a strong resemblance, but in Mozart's work everything seems condensed and intensified.

Romain Rolland once remarked about Mozart:

His true happiness was in creation. In restless and unhealthy geniuses creation may be a torture—the bitter seeking after an elusive ideal. But with healthy geniuses like Mozart creation was a perfect joy and so natural that it seemed almost a physical pleasure. . . . Beethoven had to fight with all his strength when in the throes of composition. If his friends surprised him at work, they often found him in a state of extreme exhaustion. . . . He was always making sketches of things, erasing or correcting what he had done, beginning all over again. . . . Mozart knew nothing of these torments. He was able to do what he wished, and he never wished to do what was beyond him. . . . So easy was creation to him that at times it poured from him in a double or triple stream, and he performed incredible feats of mental activity. He would compose a prelude while writing a fugue; and once when he played a sonata for pianoforte and violin at a concert, he composed it the day before, between eleven o'clock and midnight, hurriedly writing the violin part and having no time to write down the piano part or to rehearse it with his partner. The next day he played from memory what he had composed in his head. (8th April 1781.) This is only one of many examples. Such genius was likely to be spread over the whole domain of his art and in equal perfection. [1]

It is true that Mozart contributed supreme master works in

[1] Romain Rolland: *Some Musicians of Former Days*, Henry Holt & Co., New York, 1915.

almost every realm of music. His operas are among the greatest ever written, yet he composed for instruments with a mastery equal to his vocal writing. He was that rarity among human beings: a child prodigy of breath-taking precocity who did not stand still. Starting at the age of four, with the composition of some minuets, offering his first larger work—six sonatas for violin and piano—at the age of seven, he steadily grew in artistic stature up to his thirty-sixth year, when death overtook him. In the short time granted to him he wrote some twenty works for the stage; fifteen Masses and various other sacred works; some fifty symphonies; more than thirty serenades or *divertimenti* for small orchestra; fifty concertos for the most various instruments; seventeen sonatas and fifteen sets of variations for piano; seven piano trios and various other chamber music works; and more than one hundred airs, songs, or choruses.

In his early compositions the lad was strongly influenced by the music of Johann Sebastian Bach's youngest son, Johann Christian, whom he met while giving concerts in London at the age of eight. As Alfred Einstein put it:

... There existed between them a wondrous kinship of souls. ... Young Mozart felt that Johann Christian had traversed a path that he himself should follow: from a northern region to a southern—to Italy— and from the southern back again to a northern. That path led to a new, ideal land in which only men of harmonious disposition felt at home. ... Mozart yielded to an influence quite ingenuously. ... He strove least of all for originality, because he was entirely certain of the Mozartian, personal stamp of his product. ... It did not occur to him to do something new at all costs. He wanted to do it not differently, but better. [1]

The Mozartian touch can be discerned in the *Andante* of his Symphony No. 6, written at the age of eleven. He paints a delightful nocturnal scene. The first violin has the role of the serenading lover while the other instruments delicately accompany him. There is in it the sweetness of melodic idiom which Johann Christian Bach had introduced into symphonies, but added to it is a tiny touch of nostalgia which stirs our hearts as Mozart's *andantes* do so often.

Mozart: *Symphony No. 6 in F major, K. 43.* CONCERT HALL CHS 1165 (alt. OISEAU-LYRE DL 53008).

[1] From Alfred Einstein: *Mozart*, Oxford University Press, New York, 1945.

To illustrate Mozart's stupendous artistic development we may turn to another slow movement, written eighteen years later. It is the *Romanza* from the *Piano Concerto in D minor*, the sixteenth work of the kind that he composed, and one of the most outstanding. Here the composer again presents an enchantingly gentle and sweet melody which seems to dissolve our hearts. But while in the early symphony Mozart contented himself with merely spinning out a sweet tune, in the middle section of the concerto movement the atmosphere changes completely and a tempestuous, sombre mood is introduced. Only slowly and reluctantly is composure regained. The sixteenth notes change to triplets, and then to eighth notes, until the sweet *Romanza* theme sounds again.

Mozart: *Piano Concerto in D minor, K. 466.* HAYDN SOCIETY HSL 88 (alt. PHILIPS ABR 4006).

Mozart was an inspired pianist who wrote many compositions for his own performances. The piano concertos offer most rewarding and congenial tasks to the virtuoso, but his solo piano music too is wholly admirable and a never-failing source of joy to the average pianist. As is so often true of Mozart's music, some of these piano works do not present very great technical difficulties, yet they sound as though they did. The *Sonata in A major, K. 331*, shows how he managed to conjure up a whole world of different emotions within one sonata. The first movement is a superb set of variations, and this is followed by a delightful minuet. The finale is the famous *alla turca* march. Now that the Turks had ceased to be a deadly menace to Europe, their instruments were becoming fashionable, and it was Mozart's aim to evoke on the piano the sounds of a Janizary band. This *alla turca* is a highly exciting piece, with violence lurking underneath the brilliant display.

Mozart: *Sonata in A major, K. 331.* HAYDN SOCIETY HSL 126 (alt. HMV ALP 1194).

Among Mozart's many outstanding chamber music works, we may consider the String Trio in E flat major, K. 563, entitled *Divertimento*, which was completed on 27th September 1788. Like the average *divertimento*, it is quite long and consists of six entensive movements. The fourth, an *andante*, was described by the eminent French scholar, Georges de St Foix, as 'one of the greatest creations of chamber music in existence.' It is a set of variations on a folksong-like theme, and in the variations the three instruments alternately assume the leadership, each being of equal significance.   There is a constant flow of new ideas, and not a bar is repeated throughout the movement.   Worthy of particular attention is the quite stunning variation in which the viola intones the theme like a *cantus firmus*, while violin and cello weave quick ornamental figures around it.   The three instruments here achieve a power and grandeur which one would not expect to find in a *divertimento*.

Mozart: *Divertimento in E flat, K. 563*.   HAYDN SOCIETY HSL 114 (alt. BRUNSWICK AXTL 1031).

In the summer of 1788—the year the E flat string trio was written —he completed within the incredibly short time of just over six weeks his last three, and indeed his greatest symphonies; in E flat, K. 543, G minor, K. 550, and C major, K. 551.   They constitute the composer's last testament in this form, and we can well understand that after reaching such a lofty peak Mozart did not feel inclined to proceed farther on this path.   It may also be said that no symphony written in the eighteenth century surpasses these three works in content or in technical mastery.

The last of the three is usually called the 'Jupiter' Symphony (the nickname was in all likelihood devised by the pianist-composer, Johann Baptist Cramer).   Jupiter was the greatest of the gods, so this C major symphony is outstanding among Mozart's symphonic inspirations.   Moreover, the name 'Jupiter' could refer to the significance of the finale, which, contrary to prevailing custom in the eighteenth century, is not simply a gay denouement, but achieves an importance far out-ranking that of the preceding movements.   With the finale we seem to reach the throne of the supreme god Jupiter after passing a row of minor deities.

The finale starts with a deceptively simple subject consisting of four notes only.   Long before Mozart's time it had been used by Purcell, Bach, Handel, and others.   Mozart himself seems to have had a predilection for it, as he employed it in two of his church works and in various instrumental compositions.   Scholarly treatises have been written about this finale, but Eric Blom justly remarks:

There is a mystery in this music not to be solved by analysis, and perhaps only just to be apprehended by the imagination.   We can understand the utter simplicity; we can also, with an effort, comprehend the immense technical skill with which the elaborate fabric is woven; what remains for ever a riddle is how any human being could manage to combine these two opposites into such a perfectly balanced work of art. There are five subjects, each of them a mere stock phrase such as any professor of composition might give to a student to work out as a fugue. Mozart does not work any of them into a fugue, but all of them into a sonata movement with a fugal texture of incredible elaboration, combining now any two of the subjects, now a single one in canon, and again mixing both procedures together. The dizzy culmination comes in the coda, where all five themes appear together in various juxtapositions.[1]

Mozart: *Symphony in C, K. 551.* COLUMBIA ML 4035 (alt. COLUMBIA 33 CX 1257).

The very last work Mozart composed was the *Requiem.* In July 1791 he was commissioned to write a composition of this kind for a wealthy nobleman who wanted to pass it off as his own work. Mozart agreed and received a substantial advance on the honorarium. As he was also engaged in composing the operas *La Clemenza di Tito* and *The Magic Flute,* he worked very slowly on the *Requiem.* When he died on 5th December 1791 only the first movement was completely finished. The second to ninth movements were written down in Mozart's usual draft; this means that the vocal parts and the most significant sections of the instrumental accompaniment were on paper, while the rest of the orchestration was to be filled in later. Mozart's widow was afraid that she might have to return the advance on the honorarium, so she induced his pupil, Franz Süssmayer, to complete the score. As his handwriting resembled that of his teacher, Constance Mozart could pretend that the score had been finished by her husband.

Later the deception was discovered, and attempts were made to determine the exact extent of Süssmayer's participation. In the case of the movements drafted by Mozart it is quite conceivable that a faithful student could fill out what was missing without doing any harm to the master work, and this Süssmayer apparently did. We do not know, however, what constituted the basis for Süssmayer's work on the tenth, eleventh, and twelfth movements for which no sketches have been preserved. To judge by Süssmayer's modest subsequent achievements as a composer, we must assume that the last three movements of the *Requiem* were not

[1] Eric Blom: *Mozart,* J. M. Dent & Sons Ltd, London, 1935.

conceived by him.   Perhaps he had some kind of sketches from Mozart's hand or could rely on dictation the master had given to the pupil in the last days when the thought of the unfinished *Requiem* was weighing on his mind.

The two sections of the *Requiem* which we may take as examples are clearly Mozart's own, though Süssmayer may have contributed one or the other detail of orchestration.   The *Dies Irae* conjures up the vision of the Last Judgment with fearful, truly apocalyptic grandeur.   In the *Confutatis* tenors and basses, accompanied by the full orchestra, utter the desperate laments of the lost souls; whereupon angelic voices, sopranos and altos, pray for admittance among the chosen.   Finally, the full chorus implores the Lord for help in the ultimate hour, an entreaty uttered in harmonies lofty beyond all earthly notions.   Hearing the *Confutatis*, it is impossible not to feel that the dying composer wrote this plea for himself.

Mozart: *Requiem, K. 626.*   VICTOR LM 1712 (alt. Vox DL 270).

APPENDIX

BOOKS

ed. EMILY ANDERSON : *The Letters of Mozart.*
A. EINSTEIN : *Mozart.*
C. M. GIRDLESTONE : *The Piano Concertos of Mozart.*
ed. DONALD MITCHELL and H. C. ROBBINS LANDON : *The Mozart Companion.*

RECORDS

The Mozart bicentenary has seen a great increase in the already considerable representation of Mozart in the record catalogues.   As in the case of Haydn, it seems best to direct attention to one or two aspects of Mozart's work that might be overlooked.

Solo Piano Music (complete).   ANGEL 35068/78 (COLUMBIA—various).
Organ Music (complete).   COLUMBIA K3L–231.
Concert Arias.   WESTMINSTER WL 5197 (NIXA WLP 5197).
Songs.   ANGEL 35270 (COLUMBIA 33 CX 1321).
Masonic Music.   EPIC LC 3062.
Litanies, K. 195, K. 243.   OISEAU-LYRE OL 50085–6.
Mass in C, K. 317.   DECCA 9805 (DGG DG16096).
Mass in C minor, K. 427.   EPIC SC 6009 (PHILIPS ABR 4043–4).

37

Alfred Frankenstein

BEETHOVEN

I N attempting to define the place of Beethoven in the great
stream of western culture, I am reminded of the famous little
anecdote about Thomas Carlyle and Margaret Fuller. Miss
Fuller announced on one occasion that, having given the matter
due thought, she had decided to accept the universe. Carlyle's
simple comment was: 'By gad, she'd better!'

Ludwig van Beethoven is one of those universes which we had
all better accept. There are respectable musicians who do not like
Handel; there are some to whom the personality of Bach is ana-
thema, and even some who have been known to question the
genius of Mozart; but to express a fundamental distaste for
Beethoven is tantamount to expressing a fundamental distaste
for music itself. We need not all agree about every aspect of his
output, nor will the Beethoven of the young, inexperienced music
lover be the same as the Beethoven of those who have lived long
with the art he practised, but few will seriously dispute the assertion that Beethoven is peculiarly the central figure in the musical
repertoire on which the world is nourished in our time.

Like all great artists, however, Beethoven must be re-evaluated
at least every half-century. The Beethoven criticism of 1900 is
almost meaningless to-day, and the Beethoven criticism of 1850
serves mostly as naïve documentation for the philosophic school
which holds that criticism is always wrong. A world for which
Schönberg and the twelve-tone row are matters of intense contemporary concern cannot *look* back at Beethoven with the same *ears*
as a world that was just learning to accept *The Afternoon of a Faun.*
Our evaluations of the past are inevitably conditioned by the
creative preoccupations of the present; hence it follows that the
past is perpetually in flux, and our view of its shape and significance is constantly changing. This can be richly documented in

the case of Beethoven, but we may consider here just two pieces of outmoded nonsense.

Anton Schindler, the professional *ami de Beethoven* and biographer of his last years, was convinced that every single movement in every composition by Beethoven was a programme piece representing some specific event or experience.   Schindler pointed out to Beethoven that he had often given verbal clues to the 'meanings' of his music, as in the case of the *Piano Sonata, Opus 81a,* whose three sections are entitled *Farewell, Absence,* and *Return.*   Schindler asked why Beethoven had failed to give similar verbal clues to everything else he had written.   Beethoven replied: 'In my time people didn't need such things.'   Schindler interprets this remark to mean that in Beethoven's youth people in general were so marvellously sensitive to the descriptive values of music that they were able to appreciate these values without having them pointed out.   What Beethoven was in fact trying to say, gently and tactfully, was that in his heyday people were not as literal-minded as Anton Schindler.

The second piece of nonsense comes from one of the many books on Beethoven published in 1927, when the world observed the hundredth anniversary of his death.   It is the opinion of an authority, highly regarded at that time, to the effect that Beethoven lost his hearing because he had to be deaf in order to fulfil his destiny.   He had to be isolated from the world in order to write the music of his last years, according to this writer, and so a mysterious providence took away the one sense by which a musician makes his most important contact with the world.

Both of these views are obviously nonsense, but they are nonsense of two totally different orders.   One is materialistic; it drags music down to a childishly descriptive level.   The other is high-flown and mystical; it is the work of a poetic, essentially fictional imagination which confuses the writer's subjective reactions to music with the music itself.   But both absurdities arise from the same inescapable fact about Beethoven: his compositions do convey, repeatedly and perennially, an extremely powerful overtone of the ethical and rhetorical.

A great composer's music is not an intimate diary.   If at certain points his music should happen to reflect his day-to-day experiences, the experiences are likely to be of a decidedly trivial kind; the crucial incidents of his career are likely to pass without direct expression in his work. Nevertheless, musical biography is not totally meaningless; there *are* broad correspondences, and the man who in life seems far ahead of his time always seems in retrospect to be eminently typical of it.

If Beethoven's achievement must be summed up in a single phrase, it may be said that he brought a new sense of scale to the classic forms of instrumental composition; and this is related to the most dynamic forces of the society in which he lived. The new sense of scale expresses itself in every musical dimension. The time-span of the classic structure is enormously increased; the symphony, sonata, or string quartet doubles and triples in length when compared with the accepted norms. The sonority of the music takes on a corresponding weight and depth, and the classic contrast of themes and tonalities assumes the character of a dramatic conflict ultimately resolved in triumph. And as a result of this new rhetorical emphasis, the relative weight of the movements is redistributed in a highly significant way.

It has been said that in the first movement of a pre-Beethoven sonata the composer shows what he can do; in the second movement what he can feel; and in the last how glad he is that it is all over. A Beethoven first movement still shows what the composer can do—it remains supremely active and dramatic in temper— and the second movement still shows what the composer can feel, but the typical Beethoven finale is a grand summation and resolution of all that has gone before.

All this is clearly involved with the composer's new orientation towards the world. The old era of personal patronage had gone; the composer of 1800 faced a large anonymous audience gathered more often in large theatres than in intimate halls. When a musician comes to depend upon large, anonymous audiences one of two things will happen to him. If he is a commonplace man he will try to amuse the crowd with tricks and stunts. Thus the violinist, Franz Clement, made capital of the fact that he had never so much as looked at the manuscript of Beethoven's Violin Concerto until he stepped to the platform to perform it in public for the first time. At the same concert Clement presented a fantasy of his own with the violin held upside-down. The activities of men like Clement are forgotten to-day, but they should not be, for they represent the lowest level to which European art music ever sank, and they throw the achievement of Beethoven himself into even higher and more monumental relief than is apparent from our ordinary point of vantage.

Beethoven's reaction to the new social situation was exactly the opposite of that symbolized by Clement.   Rather than amuse the crowd with tricks and stunts he led, controlled, directed, and dominated; he became the archetype of the free artist as master rather than servant.   This position has its dangers, especially when the stance of mastery is assumed by artists incompetent to maintain it, but no one in history was more eminently capable of maintaining it than Ludwig van Beethoven.

To typify my comments up to this point, nothing is more fitting than the first movement of Beethoven's Fifth Piano Concerto. It is not for nothing that this is called the *Emperor* Concerto. Beethoven did not give it that title, but the world has conferred that name upon it.   The emperor involved is not an aristocrat on a throne, but the composer himself, the imperial lord of tones.

Beethoven: *Piano Concerto No. 5 in E flat.*   VICTOR LCT 1015 (alt. Vox PL 9490).

Not long after Beethoven died, a Russian critic named Wilhelm von Lenz wrote a book called *Beethoven and his Three Styles*, and the phrase 'three styles' has clung to Beethoven criticism ever since.   Vincent d'Indy characterizes the first of the three eras as a period of *imitation*, wherein Beethoven largely reflects the prevailing manner of the late eighteenth century.   D'Indy calls the second era a period of *externalization*; here Beethoven goes forth to do battle with the world in a fashion already discussed and exemplified by the first movement of the *Emperor Concerto*.   The third period, according to d'Indy, is one of *reflection*.   The spirit of the music is remote from external conflict.   It floats high in a mysterious realm of its own and it involves a series of unprecedented inventions in the domain of musical structure.   In contrast to the second period, wherein he expands the traditional forms, the Beethoven of the final period creates totally new forms.

The Beethoven of the second phase, externalization, is the immensely popular one: this is the Beethoven of the symphonies from the Third through the Eighth, of the concertos, of the opera *Fidelio*, and the most frequently exploited sonatas.   It used to be that the Beethoven of the third period had less appeal for the general public, although in recent years musicians have lost their hesitancy about performing the great quartets and piano works of that phase, and recording has spread them mightily. The quality of this last period may be suggested by the *Quartet in A minor, Opus 132,* and its slow movement, which bears the title *Holy Song of Thanksgiving of a Convalescent to the Godhead, in the Lydian Mode.*[1]

Beethoven: *Quartet in A minor, Op. 132.* COLUMBIA ML 4586 (PHILIPS ABL 3132).

An aspect of Beethoven that should not be neglected is his songs. It is often said that Beethoven did not write gratefully for the voice, and it is true that some of his vocal works are extremely awkward to encompass. There are others, however, which proceed with highly idiomatic ease. In reviewing some newly published songs by a little known composer named Franz Schubert, Robert Schumann once observed that these works clung a little too closely to the Beethoven model. In the intervening years we have been taught that Schubert was the great innovator of the German concert song and we have forgotten his indebtedness to Beethoven. But this can be exemplified by the Beethoven song cycle *An die Ferne Geliebte (To the Distant Beloved).*

Beethoven: *An die Ferne Geliebte.* DECCA 9668 (alt. HMV ALP 1066).

No composer in history has been written about in such detail as Beethoven, none is more frequently performed, none is better known. Yet there are important areas in Beethoven that remain largely unexplored, such as the songs. He wrote more than two hundred concert songs and folk-song arrangements and his influence in this department is as important as in the symphony. But only his contemporaries realized this. We of the present day still have much to learn.

---

[1] Aldous Huxley's extraordinary description of this movement, which forms part of the last chapter of his novel, *Point Counter Point,* probably did more to arouse general interest in Beethoven's quartets than any other single thing published in the twentieth century. This, at least, holds true for the English-speaking world.

APPENDIX

BOOKS

A. W. THAYER: *The Life of Ludwig van Beethoven*, 3 vols.
PAUL BEKKER: *Beethoven*.
SIR DONALD TOVEY: *Essays in Musical Analysis*. *Beethoven*.
HECTOR BERLIOZ: *The Symphonies of Beethoven*.
JOSEPH DE MARLIAVE: *Beethoven's Quartets*.

RECORDS

Alfred Frankenstein writes: 'No specific records can be recommended because there are so many of them and so many good ones. The present writer especially likes the recordings of the symphonies by Bruno Walter, of the string quartets by the Budapest Quartet, of the piano concertos and sonatas by Arthur Schnabel, Wilhelm Backhaus, and Walter Gieseking. There are many other aspects of Beethoven the hearer ought to explore and can explore by means of superlative recordings—the sonatas for violin and for violoncello, the Violin Concerto, the opera *Fidelio*, and the choral works like the *Missa Solemnis*, etc., etc.'

NOTE. Several recordings of the symphonies under Bruno Walter have appeared in the English Columbia catalogue; but they are now withdrawn, although it is possible they may be reissued at some later date, probably by Philips. Schnabel's recordings of the piano music have been transferred to LP in the U.S.A. So far they are not available on the British market; but it is expected that some at least will shortly appear from HMV. Wilhelm Backhaus has recorded all the sonatas and four of the concertos for English Decca, issued by London in the U.S.A.; and Walter Gieseking was in the process of making complete recordings for English Columbia (Angel in U.S.A.) at the time of his death. Several records have already been issued, and more are expected. For DGG Wilhelm Kempff is in the course of making also the complete cycle. The complete Violin Sonatas are recorded by Heifetz on Victor (HMV) and the Violoncello Sonatas by Janos Starker on Period (Nixa). The complete String Quartets by the Budapest Quartet are to be found on Columbia, in the course of issue in England by Philips. Two versions of the opera *Fidelio* are available: on Victor LM 6025 (HMV ALP 1304–5) and HMV ALP 1130–2. The *Missa* is available on Vox, Victor (HMV), and DGG.

A few records of rarely heard but variously important Beethoven compositions may be mentioned:

Music to 'Egmont' (complete). DUCRETET-THOMSON DTL 93085.
Variations, 'Ich bin der Schneider Kakadu.' DGG DGM 18044.
Songs. HMV ALP 1317–18.
Works for Cello and Piano. DECCA LXT 5268.

38

William Mann

NINETEENTH-CENTURY SYMPHONY AND SYMPHONIC POEM

BEFORE the nineteenth century the various arts tended to develop on parallel but not connected lines, and within music the various forms and media grew naturally but distinctly. The pronounced tendency of the nineteenth century was to bring the arts together in a process of aspiration towards what Wagner eventually called the *Gesamtkunstwerk*, the work of art in which all the arts participated. And so this was the century that brought about the literary symphony and the descriptive symphonic poem, evolved the serious ballet score as composed by Delibes and Tchaikovsky, and was able to bring forth Verdi's *La Traviata*, an opera so up to date in the style of its scenery and costumes that early audiences, accustomed to historical operas, were shocked and bewildered.

One aspect of nineteenth-century symphonic music is the development of harmony from the so-called pure classicism of Haydn and Mozart (although it was really not so pure) towards the advanced chromatic language of Wagner and Tchaikovsky, Bruckner and Liszt, Mahler and the young Richard Strauss. We divide the music of previous centuries into two categories: diatonic music, which means that the white notes on the piano, the notes of the plain scale, are most important; and chromatic music, in which the black notes, or accidentals, colour the white notes and strive to become as important as them. When all the notes, white and black, achieve equal importance, the feeling of key centre is abolished, and we call the music atonal.

Schubert's great Symphony in C begins in C major without black notes. That was a perfectly normal and eloquent musical language for the symphonist of the early nineteenth century. By 1894 in Bruckner's Ninth Symphony the key feeling, so strong in Schubert's Symphony, has altogether been dispelled. The music is by no means atonal, but is as though firmness of key had been blown away by a gust of wind.

(i) Schubert: *Symphony in C major, No. 7.*   LONDON LL 619 (DECCA LXT 2719).
(ii) Bruckner: *Symphony No. 9 in D minor.*   VOX PL 8040 (E).

Tonality was one element that advanced enormously in romantic symphonic music of the last century.   Another was the scale of the music.   Haydn's last symphonies lasted twenty minutes or so; some of Bruckner's later symphonies and Liszt's *Faust* Symphony last a little over an hour.   The size of the orchestra too increased enormously.   Schubert in 1816 was content with one flute, two oboes and two bassoons, two horns, and strings— the Haydn orchestra.   Even Mendelssohn in 1844 scored his *Italian* Symphony for a standard medium-sized orchestra.   But by 1898, when Richard Strauss composed his symphonic poem *Ein Heldenleben,* the orchestra had acquired extra instruments like the cor anglais, the bass clarinet, and the little E flat clarinet; the horns had grown in number from two to eight, the trumpets, trombones, and two tubas had joined the assembly and there was a great increase in percussion instruments.   This meant that the string department had to be increased as well, so that instead of about two dozen players in the band, about one hundred and five musicians had to be available.

The content of the symphony also expanded.   In the eighteenth century symphonies were about musical patterns that could be made by a composer's imagination to express feelings.   In the nineteenth century the feelings became more important, and the patterns had to conform.   Composers wrote symphonies about specific subjects—literary, pictorial, geographical, or patriotic.

Where did all these romantic developments originate?   The culprits, paradoxically, were musicians whom we are inclined to pigeon-hole as classical, not romantic composers.   Beethoven introduced the piccolo and the trombones into the orchestra in his Fifth Symphony, not to mention soloists and a choir in his Ninth.   In his *Eroica* Symphony he stepped up the scale to a duration of fifty minutes, and he treated a descriptive subject to the extent that his symphony was avowedly about heroism.   I gave Schubert as an example of the diatonic composer, but Schubert loved to rove from key to key without advance notice. A study of the harmonic language of the nineteenth century reveals that many of the most characteristic chords are in Beethoven, and many more in Berlioz. Berlioz, together with Liszt, dominates the story of the nineteenth-century symphony.

One of the tendencies of the symphony was to absorb other musical mediums; it was Berlioz's symphony *Harold in Italy*, which is almost a viola concerto, that set the tone for Brahms's Piano Concerto in B flat (a concerto with strong leanings towards symphony), d'Indy's *Symphony on a French Mountaineer's Song* for piano and orchestra, Lalo's *Symphonie Espagnole* for violin and orchestra, and many other works in which concerto and symphony were profitably mingled. It was Berlioz's dramatic symphony *Romeo and Juliet*, following up the principles of Beethoven's Choral Symphony, that paved the way for the mixture of cantata and symphony which found further development in works by Mendelssohn and Liszt and eventually Mahler. As for the literary symphony, Berlioz externalized the descriptive element in the *Fantastic* Symphony, *Harold in Italy*, and *Romeo and Juliet*, and so made room for the factual description of the tone poems of Strauss and Tchaikovsky. The start of the intrusion of suite into symphony can be found too in Berlioz's *Fantastic* Symphony, which has five movements instead of the usual four. The extra movement is the *March to the Scaffold*—in the eighteenth century marches belonged to serenades—while the waltz in the *Ball Scene* is a replacement of the minuet or scherzo previously conventional in symphony.

All these explorations in language and idea mark Berlioz out as a romantic, and not least the zeal with which he pursued his multifarious experiments. He is the musical parallel to such authors as Chateaubriand and Lamartine, who set the course for French romantic literature in the early years of the nineteenth century. Berlioz was a romantic in intention, but his music is classic in line; the feeling and the goal know no restraint, but the contour of the music is controlled the whole time. Like Beethoven, he did not mind what canons of taste he flouted, but the line of the music is always being driven by a well-balanced intellect.

Berlioz: *Romeo and Juliet Symphony* (*Tomb Scene*). Victor LM 6011 (HMV ALP 1179–80).

It was inevitable in the aftermath of a classical era that there should be other symphonists who blended old and new ideals. Berlioz is the most important because the most far-reaching; the

French have never recovered from his influence, and it may be that other countries have yet to feel it fully. Mendelssohn was long admired by the comfortable children of the industrial revolution and the age of bourgeois respectability because his music reflected their taste, their admiration of restraint, and their sort of Christian culture. He was probably the most widely cultured musician who had lived up to that time; travelled, well-read, fluent in the other arts. His two most popular symphonies reflect the age in that their inspiration is geographical; one is about Scotland and the other about Italy. In the *Reformation* Symphony Mendelssohn used characterizing tunes to represent the conflict of Catholic and Protestant faiths, the *Dresden Amen* and Luther's chorale *A Stronghold Sure*. This is a rather dull symphony, but it deserves mention because its aims are romantic while its tone of voice is entirely classic.

Mendelssohn: *Symphony No. 5 in D minor (Reformation)*. COLUMBIA ML 4864 (PHILIPS ABL 3082).

Among other German symphonists Schumann is appealing rather than significant. There are enterprising features in his four symphonies, none the less: the one-movement shape of the Fourth Symphony, and its construction out of a few themes which are reshaped in subsequent movements; the use of a motto theme in the Second Symphony, and the programmatic slow fourth movement of the 'Rhenish' Symphony. This is intended to represent the cathedral of Cologne and the installation of a cardinal there.

Schumann: *Symphony No. 3 in E flat, 'Rhenish.'* COLUMBIA ML 4040 (COLUMBIA 33 CX 1045)* (alt. DGG DG 16063).

Schumann's mind had a descriptive streak that emerges constantly, but the 'Rhenish' Symphony is, on examination, no more likely to be programmatically detailed than are the symphonies of his younger friend Brahms; and Brahms's greatness as a symphonist is in no way connected with literary detail or German nationalism. Brahms shaped his symphonies abstractly and rather conservatively in view of all the experiment that was in progress around him, but with a solidity of thought and feeling that stands the test of time and changing fashions. Brahms kept to a medium-sized orchestra; he preserved the time scale of the Beethoven symphony; and his style of harmony and musical argument was rigidly sober. The idea of linking the various movements of a symphony together with a common theme was not part of his method; only in the Third Symphony did he bring back the opening theme in the last bars, and that was to show with the very mildest emphasis that the original thesis of the symphony had now been proved. He preferred the classical method of symphonic construction in which the ideas were interrelated under the surface without recourse to a family tree at every new event.

Brahms's particular contribution to the symphony was the intermezzo type of third movement. He did not much cultivate the Beethovenian scherzo; instead he placed there a melodious, gracefully flowing movement in three of his symphonies so that the two inner movements might expand at ease inside two more dynamic movements. The pace of Brahms's third movements can be heard in the Third Symphony, and it may be particularly alluring and spacious because this is the only symphony by Brahms that ends softly.

Brahms: *Symphony No. 3 in F* (*Allegretto*). LONDON LL 857 (DECCA LXT 2843).

Franz Liszt's innovations in musical language, particularly in harmony, not only changed Wagner's whole outlook on music, but looked forward to Debussy and Bartók in our century. His preoccupation with form and structure, and particularly with the transformation of a few themes to meet any desired mood or tempo, have their modern outcome in the monothematic music of serial composers. Liszt evolved the single-movement literary symphonic work which we call the symphonic poem or tone poem; a *genre* with roots in the theatrical overtures—Beethoven's *Leonora* Overture No. 3 is a tone poem *manqué*. Gradually Liszt discovered that many subjects were apt for symphonic treatment in a single movement, although the subjects he used were vague; his only really detailed transcription of poetry into music is the first movement of the *Dante* Symphony.

Liszt's other symphony is based on the three principal characters from Goethe's *Faust*. The *Faust* Symphony not only shows how much Wagner learned from Liszt, but also explores symphonic psychology such as Richard Strauss was to cultivate thirty years later in his rogues' gallery of symphonic portraits. Faust's themes are presented and developed in the first movement; Gretchen's in the slow movement. When Liszt reaches Mephistopheles, he shows him as a part of Faust's psyche by using distorted versions of Faust's own themes; a passionate theme is made to sound petty and sarcastic. This is the principle of Liszt's method of symphonic metamorphosis: one theme serving opposite purposes.

Liszt: *Faust Symphony*. LONDON LL 1303–4 (DECCA LXT 5101–2).

The leading Wagnerian symphonist of the latter part of the century was Anton Bruckner, who wrote nine symphonies and an earlier one numbered 'Nought.' Bruckner developed only secondarily from Liszt. His inspiration was nature, his natural mouthpiece the organ; if his harmony and the pace at which his music moves both recall Wagner at his most majestic, the source of his heritage was surely the Beethoven of the Ninth Symphony and the Schubert of the great C major Symphony. Bruckner's orchestra is not often extravagant and the type of theme he expounded is not far from the simple song of Schubert. He thought on the vast scale of Austrian mountainous scenery; his long tunes pause for breath when they feel like it and work their way to a climax without tiring of repetition. Over the years the tunes of Bruckner's symphonies became more eloquent and intricate and his harmony more richly expressive, but his symphonic methods remained the same—atmospheric and dramatic rather than argumentative. At his most mature and finest Bruckner spoke with the voice of every countryman, simple but aware of the eternal truths of nature and divine law: the voice of a man who walked with God.

APPENDIX

BOOKS

HERMANN SCHERCHEN: *The Nature of Music*.
JACQUES BARZUN: *Berlioz and the Romantic Century*.
ERNEST NEWMAN: *Musical Studies*.
MOSCO CARNER: *Of Men and Musicians*.
ADAM CARSE: *The Orchestra from Beethoven to Berlioz*.
ed. GERALD ABRAHAM: *Schumann: A Symposium*.
HUMPHREY SEARLE: *The Music of Liszt*.
DIKA NEWLIN: *Bruckner, Mahler, Schönberg*.

RECORDS

Nineteenth-century symphonies, symphonic poems, and concertos make up the greater part of the current orchestral repertoire, and of most people's musical experience too. They are well represented in the catalogues, and few of these works are not available in a number of performances on records.

39

Andrew Porter

NINETEENTH-CENTURY SONG

ARLIER essays in this book have sketched the history of song from the troubadours to the Tudors. Then, in the seventeenth and eighteenth centuries, the history of music is not much concerned with song. Almost all the vocal music of that period was intended either for the opera-house or the church, and so for professional singers. While every composer of note has at least one or two songs to his credit, it is not until we reach Franz Schubert that we find again a composer whose songs form more than a side-line in his output.

Social reasons for this can be discovered by considering the case of Haydn. While Haydn was in the service of the Esterházys he composed operas and symphonies, but not songs. Only when he went to London, where music was organized on a democratic rather than an aristocratic basis, did he turn to song-writing in earnest. For the singing of songs is essentially a domestic activity, and it had little place in music produced under a system of aristocratic patronage. Song-writing on a large scale began only in the nineteenth century, when composers started to cater for the new, increasingly important middle-class audience which did not have private orchestras and opera-houses. It was at this time too that printed music started to circulate cheaply and extensively, and the making of so-called 'art music' became a regular activity in ordinary homes. And for this new audience a new art form was created.

All the circumstances were propitious for a song-writer of genius, and such was Franz Schubert. He was the son of an Austrian schoolmaster and sang as a boy in the choir of the Imperial Chapel. He never held any official position, but picked up a living in various ways. No publishers took any interest in his music until in 1821 some friends had twenty of his songs printed at their own expense. Although he lived only to the age of thirty-one, Schubert wrote more music than almost any other great composer, including six hundred songs; and he possessed the gift of melody as no other composer has done. Numerous stories survive to show that he could hardly read a line of poetry without conceiving at once a melody to fit it.

A good example of Schubert's art at its most simple and spontaneous is *Der Jüngling an der Quelle*, composed in 1815. The poem is not at all distinguished, but Schubert in about a minute of music creates an extraordinarily vivid little scene: the sparkling brook with its murmuring pebbles sounds in the accompaniment, while the lilting melody tells us of the boy in love. The sighs of young love are reflected in one or two magical modulations that pass like quick shadows over the very simple harmony.

Schubert: *Der Jüngling an der Quelle*. HMV DA 1521 (alt. DGG DGM 18029).

The wonderful simplicity of such a song is only one part of Schubert's creative personality. For in the new medium of the art-song, or *Lied*, nineteenth-century composers embodied musical conceptions which had formerly found expression only in works on a larger scale. The tendency of nineteenth-century music was towards greater length and greater forces, but the song-writers learned to compress; they could compass in a few minutes, and with no other resources than a single voice with piano accompaniment, the emotions, passions, and drama which other composers were putting into opera or massive tone-poems.

Schubert creates on the grandest possible scale in songs like *Der Atlas*, *Prometheus*, or *Gruppe aus dem Tartarus*. In the last, Schiller's lines tell of the torment of the damned, and Schubert's music seems actually to communicate to us what they must feel; we are among them, hearing the hollow crash of the water, seeing the harsh crags through their tortured eyes. There is a long *crescendo* as they ask whether their sufferings can ever come to an end; then with tremendous effect the word '*Ewigkeit*' crashes out—their torments will last for eternity. In the piano postlude it is as if we, the spectators, drew rapidly farther and farther away from the terrible scene. Schubert has discovered an artistic effect that became possible in a visual medium only with the invention of the cinema, or rather the cinema-camera and aeroplane used together. Schubert needed only eight bars of music.

Schubert: *Gruppe aus dem Tartarus*. VICTOR 16149 (alt. DECCA LW 5235).

There is nothing so dramatic in the songs of Robert Schumann. He treated the song medium rather as he had treated the piano; as a kind of diary to which he confided his thoughts, impressions, and emotions. Schubert in his great song cycles, *Die schöne Müllerin* (*The Fair Maid of the Mill*) and *Die Winterreise* (*The Winter Journey*), produced almost the song equivalent of novels, but more direct in their communication of feeling. Schumann did not have the same directness or objectivity. With Schubert we feel that the poem has turned straight into music; the listener is not invited to think of the poem as existing apart from the music. Schumann's is a more literary and a more self-conscious approach, and we feel that he is trying to find the music which will rightly adorn, reflect, and intensify the poem. In his masterpiece *Dichterliebe* (*A Poet's Love*) Schumann shows how sensitive he was to poetry; Heine's *words* provide the inspiration, not whatever in the first place inspired Heine.

Schumann: *Dichterliebe*. LONDON LL 940 (DECCA LXT 2875).

If 'word-painting' is the term to describe the songs of Schumann, 'mood-painting' is the term for many of Brahms's songs. He wrote nearly two hundred throughout his career, and with them a philosophical note comes into nineteenth-century song. In Brahms's lyricism there is nearly always an element of gravity which finds its final expression in the *Four Serious Songs* to biblical texts. In these songs the art-song conquered still more territory, for, although only two performers are involved, they are in effect an oratorio.

Not all Brahms's songs are solemn and reflective—he wrote many songs in the gay folk-song tradition—but his particular contribution is best represented by such a song as *Feldeinsamkeit*, composed in 1877. This shows his tender, grave lyricism at its most characteristic and beautiful, and is mood-painting of a high order. In a gently flowing accompaniment Brahms conjures up the mood induced by the still, lonely countryside, and the slowly moving vocal line suggests calm contemplation. Brahms has learned from both Schubert and Schumann; he gives us both the scene and a poetic commentary on it.

Brahms: *Feldeinsamkeit*. VICTOR 7793.

Hugo Wolf is the purest example of the nineteenth-century song-writer; for although he produced a handful of works in other mediums, he distilled the essence of his genius into some two hundred and fifty songs. He was by no means the spontaneous singer that Schubert had been. The creative power came upon him in short very intense bursts, and he would work at a feverish pitch, sometimes pouring out several wonderful songs in a single day. Then would come a period without inspiration. His songs fall into groups: the settings of Mörike, Eichendorff, and Goethe, and the Spanish and Italian song-books. These coherent collections are framed between a group of early songs and a group of late songs with texts by various poets.

Wolf was a fervent admirer of Wagner, and it is symptomatic of nineteenth-century song that the grandiose techniques of the largest-scale composer the world has ever known should have been fined down and made to serve the purposes of the composer of exquisite miniatures. Wolf may not have been a greater song-writer than Schubert, but he certainly brought the medium to a degree of flexibility and expressiveness never known before; and since Wolf there have been no further significant developments in the art of song-writing. He does everything that Schubert, Schumann, and Brahms tried to do. He puts his listeners into direct touch with the poet's source of inspiration, he paints a scene, he conjures up a mood; and at the same time he treats the poet's words with unusual faithfulness and vividness. The words to a greater extent than ever before dictate the shape of the vocal line, and without the words the music hardly makes sense. The very vowels and consonants are drawn into the texture that voice and piano spin between them.

Wolf's range is as great as that of the poets he sets. In the *Italienisches Liederbuch*, for example, he has created a gallery of men and women in and out of love. He can be tender, grand, noble, angry, melancholy, or devout. But it must be noted that his limitations spring from his very virtues: from the fact that he is, purely and solely, a song-writer. In Wolf's music we do not find, as in Schubert's, the spontaneous bubbling over of melody with a life of its own; we do not find, as in Schumann, the personal, intimate commentary on what the words mean to the composer himself; we do not find, as in Brahms, the assimilation of what may be quite commonplace ideas to a rich philosophic and intellectual background. Instead, we find an intense concentration on the particular poem before us.

Wolf too could create on an epic scale within small time-dimensions, as in *Der Feuerreiter* (*The Fire-rider*). Fire-riders have the power to detect distant fires towards which they are irresistibly impelled, but they are forbidden to extinguish the flames. The Fire-rider of Mörike and Wolf does so, however, with a chip of the true Cross, but the burning mill collapses about him in punishment.

Wolf: *Der Feuerreiter*. HMV Hugo Wolf Society (alt. HMV 7 ER 5044).

So far this essay has for obvious reasons been confined to German song, but the nationalists in other countries brought distinctive notes of their own to the art of song. In Russia Glinka inaugurated the tradition of writing art-songs; the most distinguished Russian song-writer was Mussorgsky. In his songs, as in his operas, the vocal line is inspired both by the inflexions of Russian speech and the characteristic intervals and rhythms of Russian folk music.

Mussorgsky: *The Nursery*. Capital P 8265 (CTL 7068)* (alt. DGG DGM 19050).

In Bohemia and Scandinavia, as in Russia, song-writing was closely bound up with the folk-song revival of the period. Towards the end of the century French song began to gather impetus. Earlier there was one individual genius, striking out his own path in song as in every form he attempted: Berlioz. His *Nuits d'été* deserve mention, not because they were influential, but because they are so fine. They also show that some song composers could not limit themselves to the drawing-room and the piano, but needed the full orchestra.

Berlioz: *Nuits d'été*. London LL 407 (Decca LXT 2605).

French art songs, or *mélodies*, begin properly with Gounod and Franck, but they become important only in the next generation with the work of Chausson, Fauré, and Duparc. In these *mélodies* it is not the folk-idiom that is important, but the rise and fall and the muted cadences of the French language which suggest the characteristic shape of the vocal line. French song developed late, but its development continued unbroken through Debussy and Ravel to present-day composers like Poulenc and Auric.

Fauré: *Soir*. HMV DA 1819 (alt. Decca LX 3080).

APPENDIX

BOOKS

ELIZABETH SCHUMANN: *German Song.*
ALFRED EINSTEIN: *Schubert.*
RICHARD CAPELL: *Schubert's Songs.*
FRANK WALKER: *Hugo Wolf.*

RECORDS

SCHUBERT: *Die Schöne Müllerin.*   VICTOR LHMV 6 or HMV ALP
    1036–7.   *Die Winterreise.*   HMV ALP 1298–9.
SCHUMANN: *Liederkreis.*   HMV BLP 1068.
Schubert and Fauré Recital.   LONDON LL 245 (DECCA LXT 2543).
Song Recital (Schubert, Schumann, Brahms, Wolf).   ANGEL 35023.
WOLF: *Italienisches Liederbuch.*   DECCA 9632 (DGG DGM 18192).
    Songs.   HMV ALP 1143.
MUSSORGSKY: *Sunless Cycle.*   CAPITOL P 8310 (CAPITOL CTL 7100).

40

Andrew Porter

NINETEENTH-CENTURY OPERA

OPERA up to the nineteenth century must be viewed both as a royal entertainment under direct royal patronage and as an entertainment beloved of the people. In the later seventeenth and eighteenth centuries almost every court of note could boast a private or semi-private opera; while Venice had built its first public opera-house in 1637, London in 1656, and Paris in 1669. By the beginning of the nineteenth century the distinction between the royal and the public opera-houses was beginning to disappear. The public had long been admitted to the royal opera-houses, and now they began to take an increasingly large share in their management.

Opera to the nineteenth-century public was in some ways what the circuses and games had been to the Imperial Romans, and what the cinema is to the public of to-day: the supreme form of mass entertainment. In Vienna, where the art-song flourished, this was primarily a century of private music-making, but in Italy, where there was no such tradition, opera was the chief art form—the important Italian composers of the century are all opera composers—and in Paris too the opera reigned supreme.

Paris has the grandest opera-house in the world, and during the nineteenth century it was the mecca of all opera composers in a sense which it is hard to appreciate to-day. Verdi, in a letter written in 1851, refers almost with awe to its possession of 'the most expensive singers, the most ample ballet-corps in the world, and an orchestra of unrivalled strength and eminence, accompanying never-ending masses of chorus singers.'

It is symptomatic of the exotic art of opera that the leading composers of French grand opera should have been foreigners: the Italian Lully, the German Gluck, the Italian Cherubini, the Italian Spontini, and the German Meyerbeer. By the beginning of the nineteenth century Gluck's reforms had been obscured by the more spectacular offerings of Gasparo Spontini. In 1807 Spontini's *La Vestale* was produced in Paris, and two years later his *Fernand Cortez*, and they set the tone for what was to follow: heroic or historical subject-matter, elevated emotions, music that allowed scope for vocal display, and action that allowed for plenty of elaborate scenery.

The next important contribution to this *genre* came from Rossini, who in 1829 composed for the Paris Opéra what can in some respects be regarded as his masterpiece, *Guillaume Tell*. Those who know Rossini only as the composer of the lightweight, sparkling comic operas may be surprised by *William Tell*. Its closing scene is among the great inspirations of operatic music. The storm has cleared away, and an immense view opens up: in the distance snowy peaks glisten in the sunshine. The scene is symbolic of the new freedom which awaits Switzerland. A single motive, suggesting the *Ranz des vaches*, is passed upwards from horn to wood-wind, passing through many keys major and minor; the characters contemplate the scene, their hearts filled with joy, and at last unite their voices in a great paean to liberty. After this apotheosis, it is almost understandable that Rossini should never have written another line for the theatre.

Rossini: *William Tell*. CETRA 1232.

Two years after *William Tell* was first given, Giacomo Meyerbeer made his appearance at the Opéra with *Robert le Diable*, to be followed by *Les Huguenots*, *Le Prophète*, and *L'Africaine*. In these operas flashy theatrical effects took the place of classical or epic drama. Donald Grout has given a neat description of Meyerbeer's lack of artistic integrity: 'An opera of Meyerbeer's is like a department store, where everything may be found displayed in the most tempting manner to the prospective buyer.' Whatever we may think of these operas to-day, it must be recorded as historical fact that they appealed even to people of discrimination until the end of the century. Religious conflict, historical struggles, and geographical explorations seemed to them to be elevated operatic themes, and they were willing to overlook the meretricious trappings. Furthermore, these operas were safe showpieces for singers.

It has often been said that nineteenth-century opera composers pandered to their singers and debased their music to give the prima donnas and star tenors ample opportunity to show off, but it might equally well be claimed that the prodigious vocal abilities of the singers acted as a stimulus to the composers. In Bellini's operas the coloratura is certainly no mere decoration, but unfailingly enhances the expressive power of the music.

In 1831, the year the Paris Opéra produced Meyerbeer's *Le Prophète*, La Scala in Milan brought out Bellini's *Norma*. Italian scene design was academic and conservative in comparison with that of the Opéra in Paris, and there was no Meyerbeer in Italy, anxious to astonish the public with something that they had never seen before. Italian grand opera composers tended to work in the traditional style; they expressed the drama in the traditional Italian way—first and foremost, through the melody. In Bellini and Donizetti (whose *Lucia di Lammermoor* appeared in 1835) Italy had two composers with a supreme gift of dramatic melody, and *Norma* is one of the most beautiful operas ever composed. The libretto by Felice Romani is a nobly fashioned drama which descends from the eighteenth-century librettos of Metastosio and, ultimately, from classical drama. In the final scene of the opera Norma announces to the horrified Gauls that she, their priestess, has betrayed them by becoming the mistress of the Roman Pollione. She turns to Pollione (who has in the meantime forsaken her) and makes her sublime gesture. Bellini writes the simplest of accompaniments, with a subtle, ominous mutter of drums in the second half of each bar.

Bellini: *Norma* (*Qual cor tradisti . . .*). ANGEL 3517 C (COLUMBIA 33 CX 1179–81).

But already Donizetti, although no revolutionary, was veering away from the classical drama in the melodramatic situations of his *Lucia di Lammermoor*. In 1839 Giuseppe Verdi stepped on to the scene: a composer who was to unite in a long series of operas the theatrical effectiveness and spectacular inventions of Meyerbeer, the classical serenity of Bellini, and the highly coloured expression of personal emotions of Donizetti. Verdi's heroes and heroines are, like Bellini's, often larger than life, but their emotions are treated not classically, but romantically. Furthermore, Verdi was an ardent patriot, and through almost all his works runs a strong vein of patriotic feeling: the chorus of exiled Jews weeping beside the waters of Babylon in *Nabucco*; the chorus of exiled Scots in *Macbeth*; the terrible conflict which confronts Aida when she must choose between love and patriotism. Verdi's great flair for dramatic situation has often been remarked, but Verdi was at heart, like Bellini, a very 'pure' composer who expressed the dramatic situation in terms of melody. A good example of this 'purity' is *La Vergine degli angeli*, the close of the second act of *La Forza del Destino*. Leonora is going to finish her days in penance, and her voice floats above those of the monks as together they pray for the Virgin's protection.

Verdi: *La Forza del Destino* (*La Vergine degli angeli*). LONDON XLLA 37 (alt. HMV ALP 1099).

To point the purity of Verdi's style, we may contrast *La Vergine degli angeli* with another operatic prayer, Tosca's *Vissi d'arte*. *Tosca* appeared in 1900, but it found its predecessors in *Cavalleria Rusticana* of 1890 and *Pagliacci* of 1892 and in *Andrea Chénier* and *La Bohème*, which both appeared in 1896. The aim in these works was the direct presentation of emotion. It was what Gluck had preached and what Meyerbeer and Donizetti and, above all, Verdi had often achieved; and yet it was, indisputably, opera on a less noble level. Classicism and romanticism were superseded by realism—by *verismo*. In the true sense of the word this was not grand opera at all, and it marked the final emancipation of opera from the traditions of the grand court entertainments in which the art had its origins.

Comic opera flourished locally, and thousands of comic operas were produced, were the talk of the town for a week or even a month, and were then forgotten. In Germany and Austria comic opera was almost the staple diet. In Italy in the first half of the century there was not the same distinction between serious and comic opera composers as existed later: Rossini and Donizetti were admired for both. Donizetti's *L'Elisir d'Amore*, which dates from 1832, is early nineteenth-century comic opera at its best: light, graceful, witty, and tuneful: an ideal entertainment.

Donizetti: *L'Elisir d'Amore*. VICTOR LM 6024 (HMV ALP 1067–8).

The line of comic opera dies out in Italy to flourish again in Vienna, Paris, and in London: in the works of Johann Strauss, Offenbach, and Gilbert and Sullivan. French comic opera tended to have more sting in the wit than that of other countries. When Parisians in 1864 went to see Offenbach's *La Belle Hélène*, with its guying of classical heroes, part of their fun was doubtless derived from the contrast with M. Berlioz's grand opera, *Les Troyens*, which had been seen the previous year. Offenbach's music is charming and funny enough to survive in its own right, not merely as a skit.

Offenbach: *La Belle Hélène.* RENAISSANCE SX 206 (NIXA PLP 206).

French opera proper, as distinct from the French-Italian brand of grand opera, we can date from Gounod's *Faust* of 1869, and we may trace a line through Bizet's *Carmen* (1875) and Massenet's *Manon* (1884). In these high points of a flourishing school we have characteristically French music which could not have been written by an Italian, with its vocal line closely influenced by the cadences of French speech.

German opera seems largely a matter of isolated figures: Beethoven, Weber, Wagner. But these peaks are joined by lines of hills: the works of men like Marschner, whose *Hans Heiling* influenced Wagner, and Lortzing, whose comic operas are still played in every German town. Wagner's individual genius built on the twin foundations of German romantic opera and international grand opera. Wagner was in rebellion against Meyerbeer, but he learned from Meyerbeer how to handle spectacle on a big scale. Wagner was not, however, a product of the age, but an individual genius who fitted no pattern. To be performed properly his operas had to have a special opera-house built for them.

The nationalist opera was a product of the age, and its finest fruits were produced in Russia and Bohemia. Glinka wrote two operas which together set the pattern for later Russian opera. *A Life for the Tsar* appeared in 1836, and while its formal model was French grand opera, it made conspicuous use of Russian folk melodies and rhythms. It is the progenitor of Borodin's *Prince Igor*, Mussorgsky's *Boris Godunov* and *Khovanshchina*, and Rimsky-Korsakov's *Ivan the Terrible*. Glinka's other opera, *Russlan and Ludmilla*, is a highly coloured, glittering fairy-story, and from this work sprang the other kind of Russian opera represented by Rimsky-Korsakov's *Snow Maiden* and *Golden Cockerel* and Stravinsky's *Nightingale*. Czech opera at its most characteristic presents folk-life directly on the stage, not viewing it from an epic point of view or through magic glasses. Thus Smetana's *The Bartered Bride* (1866) contains little or no quotation of folk tunes, but every number in it is closely derived from folk idiom.

APPENDIX

BOOKS

EDWARD J. DENT: *Opera.*
FRANCIS TOYE: *Italian Opera.*
MARTIN COOPER: *Opéra Comique* and *Russian Opera.*

RECORDS

Nineteenth-century opera is well represented in the current catalogues, and there are alternative recordings of many operas, so no attempt has been made to supply a comprehensive list.   But mention may be made of the following:

GLINKA: *A Life for the Tsar.*   VANGUARD 6010–2 or ENGLISH DECCA LXT 5173–6.

MUSSORGSKY: *Boris Godunov.*   VICTOR LHMV 6400 (HMV ALP 1044–7).

SMETANA: *The Bartered Bride.*   URANIA B 231 (SUPRAPHON LPV 91–3).

VERDI: *Otello.*   VICTOR LM 6107 (HMV ALP 1090–2).   *Falstaff.* VICTOR LM 6111 (HMV ALP 1229–33).

WAGNER: *Tristan und Isolde.*   VICTOR LM 6700 (HMV ALP 1030–1035).   *Die Meistersinger.*   LONDON XLLA 9 (DECCA LXT 2659–2664) or COLUMBIA SL 117 (COLUMBIA 33 CX 1021–5).   *Parsifal.* LONDON XLLA 10 (DECCA LXT 2651–6).

41

Andrew Porter

NINETEENTH-CENTURY CHAMBER MUSIC

CHAMBER music, *Kammermusik, musique de chambre*— the name reveals that it is to be played at home, in a room; and naturally it flourished in Vienna in the nineteenth century where music-making in one's own house was a widespread activity.   The royal line of chamber music composers is Haydn, Mozart, Beethoven, Schubert, and Brahms, all of whom worked in Vienna.

Towards the end of the eighteenth century composers, hitherto the paid servants of noble families, began to earn their living as independent figures.   In the nineteenth century the nobility still enjoyed hearing chamber music performed in their *salons*, but the performers were no longer members of their household, but professional musicians invited for the occasion.   Meanwhile, the educated middle classes began to enter into competition with the nobility, and soon they took the lead.   Music was cultivated in the home by friendly groups of amateurs and professionals.   The increasing cheapness of printed music, the excellence of Viennese instrument-making at the time, and, above all, the fact that there was chamber music by Haydn, Mozart, and Beethoven to play, caused it to prosper.

As the century went on, however, the family drawing-room gave way to the concert-room, and the musicians were no longer all participants, but divided into the professionals on the platform and the audience who had paid to come and listen.   And chamber music became different in kind too.   It ceased to be just entertainment, and the string quartet in particular became the regular method of expression for a composer's most profound and intimate utterances.   The responsibility for this change was Beethoven's.

Beethoven spent the first twenty-two years of his life in Bonn, the later part of it in the service of the Elector.   The Elector was 'daily entertained by a small orchestra consisting of two oboes, two clarinets, two horns, and two bassoons,' and for this band Beethoven composed music which probably accompanied the Elector's meals. When Beethoven went to Vienna, he continued for a while to write occasional pieces for wind instruments, often combining them with piano or strings. The finest of these pieces is the *Septet* composed in 1800. It was, typically, first heard at a private party, but soon afterwards at a public concert. Two years later it was published, and since not everyone was able to assemble the combination of clarinet, horn, bassoon, violin, viola, cello, and double-bass, it was put out in all sorts of arrangements. It is graceful and easy to listen to, and it makes no sort of intellectual demands on its hearers.

Beethoven: *Septet in E flat*. LONDON LL 1191 (alt. NIXA WLP 20020).

In the purer medium of the string quartet, however, Beethoven was already beginning to write works of a very different kind. Haydn's last quartets were contemporary with Beethoven's first, and Beethoven was to carry the form decisively forwards, both technically and expressively. Mozart and Haydn had agreed in principle that all four instruments of the string quartet had equally important parts to play, but in practice they generally made first violin and cello dominate the ensemble. It was left to Beethoven to establish real democracy in the chamber ensemble. (The child Mozart once remarked: 'One doesn't need to have learned the violin to play a second-violin part.' Beethoven, on the other hand, declared when sending the Septet to his publishers: '*All* the parts are *obbligato* . . . I cannot write anything not *obbligato*.')

Beethoven came to the string quartet medium surprisingly late in his career, almost as though he hesitated to use the medium which was later to enshrine his most profound thought until he felt himself ready for it. The first string quartets, Opus 18, were published in two sets of three in 1801, when Beethoven was thirty-one. They were a product of the new middle-class musical culture, for Beethoven almost certainly learned the elements of string quartet style at the home of Aloys Förster, host to the most famous virtuosi of the day, including the Schuppanzigh Quartet which performed Beethoven's Rasumovsky Quartets and almost certainly tried out and discussed the Opus 18 quartets.

Beethoven's Opus 18 quartets do not strike through to the

profundity of Haydn's, but in 1806—the year that Haydn sent his last quartet to his publishers—Beethoven produced three quartets whose boldness startled his contemporaries. They were composed to a commission from the Prince Rasumovsky, who stipulated that a Russian theme should appear in each. It is significant of the change that was taking place in the musical world that in these works Beethoven should be both writing to commission and writing for himself. His later quartets were entirely personal. The great trinity, the Quartets in A minor (Opus 132), B flat major (Opus 130), and C sharp minor (Opus 131), are still found puzzling to-day. They lead us to the shores of another world.

In March 1826 the first performance was given of the B flat quartet (Opus 130), ending with the *Grosse Fuge* that was deemed unplayable and incomprehensible. Beethoven was asked for a new finale. In July of that year Beethoven's beloved nephew, Karl, made a bungled attempt on his own life. Beethoven took him to his brother's estate to recover, and there he completed his last quartet, the *Quartet in F major, Opus 135*. His health was failing, and he wrote over the last movement of this work: 'The difficult decision. Must it be? It must be, it must be.' Marion Scott has described both the first and last movements as 'haunted by the questioning, the recoil of the human heart from death.' And yet there is another story which shows that Beethoven could bring apparent irreconcilables together. A rich amateur, on learning that it would cost him fifty florins to borrow the parts of Beethoven's latest quartet, asked ruefully: 'Must it be?' Beethoven laughed heartily, and replied: 'Yes, yes; it must be. Over with the money! Yes, yes, it must be.' He jotted down a canon to the words, making his first use of the theme for this 'death-haunted' last movement. In the quartet cello and viola put the question, at first softly and then more and more insistently; and the violins reply decisively.

Beethoven: *Quartet in F major, Op. 135.* COLUMBIA ML 4587 (PHILIPS ABL 3133).

Schubert did not have the same specific feeling for the medium of the string quartet as Haydn and Beethoven; he used it with great skill, but he did not experiment boldly with its possibilities. On his chamber music he bestowed the same gifts of inexhaustible melody, grace, and poetic feeling as went into his songs and orchestral writing. His *Piano Quintet in A*, the so-called 'Trout'

Quintet, shows the sort of circumstances that could influence the writing of chamber music.   It might be thought from the unusual combination of instruments—not string quartet and piano, but violin, viola, cello, *double-bass*, and piano—that the composer had some special reason for choosing these sonorities.   In fact, Schubert wrote the quintet while on holiday in a small town for the players who happened to be available.

Schubert: *Piano Quintet in A*.   London LL 223 (Decca LXT 2533).

Schumann's Piano Quintet is very different in style.   The bulk of Schumann's chamber music dates from the single year 1842; three string quartets, the piano quintet, and the piano quartet. The string quartets are not very interesting, but when the piano enters the texture it is a different matter.   The Piano Quintet may be said to have begun a new epoch in chamber music, a line to be continued by Brahms, Dvořák, and César Franck.   In these piano quintets the composers are writing concert music for public performance, and we have only to compare Schumann's quintet with Schubert's to hear the difference between 'public' and 'private' chamber music.

Schumann: *Piano Quintet in E flat*.   Capitol P 8316 (alt. Columbia 33 CX 1050).

In the chamber music of Brahms all the various strands draw together.   Like Schubert, Brahms wrote works whose instrumentation was determined by particular performers; like Schumann he wrote concert music; and like Beethoven he made it an intimate, profound medium.   Brahms's Clarinet Quintet sums up all that has been said.   Its first performance was in the intimacy of a *salon*; the performers were court musicians.   Its second performance was at a public concert in Berlin.   It was written for Richard Mühlfeld, the principal clarinet of the excellent Meiningen orchestra, whom Brahms much admired.   He dubbed him 'Fraülein Klarinette' on account of the exceptional sweetness of his tone, and declared that he had never heard such beautiful sounds from the instrument, or such poetical phrasing.   For Mühlfeld Brahms wrote the Clarinet Quintet and the Clarinet Trio, both in 1891, and three years later the two Clarinet Sonatas. The quintet is Brahms's most graceful, mellow composition, free from conflict and glowing with sunset radiance.   Its predecessor in the *genre*, Mozart's Clarinet Quintet, is a high-summer composition, written in A major, one of his most sun-filled keys.   In

Brahms's B minor quintet it is October.   He uses to the full the gentle, melancholy, expressive possibilities of 'Fraülein Klarinette'; while making much of its poignant *chalumeau* register, he does not neglect the brilliant upper reaches where it can ring out with clarion tones or its affectionate middle register.   In this celestial music the vigorous striving of Brahms's early chamber music and the earnestness of the three string quartets all find their fulfilment.

Brahms: *Clarinet Quintet in B minor.* WESTMINSTER 5155 (alt. DECCA LXT 2858).

The Russians were not especially noted for chamber music, although Borodin wrote two beautiful quartets, and Tchaikovsky wrote three quartets and a piano trio.   In France, Saint-Saëns produced a good deal of chamber music, as he did everything else, but French chamber music really began to flourish later with Fauré, Debussy, and Ravel.   Chamber music was not a convenient medium for nationalistic expression, but Beethoven, followed by Brahms, had set the tradition for making chamber music a personal form of utterance.   In the works of so intensely nationalistic a composer as Smetana we find that both his string quartets are autobiographical.   The First Quartet is generally known by its German title, *Aus meinem Leben* (*From my life*).   It follows a programme: the first movement tells of 'love of art in youth, the unsatisfied longing for something inexpressible'; the second movement uses a national idiom to describe his merry youth; the third describes his happy married life.   The finale 'illustrates the composer's response to national music and his joy in success.'   This is suddenly broken by the fatal note which sounded in his ear, the herald of his approaching deafness.   The joyful music is suddenly broken by silence; over shuddering chords we hear a prolonged high E, and then a lamenting recitative.   There follows a tender moderato; the composer is not defiant, not despairing, and the work ends on a note of quiet grief.

Smetana: *String Quartet No. 1 in E minor.* LONDON LL 865 (DECCA LXT 2876).

K

APPENDIX

BOOKS

A. HYATT KING: *Chamber Music.*
MARION SCOTT: *Beethoven.*
KARL GEIRINGER: *Brahms.*

RECORDS

The chamber works of the nineteenth-century composers discussed have all been extensively recorded. None of the complete sets of the Beethoven String Quartets is ideal; on the whole that by the Budapest Quartet on Columbia (Philips) is probably the most satisfactory. The following records deserve special mention:

BEETHOVEN: *Piano Trio in B flat, Op. 97, 'Archduke.'* WESTMINSTER 5131 or NIXA WLP 20018.

SCHUBERT: *String Quintet in C.* CAPITOL 8133 (CAPITOL CTL 7011) or PHILIPS ABL 3100. *Piano Trio in B flat, Op. 99.* COLUMBIA ML 4715 or HMV BLP 1077. *Piano Trio in E flat, Op. 100.* COLUMBIA ML 4716 or PHILIPS ABL 3009.

42

Lionel Salter

NINETEENTH-CENTURY PIANO MUSIC

THE piano, at the start of the nineteenth century, was an instrument with only about twenty years' use behind it. Publishers were still warily announcing their works as 'for harpsichord or pianoforte': Beethoven's first eight sonatas were so described, although we may be confident that he never had the harpsichord in mind. But the piano was frail in construction, with a light action and a light tone, and a five-octave compass which manufacturers were just beginning to extend. The kind of music to which it was suited was the delicately decorative Viennese style.

Hummel: *Rondo in E flat.* HMV DB 5510.

Beethoven's influence on piano writing was as great as on every other aspect of music which he touched: he enormously extended the structure and emotional range of the sonata, and technically he exploited chord and broken octave figurations, the full range of the keyboard, the *una corda* or 'soft pedal' effect, inner trills, fugal textures, and all the other devices which are now the basis of piano writing. Many of these can be observed in the Sonata, Opus 106, which Beethoven in an excess of nationalism called the *Hammerklavier*, a German term which implied no difference from the accepted instrument of the time.

Beethoven: *Sonata in B flat, Op. 106.* LONDON LL 422 (alt. DGG DGM 18146).

Such flights as the *Hammerklavier Sonata* were way over the heads of most of the new public. The more informed of them could take variations on favourite operatic airs or popular tunes of the day, and these were dutifully provided by every composer; less cultivated listeners formed the vast public for dance music, for there was at this time a great craze for dancing. Waltzes, *écossaises*, and *contredanses* poured out from the publishers; no composer ignored the demand, and some of Schubert's chains of waltzes and *ländler*, in particular, have remained in the repertoire through their fresh simplicity and unflagging invention. The first composer to elevate the waltz to concert level was Weber, in 1819. He was himself a virtuoso player, with long fingers and a big stretch, so that in his music are to be found extended chords, wide leaps, and a great deal of florid passage work.

Weber: *Invitation to the Dance.*   VICTOR LM 1918 (alt. HMV DB 6491).

Weber's sonatas, though classical in form, are romantic in style. One of the best definitions of romanticism in music is that of Kathleen Dale:

Romanticism is exemplified in music by the insistence laid upon the expression of personal feelings and emotions, by impatience with the restraints imposed by conventional forms, by the introduction of the picturesque and the exotic, and by the attempt to translate other arts into music or to combine the phenomena of other arts with music itself.

Partly because of his operatic background, Weber favoured the writing of programme music—that is, music which tells a story. To the immature public of limited understanding programme music made a great appeal: storms, with rumbles in the left hand for thunder and chromatic scales for lightning, were immensely popular, and so were battle scenes. Until 1815 Europe was never without a war somewhere, and innumerable piano representations of famous battles were put on the market by astute publishers.

Too close a preoccupation with the accepted masterpieces of the nineteenth century may lead us to overlook the tremendous influence exerted by musical amateurs and tyros. To be able to play the piano was regarded as an accomplishment for the womenfolk of the new bourgeois class, and fashionable teachers such as Clementi and Moscheles made a lot of money. Published studies for the piano also did well: here two of the earliest in the field were Cramer and Czerny, whose time-and-motion studies analysed technique scientifically. Moscheles complained bitterly of the tastes of his patrons; they wanted nothing but fugitive pieces, and their constant cry was for 'something with a pretty tune, brilliant but not difficult.' As audiences at piano recitals (which seem to have come into fashion in the 1830's) this class also made its tastes felt. To top its persistent chatter and seize its wandering attention, performers were forced to ever greater lengths of showiness. The greater strength of pianos, achieved by the use of an iron frame, increased tension on the strings, and heavier hammers, helped in this trend, and one of the characteristic phenomena of the first half of the nineteenth century was the rise of the keyboard virtuosi (as opposed to interpreters). Their aim appeared to be to play louder and faster than their rivals, and flashy arpeggios, leaps, and flourishes were the order of the day. Apart from glib improvisations (some of which were prudently rehearsed beforehand), they specialized in transcriptions of operatic arias, or pot-pourris from popular operas by Meyerbeer or Rossini. This tradition was continued for several decades by Liszt, although his transcriptions were usually more artistic, with subtleties of harmony and keyboard lay-out.

Liszt: *Rigoletto paraphrase.*   LONDON LD 9159 (DECCA LXT 2971).

Another manifestation of this exhibitionist trend was the use of two or more pianos together. The pianist and teacher Kalkbrenner was one of the first to indulge in this, but in 1838 we hear of Liszt and five others taking part in a twelve-handed version of the *Magic Flute* overture. In the category of the sensational may also be included child prodigies, of whom Liszt himself was one, appearing in public for the first time at the age of eleven.

The interest focused on technique had, however, the beneficial effect of developing the medium for which composers were writing. Liszt, like everyone else, had been much struck by the virtuosity of the violinist Paganini, and he not only transcribed some of Paganini's Studies, but wrote some Studies of his own to show off the most advanced piano technique. By his freedom of the keyboard, his unparalleled facility in decoration, his daring harmonies, and his feeling for colour Liszt brought piano technique to its highest peak of development. Contemporary accounts tell us, however, that he frequently broke strings and hammers by the violence of his performance, and usually had a reserve instrument standing by. Such excesses were coldly viewed by serious-minded artists like Clara Schumann, who was one of the first to play Beethoven sonatas to concert audiences. 'Before Liszt,' she complained, 'people used to play: after him, they

pound and whisper.   He has the decline of piano playing on his
conscience.'

There was undoubtedly an increased demand for music.
Berlioz in 1838 spoke satirically of the 'rain of albums, avalanches
of romances, torrents of airs with variations, spouts of concertos,
cavatinas, dramatic scenes, comic duos, soporific adagios, diabolic
evocations, and rondos romantic, fantastic, frenetic, and fanatic.'
It might be thought from all this that the traditional sonata was a
form of the past, but although it underwent some modifications
of thought and style, the 1830's saw the appearance of Schumann's
three sonatas, Liszt's *Dante Sonata*, and Chopin's *Funeral March
Sonata*.   Nevertheless, it was noticeable that shorter pieces with
fancy titles were becoming more numerous.   Besides the spring
songs, hunting songs, and dances of elves or witches, in the completely serious field new types were springing up or old types being
transformed.   Schumann's *Carnaval*, for example, is a combination of free variations and musical character studies; his *Humor-
esque* and *Arabesque* are in effect rondos: in his many separate
pieces or sets of pieces his poetic imagination was frequently
fired by pictorial or literary ideas, or by the changing nuances of
his own emotions.   Schumann's texture tends to be somewhat
thick—the result of composing at the piano and experimenting
with the sustaining pedal—but among his fingerprints is his
fondness for canonic writing and for cross-rhythms.   His friend
Mendelssohn contributed little to the piano repertoire save elegant
salon trifles; more important are his *Variations Serieuses* and the
elfin scherzos which only he seemed able to write with such
delicacy and grace.

Mendelssohn: *Scherzo in E minor*.   London LL 824 (Decca LXT
2838).

The supreme nineteenth-century writer for the piano, whose
whole output featured his chosen instrument, was Chopin.   The
beauty of his melodic lines, with their graceful decorations,
stemmed from the Italian opera (he was a great admirer of Bellini)
but of equal importance were his strikingly bold harmonic sense
and his feeling for rhythmic subtleties.   The term *tempo rubato*,
so associated with his music, is commonly taken to-day to mean a
constant flexibility of rhythm, and as a result the most appalling
artistic crimes are committed.   True *tempo rubato* consists only
in slightly moving forward or holding back a melodic line while

the basic tempo continues unchanged. The principle is by no means confined to Chopin, but goes back certainly to the fourteenth century and forward to jazz. Chopin said that, despite the lingerings, the hesitations, the anticipations of the right hand, the left hand 'should act like a conductor and not waver for a second.'

Besides his contributions to the development of melody, harmony, rhythm, and keyboard technique, Chopin is also important for the forms he employed. He took over the nocturne from the Irishman, John Field, greatly extending its treatment and its expressive scope; he wrote impromptus, ballades, fantasies, and preludes, as Schumann wrote novelettes, humoresques, and album-leaves, but Chopin (unlike Schumann) never had a programme or descriptive element for these pieces. In addition, he composed in various dance forms, although in every case transcending mere music for dancing and transforming it into something infinitely more imaginative; and he introduced the dance rhythms of his native Poland—mazurkas and polonaises.

Chopin: *Polonaise in F sharp minor*. Victor LM 1205 (HMV ALP 1028).

Even when the minimum of form or harmony is in question, Chopin is content to sit making beautiful sounds and arabesques. An example is the *Berceuse* which, except for the coda, consists of fifty-four measures of nothing but alternate tonic and dominant chords.

Chopin: *Berceuse*. HMV C 3308.

Chopin was not alone in introducing folk elements from countries hitherto outside the main stream of artistic development. In Bohemia, Smetana and later Dvořák wrote polkas (a dance which became all the rage in the 1840's), furiants, and other national dances; from Russia, Balakirev brought in an exotic flavour which, allied to brilliantly virtuoso keyboard writing, made for a distinctive contribution to the repertoire. Liszt had already shown the way in the use of exotic idioms, using gipsy rather than true Hungarian themes, and had extended the piano's colour by making it imitate the sound of other instruments, notably the Hungarian cimbalom.

Liszt: *Hungarian Rhapsody, No. 11*. Westminster WL 6213 (Nixa WLP 6213).

The orchestra was also progressing towards its highest development at this time, and with the growth in power, range, and colour of the piano some composers were beginning to look upon it almost as a substitute for the larger body. Orchestral thinking was responsible not only for the effects of drums, bells, and horns which were widely used, but also for piano lay-outs, particularly in the case of Brahms, which suggested cello melodies, pizzicato basses, wood-wind writing, or broad string passages. The ultimate was reached in the finale of Mussorgsky's suite *Pictures from an Exhibition*, where the full weight of piano sonority and the entire range of the instrument were employed to create a massive effect more appropriate to the full orchestra.

Mussorgsky: *Pictures from an Exhibition* (*The Great Gate of Kiev*). LONDON LL 330 (DECCA LK 4046).

Nevertheless, from about the middle of the century there was a definite decline in the amount of empty virtuosity being demanded by the public, and the major performers of the day, like Clara Schumann or Hans von Bülow, prided themselves more on their interpretative powers than on their ability to dazzle. It is worth noting that, unlike the earlier keyboard celebrities who wrote their own show pieces to demonstrate their best points, this new generation for the most part played other men's music— Beethoven, Schumann, Chopin, Schubert. Brahms was representative of the new temper of the time; he combined classic proportions and restraint with romantic expression and spirit. He was a fine pianist himself, with big, powerful hands, and his music abounds in broad melodies, counterpoint, and impressive chordal writing.

Brahms: *Variations on a Theme of Handel*. LONDON LS 552 (DECCA LX 3078).

Brahms was less interested in colour than in form and matter; yet he had a complete understanding of what was effective in piano writing, as can be seen from the virtuosity demanded in his *Paganini Variations*. Later in life he abandoned large-scale keyboard works for miniatures, frequently entitled *Intermezzi* or *Capriccios*, in which a refined poetic sense is coupled with a disciplined intellect. A different kind of intellectualism, expressed in a more chromatic idiom, was that of César Franck. Previous composers had stressed the inner unity of a work by employing the same theme or themes in its different movements, but Franck made a habit of this, and the peroration of his *Prelude, Chorale, and Fugue* has the material of all three movements ingeniously and brilliantly combined.

Franck: *Prelude, Chorale, and Fugue.*   WESTMINSTER WL 5163 (NIXA WLP 5163).

At the other extreme from Franck's style are the naïve but appealing piano pieces of Grieg. He adopted the accents of his native folk music, reproducing the sound of the *hardanger* fiddle, the rhythm of the *halling* and *springdans,* and all the atmosphere of Norwegian village life. A few of Grieg's *Lyric Pieces* tend towards a new style that was to come to the fore after the turn of the century—Impressionism. The indefinite tonality, looser construction, and overlapping sonorities of pieces like his *Bellringing* anticipate to some extent the style of Debussy. Debussy's experiments with non-diatonic scales and harmonies, and his evocative impressions of pictorial subjects lay just ahead, but by the end of the nineteenth century he had found the mood of poetic reverie at which he was to excel. By subtleties of pedalling he had taken the first step to the creation of new colours and to his ideal of a piano of fluid sonorities, a piano 'without hammers.'

Debussy: *Clair de lune* (*Suite Bergamasque*).   ANGEL 35067 (alt. DECCA LW 5278).

APPENDIX

BOOKS

A. EINSTEIN: *Music in the Romantic Era.*
ROSAMUND HARDING: *The Pianoforte.*
KATHLEEN DALE: *Nineteenth-century Piano Music.*

RECORDS

As nineteenth-century orchestral music is the staple of our symphony concerts, so nineteenth-century piano music is the staple of our recitals. The recording companies have made available many records of the piano music of such composers as Beethoven, Chopin, Schumann, Liszt, and Brahms. Mention should perhaps be made of one series of works that is neglected in the programmes of piano recitals: the sonatas of Schubert. But these can be explored on a series of Vox records (PL 9800/9130/8420/8590/8210, all (E)).

*K

43

William Mann

NINETEENTH-CENTURY NATIONALISM AND THE DIFFUSION OF ROMANTICISM

THE story of late nineteenth-century music is one of gradual withdrawal from the apron strings of German models. I tried in my earlier essay to stress the historical importance of Berlioz and Liszt, two non-German composers, and that process of reaction away from German domination has continued right up to the present day. But the more one looks at the growth of musical nationalism in the nineteenth century, the more one finds Beethoven and Wagner at the root of these non-German reactionaries. Heroes of weighty influence, like Berlioz and Liszt, are not to be found in the story of nationalistic music, but Beethoven can almost be called the hero of the age, much against anyone else's will.

The spirit of nationalism was and is supposed to be rooted in folk-song. But the other contradiction forced upon us is that, although traditional music undoubtedly played a part in the formation of the various national styles, those composers who most successfully found their own style were those who did not actually base all their music on the songs of their own country.

The country that found nationalism *most* easy to establish was probably France because there the tradition was *most* established. The heritage of old Burgundy and of Couperin and Rameau had not been obliterated. The strongest figure in French instrumental music during the latter part of the nineteenth century was an adopted Frenchman, César Franck. Those of us who admire the individuality of French music from Chabrier to Boulez may find it galling to recognize the fact, but that tradition is largely due to the personality of a Belgian, Franck, and two Germans, Beethoven and Wagner. Franck's most admired work, the Symphony in D minor, gave its contemporaries a working plan that they did not disdain; the principle of cyclicism. Franck and others brought the common denominator of the themes of a symphony into the open and made a motto of it. The working method of Franck's symphony can be traced back to the Fifth and Seventh symphonies of Beethoven.

Franck also developed a characteristic orchestral sound which owed its being to the particular sound quality of French organs which people find thick and treacly unless they are used to it. His harmonic language is usually ascribed to the doodling that he did at the organ, but it can be traced more efficaciously back to the Wagner of *Tristan und Isolde* and *Parsifal*. It is as a French Wagnerite that Franck had most influence, and what the Franckists and their contemporaries admired in Wagner was his nobility and sensuous subtlety of expression. That is what Franck set out to bring into French music. When he combined his mastery of that idiom with the freshness of an unusual form, as in the *Symphonic Variatious*, which are a mixture of piano concerto and non-virtuoso symphonic thought, the result is a masterpiece by any standard, and an influence that is still not played out in France.

Franck: *Symphonic Variations*. COLUMBIA ML 4536 (COLUMBIA 33 CX 1190).

The most admired composition of César Franck, in terms of importance, is surely his Symphony. Gounod called it 'the affirmation of incompetence pushed to the lengths of a dogma,' but it was very influential and beneficially so. The most successful symphony to use the same method is the *Symphony in B flat* of Ernest Chausson, that very gifted artist who left his mark on chamber music as well before his tragic early death. Indeed Chausson's symphony carried out the Franckian practice with such conviction, and such individual freshness, liberated from the organ loft, that it seems to wear as well as its model.

Chausson: *Symphony in B flat*. VICTOR LM 1181 (alt. PHILIPS NBR 6018).

The forward-looking part of Franck's influence can be seen to-day in the music of Messiaen, who has been able to speak with his own contemporary voice and to absorb other influences without breaking free of the tradition. We can see another wing of the French Wagnerian faction in the music of Chabrier. His sort of romanticism was less intense; the sort of mind that could adore Wagner while writing quadrilles on themes from *Tristan und Isolde,* and Chabrier could glean and profit from foreign influences, as in the *Fête Polonaise* or the *España* rhapsody, without endangering his own vitality or personality. What marks him out is the utter professionalism of his music. Many of the late romantics can be taunted with amateurishness, but not Chabrier; and it is that proficiency and certainty of direction that has so influenced the dapper French music of Satie and *Les Six* and Ravel in our own times. The music of Milhaud and Roussel finds its ancestor in Chabrier's *Bourrée fantasque.*

Chabrier: *Bourrée fantasque.* WESTMINSTER 5294 (NIXA WLP 5294).

One thing that history teaches us is that the most important figures are not necessarily the most admirable ones. One of the most distinguished French composers of this period was Fauré, who ploughed his own furrow, apparently unconcerned but with highly original results. Yet the long line of history cannot single him out for significance, though it can acclaim his music. For sheer quality of output most musicians would rate Fauré higher than old Saint-Saëns, whose lifetime embraced Bellini and Schönberg and who went on producing music (in his own phrase) 'as an apple-tree produces apples.' He toyed with exotic influence in the best romantic tradition, but remained all his life a reactionary, and as such his influence on musical history was small and impermanent. The folk-song wing of French nationalistic music does not seem very strong; a focal point is Vincent d'Indy, who brought together the symphonic application of traditional music, the piano concerto, and the Lisztian idea of thematic metamorphosis in his *Symphony on a French Mountaineer's Song.*

D'Indy: *Symphony on a French Mountaineer's Song.* COLUMBIA ML 4928 (COLUMBIA 33 CX 1190).

The French composers of this period, taken together, demonstrate the fundamental unromanticism of French music. France was largely responsible for the start of the romantic movement in art, but the music of romantic France strives constantly, if we except the school of César Franck, for ideals of elegance and deprecating affability that are more markedly classic. And this is why France progressed so quickly to the anti-romantic aims of the twentieth century; the sympathy with them was always there.

With the Russian nationalist movement the German influence is much less marked. Russia had fallen under the spell of the

Italian opera in the early part of the century, and the sophisticated circles were temperamentally linked with French trends in art. The history books tell us that Glinka's opera *A Life for the Tsar* (or *Ivan Susanin*) was the beginning of Russian opera, but there is a strong flavour of Bellini about it. It was the next generation that secured Russian independence with the school of composers called the 'Mighty Handful.' Their leader was Balakirev, an extraordinarily intelligent and gifted musician.

As with much romantic art, the Russian nationalist school of composers contained a strong element of amateur musicianship, and of the group only Rimsky-Korsakov had the professional's unerring touch. The aim of musical independence was quite clearly to be attained, according to Balakirev, through the inspiration, direct or indirect, of Russian traditional melody. The specific character of Russian folk melody translated itself smoothly to art music, so far as opera went; this is evident from the works of Mussorgsky, who was probably the greatest genius of the whole Handful. The pungent flavour of eastern Russian music brought in a characteristic that the rest of the world has acclaimed in Rimsky-Korsakov's *Scheherezade* or even more distinctively in Balakirev's superb tone poem *Thamar*, which deals with a similar subject from a similar clime.

Balakirev: *Thamar*. ANGEL 35291 (COLUMBIA 33 CX 1280), or ML 4974, or LONDON LL 1068 (DECCA LXT 2966).

Russian folk music was not so useful for symphonic architecture; accordingly, it is the non-symphonic orchestral works, the suites and tone poems and operas of these composers, that now seem most successful. Folk tunes are not really suited to the process of taking apart and putting together in a different order which we call symphonic technique; they are too much of an indestructible piece. That is the trouble with that popular masterpiece Borodin's Second Symphony and with the even more admirable Symphony in C of Balakirev. As examples of Russian nationalistic art those two symphonies are more to be admired than the symphonies of Tchaikovsky, which seem to western peoples much more European in tone of voice. But Tchaikovsky's Russianness is perfectly accepted by his own compatriots. The particular character of his greatest works is that strange blend of melancholy passion and sardonic humour which is perfectly Russian and which we acclaim in Tchekov's plays as nationalistic. Those two qualities come together most strongly, I think, in the first movement of the *Fifth Symphony*, which is often dragged down to the pace of a dirge, but which, taken at the speed specified by the composer, tells us a good deal about the Russian character.

Tchaikovsky: *Symphony No. 5 in E minor.* Victor LHMV 1003 (HMV ALP 1001).

Tchaikovsky did a great deal to extend the boundaries of music: he made ballet music into a serious musical art; he brought the sphere of dance music more closely into contact with symphonic behaviour in his waltz and march movements; he made the symphony a dramatic art form as well as an argumentative one. The national roots of his style are more marked the more one studies his music, and not just in the folk tunes that he occasionally used or in the Russian dance measures of his ballets. In the finale of his Violin Concerto, for example, there is a tune which could easily have appeared in a symphony by Borodin or Balakirev, but which also has the unmistakable signature of Tchaikovsky, and no other Russian, upon it.

Tchaikovsky: *Violin Concerto in D.* Decca 9755 (DGG DGM 18196).

Russia was far enough away from Germany to feel no very cogent pull musically. The nearer you get to central Europe, the more the national movement owes to the country against which it was reacting. Sibelius went to study in Germany, but when he returned to Finland he showed no sign of wanting to fall under Teutonic influence. In Bohemia the German pull was almost harmless. The gentle, contented nationalism of Dvořák is not far away from the Carinthian mood of Brahms on holiday; the two composers were good friends, and some of Dvořák's music has a Brahmsian feel about it, but in the most characteristic of Dvořák's music the Czech atmosphere is not just an accent, but a living language. Dvořák could go to Germany or to England or to America, but the music that came back was entirely Bohemian.

Dvořák: *Symphony No. 4 in G.* Victor LHMV 1014 (HMV ALP 1064).

In other countries nationalism was either unripe, as in Hungary or England, or else the national tradition was so established that no composer needed to stress his nationalism, as in Italy. Italian music in any case was almost exclusively operatic and gradually developed vividness to the point of the so-called school of *verismo* in which blood and thunder—the more lurid and true to life the better—were the order of the day. *Verismo* claimed a French convert at the end of the century in Charpentier, whose *Louise* made a heroine of the French working girl. The task of Germany was to consolidate and build on the developments of German composers, chiefly Wagner and Brahms, and of the adopted German composer Liszt. The orchestra was growing larger and larger; two composers who led this inflation to its explosion, and to the small orchestras of the twentieth century, were Richard Strauss and Gustav Mahler. Richard Strauss took his musical language first of all from the classics up to and including Mendelssohn and Brahms, but then fell under the influence of Liszt and Wagner. He became a master of musical portraiture, taking over the Lisztian symphonic poem and developing it in much sharper focus, so that where Liszt and Saint-Saëns and Tchaikovsky were describing rather vague programmes, Richard Strauss portrayed his heroes and heroines in minute detail. He could declare of Donna Elvira in *Don Juan* (though he may be contradicted) that anyone must hear in the music what colour her hair was. The sheep in *Don Quixote* are perfectly realistic, as is the crying of the baby in the *Sinfonia Domestica*. Perhaps the most detailed passage of all is the violin solo that represents Mrs Strauss in *Ein Heldenleben*; the music moves rapidly through a wide emotional gamut.

R. Strauss: *Ein Heldenleben*. LONDON LL 659 (DECCA LXT 2729).

Strauss wrote *Ein Heldenleben* in 1898, when he was thirty-four years old. His full importance did not become apparent until after 1900, but already he had pointed some of the way to modern music. Mahler only had eleven years of the new century to live, and yet his work was hardly begun when *Ein Heldenleben* was produced. Just as Strauss enlarged the symphony orchestra to the army of *Ein Heldenleben* and later *Elektra*, only to return to a tiny band for the opera *Ariadne auf Naxos*, so Mahler stepped up his orchestral forces with extra wind, brass, and percussion and with the addition of voices in certain symphonies; and yet by temperament he was a delicate orchestrator. Strauss's later career and influence were reactionary, but Mahler went on to probe farther into the refinement and extension of tonal language, and the logical corollary of his later symphonies is in the twelve-note music of Schönberg and his followers, while his influence has been beneficial and profound on such tonal composers as Shostakovich and Britten. The most forward-looking side of Mahler was not the torrent of sound he drew from his three hundred performers, but the cleanly poised and refined sound that emanates from his orchestra, for example, in the song *Urlicht* which forms the fourth movement of his Second Symphony. This clarity and emphasis on the contrast of significant lines is the story of twentieth-century music up to our day.

Mahler: *Symphony No. 2 in C minor.* Vox PL 7010 (E).

APPENDIX

BOOKS

MARTIN COOPER: *French Music from the death of Berlioz to the death of Fauré.*

R. A. LEONARD: *History of Russian Music.*

SIR DONALD TOVEY: *Essays in Musical Analysis* (especially Tchaikovsky's Fifth Symphony).

RECORDS

The remarks on nineteenth-century orchestral music apply here too. Such composers as Franck, Borodin, Dvořák, Tchaikovsky, Richard Strauss, and Fauré are represented in the catalogues by many fine records —their most familiar works in alternative recordings. But it is probably as well to mention two recordings that might escape notice.

BALAKIREV: *Symphony No. 1 in C.* ENGLISH COLUMBIA 33 CX 1002.

SMETANA: *Ma Vlast* (complete). MERCURY OL 2–100 (MERCURY MRL 2504–5).

44

Aaron Copland

THE TWENTIETH CENTURY:
REORIENTATION AND EXPERIMENT

THERE are two kinds of revolution that typify the early 1900's. The first is a technical revolution; the new musical resources developed out of old resources were strikingly different. New chords, unheard of before 1900, gradually found acceptance. There were new rhythms unlike the more conventional and sometimes plodding rhythms of the nineteenth century. There began to be an emphasis once again on contrapuntal texture, and also an emphasis on individual tone-colour values. These four new developments were characteristic of the technical advance in music of the 1900's; but there developed also a second and very important difference: an aesthetic difference. Composers began to take a more critical attitude towards the romantic nineteenth century, gradually pulling farther away from the hegemony of German music that had been so powerful an influence, stressing instead a more discreet and objective expressive attitude.

It might almost be said that Germany *owned* music towards the end of the nineteenth century. It was as if Wagner had epitomized everything that had happened before him in the music of that century and had left nothing truly new to be done after him. The first striking signs of a newer and braver post-Wagnerian music can be found in the work of Richard Strauss and Gustav Mahler.

In Strauss we find an aesthetic which is not basically different from Wagner's; Strauss's music has all the earmarks of the Wagnerian style. Nevertheless, it was apparent before long that Strauss belonged to the future, at least in part, for his harmonies were more daring, his textures more brilliant and more complex, and in general he indicated to the composers who followed him a rhythmic and musico-dramatic adventuresomeness that surpassed anything they had previously known.   In his operas *Salome* and *Elektra*, both of which date from the first decade of the twentieth century, Strauss really ventured on new territory; not aesthetically, but tonally and rhythmically and in the brilliance of his orchestration.   It can be seen especially in the scene in *Salome* which portrays musically the beheading of the prophet Jokanaan.

R. Strauss: *Salome*.   London XLL 1038–9 (Decca LXT 2863–4).

Mahler to-day looms much larger on the musical horizon as a composer than was true during his lifetime.   He loved the grandiose, and that was one of his links with the nineteenth century.   Another was his sense of intimacy with nature, a trait that had its origin in early romantic literature.   But his was an earnest, passionate, and even metaphysical personality.   His philosophic quality was curiously balanced by a love of simple things like the folk-songs he came to know as a child.   As he used them in the works of his maturity they suggest an escape to youthful and happier times.

Mahler made two main technical contributions to the new music of the twentieth century.   The first was his conception of texture as contrapuntally conceived, in contrast to the harmonically based texture of Richard Strauss.   It is as if Mahler plays on an orchestra without using the pedal; he emphasizes the separate lines and does not blur them with a heavy chordal background.   The clarity of independent melodic lines is a very typical feature of later twentieth-century music, and Mahler was perhaps the first composer to realize that the new sound world would reflect primarily contrapuntal rather than harmonic interests.

Mahler's second contribution was a new kind of orchestration, very different from that of Strauss.   By comparison Strauss's orchestration is sometimes over-ornate: there is so great an elaboration of sonorities in the orchestra that it is difficult for the ear to unravel the separate strands.   That is almost never true of Mahler's most characteristic pages.   We find in Mahler a dry, clear orchestration demonstrating a striking economy of means.   Even though he wrote for enormous numbers of performers (in a work such as the Symphony No. 8) there are always sections where single instruments play thinly spaced sonorities.   The way in which he uses solo instruments to bring out these original sounding intervals can be heard even more clearly in *Das Lied von der Erde* (*The Song of the Earth*), one of his last works.

Mahler: *Das Lied von der Erde*.   LONDON LL 625–6 (DECCA LXT 2721–2).

Strauss and Mahler, although their aesthetic was based on German music of the nineteenth century, showed the direction that twentieth-century music would take in certain matters of technique. But nothing really new could happen in twentieth-century music without a complete break with the nineteenth century, and Claude Debussy was the first composer who fully understood the need to take music down a more objective path.

Debussy was influenced, no doubt, by the visit he made to Russia towards the end of the nineteenth century. While it is not clear precisely what music he heard while in Russia, it would have been unlikely for a man of Debussy's temperament to have lived there and disregarded original work, such as that of Mussorgsky. It is easy to trace the beginnings of some of the most characteristic features of contemporary music to the Russian school of that time, and especially to Mussorgsky. His realism, his simplicity, and his desire for a natural approach to music aided other composers in moving out of the sphere of the nineteenth century. Perhaps it was Mussorgsky's amateur status that helped him to freshen the sources of serious music; certainly his love of naturalness and simplicity led him to take a special interest in the folk-song of the Russian peasant. The unconventional rhythms and harmony of his music were so sparklingly new that his colleague Rimsky-Korsakov thought they had to be 'corrected.' Mussorgsky is farther from German music of that period than any other well-known composer. Whether or not Debussy discovered Mussorgsky's music during his visit to Russia, there is certainly some influence of Mussorgsky to be discerned in even so characteristic a work by Debussy as *Pelléas et Mélisande*.

Debussy: *Pelléas et Mélisande*.   LONDON LLA 11 (DECCA LXT 2711–4), or EPIC SC 6003 (PHILIPS ABL 3076–8).

Debussy is in a certain sense a transitional composer; he did not go all the way from German subjective romanticism to a more objective attitude. It is only natural that he could not, for a composer is unable suddenly to turn the history of music about and do as he pleases. While Debussy reacted strongly against Wagner, there is still a romantic expressiveness in Debussy's music, but it is of a more passive and hypersensitive kind. In his exquisite transcription of an ideal world of sensations he was helped by the example of the French impressionist painters and symbolist poets. His delicate and sensitive music had revolutionary implications, for Debussy was one of the first composers of modern times who dared to make his ear the sole judge of what was right and wrong. Debussy was influenced by his colleague, Erik Satie, both harmonically and in his aesthetic ideas. Satie desired to be relaxed in his music, to make an end of overblown 'rhetoric.' His *Gymnopédies* are good examples of the music he was writing round the year 1900. They do not sound revolutionary any more, but their quietude, distinction, and general simplicity prophesy the music to come.

Satie: *Gymnopédies*.   CAPITAL P 8244 (CAPITOL CTL 7055).*

Arnold Schönberg grew up in the nineteenth-century German tradition, and indeed had great difficulty in throwing off the influence of Wagner. Early works such as *Gurrelieder* and *Transfigured Night* were written under the direct influence of Wagner and Strauss. But Schönberg was an intensely serious composer who soon realized that certain conclusions were to be drawn from what Wagner had contributed in harmonic development. The modulatory scheme in Wagner leads us to the brink of losing our sense of tonal centre. Schönberg's historic role was to lead Wagner's modulatory scheme to its inevitable conclusion, namely, the complete abandonment of tonality. It might almost be said that modern music has never been more revolutionary than at the moment when Schönberg decided that tonality was not an essential element of serious music. His music of that time was (against his will) generally called atonal—i.e. without tonal centre of any kind. Atonal music was a truly unprecedented conception; it still remains disturbing to some present-day audiences. Anyone hearing his *Five Orchestral Pieces* would be unlikely to suspect that they were written as long ago as 1909.

Schönberg: *Five Orchestral Pieces*, *Op*. 16.   MERCURY 50024 (alt. HMV ALP 1251).

Igor Stravinsky is certainly one of the most fascinating figures in the musical history of the twentieth century. The fact that he has written, since the twenties, so much so-called neo-classic music tends to make us forget that the music he wrote around 1911 was filled with revolutionary implications, and came as a great shock to its first listeners. It was as though Stravinsky had suddenly applied a rhythmic hypodermic to the music of the nineteenth century; the power of sheer rhythm to arouse us had been forgotten. Stravinsky, a Russian who had absorbed the music of Mussorgsky and other Russian masters, reinstated the role of rhythm in the music of that time. Audiences had begun to associate the new music, especially that from France, with a delicately tinted, quiet, and sensuous expression. When Stravinsky appeared, an enormous dynamism entered music; and it has never been the same since experiencing the elemental, almost brutal, certainly non-erotic vitality of *Petrouchka* and *The Rite of Spring*.

Stravinsky: *The Rite of Spring*. LONDON LL 303 (DECCA LXT 2563).

Finally, the American composer Charles Ives should be mentioned. Through a curious quirk of history the music that he was writing during the period 1895–1910 only became known during the early 1930's. But all commentators are agreed that Ives in his experiments invented rhythms and harmonies which ante-dated in daring those of Schönberg and Stravinsky. Ives was a poetic realist in his music; we can often trace his innovations to real sounds that he heard. If, for example, he heard several brass bands on the 4th of July marching through the centre of his small town of Danbury, Connecticut, he attempted in his music to re-create what might be called the poetic confusion of these sounds from different points of the compass meeting simultaneously. Ives was particularly experimental in his rhythms; some of his works are so polyrhythmically conceived that it is difficult to play them even now. For that reason some of his scores are still unperformed. But as time goes on Ives will probably be credited more and more with having indicated the direction the contemporary movement was later to follow, especially in the United States.

APPENDIX

BOOKS

CLAUDE DEBUSSY: *Monsieur Croche, Anti-dilettante.*
VICTOR SEROFF: *Debussy.*
ROLLO MYERS: *Erik Satie.*
A. SALAZAR: *Music in Our Time.*
WILFRID MELLERS: *Studies in Contemporary Music.*
AARON COPLAND: *Our New Music.*
HENRY and SIDNEY COWELL: *Charles Ives.*

RECORDS

Such composers as Debussy, Ravel, and Mahler are well represented in the catalogues now. For recordings of works by Schönberg and Stravinsky, see Chapter 45.

SATIE: *Parade.* ANGEL 3518 C (COLUMBIA 33 CX 1197). *Piano Music.* MGM 3154. *Socrate.* ESOTERIC 510.
IVES: *Piano Sonata No. 1.* COLUMBIA ML 4490. *Piano Sonata No. 2.* COLUMBIA ML 4250. *Violin Sonatas.* MERCURY 50096–7. *Songs.* OVERTONE 7. *Symphony No. 3.* VANGUARD 468.
BUSONI: *Arlecchino.* VICTOR LM 1944 (HMV ALP 1223).

45

Alfred Frankenstein

NEW ORTHODOXIES:
TWELVE-NOTE COMPOSITION

TWENTY-TWO years ago, when Arnold Schönberg had only just arrived in the United States, he was invited to give a public lecture at the University of Chicago, where I then had the privilege of teaching. The title of his lecture was *Composition with Twelve Tones Related Only to Each Other*, and it set forth the theory of composition with tone-rows which he and his pupils had been employing for about a decade, but which was still very little known to the musical world at large. The reaction of the music faculty at the University of Chicago was typical of the general reaction of that period: we respected Schönberg's knowledge, integrity, and daring, but we were unanimously of the opinion that the theory we had just heard expounded represented a deviation or spur from the main line of musical history and was not part of the main line itself.

We were all very young in those days and we did not know what at least one of us has since come to believe: that if a theory in the arts seems on first exposure to represent an extreme or even absurd blind alley, it will shortly prove to be of very general usefulness and significance. The reasonable, readily acceptable theories seldom have much vitality. The unreasonable theories provide the arts with their true dynamics.

This has certainly proved true of the Schönbergian theory of composition with twelve tones related only to each other. Far from being limited to a mere handful of composers, it has spread during the last quarter of a century to colour the music of the entire world, and now there are devotees of the twelve-note system everywhere. Composers once regarded as enemies of this system, like Béla Bartók and Igor Stravinsky, have flirted with it, and it has allied itself with idioms of the most improbable kind, like jazz.

This theory was the product of a long development in which many different forces played their parts.

The young Arnold Schönberg was responsive to and sympathetic towards numerous currents in the musical life of his time, but was especially attuned to the idioms of Richard Wagner and Gustav Mahler. Wagner had said that for him the art of musical composition was an art of continuous transition. Hence the continuously liquid, dynamic progression of Wagner's harmony which dissolves all discrete forms into a single entity, and in so doing tugs hard at the underpinnings of tonal relationship on which a structure of smaller structures, like a symphony or an opera, is based. It is not surprising that early works of Schönberg, his First String Quartet, for example, dissolve the conventional four-movement pattern into a single pattern; this is an inevitable development from the practice of Wagner.

From Gustav Mahler Schönberg learned to use the orchestra, not exclusively as the vastly sonorous, heroic body which it had been to Wagner and his older followers, but also as a gigantic chamber ensemble in which individual sonorities and soloistic lines are accorded an importance equal to, if not greater than, the sounds of massive groups. Ultimately Schönberg was to detach the chamber ensemble of string and wind instruments from its context in the full symphonic band of the Mahler tradition, while the treatment of the big orchestra by Schönberg himself and his major disciples always reveals a Mahler-like touch.

An early work by Schönberg shows us a composer strongly beholden in his harmony to Wagner and in his orchestration to Mahler. Such a piece is the prelude to the huge vocal piece called *The Legend of the Castle of Gurre*, composed in 1901, but not orchestrated until ten years later. The prelude is clearly associated with the idea of sunset and gathering twilight over a wild landscape.

Schönberg: *Gurrelieder*.   HAYDN SOCIETY 100 (NIXA HLP 3100).

In later works of the same period—1900–10—Schönberg's music continues, in its extremely free and fluid modulation, to undermine the sense of key centre and key relationship on which the very concept of modulation is based. Wandering chords, at home in all keys and owing special allegiance to none, come to play an increasingly important role; dissonance is freed from its laws of preparation and resolution, and at length the whole fabric of key relationships on which the musical theory of the eighteenth and nineteenth centuries had been based, dissolves. There follows a period of free atonality in Schönberg's work. Key centres have disappeared, but a systematized order of tonal relationships without them has not yet evolved. This does not mean that the music is devoid of structure. On the contrary, the works of Schönberg's freely atonal period are among his most elaborately contrived from the formal point of view. However, and this is very important, the forms that Schönberg employs at this time are all extremely short. The older system of fixed tonalities had provided a logic or rationale for musical patterns greatly extended in time; free atonality provided no such rationale. Furthermore, Schönberg was obviously entranced at savouring the remarkable harmonies and colouristic effects of the new style on a small scale, as if these were precious jewels that were not to be spread about too lavishly.

There is also an emphasis on an emotional atmosphere, often made specific in song texts, of a highly expressionistic kind. Expressionism is almost a technical term for the German painting and sculpture of this period, and Schönberg was himself an expressionist painter of no mean ability. Probably the best definition of expressionism was provided by the German sculptor, Ernst Barlach, who once said: 'I must be able to join in the suffering.' All expressionists make us join in the suffering, Schönberg the composer no less than Barlach the sculptor. The psychology of Sigmund Freud is another expression of the same attitude, and there are some works of Schönberg's freely atonal period which are clearly coloured by Freud's compassionate joining in the suffering expressed by the morbid and irrational aspects of the human psyche.

Pierrot Lunaire (*Mad Pierrot*), composed in 1912, is one such work. It is a setting of twenty-one triolets by the Belgian poet, Albert Guiraud, as translated into German by Otto Erich Hartleben. The setting is for a vocalist who neither speaks nor sings but employs a completely novel idiom, part way between speech and song, which Schönberg invented for this work and which has often been used by his followers. The instrumental part calls for five players who perform on seven different instruments. No two of the twenty-one movements are quite alike in scoring.

Here is the chamber music ensemble of Mahler in its most brilliant, independent, and ingenious form.   The musical structure is completely atonal and often very learned in its use of such patterns as canons and passacaglias, although these aspects of the music are very difficult to appreciate by means of the unaided ear.

Schönberg: *Pierrot Lunaire*.   Westminster 18143 (alt. ARGO RG 54).

All the works of Schönberg's freely atonal period are either very short or are composed of many very short movements strung together.   A return to extended forms required some kind of theoretical structure, and this Schönberg ultimately provided in the twelve-note system.   I think that the evolution of this theory was also conditioned, as the crystallization of principles often is, by the extreme hostility with which so much of Schönberg's music was met.   If a new idiom can be shown to have an unassailable rationale, those who practise it can feel secure against the attacks of the world.   I think this is what Schönberg meant when in the course of his address at the University of Chicago in 1934 he said: 'You do not think my music is beautiful, but I *know* it is.'

At all events, the twelve-note theory provides a logical structure for atonality.   Schönberg himself used it from 1923 until his death in 1951.   In simplest essence it is a method whereby notes are related, as Schönberg put it, *only to each other*, which means that they are no longer related to a common centre.

A major scale is the simplest and most perfect example of notes related to a common centre.   All the notes in a major scale have their places, derive their order and their functions from the note with which it begins and ends; and the scale is named after that note—C major, D major, E major, etc.   Any scale has two forms and two forms only; it can go up and it can come down, and that is all it can do.

Schönberg replaces the concept of scale with the twelve-note row, an arbitrary selection of the twelve notes within an octave arranged in a fixed, unchanging order.   Each composition is based upon a different twelve-note row, and sometimes the row undergoes modification from movement to movement in the course of a composition in large form.   Unlike a scale, a twelve-note row does not have two forms but four.   It can be played backwards, it can be turned upside down, and the upside down version can also be played backwards. The terms commonly used for these four forms are prime (the original form of the row), retrograde, inversion, and retrograde inversion.

Composition in the Schönbergian system is the art of bringing the twelve-note row to life in rhythm, as the composition of a melody in the tonal system might be called bringing a scale to life in rhythm. The four forms of the row may be used melodically, contrapuntally, and harmonically in endless numbers of ways. There are, of course, many other aspects of this technique, and what has been said no more defines the whole of the twelve-note system than the playing of a major scale defines the whole of the harmonic and contrapuntal system of Beethoven. But this is the basic axiom of the Schönbergian philosophy: the twelve-note row provides a method whereby *notes are related to each other*, and not to a common centre, during the course of a composition in large form or small. Some theorists regard this as a technique of continuous variation, and that is one good way of looking at it. It is a discipline for the creation of the utmost unity and the utmost variety.

The twelve-note row may be heard in practice in the last movement of the *Suite, Opus 29*; a *gigue* for three clarinets of different sizes, violin, viola, cello, and piano.

Schönberg: *Suite, Op. 29*. COLUMBIA ML 5099.

Schönberg had two major disciples, both of whom predeceased him. One was Alban Berg, whose music is probably played more frequently to-day than that of Schönberg himself, and the other was Anton von Webern. These two men occupy very different places in the Schönbergian hierarchy. As René Leibowitz puts it, Schönberg was the innovator, while it was the function of Berg to relate the innovations of his teacher to the art of the past and the function of Webern to jump ahead and explore their possibilities towards the future. The music of Berg is more 'expressive' in the conventional sense than that of Schönberg, and it is scarcely accidental that his operas, notably *Wozzeck*, have been presented all over the world, while the operas of Schönberg remain all but totally unknown. Berg seldom remains strictly within the twelve-note tradition; he uses it as one of many means and plays in and out among all the systems as his purpose dictates. It is characteristic of Berg that he should have written a *Lyric Suite* for string quartet and entitled its six movements Allegretto giovale, Andante amoroso, Allegro misterioso, Adagio appassionato, Presto delirando, and Largo desolato.   This emphasis on high-pitched emotionalism, coupled with the utmost fineness in texture, is typical of Berg, and is responsible for the relatively high degree of public success his work has won.

Berg: *Lyric Suite*. COLUMBIA ML 2148.

Anton von Webern is the least successful of the disciples of Schönberg from the point of view of public approbation.   Webern is one of those paradoxical artists who elaborate things to such an extent that they produce the starkest kind of simplicity.   His work is like that of those modern painters whose canvases are mostly bare, with a few telling strokes that not only express their own shapes and relationships but give shape, likewise, to the surrounding void.   Webern composes as much with silence as with tone. His orchestration is likely to be, as Leibowitz puts it, a matter of isolated sounds contributed by one instrument at a time.   His forms are extremely condensed, but everything in his textures is wonderfully open and clear.   Every sound tells; Webern's is perhaps the most sinewy music of modern times.   An example is the Concerto, Opus 24, composed in 1934.

Webern: *Concerto for nine instruments, Op. 24*. DIAL 17.

Schönberg and his personal disciples, Berg and Webern, are doubtless the major figures in the twelve-note school, but their technique has been taken up by other composers throughout the world.   It has proved to be an infinitely plastic medium for the expression of an infinite number of musical personalities.   And for a good example of twelve-note music written outside the Schönbergian circle, we may take the Third Symphony of the American composer, Wallingford Riegger.

Riegger: *Symphony No. 3*. COLUMBIA ML 4902.

APPENDIX

Books

RENÉ LEIBOWITZ: *Schönberg and His School*.
JOSEF RUFER: *Composition with Twelve Notes Related Only to Each Other*.
ARNOLD SCHÖNBERG: *Style and Idea*.

RECORDS

SCHÖNBERG: *Four String Quartets.* COLUMBIA 4 SL–188. *Transfigured Night.* CAPITOL P 8304 (CAPITOL CCL 7507).
BERG: *Wozzeck.* COLUMBIA 5 SL–118. *Violin Concerto.* COLUMBIA ML 3857 (COLUMBIA 33 CX 1030). *Chamber Concerto.* VOX PL 8660 (E).
WEBERN: *Five Movements for String Quartet.* COLUMBIA 4 SL–188 (with Schönberg).

A set of recordings containing the complete works of Anton von Webern has been released by Columbia (U.S.A.), K4L–232.

46

Alfred Frankenstein

NEW ORTHODOXIES:
NEO-CLASSICISM

CARL VAN VECHTEN is remembered to-day as the author of some slight, smart, amusing novels, but he began his career between hard covers with some of the most brilliantly written books on musical subjects ever produced in North America. One of these books is called *Music After the Great War* and it was published in 1915. In the title essay of this collection Van Vechten made a bold attempt to predict what music would be like after World War I. His major prediction was one hundred per cent correct. He said that the two most important figures in the musically creative life of the world would be Arnold Schönberg and Igor Stravinsky. But this prediction, correct though it was, was nevertheless based upon a philosophy which events proved to be one hundred per cent wrong.

This is a fascinating phenomenon: a completely accurate prophecy arrived at through the application of a completely false premise. It demonstrates that the history of the arts does not work according to the dictates of logic, and especially according to the evolutionary hypothesis which underlay Van Vechten's thought.

His argument was that over the years harmony had grown more and more complex and had placed increasingly heavy emphasis upon dissonance until the new school of his time had come to create a veritable science of 'disharmony.' He saw nothing in the future but further and more complex explorations of 'disharmony,' and observing that Stravinsky had written his best works, such as *The Rite of Spring*, on barbaric, oriental themes he predicted that a similar barbaric orientalism would suffuse the entire musical world. 'I do not predict a return to Mozart as one result of the war,' said Carl van Vechten, and that line was written with the utmost irony, as representing the ultimate in unthinkables.

Two years later Serge Prokofieff produced his *Classical Symphony*, and the return to Mozart was on in earnest. Stravinsky, the barbaric orientalist, rediscovered Bach in his Piano Concerto, and some of his major works to come would bear such titles as *Apollo, Ruler of the Muses, Oedipus Rex,* and *Orpheus.* Mozartian forms, Bach-like textures, and classical subjects became the rule; for a time it even seemed as if a race were on among contemporary composers to find the most obscure and academic among the composers of the past to be used as models.

There were many good reasons for this. Music does not evolve in a straight line, but is subject to mutations, pendulum swings, and sudden switches as the result of all manner of forces, including satiety. It is easy to see the musical world of 1917 through the eyes of young Prokofieff: the impressionist tradition of Debussy going to seed in diaphanous ultra-refinement, the tradition of Wagner dying of elephantiasis, the Russian folklore tradition of his immediate background breaking up in preciousness and triviality. To all of this Prokofieff replied with a bold, smiling gesture: back to simplicity, to clear forms and uncomplicated emotions.

Prokofieff: *Classical Symphony.* VICTOR LM 1215 (HMV ALP 1107).

Prokofieff was one of the most striking forerunners of the modern neo-classical movement, although other composers of 1917 exhibited somewhat similiar impulses, including Debussy himself in the three sonatas composed at the end of his life. The composer, however, who has come to be most strongly identified with this movement—who is, indeed, its major lawgiver—is Prokofieff's compatriot, Igor Stravinsky.

Stravinsky won world celebrity within the Russian nationalist framework with *The Fire Bird, Petrouchka,* and *The Rite of Spring,* but after World War I he turned his back on folkloric nationalism and gave the neo-classical ideal a powerful philosophic propulsion. Neo-classicism was entertaining with Prokofieff; with Stravinsky it took on seriousness and depth. Perhaps the best statement of the neo-classical philosophy (Stravinsky version) is to be found in a famous passage of his autobiography. In discussing the composition of one of his later ballets, Stravinsky says:

Here, in classical dancing, I see the triumph of studied conception

over vagueness, of the rule over the arbitrary, of order over the hap-
hazard. I am thus brought face to face with the eternal conflict in art
between the Apollonian and the Dionysian principles. The latter
assumes ecstasy to be the final goal—that is to say, the losing of one's
self—whereas art demands above all the full consciousness of the
artist. There can, therefore, be no doubt as to my choice between the
two. And if I appreciate so highly the value of classical ballet, it is not
simply a matter of taste on my part, but because I see in it the perfect
expression of the Apollonian principle.

This antithesis between the Apollonian and the Dionysiac is
not original with Stravinsky. It comes from Nietzsche's *The
Birth of Tragedy*, but Stravinsky's moral is the polar opposite
of the German philosopher's. Ardent Wagnerite as he was at
this time, Nietzsche is all for the Dionysiac point of view; for
inspiration, creative intoxication, and the surpassing of one's self
in the ardour of imaginative effort. Stravinsky, on the other
hand, preaches rule, order, precise definition, and precise delimita-
tion. This contrast between Apollonian and Dionysiac, or classic
and romantic, can be found in all the arts, sometimes at the same
period, more often in alternation as one generation succeeds
another. Since the name of the god Apollo has been invoked in
Stravinsky's philosophic expression of the neo-classical ideal, we
should discover how he hymns Apollo in music. *Apollon
Musagète* is not one of the most dynamic of Stravinsky's neo-
classical works, but it is one of the clearest expressions of his
principle. It is scored for strings alone, and this is one facet of
the discipline that appeals so strongly to this composer. Quite
deliberately he rules out the varied colours of wind instruments
and deeply explores the sonorities of violins, violas, celli, and
basses.

Stravinsky: *Apollon Musagète*. LONDON LL 1401 (DECCA LXT
5169).

Apollo, Ruler of the Muses, represents only one phase of neo-
classicism in the works of Stravinsky. There are many others.
There is, for instance, his revival of the strictly formal operatic
scene in several movements. His one big opera, *The Rake's
Progress*, brings us back after more than a century of experiment
in other directions to the fact that opera is a highly stylized or
conventionalized form of art. *The Rake's Progress* is cast in a
pattern deliberately reminiscent of the most famous rake's progress

in the literature of opera, Mozart's *Don Giovanni*, even including *recitativo secco* with harpsichord accompaniment. The principal aria for Anne Truelove, Stravinsky's heroine, is in three sections. After the orchestral introduction, the singer begins with a recitative. The second section is an *andante*, and then, after another short recitative, the scene concludes with a brilliant *allegro*. This is exactly the way in which the major arias of Beethoven's *Fidelio* and other operas of its period are constructed. The recitative and *andante* have to do with Anne's tenderness towards Tom Rakewell, who has deserted her, while the *allegro* expresses her resolve to find and serve him.

Stravinsky: *The Rake's Progress, Act I, Scene 3.* COLUMBIA SL 125 (PHILIPS ABL 3055–7).

There are other aspects of contemporary neo-classicism beside those represented by the ideas of Stravinsky. Some composers, such as Paul Hindemith, arrive at it through a powerful sense of identification with the music of the more or less remote past. One of the most remarkable characteristics of the music of our time is that the scholar and composer no longer hate each other; indeed, composers like Hindemith are among the most learned of musical historians. Hindemith's history is expressed in composition rather than verbal treatises, but like a thorough work of scholarship, it is based upon extensive and often highly involved research. An example is the *Concert of the Angels* from Hindemith's symphony, *Mathis der Maler*. This is actually a suite drawn from his opera about the life and work of the sixteenth-century painter, Mathias Grünewald. 'Concert of the Angels' is the title of one panel in Grünewald's most famous work, the altarpiece he painted for the abbey church of Isenheim in Alsace. Hindemith's music is, as he himself put it, based on 'old folksongs, war songs of the Reformation period, and Gregorian Chant.' The association of this old German musical material with the paintings of Grünewald and the atmosphere of his life and time all combine into a powerful evocation of the Gothic past.

Hindemith: *Symphony: Mathis der Maler.* DECCA 9818 (DGG DG 16130).

Still another aspect of neo-classicism remains to be touched upon. It is one with which Stravinsky has no sympathy at all, but with which the name of Paul Hindemith is strongly identified. Many contemporary composers, following Hindemith's lead,

L

have come to believe that in our time creative music and the audience have grown so far apart that the contemporary composer is in danger of losing touch with society altogether. Consequently many composers are now making a deliberate, self-conscious attempt to forge an idiom that the public will readily understand, and thereby return the composer to an immediately functional status in his world. This is something entirely new. I know of no period in the past when such a philosophy was preached or even dreamed of; up to now the composer's place in society, for better or for worse, has simply been taken for granted. The deliberate effort to woo the audience has led Aaron Copland and others of his persuasion back to folklore; if one is going to write music for the people one may as well employ material which the people themselves have created. The result may perhaps be better described as neo-romantic than neo-classical; the dividing line is subtle and difficult to maintain in any dogmatic way.

A good example of neo-classicism in this phase is the slow movement of the *Cello Concerto* by the American composer, Virgil Thomson. This is called *Variations on a Southern Hymn*. The tune is an old one entitled *Tribulation* which appears consistently through the shape-note hymnals which have been used in the southern states for one hundred and fifty years.

Virgil Thomson: *Cello Concerto*. COLUMBIA ML 4468.

APPENDIX

BOOKS

IGOR STRAVINSKY: *An Autobiography* and *The Poetics of Music*.
PAUL HINDEMITH: *A Composer's World*.

RECORDS

Alfred Frankenstein writes on the subject of records: 'Igor Stravinsky is one of the most richly and extensively recorded of all composers. He has himself conducted recordings of nearly all his orchestral works, and these recordings are recommended above all others—Columbia (Columbia or Philips). Stravinsky regards the disk as a method for establishing the true and correct interpretation of his music, and he makes an eloquent case for his views in this regard. His recordings are too numerous to list.

'A similar situation exists with regard to recordings of the music of Paul Hindemith; he is by far his own finest interpreter, but his list of recordings is relatively small. Of special importance are the following, all played by the Berlin Philharmonic Orchestra under Hindemith's direction:

Theme and Variations After the Four Temperaments. DECCA 9829.

Symphonic Metamorphosis of Themes by Carl Maria von Weber. (DGG DGM 18301.)

Symphony from Die Harmonie der Welt. DECCA 9765 (DGG DGM 18181).

Kammermusik, Op. 24, Nos. 1 and 2. CONTEMPORARY 101.

'An extremely important Hindemith work not conducted by the composer is:

Nobilissima Visione. ANGEL 35221 (COLUMBIA 33 CX 1241).

'The listener should also investigate Hindemith's rich and varied contributions to the literature of the string quartet and the sonata for solo instruments and piano.

'Other important recordings in the neo-classic and neo-romantic area are as follows:

POULENC: *Trio and Sextet.* REB 7.

VILLA LOBOS: *Bachianas Brasileiras No. 1.* CAPITOL P 8147 (CAPITOL CTL 7014).*

ROREM: *Sonata for Piano, No. 2.* LONDON LL 759 (DECCA LXT 2812).'

47

Andrew Porter

TWENTIETH-CENTURY NATIONALISM

A T the opening of the twentieth century the outlying
countries of Europe began to develop schools and styles
of their own which found their inspiration either directly
in national folk music or else more loosely in what might
be termed national characteristics. Those peripheral countries,
which had formerly produced only small-scale compositions or
works based on foreign models, now evolved styles of their own;
and composers emerged who wrote music that was distinctively
Spanish or English or Scandinavian.

For a long time the only truly Spanish music was the extremely
rich and varied folk music; in each province it had distinctive
characteristics. The one native art form, the *Zarzuela*, or Spanish
operetta or musical comedy, was eclectic; its ingredients were
largely derived from French vaudeville and Italian *opera buffa*.
The first decisive national movement came from Felipe Pedrell
(1841–1922), who, though not a great composer, was a great
teacher and is venerated to this day by all Spanish composers.
In his two operas he attempted to write music that would make
distinctive use of the rich treasury of folk-song. Pedrell was
succeeded by Albéniz and Granados. Albéniz, born in 1860,
was by seven years the senior. His masterpiece is *Ibéria*, four
books of piano pieces which are brilliant, picturesque descriptions
of the people and atmosphere of Andalusia. Granados had a
sharper invention and a more purely musical talent. We do not
know how much he might have achieved, had he not lost his life
in the sinking of the *Lusitania* in 1915 when he was on his way back
from the New York *première* of his opera, *Goyescas*. But we can
tell how strong, decisive, and distinctive is the national feeling
in Granados from his song, *El majo discreto (The Discreet Lover)*.

Granados: *El majo discreto (Tonadillas)*. HMV BLP 1037.

Meanwhile, there had already appeared a still sharper and more

brilliant Spanish talent in Manuel de Falla, born in 1876.   A pupil
of Pedrell, Falla flung himself passionately into the rediscovery of
Spanish folk-song, and it penetrated the whole of his artistic
personality.   Spanish composers have never made any world
impact as symphonists, but in the field of ballet Falla found his
ideal medium.   With his first ballet, *El amor brujo* (*Love the
Magician*), he won a local success, and then, with *El sombrero de
tres picos* (*The Three-cornered Hat*), world success.   His genius
for orchestration should be mentioned.   His predecessors had
tended to score rather lushly, but Falla's use of instruments was
keen and clear and brilliant.

Manuel de Falla: *The Three-Cornered Hat*.   LONDON LL 598 (DECCA
LXT 2716).

Falla's creative career has a strange curve to it.   He began with
the rich, colourful opera *La vida breve*, given first in 1913.   During
World War I he produced his masterpieces, *Nights in the
Gardens of Spain* and the two ballets.   Then compositions grew
less frequent and his style became more severe.   The influence
of Scarlatti began to make itself felt in such a work as the Harpsichord Concerto.   Eventually Falla withdrew almost completely
from the world and died in 1946 in a remote village in Argen-
tina.   His wonderful works of art have found no comparable
successors in Spain.

In England folk-songs have never played such a part in the life
of the people as they do—to this day—in Spain.   The English
folk-song heritage is rich and remarkable, but in a quiet, lyrical
way, and the English musical renaissance did not find its starting-
point in folk-song.   The eclipse of English music during the nineteenth century was not so complete as we are often told, but
certainly two giant shadows hung over most of the music that was
produced: Handel and Mendelssohn.   The first two decisively
English composers to appear were Parry and Stanford, both
excellently trained academic musicians whose work appears now
to have been largely preparatory.

The first great English composer of the century, Edward Elgar,
came from outside the academic circle and was conscious of being
a self-made musician.   His early compositions were not too well
received, but at the turn of the century he established himself with
two extraordinary masterpieces, though of very different weight
and calibre: the oratorio *The Dream of Gerontius*, and the *Enigma*

Variations. Two symphonies, two concertos, the *Introduction and Allegro* for strings, and the *Symphonic Study : Falstaff* consolidated his reputation.

Foreigners often declare that they can find nothing specifically English in Elgar's music, a view that finds its extremest form in the epigram: 'When you have rendered unto Brahms the things that are Brahms's, and unto César the things that are César's, what is left but a handful of unimportant mannerisms.' Elgar unquestionably learned from both Brahms and César Franck, and in its actual facture his music is certainly German. All Englishmen, however, must feel a strongly English flavour in his music; for instance, in the first subject of his Cello Concerto. One proof of its Englishness is that no foreign cellist ever seems able to phrase it as we feel it ought to be phrased. Even a great interpreter like Casals makes it too emphatic and too rhetorical, whereas it should sound—as Elgar once said of a passage in his First Symphony— 'like something you hear down by the river'—a melody exhaled from the English landscape.

Elgar: *Cello Concerto in E minor.*   London LS 95 (Decca LX 3023).

There is more to Elgar's music than its Englishness; but we are concerned here with such passages as the first movement of the Cello Concerto, the *Introduction and Allegro*, and the pastoral interludes in *Falstaff*, rather than the mystic quality or the Edwardian swagger. These lyrical passages have much in common with English lyric poetry; they are shy, unemphatic, and delicate.

Ralph Vaughan Williams, fifteen years Elgar's junior and still to-day a prolific composer, gives us English music genuinely rooted in English folk-song. With his discovery of English folk-song Vaughan Williams found himself as a composer. Many of his compositions make direct use of folk-songs; others are influenced by the modes, the characteristic intervals, and the rhythms of folk-music. Vaughan Williams has not made the mistake of thinking that folk-melodies make good symphonic material, and in his set of eight symphonies there is rarely a direct folk-song quotation. But at the opening of the *Romanza* of his *Fifth Symphony*, for example, we hear a melody that seems again to be exhaled from the English countryside, although, unlike Elgar's melody, it is redolent of folk-song associations. Again, there are many other elements in Vaughan Williams besides

Englishness; and the most marked is a visionary quality which embraces compassion, fortitude, and the ability to look bravely on almost unendurable prospects.

Vaughan Williams: *Symphony No. 5 in D major*.   LONDON LL 975 (DECCA LXT 2910).

Carl Nielsen (1865–1931) is a composer whose concern is more with national characteristics than with national folk-music.   He made many arrangements of Danish folk-songs, but in his symphonic music he struck through to something deeper than actual folk-idioms.   He tried to give some idea of what it was in a little essay he wrote about Funen, the island on which he was brought up.   'Everything in Funen is different from the rest of the world. The bees hum in a way of their own . . . and when the horse whinnies and the red cows low, why, anyone can hear that it is different from anywhere else.   The stillness sings the same tune too, and even the trees dream and talk in their sleep with a Funen lilt.'   And Nielsen's music too is different from anything else. His themes 'have a large free air about them; they diverge into some quaint lyrical backwater, or suddenly reveal an unexpected, even formidable strength and purpose.'   Carl Nielsen in six symphonies, three concertos, and two operas gave Denmark a national music of its own.

Jean Sibelius was born in the same year as Nielsen, but while Nielsen is generally considered a humanist, and an optimistic one, Sibelius is regarded as the poet of nature.   There is a good deal of the Russian in his musical personality; he is also a Finnish patriot: many of his works find their inspiration in the Finnish folk-sagas. But in the end it is because of his intensely personal works that we rate Sibelius so high: his seven symphonies and *Tapiola*.   As constructions they are highly interesting and successful, but their real claim to greatness lies in something less fathomable.   Sibelius has come nearer than anyone else to giving expression to those mysteries which man senses in nature.   In Wordsworth's lines:

> No familiar shapes
> Remain, no pleasant images of trees,
> Or sea, or sky, no colours of green fields:
> But huge and mighty forms, that do not live
> Like living men.

There are several stories which show that Sibelius found direct inspiration in the landscapes of his native Finland.   Bengt de

Törne related how he once told Sibelius how impressive he always found the first sight of Finland from the sea: reddish granite rocks rising out of the pale blue water, and a solitary island of a hard, archaic beauty. 'Yes,' Sibelius answered eagerly, and his eyes flashed. 'And when we see those granite rocks we know why we are able to treat the orchestra as we do.'

The Swan of Tuonela shows his individual treatment of the orchestra, and at the same time his concern with Finnish mythology and his ability to evoke an eerie, inhuman scene. Tuonela, the hell of Finnish mythology, is surrounded by a black river on which floats a swan, singing with weird beauty. The song is represented by the cor anglais, and the accompaniment contains only one oboe, one bass clarinet, four horns, three trombones, harp, drums, and muted strings divided into many parts.

> Sibelius: *The Swan of Tuonela.* LONDON LL 843 (DECCA LXT 2831).

Sibelius is a strange, solitary, off-centre figure and his long silence forms one of the puzzling episodes in musical history. From about 1893 to 1925 he was immensely prolific, but his last work of any consequence, incidental music to *The Tempest*, was composed in 1926. Then, like Prospero, he 'abjured his art.' There has been much talk of an Eighth Symphony, and in 1945 he wrote to the English conductor, Basil Cameron: 'My 8th Symphony has been "finished" many times, but I am not content with it yet. When the time comes, it will be a pleasure to deliver it into your hands.'

Leoš Janáček is a rather different case from any of the other composers considered in this essay, for Czechoslovakia had already produced Dvořàk and Smetana, and so there was no question of 'founding' a national school in the twentieth century. Janáček's music derives from a close study of folk-songs, but even more from the actual inflexions of the speech of his native Moravia. He would jot down in musical notation the words that he heard spoken around him. 'The best way of becoming a good opera composer,' he wrote, 'is to study analytically the melodic curves and contours of human speech. . . . The melodic curves of speech as used in song give only a reflection of the spirit, weakened by the heat of the music itself. But the melodic curves of speech as used in the spoken word are a direct reflection of life.' Such was his genius that from short speech-phrases he could build large, coherent musical structures; and not only the voices, but the instruments too in his operas seem actually to be *uttering*. Such phrases also form the thematic material of some of his later purely instrumental works, and it must be admitted that in these works there is often a curious elliptical quality that proves hard to accept at first. But all his music is marked by spontaneity and originality.

Coupled to his purely musical gifts was a deep love and compassion for humanity, and a profound feeling for nature. The former finds expression in his operas *Jenufa*, *Katya Kabanova*, and the austere *House of the Dead*; the latter is found most specifically in the opera *The Cunning Little Vixen*, in which some of the characters are human, some animal. We hear both in his song cycle *The Diary of One Who Vanished*. This is a setting of twenty-one poems left behind by a farmer's son who was seduced by a gipsy and left his parents for her. Into a thirty-minute cycle Janáček compressed the drama, which takes on a clean, fierce purity like that of Hardy's *Tess of the Durbervilles*.

Janáček: *The Diary of One Who Vanished*. EPIC 3LC 3121 (PHILIPS ABR 4041).

APPENDIX

BOOKS

JAIME PAHISSA: *Manuel de Falla*.
DIANA McVEAGH: *Edward Elgar*.
FRANK HOWES: *The Music of Ralph Vaughan Williams*.
ROBERT SIMPSON: *Carl Nielsen: Symphonist*.
CECIL GRAY: *Sibelius*.

RECORDS

FALLA: *Love the Magician*. WESTMINSTER 5238 or ANGEL 35089. *Master Peter's Puppet Show*. (DUCRETET-THOMSON DTL 93010). *Nights in the Gardens of Spain*. *Homenajes*. ENGLISH COLUMBIA 33 CX 1221.
ELGAR: *Enigma Variations, etc.* COLUMBIA ML 5031 (PHILIPS ABL 3053). *Falstaff*. ENGLISH DECCA LXT 2940.
VAUGHAN WILLIAMS: *The Symphonies*. LONDON (DECCA, 8 records). *Job—A Masque for Dancing*. ENGLISH DECCA LXT 2937.
NIELSEN: *Symphony No. 5*. LONDON LL 1143 (DECCA LXT 2980). *Flute Concerto*. *Clarinet Concerto*. LONDON LL 1124 (DECCA LXT 2979).
SIBELIUS: *Symphony No. 4*. *Tapiola*. ANGEL 35082 (COLUMBIA 33 CX 1125). *Symphonies Nos. 6 and 7*. ANGEL 35316 (COLUMBIA 33 CX 1341).
JANÁČEK: *Sinfonietta*. *Taras Bulba*. VOX PL 9710 (E).

*L

48

Andrew Porter

TWENTIETH-CENTURY MUSIC: THE SECOND GENERATION

THE greatest of the twentieth-century nationalist composers was Béla Bartók, who was born in Hungary in 1881 and died in New York in 1945. The central problem of his creative career was his struggle to unite the melodies and rhythms of eastern European folk-music and the harmonic and contrapuntal idiom of the west. The western music to influence him was that of Brahms, Wagner, Liszt, Debussy, Richard Strauss, and Stravinsky, but all these elements took on new properties when fused in the crucible of his entirely individual imagination.

In 1920 Bartók wrote an article on folk-music which must furnish the text for any consideration of twentieth-century nationalism. He argued that there was no solution but a complete break with the nineteenth century. Invaluable help was given to this rejuvenation by a kind of peasant music hitherto unknown. The right type of peasant music, Bartók continued, 'is most varied and perfect in all its forms. Its expressive power is amazing, and at the same time it is void of all sentimentality and superfluous ornaments. It is simple, sometimes primitive, but never silly, and it is the ideal starting-point for a musical renaissance.'

Bartók went on to describe three ways in which peasant music could be taken over and transmuted into modern music. First, one could simply take the tune, either as it stood or slightly varied, and provide it with an accompaniment. Second, the composer could use, not an actual peasant melody, but one of his own invented in emulation of the real thing. Or third, neither peasant melodies nor imitations would be found in the music, but it would be pervaded by their atmosphere. By this third method the composer completely absorbs the idiom of peasant music, which becomes his musical mother tongue.

Bartók cited his compatriot, Zoltán Kodály, as a composer of this last kind of folk-inspired music. Together Bartók and Kodály travelled through the countryside, collecting peasant music, and Kodály's *Psalmus Hungaricus* and his opera *Háry János* are both large works steeped in the atmosphere of Hungarian folk-music. Bartók himself composed music in each of his three categories. The first—an original tune with ornamental setting—is well exemplified in his collection of short piano pieces, *For Children*. The harmonies are by no means those of our ordinary western common chords. The tune itself, with its characteristic intervals, has been allowed to suggest the chords and counterpoints with which it is to be accompanied.

Bartók: *For Children*. BARTÓK 919–20 (alt. COLUMBIA 33 CX 1176 and 1316).

For Children appeared in 1908, the year that also saw the production of his First String Quartet. Bartók's six string quartets—the last dates from 1939—are generally considered the most important contribution to the *genre* since those of Beethoven. The Sixth Quartet shows us utterly contemporary music that has sprung from peasant soil. In the sad theme which opens each of its four movements we seem to hear a farewell to Hungary. It is certainly not a real folk theme, nor an invented one, but it breathes the spirit of the country. Then comes a characteristic late-Bartók exposition: three notes in octaves; the same phrase in reverse order, pitched a tone higher, and so on; then a lively twirling theme, extracted from the opening, which is whisked away in brisk counterpoint. This is enough to show that Bartók was no simple 'folky' composer.

Bartók: *String Quartet No. 6*. COLUMBIA ML 4280 (PHILIPS ABL 3093).

Bartók's toughest music was written during his middle period, the late 1920's and early 1930's. Then his style clarified and he went out to meet his listeners in such works as the *Music for Percussion and Strings* (1936), the *Concerto for Orchestra* (1943), and the Third Piano Concerto (1945). Bartók founded no school and has had no successors; and so he is the type-figure of the undoctrinaire composer, the nationalist whose music can be understood without reference to its national background.

In considering the undoctrinaire composers we should remember, first, that nothing links them together except, tenuously, nationalism; and second, that there is no important living composer who has not been influenced, directly or indirectly, by Stravinsky, Hindemith, and Schönberg. Stravinsky's influence is strong in the music of Aaron Copland, who may serve as an example of the American nationalist composer, European-trained, but aiming to write specifically American music.

Copland was born in Brooklyn in 1900 and began to study composition in America. In 1921 he left for Paris and stayed three years, studying with Nadia Boulanger. The principal fruit of this period was a Symphony for Organ and Orchestra. Walter Damrosch first performed it in New York in 1925 and remarked to the audience at the end of the performance: 'If a young man at the age of twenty-three can write a symphony like that, in five years he will be ready to commit murder.' Copland waited ten years, and then produced the bright, jazzy *El Salon Mexico*. At this time he decided to reach out to the public which had grown up around the radio, the gramophone, and the cinema. He wrote: 'It made no sense to ignore the new public and to write as if they did not exist. I felt that it was worth the effort to see if I couldn't say what I had to say in the simplest possible terms.'

As Bartók collected Hungarian peasant music, so Copland investigated cowboy tunes, spirituals, revivalist hymns, and Shaker songs. The score to the ballet *Billy the Kid* (1938) was the first product of this reaching out to the new public, and in it Copland used cowboy songs as the basis for long sections of the score. Just as the feel of an English folk-song is sensed under many of Vaughan Williams's pages, so cowboy tunes lie beneath some of Copland's, but do not come to the surface in specific quotations. Copland turned to ballet, as Falla had in Spain, and in *Rodeo* (1942) the handling of cowboy tunes was more extended and more varied, and the tunes called *If he'd be a buckaroo by trade* and *Sis Joe* are subjected to a highly complex development.

Copland: *Rodeo*.   Capitol L 8198 (Capitol CCL 7516).*

The best of all Copland's ballet scores is *Appalachian Spring* (1943-4), a lyrical evocative score of great beauty. Copland's movement towards simplicity reaches its fitting consummation in five variations on the lovely Shaker tune: *The Gift to be simple*. At its best Copland's music has almost the punch and precision of Stravinsky's in the sureness of the instrumental texture and the sophistication of rhythmic interplay. The simplicity and the sophistication come together in the Third Symphony, perhaps his most important work to date.

Copland has been likened in one respect to Vaughan Williams: Samuel Barber can perhaps be likened to Elgar. He is a composer whose music does not make specific use of national music, but somehow breathes the spirit of the country in which it is written. Barber, like Elgar, is a late romantic and a composer with a rare lyrical gift and a rich sonic imagination. His more daring pieces, such as the ballet suite *Medea* and the Piano Sonata, can hardly be called venturesome, but they are nevertheless fine music. *Knoxville, Summer of 1915*, a remembrance of childhood, is one of the most evocative pieces of American music there is, and as American as Elgar's Cello Concerto is English. The shape and the rise and fall of Barber's phrases seems to have been suggested by the actual inflexions of American speech.

Barber: *Knoxville, Summer of 1915*. COLUMBIA ML 2174.

Benjamin Britten, born in 1913, is Britain's leading composer, and certainly undoctrinaire. Mozart, Verdi, Mahler, and Alban Berg have all been absorbed in a style which is strikingly personal, but hard to define. It is very English in its feeling for the language; no one since Purcell has set English lyric poetry so sensitively. The landscapes that Britten evokes are English, but folk-music has played no part in his melodic or harmonic invention. The melodic felicity, dramatic sense, and individual colouring of Britten's music can be heard in the *Sea Interludes* from his opera *Peter Grimes*.

Britten: *Sea Interludes and Passacaglia: Peter Grimes*. LONDON LL 917 (DECCA LW 5244).

Britten reached a world public in 1937 with his *Variations on a Theme of Frank Bridge* for string orchestra which has been called 'one of the landmarks of string orchestral writing in musical history.' In 1945 *Peter Grimes* was produced, and it became the first English opera to meet with international success. *Peter Grimes* was followed by three chamber operas: *The Rape of Lucretia*, *Albert Herring*, and the children's opera, *Let's Make an Opera*. Then for Covent Garden Britten wrote *Billy Budd* and the ill-starred Coronation opera, *Gloriana*; and most recently he has composed another chamber opera, *The Turn of the Screw*.

The success of *Peter Grimes* made possible that revival of English opera which has been so prominent a feature of the British musical scene since the war. One of its products has been Sir William Walton's *Troilus and Cressida*, already heard in San Francisco, New York, and Milan. Walton, born in 1902, leapt before the world at the age of twenty with his *Façade*; poems by Edith Sitwell recited to the accompaniment of brilliant, barbed chamber music. In 1931 he revitalized English oratorio with the powerful *Belshazzar's Feast*; between 1932 and 1935 a Symphony appeared. In 1939 he wrote a Violin Concerto, and it became clear that his affiliations were now with the Romantics. Other interesting composers to-day are Michael Tippett, composer of the opera *The Midsummer Marriage*, and Lennox Berkeley, who writes beautifully fashioned chamber music, and in his latest work, *Ruth*, has carried forward the line of English chamber opera that begins with Purcell's *Dido and Aeneas*.

In Italy Luigi Dallapiccola, born in 1904, ranks as a twelve-note composer, but he could not be called doctrinaire. His use of the twelve-note system stems from Alban Berg rather than Schönberg, but is modified at every turn by his concern for expressive colouring and dramatic suggestiveness. His opera, *The Prisoner*, is one of the most remarkable compositions of our time. It was preceded by the *Songs of Imprisonment*, a choral triptych inspired by sympathy for those who suffered in the Second World War. The opening of the first song, the *Prayer of Mary Stuart*, is typical of Dallapiccola's methods. The *Dies Irae* theme sounds from the harps and timpani, and against it a twelve-note theme moves upwards on two pianos. Then the voices enter, whispering the queen's prayer.

Dallapiccola: *Canti di Prigionia*. ANGEL 35228 (COLUMBIA 33 CX 1353).

Many other composers could legitimately be discussed in this essay. Not many German composers; their allegiances have generally been to Hindemith or to twelve-note music. In Scandinavia, too, Hindemith has been an almost decisive influence, while in France neo-classicism and Stravinsky have tended to prevail. But there are, for example, the Swiss composers led by Ernest Bloch (whom we could reckon a Jewish nationalist) and Frank Martin. In Russia we must settle for the one indisputably great composer produced there in our day. Shostakovich's

music has always been distinctively Russian in flavour, although
it has drawn on western tradition, being particularly influenced
by Mahler. At one time it seemed that Shostakovich's talent
might have been spoiled by the directives of Soviet culture, but
in his Tenth Symphony and the Violin Concerto Shostakovich
has discovered his authentic voice again. The long, gradually
unrolling melody that opens his Tenth Symphony is as far removed
from Russian folk-song as was the opening theme of Bartók's
Sixth Quartet from Hungarian folk-song. It is as evidently the
product of an individual mind as any music can be, and yet, like
our other examples, it seems to breathe the atmosphere of the
country in which it was composed.

Shostakovich: *Symphony No. 10.* COLUMBIA ML 4959 (PHILIPS
ABL 3052).

APPENDIX

BOOKS

HALSEY STEVENS: *The Life and Music of Béla Bartók.*
ARTHUR BERGER: *Aaron Copland.*
NATHAN BRODER: *Samuel Barber.*
ed. DONALD MITCHELL and HANS KELLER: *Benjamin Britten.*
ed. OSCAR THOMPSON: *Great Modern Composers.*

RECORDS

BARTÓK: *Six String Quartets.* COLUMBIA ML 4278–80 (PHILIPS ABL
3064/3093/3112) or ANGEL 35240–2 (COLUMBIA 33 CX 1245/1267/
1285). *Third Piano Concerto.* LONDON LL 945 (DECCA LXT
2894).

COPLAND: *Appalachian Spring. El Salon Mexico.* * VICTOR LCT
1134 or PHILIPS NBR 6019.* *Third Symphony.* MERCURY 50018
(MERCURY MG 50018).

BRITTEN: *The Turn of the Screw.* LONDON XLL 1207–8 (DECCA
LXT 5038–9). *Serenade for Tenor, Horn, and Strings. Les Illumina-
tions.* LONDON LL 5358 (ENGLISH DECCA LXT 2941). *A Ceremony
of Carols.* LONDON LL 1136 (ENGLISH DECCA LW 5070).

SHOSTAKOVICH: *Violin Concerto.* COLUMBIA ML 5077 (PHILIPS ABL
3103). *Piano Quintet.* CAPITOL P 8171 (ENGLISH DECCA LXT
2749). *Symphony No. 10.* HMV ALP 1322.

49

Wilfrid Mellers

MUSIC AND SOCIETY NOW

IN Shakespeare's time, in England, the young composer was taught to write like Byrd, who in turn based his idiom on the European convention which we associate with Palestrina. In Handel's time the young composer was trained to write like Handel. There was no other way: for conformity to an established convention meant the acceptance of inherited ideas about man's place in the universe and the relationship of man to man. Personal feeling could flower when rooted in such acceptance; and every vital work of art is a point of intersection between the private and the public life. But though Bach, for instance, tells us through his music what he felt about God and man, that was not his primary intention. For him music was not a conscious expression of the self: it was a liturgical and social act.

There is to-day no such clearly defined relationship between musical technique and the values and beliefs in the light of which we live. Almost certainly we exaggerate the heterogeneous nature of twentieth-century styles: an observer a hundred years hence may discover points of accord between composers who seem to us as extravagantly dissimilar as Stravinsky and Vaughan Williams. None the less, it is broadly true that to-day the relationship between techniques and values is confused rather than clear, for the obvious reason that our values are themselves confused. We doubt whether there can be *the* right musical technique because we doubt whether there can be *the* right conception of moral order. When in the mid eighteenth century Rameau deduced his theory of harmony from the practice of his contemporaries he was convinced that he had given a scientifically unanswerable account of the laws governing musical composition. He was equally convinced that the past was irrelevant: that music composed according to his prescription would culminate in the

312

perfection of his art, for the perfectability of music must complement that of man. As a matter of scientific fact, he was wrong
on both counts. But what he said was true while it lasted, in so
far as it was deduced from man's creative instincts and needs.
His truth was of the kind that matters to artists, because it was at
once a technique and a morality. For artists it is a hindrance,
not a help, to know more but believe less.

Now whatever explanation one may give of the disintegration
of tradition that occurred during the nineteenth century—it
certainly had something to do with individualistic capitalism and
the Industrial Revolution—there can be no doubt that it sprang
from a failure of what is usually called belief. Perhaps the
process starts with Beethoven: for whereas Mozart still preserved
an equilibrium between acceptance and protest, Beethoven, seeking a personal belief, delivered a frontal assault on a world which,
he thought, needed change. Beethovenian egoism led to Wagnerian egomania: for Wagner believed in himself so heroically
that he could offer his emotions as a substitute for what concepts
such as God and Civilization had meant in the past. Perhaps the
quintessential romantic artist is Wagner's successor, Delius, who
believed not at all in God and very little in mankind: and not even
in his own senses sufficiently to offer them as a Music of the Future,
so that the dominant emotion in his work is a powerful regret.
A more extreme form of this reliance on personal sensation is found
in some of the middle period music of Debussy, in which God and
Society are reduced to a momentary tremor of the nerves.

Belief in oneself is a dangerous substitute for belief in God or
Reason or Truth or any other absolute. Similarly, the cultivation
of your own sensations in the Ivory Tower is all very well if your
sensibility is as delicate and subtle as that of Debussy. But for
most people the spirit atrophies unless it has contact with other
human beings. It is not therefore surprising that the history of
modern music should have been largely a series of attempts to
evade the implications of the Ivory Tower. The difficulty is that
with the collapse of inherited ideas of order every composer, or
group of composers, has to work out the problem afresh, spending
weary years in arriving at the point where Byrd, Handel, Mozart,
Beethoven, or even Wagner started.

The attempt to achieve a consistent stylization which is at the
same time adequate to our relatively chaotic world lies behind

Debussy's rediscovery of the melodic rather than harmonic tonality of medieval music: behind Sibelius's search for a 'monistic' symphony: behind Bartók's attempt to fuse melodic and rhythmic techniques suggested by Magyar folk-music with Debussyan harmony, Bachian counterpoint, and the formal explorations of late Beethoven. The same need impelled Stravinsky to approach music once more as ritual—whether primitive, liturgical, or theatrically baroque: impelled Schönberg to evolve the twelve-note technique: impelled Hindemith to formulate a theory of tonality which should be as apposite to the twentieth century as was Rameau's theory to the eighteenth. The central composers of our time—Debussy, Schönberg, Stravinsky, Bartók, and Hindemith—have all evolved over the past forty years techniques which bear some resemblance to the principles governing medieval and oriental music. Debussy and Stravinsky in particular created a world of sound remote from the post-Renaissance idea of time progression; and some later developments of twelve-note music have carried this tendency to an extreme point. Perhaps it is not altogether fanciful to sense a relationship between Webern's grotesque treatment of the human voice and the deliberately unnatural vocal techniques employed by medieval and by eastern singers. The voice is dehumanized because it must become supernatural law.

Young composers such as Stockhausen, Boulez, and Nono have taken Webern as a spring-board to create a music even more mathematical in its order than his, since it is organized by rhythmic and dynamic, as well as by linear series. Such a very different composer as Messiaen has employed a highly sensuous harmonic vocabulary in a manner divorced from the traditional notion of progression, organizing his music by rhythmic rather than by harmonic means. In the United States Elliott Carter has experimented with another complex technique that recalls the medieval principle of isochronous rhythm. By way of 'metrical modulations' the tempo and even the dimensions of every section of a composition are controlled by a mathematical interrelation of the rhythms of the parts. Other Americans, taking a hint from the pioneer work of Charles Ives and Edgar Varese, have thrown over pitch notation to create music out of a *collage* of sounds existing in time, the spacing and duration of the noises being dictated by mathematical laws or even by chance: the throw of the dice, being a 'law' of chance, is more significant than a 'morbid' preoccupation with personal feeling! The music of John Cage, like that of the extremist followers of Webern in Europe, naturally enough dispenses with the human intermediary, the performer, and relies on electronic reproduction. Reaction against Wagnerian egomania could hardly go further than this. Indeed, there are signs that the electronic composers are becoming aware of the paradox in their position: for the logical outcome of the rejection of the personality is silence.

Perhaps it may come to that: a world without art is conceivable, though most of us, reared in a long humanist tradition, preserve a weakness for the perverse tragi-comedy of our fallible lives. However this may be, we have to admit that, below and beyond the 'conscious' attitudes of extremists, we can detect a change of approach, evolved instinctively over a long period of years, in the music of men such as Stravinsky, Schönberg, Hindemith, and Bartók. We do not yet know what it means; but it is at least possible that we are living at the end of a cycle that began with the Renaissance. The music of these great men contains many elements which preserve continuity with the past. It may also contain elements which reflect a changing conception of man's nature and destiny, whether involving a renewed respect for supernatural authority or subservience to the laboratory's mathematical law.

All this seems very remote from the conditions of practical music-making to-day. Few people listen to the music of Schönberg, Bartók, Stravinsky, or Webern; almost no one apart from themselves listens to the electronic composers, who perhaps need an audience no more than they need performers. Quite understandably the 'average' musical person in the twentieth century has tended to use music—mainly nineteenth-century music—as an evasion of the perplexities of modern life. None the less one should remember that this desire to listen exclusively to the music of the past rather than to that of one's own time is a phenomenon that has never happened before.

To fill the gap that 'art' music ought to fill if it had a sense of social obligation, a vast mechanized industry of music manufacture was developed to provide entertainment at a debased level. This industry is nothing like a genuine folk-culture, because it is not a spontaneous expression of man's creativity but is imposed on people for reasons of commercial expediency. Commercial music to-day panders to people's feeling of insecurity—cultivating a fatuous optimism or a flabby despair—because it is the product of a society that does not know what it believes in. The position is the more depressing because the public for commercial music, no less than that for nineteenth-century orchestral music, is passive rather than active.

Moreover, commercial music, like the academic tradition and the majority of the concert-going public, lives on the past: since the separation of 'art' music from entertainment it could hardly do otherwise. The music of *hoi polloi* derives its harmony, with pointed irony, from Massenet, Debussy, and Delius—from a kind of plastic Ivory Tower. It is precisely its synthetic, manufactured quality, rather than its vulgarity, that makes it so immorally potent a weapon. It cultivates bogus emotion and makes genuine feeling difficult to recognize, using the same technique as commercial advertising and the glycerine tears of Hollywood. And the ultimate irony is that synthetic music is the only kind that bears an economically sound relation to the community. The position of the 'serious' composer is fallacious because he is, by the nature of his calling, still living in the handicraft age in an age of mechanization.

It may seem that there can never be a *via media* between the mathematical abstraction of the electronic composers and the synthetic mass emotions of commercial music; none the less, I suppose the relatively traditional, non-electronicized composers go on working because they think there may be. Certainly, the more good music that can be written for a commercial function, the better for both art and commerce. As things are, the composer can seldom be employed by commerce without being involved in some degree of emotional simulation; while his traditional employers, the Church and State, have no use for him.

The twentieth-century composer's position is unprecedented in the sense that he is willy-nilly a parasite. A real musical culture should not be a museum culture based mainly on the music of past ages; nor should it be, like most commercial music, a drug. It should be the active embodiment in sound of the life of a community—of the everyday demands of people's work and play and of their deepest spiritual needs. Clearly, a more creative conception of musical culture can come only with a more creative society.

The composer to-day has to accept the fact that both a haughty isolation and a subservience to the values of commerce may involve a kind of dishonesty. But—except when he is young—he will not, if he is truly creative, be greatly concerned about his 'predicament.' He will be too busy writing as well as he can for the public that wants him, small though it may be. He will do so because he believes that authentic creation keeps alive the human spirit; and because he believes, or at any rate hopes, that the public that wants him is growing and will continue to grow, in so far as his apprehension of the world is more honest, more sensitive, and ultimately stronger than that of commercial art. In his more sanguine moments he can envisage a day—perhaps for his children's children—when the distinction between art and commerce shall have become meaningless.

INDEX

INDEX

Abélard, 34
Adam de la Halle, 30, 49–50
Adam of Fulda, 95
Agazzari, 156
Agricola, 193
air de cour, 91
Albéniz, 300
Albinoni, 158–9, 164
Alfonso X (*Alfonoso el Sabio*), 30
Alison, Richard, 125
Altnikol, 193
Ambrose, Saint, 17
Ambrosian chant, 17
Andrea da Firenze, 56
Andrew of Crete, 12
Anonymous IV, 43
Anthonella da Caserta, 56
Apollo, hymns to, 9–10
Arcadelt, Jacques, 110–11
aria, 150–4; *da capo* aria, 153–4, 203, 220
Ars Antiqua, 50
Ars Nova, 49–66, 74, 88, 117; in France, 49–54; in Italy, 55–60
Ars Novae Musicae, 50
atonality, 284, 288-90
aulos, 9
Auric, 253
ayre, 128–9

Bach, Carl Philipp Emanuel, 193, 210–12, 216–17, 227
Bach, Johann Christian, 193, 217–218, 232
Bach, Johann Sebastian, 6, 37, 152, 164, 179, 186, 187, 188–9, 191, 193–9, 205, 208–11, 214, 237, 295, 312, 314
Bach, Wilhelm Friedemann, 215–216
Baïf, Jean Antoine de, 90

Balakirev, 271, 277
ballade, 49
ballata, 56–7
balletti (ballet), 127
Banchieri, 122
Barber, Samuel, 309
Barlach, 289
baroque, characteristics of baroque music, 3–4, 137–142, 170, 220
Bartlet, John, 129
Bartók, 247, 287, 306–8, 311, 314–15
Beethoven, 4–6, 37, 207, 212, 231, 237–42, 244–7, 259, 261–4, 267, 269, 272, 274, 297, 313
Bellini, 257–8, 270, 276–7
Berg, 291–3, 309–10
Berkeley, Lennox, 310
Berlioz, 245–6, 253, 258, 270, 274
Bernart de Ventadour, 27–9, 31
Binchois, 61–2, 71, 75
Bizet, 259
Bloch, 310
Blom, Eric, quoted, 234–5
Boccaccio, 55, 74
Böhm, 188, 207
Boileau, 196
Borodin, 259, 265, 277–8
Boulanger, 308
Boulez, 274, 314
Boyce, 159
Brady, Nicholas, 170
Brahms, 245–7, 251–2, 261, 264–265, 272, 278–9, 302, 306
Britten, 280, 309
Bruckner, 243–4, 248
Buchner, Hans, 96
Bukofzer, Manfred, 65, 68
Bull, 125, 131–2, 188
Bülow, Hans von, 272
Buxtehude, 188–9, 193
Byrd, 2–3, 5–6, 124–6, 132, 312–313